AIDA Europe Research Series on Insurance Law and Regulation

Volume 6

The AIDA Europe Research Series on Insurance Law and Regulation is the first book series of its kind and area of specialization. It comprises volumes on topics researched and written with an international, comparative or European perspective.

The regulatory response to the financial crisis in 2008 has pushed towards the adoption of transnational principles and rules also in the field of insurance by encouraging the convergence of national regulations to common regulatory framework. The need for a common legal language emerges to fully understand the process of transnational convergence in place and its impact on national legislation. On the other hand, persisting national peculiarities must be examined in the light of the transnational convergence of rules and concepts. Moreover, new risks, business practices and customers' issues are emerging worldwide, so requiring increasingly global responses.

The scope of the series is to bring together academics, practitioners and policy makers in order to exchange views and approaches to the topics concerned, which are based on the new transnational dimension of insurance law, business and regulation. All contributions are peer reviewed.

More information about this series at https://link.springer.com/bookseries/16331

Pierpaolo Marano • Kyriaki Noussia
Editors

The Governance of Insurance Undertakings

Corporate Law and Insurance Regulation

Springer

Editors
Pierpaolo Marano
Department of Legal Studies
Catholic University of the Sacred Heart
Milan, Italy

Kyriaki Noussia
University of Reading
School of Law
Reading, UK

ISSN 2662-1770 ISSN 2662-1789 (electronic)
AIDA Europe Research Series on Insurance Law and Regulation
ISBN 978-3-030-85816-2 ISBN 978-3-030-85817-9 (eBook)
https://doi.org/10.1007/978-3-030-85817-9

This Springer imprint is published by the registered company Springer Nature Switzerland AG.
The registered company address is: Gewerbestrasse 11, 6330 Cham, Switzerland

Preface

Insurance law is multidisciplinary by nature, as it necessarily must interact with other disciplines, such as actuarial sciences or finance. However, this multi-disciplinarity also concerns the intersection with other branches of law. Most of the insurance undertakings are corporations and, as such, they are subject to corporate law rules, while insurance law is increasingly taking on a transnational connotation in regulating the organisation and activity of insurance companies. The combination of company law and insurance-specific rules is at the heart of this investigation.

This book is a collection of contributions from authors with different legal cultures, and it aims to identify the legal issues that arise from the intersection of these two disciplines, i.e., insurance law and corporate/company law. The issues entailed are examined mainly based on the European Union (EU) law, although there are also contributions from other legal systems that enrich the perspective with which to approach those issues.

The book includes two parts. The first part collects six contributions that analyse different profiles of the system of governance of insurance undertakings. The analysis concerns the regulations introduced by the Directive Solvency II and the corporate law of relevant EU jurisdictions. However, one of the chapters contributed tackles the issue from the perspective of Singaporean law that aspires to become the leading (re)insurance and risk transfer hub in Asia. The second part contains eight contributions that examine the intersections between the insurance business and corporate law. They include extraordinary corporate operations, supervision, reporting, customer relations, and claims handling management, whilst one contribution focuses on private international law issues. Again, the issues entailed are examined mainly based on and from the perspective of the European Union (EU) law. Still, the supranational nature of the insurance business also allows the experiences of other legal systems to be included in the analysis, since they can provide valuable insights to other regulators.

This book fills a gap in the legal literature that has examined the two branches of law, i.e., insurance regulation and corporate law, separately so far. With the objective difficulty of examining rules with different levels of transnational harmonisation, the effort made is to provide as much a "unitary" vision as possible of the legal issues entailed and herein examined. This effort is made, nonetheless, with the awareness that those issues are mainly perceived and managed as such in practice. It is left upon the reader to undertake the task of evaluating the efficacy of this effort. The law stands as on 27th April 2021.

Milan, Italy Pierpaolo Marano
Exeter, UK Kyriaki Noussia
April 2021

AIDA Europe

AIDA Europe was established in 2007 with the aim of promoting, either directly or through its members, the development of insurance and related laws. It attempts to achieve this, mainly through:

- furtherance of the study and knowledge of international and national insurance law and of related matters;
- proposition of measures aiming at the harmonization of insurance law or the means for resolution of insurance disputes;
- facilitation of exchange of academic know-how between its members or any other European organization dealing with insurance-related matters, similar to those of AIDA Europe;
- support of academic work in the field of insurance, e.g. through cooperation with universities or the sponsoring of academic research and papers.

AIDA Europe organizes conferences mainly geared to the European-based jurisdictions, offering to all interested stakeholders a platform for an open- and solution-minded scientific- and practice-related dialogue on key developments in the area of insurance, reinsurance and related law also supporting its members in their respective endeavours. Conferences are open to all stakeholders and regularly attract representatives from the insurance sector, academia, private practice, regulatory authorities or law-making bodies.

AIDA Europe also maintains a keen focus on supporting the development of young academic talents by sponsoring academic work and by inviting young academics to its conferences. AIDA Europe's Scientific Committee, which supports

AIDA Europe through the scientific agenda setting, also manages AIDA Europe's Calls for Papers.

AIDA Europe is a non-profit organization, pursuing altruistic goals and has its seat in Zurich, Switzerland. Its events are open to all interested parties. For further information, please see https://aidainsurance.org/regional-groupings/aida-europe.

Contents

Part I
The System of Governance of Insurance Undertakings

Corporate Governance and the So-Called 'Four-Eyes Principle'

Niccolò Abriani and Armando Catania

Abstract This chapter aims to analyse the current role played by insurance undertakings and their senior managers—with a specific reference to the Italian, French, Spanish and British insurance industry, taking into consideration the important changes introduced by the Solvency II framework.

In doing so, the study identifies features of the international regulation of insurance development based on the recommendations of the International Association of Insurance Supervisory (IAIS) and the Directives of the European Union (EU).

The board delegates the running of the business to the senior managers, expecting them to operate on behalf of the company's interests.

The literature has identified several problems resulting from this relationship.

We intend to consider the internal behaviour affected by the board-senior managers' relationship, by looking for direct connection between the elements of senior managers behaviours' and the organisational and operational structure of the enterprise.

Inside the theoretical framework and given the existing related literature, our work aims to answer the above research question.

According to our statements, it will be demonstrated that, with specific focus on the management sector, there are still wide possibilities for improvement and more studies concerning board-senior managers relationship.

The Authors have shared all 'significant decisions' in actual application of the so-called 'Four-Eyes Principle'. Nonetheless, Paragraphs 1, 2 and 4 are attributed to Armando Catania, and Paragraph 3 to Niccolò Abriani.

N. Abriani (✉)
College of Law, University of Firenze, Firenze, Italy
e-mail: niccolo.abriani@unifi.it

A. Catania (✉)
Palermo Bar Association, Palermo, Italy

P. Marano, K. Noussia (eds.), *The Governance of Insurance Undertakings*, AIDA Europe Research Series on Insurance Law and Regulation 6,
https://doi.org/10.1007/978-3-030-85817-9_1

1 The Corporate Governance Structure

In the Solvency II framework,[1] an effective system of governance[2] is considered essential for the proper management of insurance undertakings, as well as for the resulting regulatory system.[3]

Governance is the system through which the insurance company is internally regulated.[4] It incorporates many aspects of the business of an insurance company, such as corporate structure.[5]

Solvency II identifies an effective system of governance in an adequate organisational and operational corporate structure[6]—aimed at supporting the

---

[1] The Directive 2009/138/ EC (Solvency II) is the regulatory framework for the European insurance industry. It has been amended over and over and its entry into force, postponed several times, has been set for all Member States on 1 January 2016. The principles of the Solvency II Directive are complemented by a second level sectoral regulation represented by Delegated Regulation 2015/35/ EU (as amended by Delegated Regulation 2016/467/EU), as well as technical implementing standards issued by the European Commission, both directly applicable at national level.

At a supranational level, the regulatory framework is completed by the Guidelines, Recommendations, Opinions issued by the European Insurance and Occupational Pensions Authority (EIOPA) aimed at fostering convergence in the application of the Directive and supervisory practices.

[2] Solvency II identifies some core principles that should characterise an effective system of governance.

These principles include: (i) transparency (to be achieved through a clear division and appropriate separation of responsibilities, as well as through an effective information system); (ii) proportionality (with respect to the nature, scope and complexity, of a company's activities); (iii) written policies on risk management, internal control, internal audit and (where relevant) outsourcing and business continuity.

See Dell'Atti et al. (2018), p. 135.

On the requirement for all insurance and reinsurance undertakings to have in place an effective system of governance, see Manes (2017), p. 115 ff.

The internal governance implications of Solvency II have been widely debated by Dreher (2015), p. 155 ff.

[3] See Siri (2017), p. 12.

Vella (2014), p. 291, points out that the term 'governance' encompasses a plurality of phenomena, on which regulatory choices may have an impact.

[4] A recent research conducted by Anderloni et al. (2019) shows how governance mechanisms can be divided into external and internal mechanisms.

External governance mechanisms are: (i) market mechanisms; (ii) threats of take-overs; (iii) the action of external stakeholders other than shareholders; (iv) the market for managerial work.

The internal governance mechanisms include: (i) the characteristics of the board; (ii) the extent of the CEO's powers; (iii) the presence and characteristics of the internal board committees; (iv) the management incentive and remuneration tools; (v) the financial policies.

[5] See Dodevska and Nuredini (2019), p. 2.

[6] Selleri (2010), p. 608 ff. highlights the fact that insurance undertakings are accustomed to alternating between use of a so-called 'divisional' or 'functional' organisational and operational structure.

The first is characterised by an articulation of the entire activity of the enterprise in business areas differentiated by product lines or market spheres, cultivated through Strategic Business Units (S.B. U.), which in turn are further broken down into functions or departments.

undertaking's strategic objectives and operations—clearly distributed, transparent and equipped with an effective system to ensure the transmission of information internally.

The organisational and operational structure plays a decisive role to guarantee the sound and prudent management of the insurance undertaking.[7] It is the duty of the board of directors[8] to arrange an appropriate organisational and operational structure, to be adapted periodically to the changing conditions on an international, national and corporate level. The organisational structure determines the tasks and assignments, while the operational structure settles the way of performing the tasks; in any case, it is ultimately the administrative, management or supervisory body[9] that has the responsibility for the execution.

The four key functions (Risk Management, Compliance, Internal Audit and Actuarial) must have an appropriate standing in the undertaking's organisational structure, even though it is not required any mandatory organisational structure, as the insurers[10] have the freedom to decide how to organise any function,[11] unless otherwise specified by the law.[12]

2 The Board-Senior Managers Relationship

Corporate governance involves making decisions and taking actions related to the corporate culture, environment and structural framework, policies and controls. It is not indeed a once-established system, but a continuous process that needs to be

---

The second, instead, can be distinguished by the division into several functions (i.e. specialised areas of activity), characterised by the homogeneity of the processes carried out.

The aspect on the basis of which the articulation of the business activity would be determined by function both in the 'divisional' and 'functional' organisational structure is a symptom of a vertical division of the same, although, in one case, it takes place at the level of the entire enterprise, while, in the other, within each business unit.

[7] See Marino and Costa (2015).

[8] There are a lot of different set of rules at different levels in each European country largely affecting the activities, duties and accounting of insurance companies' directors.

See furthermore Montalenti (2021), p. 18 ff.

[9] The nature and structure of the administrative, management or supervisory body varies with the national company law applicable.

[10] In this paper, hereinafter, unless stated otherwise, the terms 'insurance undertakings' and 'insurer' are assumed to include both insurance and reinsurance undertakings.

[11] In the context of a system of governance, a 'function' is to be understood as an administrative capacity to undertake particular tasks, considered important or critical.

[12] Article 268 of the Delegated Acts reserves to the autonomy of the insurance undertaking any decisions on the organisational position deemed most appropriate to be given to the fundamental functions, in compliance with the principle of separation between operational and fundamental functions.

constantly upgraded.[13] This is why an effective corporate governance structure requires appropriate standards to recognise, protect and promote the rights, relationships and interests of the administrative, management and supervisory bodies.

This chapter aims to explore only the different ways in which the governance of insurance undertakings is involved with the board-senior managers relationship.[14]

The day-to-day business of the firm, and so the state of affairs that might lead to any key decision the board is asked to make, is largely determined by the work of the company's senior managers.[15]

Senior managers work with various parties in the interest to manage the firm's relationships with the outside world,[16] so they have often more intimate knowledge of the deals than the board and may have to explain the interactions of the different relationships to the board.[17]

When the board is asked to make significant decisions[18] that involve mediating among various interests, it is supposed to be challenging and reviewing critically the

---

[13] See Dodevska and Nuredini (2019), p. 1 ff.

[14] Confirmation that both directors and managers contribute to the composition of corporate governance on different, albeit complementary, bases can already be found in the Preamble to the G20/OECD - Organization for Economic Cooperation and Development (2015), where it is explained that 'Corporate governance involves a set of relationships between the managers of a company, its board of directors, its shareholders and other interested parties'.

The current version of the OECD Principles is the one approved by the Council of the same organisation during the meeting held on July 8, 2015, subsequently implemented by the representatives of Governments belonging to the G20, therefore also known as G20/OECD Principles.

[15] See Fama and Jensen (1983), p. 127.

[16] See, in general, Lin (1996), p. 914 ff.

Anderloni et al. (2019), p. 4, attribute a certain influence of insurance undertakings' stakeholders (such as policy holders, injured third parties, reinsurers, supervisory authorities and shareholders) on decisions that modify the level of management risk assumed and the solvency of the institution.

[17] This seems to be a component common to all the most advanced economies, considering that it is also found in North American literature that investigates the specific phenomenon of business organisation.

See Alces (2011), p. 783, which gives evidence of how in the largest multinationals in the world, when the board must vote on a particular matter of corporate business, officers and experts selected by the officers brief it on the subject.

The above consideration seems to assume a critical value in the opinion expressed by Henderson (2013), p. 28, according to whom while most boards are composed of smart and experienced individuals with diverse experience and significant reputations, they are simply outgunned in terms of information and incentives relative to the managers they are supposed to control.

[18] Significant decisions are the ones are unusual or that could have a material impact on the undertaking (i.e. decisions that—according to E.I.O.P.A. - European Insurance and Occupational Pensions (2015)—could affect the strategy of the undertaking, its business activities or its business conduct; or even could have serious legal or regulatory consequences; or even more could have major financial effects or major implications for staff or policyholders; or ultimately could potentially result in repercussions for the undertaking's reputation).

The 'significant decisions' must be considered as opposed to the 'day-to-day decisions' (i.e. the spate of usual decisions to be taken at the top level of the undertaking in the running of the business, according to the same Guidelines above mentioned).

information it needs to fully perform its function by a correct interaction with the senior management[19] and key functions holders (Risk Management, Compliance, Internal Audit and Actuarial).

The board may perform in such effective style if senior managers maintain industrial development, business decisions and internal policies consistent with company's strategies and risk appetite.

The ability of senior managers to perform this role is to a large extent dependent upon the flow of information—coming across control functions, among internal functions and within the business units—to determine whether, based on each individual senior's manager experience, knowledge and expertise, any strategic decision is advisable for such company.

Consequently, the collection of credible information provides the foundation for effective decision making by the board.

Senior managers serve, therefore, such as a backstop, or a final quality check, before a major decision is formalised.

Thus, a relational environment throughout the company that fosters open communication between senior managers and the board encourages a critical review of the company's site and scope of operations.

A relevant mediation function among the board and senior managers is now performed by the in-house counsels of the firm, such as a person, who, over time, has acquired an increasingly distinctive role, i.e. the Secretary of the Board of Directors.

The *Codice di Corporate Governance* (Corporate Governance Code)[20] of listed Italian companies (and the major national insurance companies fall into this category), for instance, assigns to the Secretary of the Board of Directors the task of ensuring, together with the Chairman of the Board of Directors, that the preliminary information and the information provided during board meetings is suitable to empowering the directors to act in an informed manner, also by way of attendance at board meetings by the officers of the company (as well as those of the group companies it heads) who occupy the role of heads of the various company functions.

For listed companies, the UK Corporate Governance Code[21] provides that the board, supported by the company secretary, should ensure that it has the policies,

---

[19] Arg. by Siri (2017), p. 20.

According to Bailey (2015) on a forward-looking basis a firm's culture should promote discussion, debate and honest challenge.

[20] Available at https://www.borsaitaliana.it/comitato-corporate-governance/codice/2020.pdf, approved by the *Comitato per la Corporate Governance* di Borsa Italiana (Corporate Governance Committee of Borsa Italiana 2020) in January 2020.

The companies that will adopt the Code will apply it as from the first financial year starting after 31 December 2020, informing the market in the corporate governance report to be published in 2022.

The compliance with the rules of Solvency II is most likely to be easier for the Italian companies who adopt the Italian Corporate Governance Code (as last time updated in January 2020) because of the greater familiarity with reporting obligations and other constraint.

See Venuti et al. (2016), p. 143.

[21] F.R.C. - Financial Reporting Council - (2018a).

processes, information, time and resources it needs to function effectively and efficiently, and all directors should have access to the advice of the company secretary, who is responsible for advising the board on all governance matters.[22]

According to the Spanish *Código de buen gobierno de las sociedades cotizadas* (Listed Companies Corporate Governance Code),[23] the company's secretary is the one who has the key task of facilitating the efficient functioning of the board through a strict control exercised on the performance of the board itself in any matter relating to corporate governance.

An adequate knowledge of the company reality on the part of those who, for various reasons, contribute to the organisation of the enterprise structure, is nourished through effective professional cooperation between them.

In the French legal system, Article 2.5 of the *Notice 'Solvabilité II - Système de gouvernance'* (Notice 'Solvency II' - System of governance)[24] encourages cooperation between members of the top management of insurance undertakings as a means of preventing unnecessary overlapping of tasks between them, with a view to achieving a balanced distribution, in accordance with the corporate strategy pursued.[25]

---

[22] In Great Britain, under Section 271, Companies Act 2006, each 'public company' is required to have a 'secretary', whereas under Section 270 above, the same obligation does not apply to 'private companies'.

The Financial Reporting Council (FRC) (2018b) provides a more detailed description of the role of the company secretary in his or her support of the board.

See Kakabadse et al. (2014).

[23] Approved by the *Comisión Nacional del Mercado de Valores* (National Stock Market Committee) in June 2020.

[24] The *Code des Assurances* (Insurance Code)—the first version of which is based on decree n. 76/667 of 16 July 1976—covers all the laws and regulations that have, among other things, contributed to the implementation in France of the requirements of Solvency II, while the regulation of the system of corporate governance of insurance undertakings has found its home in the *Notice 'Solvabilité II - Système de gouvernance'* (Notice 'Solvency II' - System of governance) drawn up by ACPR - Autorité de Contrôle Prudentiel et de Résolution - Banque de France (2015).

[25] The principle of informed action—of which the call for cooperation is a concrete method of implementation—seems for the French regulator to become the keystone on which to build the functional system of insurance undertakings, structured in a neutral manner by Solvency II.

The provision contained therein in Article 41, which states 'Member States shall require all insurance and reinsurance undertakings to have in place an effective system of governance which provides for sound and prudent management of the business', seems in the regulatory act to consist almost entirely in the duty for top management to act in an informed manner, thus giving the impression of abandoning the function of a merely concurrent component of a good system of corporate governance, to become a fundamental requirement for the construction of a good system of corporate governance.

Article 2.7 of the Notice 2015 seems to give force to the above impression, where the focus of the policies implemented for the creation of a good corporate governance system coincide with the processes and procedures envisaged to foster the exchange of information between the members of the corporate functions.

These procedures connote a real obligation if they refer to information to be provided to the heads of the risk management, compliance verification, internal control and actuarial functions.

3 The So-Called 'Four-Eyes Principle'

Under Solvency II the insurance undertakings must implement the Own Risk Self-Assessment (ORSA) and make it an integral part of their business strategy, which must be considered on an ongoing basis in the strategic decisions of the undertakings.[26]

Through the ORSA process it is expected that senior managers update[27] the board regularly at board and committee meetings in light of the progress of the ORSA and of any material findings that may influence the undertaking's strategy before the making of any key decisions.[28]

In this regard, it has to be investigated whether it is possible to infer from Solvency II the principle that, prior to the implementation of any significant decision concerning the undertaking, at least 'two persons' must review such decision (so called 'Four-Eyes Principle');[29] that it must necessarily be referred to directors, or that at least one of these 'two persons' could be a senior manager.[30]

A very relevant consequence could arise from the first or the latter of these two working hypotheses.

In the first scenario, it will be confirmed that the ownership of any significant decision concerning the undertaking rests with the board, as the directors are part of it; in the second, it could be demonstrated that, even if it is still true the ownership of this particular kind of decisions rests with the board, some significant decision could be taken by the senior management too.

To find it out, we could assume that, according to Section 1.29 of the EIOPA Guidelines on System of Governance 2016,[31] the two persons to be involved in any significant decision, before it is implemented, are those who effectively run the undertaking.

---

[26] Own Risk Self-Assessment (ORSA)—that may be treated as part of the management system—aims to: (i) improve risk management system; (ii) better understand the overall capital adequacy and capital allocation; (iii) harmonise risk and capital management systems.

[27] The maintenance of a constant internal discussion within the management for adequate knowledge of the trend of relevant economic scenarios contributes to implement on the best way the strategic plan drawn up by the administrative body (arguments *ex* Siri 2018, p. 73 ff).

The EIOPA—as part of the process aimed at applying Solvency II—with the public consultation on the Set 1 of the Solvency II Guidelines of 2 June 2014, refers to the concept of 'collective knowledge' of the administrative body as a whole, as an indispensable prerequisite for guaranteeing healthy and prudent management of the insurance undertakings.

[28] See Clarke and Phelan (2015), p. 17.

[29] It is the application of the principle expressed in the premises to Delegated Regulation 2015/35/EU, according to which none in the company should have an uncontrolled decision-making power.

[30] Siri (2017), p. 14, states that arguably the 'two persons' who shall ensure to take every significant decision should not be necessarily both directors.

Dodevska and Nuredini (2019), p. 8, agree with Siri (2017), p. 4, on the basis that the provision refers generally to 'persons'.

[31] E.I.O.P.A. - European Insurance and Occupational Pensions Authority (2016).

For the aforementioned Guidelines, the persons who effectively run the undertaking cover members of the administrative, management or supervisory body taking into account national law, as well as members of the senior management. The latter includes persons employed by the undertaking who are responsible for high level decision making and for implementing the strategies devised and the policies approved by the administrative, management or supervisory body.

So, the governance of insurance undertakings is composed, like that of any other undertaking, of two distinct interdependent spheres, namely management and administration.[32]

It appears that this can be deduced from the consideration that, while the governance system as a whole is essential for the management of the entire enterprise, the functions—even those defined as 'key'—are parts of the governance system and indeed are fundamental for the administration of the various phases of the enterprise.

Between the phases of administration of insurance undertakings, there should be a further distinction between the performance of executive activities, on the one hand, and non-executive activities, on the other.

A precise indication of this impression seems to be found in Recital 35 of Solvency II, which differentiates between the persons who 'effectively run the undertaking' and those who 'have other key functions'.

It seems that the use of the adjective 'other', modifying the noun 'functions', should relate to a term that is missing in the first part of the same sentence (that is 'key functions'), which should also apply to those who actually run the business.

In other words, it seems that the European legislator may have wanted to differentiate between those who direct the functions through which executive activities of the companies are performed, and those who direct functions through which non-executive activities are carried out.

True confirmation of the opinion just expressed seems to be found in the Guidelines published by EIOPA regarding the articulation of the corporate gover-

[32] A differentiation of roles between the board of directors and management persists, which helps to identify the scope of managerial functions in the performance of the acts related to the organisation of the company. These are limited—upwards—by the acts relating to the conduct of business operations falling within the powers of the general meeting, and—downwards—by the acts concerning the administration of the company that are incumbent on the executive staff.

See furthermore on the topic Champaud (1962); Pailluseau (1967); Iglesias Prada (1971), p. 43 ff.; Rodriguez Artigas (1971), p. 126; Angelici (1990), p. 997 ff.; Cabras (1995), p. 38 ff.; Charreaux (1997); Vicent Chuliá (2008), p. 451; Alces (2011), p. 783 ff.; Winter (2011), p. 3 ff.; Fleckner and Hopt (2013); Juste Mencía (2013); Latorre Chiner (2013); Martynova and Renneboog (2013), p. 97; Mc Nulty (2013), p. 133 ff.; Henderson (2013), p. 28 ff.; Goergen (2018); Abriani (2019), p. 36 ff.; Tricker (2019), p. 317 ff.

nance system, which aim to limit the possibility that the exercise of the four key functions taken into account by Solvency II (Risk management, Compliance, Internal Audit and Actuarial) may be combined with the performance of roles of administration, management and control, or, in any case, with the performance of operational activities.[33]

To achieve the desired result, the EIOPA Guidelines aim to prevent a situation where the holder of a key function may be in a subordinate position compared to the head of an operational function,[34] unless—in addition to creating no other filter in the direct reporting of the holder of the key function to those with roles of administration, management and control—adequate risk mitigation criteria are also adopted to ensure that the owner of a key function does not find himself, even if only on a purely formal level, in a non-autonomous position in relation to the head of an operational function.[35]

Thus, according to EIOPA Guidelines, any further reflection on the persons intended to effectively run the undertaking could be developed when we turn to analyse the equivalent regulatory framework shaped by each national law.

---

[33] The Peer Review of key functions: supervisory practices and application in assessing key functions, conducted by the EIOPA in 2016, has shown that a certain combination of the exercise of key functions and the performance of tasks of administration, management and control, or, in any case, the performance of operational activities, takes place, albeit occasionally, in insurance undertakings in almost all countries, where the respective national market regulatory authorities. However, it seems inclined to maintain an approach based on an assessment of the compatibility of the individual case with the general principle of proportionality.

The principle of proportionality constitutes, according to Article 5 of the Treaty on European Union (TUE), the main parameter for assessing the legitimacy of European acts, in terms of suitability and necessity, in relation to the achievement of the objectives pursued by the Treaty itself.

Nevertheless, the European Regulatory Authority considered it essential to draw the attention of each national authority to the possibility that such situations may occur, especially in companies with more complex organisations, ensuring, in any case, the adoption of adequate safeguards to ensure an effective system of corporate governance.

In the opinion of the EIOPA, a useful mechanism to prevent the onset of potential critical phenomena is the timely invitation of individual national authorities to each of the companies concerned to promptly communicate the non-existence of a conflict situation, and, in any case, the proper management of the relative phase.

See, furthermore, Lener (2016), p. 239 ff.

[34] The above-mentioned Peer Review has ascertained that such cases exist in half of the countries observed.

[35] Equivalent tension seems to have pervaded the orientation of the IAIS, to the extent that that ICP 7.1. is careful to alert the national market regulatory authorities to ensure that the three main players in the corporate governance system—(i) the administrative body; (ii) senior management; (iii) key persons in control functions—adopt criteria capable of guaranteeing a clear separation between the management tasks of the company assigned to the administrative body—whose functions of effective administration reserved to a part of the management constitute just one stage—from the supervisory tasks, reserved, on the contrary, to the holders of the fundamental functions.

4 The Persons Who Effectively Run the Undertaking

4.1 In Italy and in France

In the Italian legal system, according to Article 30, paragraph *Codice delle Assicurazioni Private* (Private Insurance Code),[36] the board of directors has both the power to set up operational functions—by assigning tasks and responsibilities—whereas, according to Article 26, paragraph II, I.V.ASS. Regulation No. 38/2018, has the duty to formalise the establishment of fundamental functions.[37]

This seems such a natural consequence arising from the content of the previous Article 29-*bis* which, in accordance with Article 40 Solvency II, provides that the board has the ultimate responsibility for the compliance, by the insurance undertakings, with the laws, regulations and provisions, both at a national and a supranational level.

The nature of the verbs used by the Italian legislator ('attribute' and 'formalise') does not seem accidental: one can only attribute to someone something that one already possesses; on the other hand, one can only formally acknowledge the fact that someone else already possesses something.

It seems that this may be the reason the board of directors is able to attribute tasks and responsibilities to operational functions, whereas, in relation to fundamental functions, the same body may merely formalise the institution thereof.

The tasks and responsibilities are, therefore, attributed by the board of directors to the heads of the operational functions, so that they can contribute, through their activity, to the sound and prudent management of the company; the tasks and responsibilities, on the contrary, are conferred by the board on the heads of the fundamental functions, because they ensure, through their activity, the sound and prudent management of the company.[38]

---

[36] In the Italian legal system, the Legislative Decree No. 209/2005, containing the *Codice delle Assicurazioni Private* (Private Insurance Code), pursuant to the amendments and additions to it since its promulgation, has helped to implement Solvency II in Italy,

The Private Insurance Code has delegated to *Istituto per la Vigilanza sulle Assicurazioni* (Italian Insurance Supervisory Authority)—hereinafter, for the sake of brevity, referred to only as I.V.ASS (2018).

The Regulation constitutes the pre-eminent regulatory act which the I.V.ASS. has at its disposal to implement the primary legislation.

The regulatory competence of the I.V.ASS. is also exercised through the Letters to the Market (general recommendations containing the Institute's expectations aimed at guiding the work and organisational structure of the supervised companies) and the supervisory procedures.

[37] Marino and Cimarelli (2018) share the assumption that the board of directors remains ultimately responsible and central pivot of the corporate governance system, since it is their task to define strategies, provide guidelines and guidance, and approve the organisational structure of the companies.

[38] Senior management works alongside the board of directors with the task of implementing, maintaining and monitoring the corporate governance system, as it has the first responsibility for the compliance, by the insurance undertaking, with the laws, regulations and company's strategies.

See Farenga (2016), p. 24 ff.

So, while the division of the organisational structure of the company into operational functions is freely left to the board of directors, the division into fundamental functions is provided for by the legislator as an obligation, both of which are instrumental to ensuring the sound and prudent management of the company.

The idea that it is within the board of directors' power to configure, in compliance with the law, not only the organisational structure of the operational functions, but also the fundamental functions, could be a valid indication of the equivalence of the levels occupied by both functions in the structure of the insurance undertakings, which would also signify an equivalent hierarchical level between the heads of the operational functions and those of the fundamental functions (or, it is the same, no hierarchical level is inserted between the heads of the fundamental functions and those of the operational ones[39]), even though the latter contribute to the performance of the company's administrative acts from a position that ensures compliance with the principle of separation from the operational functions, so as to preserve their autonomy, independence and objectivity of judgement.

It would seem, therefore, that the heads of fundamental functions would be part of the management category of the insurance undertakings, even though they carry out non-operational administrative activities.

The heads of the fundamental functions would therefore be at the same level as the heads of the operational functions, with whom they collaborate on a horizontal level, given their autonomy and independence, but unlike the latter, they would not remain subject to the vertical hierarchical line which extends all the way up to the General Manager, precisely in order to preserve their autonomy and independence.

Ultimately, this could be the reason for the choice made by the Italian legislator to coin the notion of '*personale rilevante*' ('relevant personnel') in Article 2, paragraph I, letter m), of I.V.ASS. Regulation No. 38/2018 to bring together under this common definition both those who perform operational functions and those who perform non-operational functions.

Therefore, the notion of 'relevant personnel' includes 'the general managers, managers with strategic tasks, the owners and the highest level staff of the fundamental functions and the other categories of personnel whose activity may have a significant impact on the company's risk profile, chosen by the company on the basis of motivated and adequately formalised choices' (*'i direttori generali, i dirigenti con compiti strategici, i titolari e il personale di livello più elevato delle funzioni fondamentali e le altre categorie del personale la cui attività può avere un impatto significativo sul profilo di rischio dell'impresa, identificato dall'impresa, in base a scelte motivate ed adeguatamente formalizzate'*).

[39] See Marly (2017b), p. 42.

French legislation explicitly distinguishes the 'administration' of a company from its 'management'. The first, if the company is set up as a joint-stock company, is the job of the board of directors; the second, on the contrary, that of one or more managers,[40] and indeed the verb used to refer to management activity is '*diriger*'.[41]

The French *Code de commerce* (Commercial Code) seems to end its use of the lexicon to identify the senior managers of the company at the alternation of '*directeur général*' (general manager)—but also '*directeur général délégué*' (deputy general manager), since French company law expressly regulates the possibility of appointments up to a maximum of five—and '*dirigeants*' (managers).[42]

The *Code des assurances* (Insurance Code) provides that the *dirigeants* can take on the additional status of *'dirigeants effectifs'* (effective managers).

The term *dirigeants effectifs* seems to pair the adjective and the noun based on the will expressed by the legislator—in Article R 322-168 Insurance Code—which determines that the effective management of the insurance undertaking[43]—conferred, at the discretion of the board of directors, or of the supervisory board, to the general manager, or to the deputy general manager, or to the members of the board, may also be conferred to one or more officers, having the experience, skills and honourability necessary to ensure the necessary diversity of knowledge, experience and qualifications which are essential to being able to manage the undertaking in a professional manner, and having also sufficiently broad powers over the activities and risks of the company to being involved in decisions with a significant impact, particularly in strategic, budgetary or financial matters (Article L322-2, paragraph VII, Insurance Code, supplemented by Article 4.1 Notice 2015)—who thus assume the profile of *dirigeants effectifs*.[44]

---

[40] In the French legal system, the managers are quite often called '*cadres*'.

See furthermore on this topic Robin Olivier (2009), p. 37 ss.

In the management companies, but also in the investment service providers, credit institutions and insurance companies, '*cadres*' are natural persons with operational and effective functions.

See AMF – Autorité des Marchés Financiers - Règlement général (FMA - Financial Markets Authority - General Regulation) (2021), available at https://www.amffrance.org/fr/eli/fr/aai/amf/rg/20210101/notes.

See also Marly (2017a), p. 6.

[41] See, for instance, Articles L 210-9(I) of the Commercial Code and L322-2(VII) of the Insurance Code, respectively. The first is devoted to the impossibility of invoking any defects affecting the appointment of '*personnes chargées de directeur la société*' (people responsible for managing the company) once the disclosure formalities have been completed; the second, on the contrary, is intended to describe the personal requirements of '*Les personnes appellees à directeur une enterprise (...)*' (The people called to manage a company).

[42] It is the *Code de gouvernement d'enterprise des sociétés cotées* (Listed Companies Corporate Governance Code) to create the further category of '*Dirigeants mandataires sociaux exécutifs/non exécutifs*' (Executive/non-executive senior corporate managers) for the purposes there conceived.

[43] The effective management of the insurance undertaking consists in the determination of the direction of the company's activities.

[44] The general manager or members of the management board, as well as any deputy general manager in the bodies governed by the Insurance Code (Article R 322-168); the chairman of the board of directors and the operational manager in organisations subject to the Mutual Insurance

The Notice 2015 in Article 2.3 determines that it is the responsibility of the companies carrying out insurance activities listed in Articles L 310-3-1 Insurance Code, L 211-10 *Code de la mutualité* (Mutual Insurance Code) and L 931-6 *Code de la sécurité sociale* (Social Security Code), to ensure that at least two people effectively manage the company and intervene in all significant decisions before they are taken (*'L'enterprise veille à ce qu'au moins deux personnes dirigent effectivement l'enterprise et interviennent dans toute décision significative avant que celle-ci ne soit mise en oeuvre'*).[45]

The syntactic construction used by the Notice 2015 ('The company shall ensure that at least two persons (...) intervene in all significant decisions before they are taken'), without prejudice to the particular—and certainly far from negligible—reference to the requirement that the persons whose duty it is to intervene in all significant decisions of insurance companies, before they are taken, are the same persons who actually direct them (at least two, therefore, chosen from among the general manager, deputy general managers, members of the board of directors or officers), does not appear to be a mere semantic variation of the definition of 'effective managers' (*'dirigeants effectifs'*), since the duties incumbent on those who effectively direct insurance undertakings—therefore, also the related powers granted to implement them—are enriched by a further feature, consisting of intervention in any significant decision before it is taken, generally not granted to 'effective managers' (*'dirigeants effectifs'*).

The Notice 2015 do not seem to provide any indication as to whether such a duty is actually being performed neither with reference to the recipients on the possible power of intervention, nor in relation to the possible effects thereof, nor, finally, in

---

Code (Article R 211-15); the general manager and the delegated general manager in organisation subject to the Social Security Code (R. 931-3-45-3) are effective managers as of right.

The '*dirigeants effectifs*' form a specific category, which is superimposed on the ordinary classifications of law.

Marly (2017b), p. 42, observes that this interference raises many questions to which the regulator has endeavored to answer in the form of the ACPR - Autorité de Contrôle Prudentiel et de Résolution - Banque de France (2016).

[45] The so-called 'Four-Eyes Principle' is not new in France. Under the *Code Monétaire et Financier* (French Monetary and Finance Code), Article L 532-9 imposes the 'four-eyes rule'.

It means that the portfolio management company must be effectively managed by at least two people with a view to guaranteeing its sound and prudent management (*'La société de gestion de portefeuille est dirigée effectivement par deux personnes au moins possédant l'honorabilité nécessaire et l'expérience adéquate à leur fonction, en vue de garantir sa gestion saine et prudente'*).

The General Court of the European Union, by the Judgment 24 April 2018 in Joined Cases T-133/16 to T-136/16, has declared that the same person may not occupy at the same time the place of chairman of the board of directors and that of 'effective director' in credit institutions subject to prudential supervision.

The concept of 'effective director' refers to members of the senior management, a function which may not be combined with a non-executive supervisory function.

See, about the so called 'Four-Eyes Principle' in the French legal system, AMF (2004), p. 57; Samin (2000); Bonneau (2005); Marly (2015); Storck (2016), p. 1.

relation to the presumed responsibilities that may arise from the failure to exercise this duty.

Nor does the Insurance Code seem to offer any insight into the scope of the power to intervene in any significant decision given by the Notice 2015 to at least two of the persons who effectively direct insurance companies.

Nor does the Commercial Code seem to provide for what appears to be a kind of veto power that could be vested in those who actually run insurance undertakings, given that, from time to time, they should be allowed to intervene in any significant decision before it is taken, as it should be possible—as a result of the power of intervention—to prevent the decision from being taken, or from being taken in the same form conceived prior to the exercise of the power of intervention itself.[46]

Yet, in the absence of any clue in the regulatory act regarding the possibility of reconstructing the existence of a veto power on the part of those who actually direct insurance undertakings, instrumental to the previous duty to intervene in any significant decision, there seems to be no alternative for the interpreter except to change the hermeneutical approach.

To this end, it seems that the duty/power to intervene in relation to the taking of any significant decision by those who actually direct insurance undertakings—mentioned in the Notice 2015—can only be preceded by a power/duty to act in an informed manner.[47]

It is the same Notice 2015—in Article 2, entitled *'Exigences générales en matière de gouvernance'* ('General governance requirements')—that place the duty to act in an informed manner at the top of the list of elements that contribute to shaping the system of corporate governance of insurance undertakings, to the extent that the following Article 2.1 is specifically entitled '*L'organe d'administration, de gestion ou de contrôle*' ('The administration, management or control body'), as if to highlight the fact that the administration, management and control bodies base their functioning on the exchange of information not only between themselves but also with the members of the key functions of the companies.

The regulatory measure, however, fulfils the legislator's intention set out in Article 354-1 of the Insurance Code, in accordance with Article 41 of Solvency II, to provide insurance undertakings with a system of corporate governance that includes an effective system for the transmission of information.

---

[46]The reflections expressed here are evidently influenced by the experience gained in Italy in relation to Article 2257, paragraph II, of the *Codice Civile* (Italian Civil Code), which dictates *'Se l'amministrazione spetta disgiuntamente a più soci, ciascun socio amministratore ha diritto di opporsi all'operazione che un altro voglia compiere, prima che sia compiuta'* ('If the administration is the responsibility of several shareholders, each managing shareholder has the right to oppose the operation that another wants to carry out, before it is completed').

[47]The power/duty to act in an informed manner, after all, allows each of the responsible officers to exercise control over the operations of the others.

See Storck (2016), p. 2.

From this reconstructive point of view, therefore, the idea that the power to intervene in the taking of any significant decision established in favour of those who actually direct insurance undertakings, from Article 2.3 of the Notice 2015, seems to be best interpreted as their duty to intervene (after all, the verb used in the French language '*intervenir*' can be translated as both 'to intervene' and 'to become involved').

Whoever becomes involved in a decision merely contributes—whether in a favourable or contrary way to the party or parties responsible for making that decision.

However, a person who intervenes in a decision can influence the outcome.

Assuming that those who actually manage insurance undertakings are burdened with 'becoming involved' in any significant decision, rather than being required to 'intervene' therein, seems, on the one hand, to be a way of providing them with an exegesis of the regulatory measure that could protect certain subjects from the probable failure that a differently-oriented reading of the provision in question could cause during a conflict of powers between those who, for various reasons, are called upon to make a significant decision for insurance undertakings; on the other hand, it could be an adequate response to the spirit shown by the Regulator through the continuous call for collaboration between the top management of the company, which is instrumental to achieving an effective system of corporate governance. At the end, it could be argued that the basic requirement for being appointed as 'effective manager' (*'dirigeant effectif'*) in French insurance undertakings is to be involved in strategic decisions.

This could confirm the working hypothesis on the basis of which the idea was put forward that not only the directors, but also the senior managers, could be considered as parties included in the scope of operations of the so called 'two eyes principle'.

4.2 In Spain and the United Kingdom

The contrast between company administration, on the one hand, and management, on the other, seems to be found intact in the provisions[48] that the Spanish legislator dedicates to the system of government of insurance undertakings.[49]

[48] Articles 65–67, Chapter I, Title III, *Ley 20/2015, de 14 de julio, de ordenación, supervisión y solvencia de las entidades aseguradoras y reaseguradoras* (Insurance Undertakings Act)—hereinafter, for the sake of brevity, referred to only as L*OSSEAR*, in accordance with the acronym used by the same legislator—as well as Articles 44–47, Chapter I, Title III, *Real Decreto 1060/2015, de 20 de noviembre, de ordenación, supervisión y solvencia de las entidades aseguradoras y reaseguradoras* (Insurance Undertakings Regulation).

[49] The only exception is one of the final provisions of the text—namely Article 192, letter c)—where they are considered jointly, when they refer to the general representative, or, in any case, to those who exercise powers of effective management of a foreign insurance company established in Spain.

Article 2 LOSSEAR—intended to delimit the perimeter of the law—in letter c) begins by declaring that it is addressed to natural or legal persons who, for any reason,[50] perform administrative or management functions for insurance companies.

An unexpected clarification regarding the persons regarded as holders of administrative and management powers, respectively, appears to be found in a sentence in the second paragraph of Article 24, which is devoted to a quite different aspect, i.e. the absence of any required administrative authorisation to carry on insurance undertakings.

It does not seem essential for the moment to transcribe the entire paragraph, nor to provide an illustration of the premise of the legal precept that is understood as subject to common interpretation.

It seems sufficient to transpose here the only sentence of the above-mentioned regulation that seems to provide a regulatory foothold to the uncertain assumptions made so far.

This refers to the subordinate sentence *'… como los mencionados administradores o directores'* ('such as the aforementioned administrators or directors') placed in relation to the main sentence *'Esta obligación será solidaria entre la entidad y quienes, desempeñando en la misma cargos de administración o dirección …'* ('This obligation will be jointly and severally between the company and those who, holding the same administration or management positions …').

The legislator, according to the sentence under review—which, now, for ease of understanding, is transcribed in the correct order *'Esta obligación será solidaria entre la entidad y quienes, desempeñando en la misma cargos de administración o dirección, hubieren autorizado o permitido la celebración de tales contratos u operaciones, todo ello sin perjuicio de la infracción administrativa en la que hubieran podido incurrir tanto la entidad como los mencionados administradores o directores'*—in making the directors and officers of insurance companies aware of the liability they may incur if they were to conduct insurance business in the absence of administrative authorisation, refers to them as cited above (*'… como los mencionados administradores o directores'*).

Article 24 LOSSEAR, on the other hand, mentions for the first time the directors and officers of insurance undertakings,[51] since it previously made a different reference to those who perform administrative or management functions (*'quienes desempeñando cargos de administración o dirección'*).

---

[50]This provision could find a similar reference with Article 236.4 *Ley de sociedades de capital* (Limited Liability Companies Act), referred to the provisions on duties and responsibility applicable to the person—whatever his name—who has the powers attributed to the highest management of the company.

See furthermore Juste Mencía (2016), p. 433 ff.

[51]Spanish law has not dealt with non-organic management, at least from the legal commercial perspective, which is insufficient to build the figure of the director within capital companies.

See furthermore Juste Mencía (2000), p. 450; Menéndez (2003), p. 195 ff.; Latorre Chiner (2013).

If those who exercise functions of administration and management of insurance undertakings are the 'mentioned' directors and officers, it would seem that the structure of relations between holders of administrative and management powers was officially established (up to now this relation could only be unofficially based on a series of conjectures).

The conceptual framework thus formulated seems to receive a decisive endorsement from the following Article 38 LOSSEAR.

This article—which dictates the requirements that must be met by those who exercise the effective management of insurance companies, i.e. perform functions that constitute an integral part of the system of corporate governance (both concepts on which it is not considered useful to dwell, as their content derives directly from Solvency II)—in providing, in the second paragraph, an indication of those who exercise effective management, mentions 'those who hold positions of administration or management' (*'quienes desempeñando cargos de administración o dirección'*), to clarify immediately thereafter—in letters a) and b), respectively—that such positions are considered to be (i) 'directors or members of the board of directors' (*'los administradores o miembros de los órganos colegiados de administración'*); (ii) 'general managers and persons regarded as such' (*'los directores generales y asimilados'*), considering as general managers 'all those who perform senior management functions under the direct supervision of the Board of Directors, executive committees or managing directors' (*'entendiendo por tales todas aquellas personas que ejerzan en la entidad la alta dirección bajo la dependencia directa de su órgano de administración, de comisiones ejecutivas o de consejeros delegados de aquel'*).[52]

It seems, therefore, that we can conclude that in insurance undertakings under Spanish law, administration is the responsibility of the *'administradores'* (directors), while management is the responsibility of the *'directores'* (senior managers).[53]

Support for this idea could also be found in Article 540, paragraph IV, letter c) of the *Ley de Sociedades de Capital* (Companies Act), which, although referring only to listed companies, requires an annual report to be made public providing information on the corporate governance structure adopted, with a distinction to be made between holders of directorships and management positions.

---

[52]The characterising elements of the senior management personnel that derive from the above definition are, on the one hand, the exercise of powers inherent to the ownership of the company and related to the general objectives of the same, and, on the other hand, the performance of the same with autonomy, and fully responsibility, only limited by the criteria and instructions of the higher government and administrative bodies.

See Martinez Moreno (1994), p. 55; Gutiérrez García (2009), p. 1; Juste Mencía (2013); Latorre Chiner (2013).

[53]The decentralisation of functions and the structural complexity of large companies lead to the creation of management teams that, under various names, are made up of the directors of the main areas of the company.

See Juste Mencía (2006), p. 1031; Latorre Chiner (2013).

A significant contribution to understanding the powers of administration conferred on 'senior managers' could have been found in the Financial Services and Markets Act 2000[54] (hereinafter, for the sake of brevity, referred to only as FSMA in accordance with the indications of the British legislator), which, together with the Financial Services and Markets Statutory Instrument 2015 No. 575 (better known as 'The Solvency 2 Regulations 2015'), formed—until 31 December 2020[55]—the reference regulatory framework for the application of the precepts of Solvency in the United Kingdom.

The functions of 'senior management',[56] in the case of companies subject to the application of the FSMA 2000, are characterised, under Section 59ZA, by profiles of daily management, which require the taking of decisions, or even mere participation in the taking of decisions.[57] These decisions may have serious consequences on the performance of the company itself, if not indeed on the functioning of the economic market in the whole of Great Britain.[58]

---

[54] The Financial Services and Markets Act 2000 (FSMA), regulates the public offering and listing of shares and other securities.

It applies to both private and public companies.

The legal and regulatory framework which applies to private and public companies is primarily set out in the Companies Act 2006 and the Financial Services and Markets Act 2000.

In addition, the Disclosure Guidance and Transparency Rules sourcebook applies to a public company that is listed or that has shares traded on a UK market. It sets out the disclosure guidance, transparency rules, corporate governance rules and certain other requirements applicable primarily to companies that are admitted to the Official List and traded on the Main Market (with some parts applying also to companies quoted on AIM).

[55] The United Kingdom has ceased to belong to the European Union on 31 December 2020.

On 5 March 2019, the EIOPA and all national competent authorities of the European Economic Area with competencies in insurance agreed memoranda of understanding with the Bank of England in its capacity as the Prudential Regulation Authority (PRA) and the Financial Conduct Authority (FCA) of the United Kingdom.

The MoUs took effect starting on 1 January 2021, at the end of the transition period following the departure of the UK from the European Union.

Since this date, all Union primary and secondary law no longer applies to the United Kingdom, including the Solvency II Directive as well as the Directive on Insurance Distribution.

See furthermore Herbst and Lovegrove (2020).

[56] See furthermore about this topic Bournois and Livian (1997), p. 31; Sisson and Marginson (2003), p. 78; Koukiadaki (2009), p. 21.

[57] Deighton et al. (2009), p. 15, seem to substantiate the assertions made in this text, in the part where they state that 'It is clearly not practical for the board, which includes non-executive members, to actually perform the day-to-day management of the company, to develop and to maintain the system of internal control or to undertake risk management. This is, therefore, delegated to the executive directors and the other senior management'.

[58] In the British insurance market system, the LMA - Lloyd's Managing Agents (2019), although has been designed for Lloyd's managing agents, was intended to highlight certain important aspects of the Senior Managers & Certification Regime (SM&CR).

So, for instance, these were some of the definitions given for the holders of the Senior Management Functions.

Thus, 'Head of Key Business Area', individuals who are responsible for the management of business areas and divisions that are sufficiently large and complex to have a potential impact upon

Ultimately, it does not seem to be the membership to the board of directors that distinguishes the 'two persons' ensuring to take every significant decision, but rather it is the nature of the functions performed, in relation to the type of activities carried out, to allow the senior managers to be involved in some aspects of the firm strategy, such as viability and sustainability of the business model and the establishment, maintenance and use of the risk appetite.

References

Abriani N (2019) Le modificazioni al codice civile introdotte dal d.lgs. n. 14/2019. In: D'Arrico C et al (eds) Commento al codice della crisi d'impresa. I quaderni di *in executivis*, Genius (3), pp 36–63

ACPR - Autorité de Contrôle Prudentiel et de Résolution - Banque de France (2015) Notice 'Solvabilité II' - Systeme de gouvernance du 17 decembre 2015. https://acpr.banque-france.fr/sites/default/files/20151218-notice-solvabilite2-systeme-gouvernance_1.pdf. Accessed 18 May 2021

ACPR - Autorité de Contrôle Prudentiel et de Résolution - Banque de France (2016) Notice sur la désignation des 'dirigeants effectifs' et des 'responsabile de fonction clés' dans le régime 'Solvabilité 2' (PCRA - Prudential Control and Résolution Authority - Bank of France. Notice ACPR on the designation of 'effective managers' and 'key function managers' in the 'Solvency 2' regime). https://acpr.banquefrance.fr/sites/default/files/media/2020/08/07/11._notice_gouvernance-post-ccap.pdf. Accessed 18 May 2021

Alces K-A (2011) Beyond the board of directors. Wake Forest Law Rev:783–836

AMF - Autorité des marchés financiers - (2004) Application de la règle des 'quatre yeux' dans les sociétés de gestion de portefeuille. https://www.amf-france.org/sites/default/files/doctrine/fr/Position/DOC-2004-05/1.0/Application%20de%20la%20regle%20des%20quatre%20yeux%20dans%20les%20societes%20de%20gestion%20de%20portefeuille.pdf. Accessed 18 May 2021

AMF - Autorité des marchés financiers - (2021) Règlement général (FMA - Financial Markets Authority - General Regulation). https://www.amf-france.org/fr/eli/fr/aai/amf/rg/20210101/notes. Accessed 18 May 2021

Anderloni L, Moro O, Tanda A (2019) Governance e performance nelle imprese di assicurazioni: un'analisi bibliometrica ed una meta analisi. http://dem-web.unipv.it/web/docs/dipeco/quad/ps/RePEc/pav/demwpp/DEMWP0177.pdf. Accessed 18 May 2021

Angelici C (1990) Società per azioni e in accomandita per azioni. In: Enc. dir., vol XLII, Giuffrè, Milano, pp 997–1042

Bailey A (2015) Governance and the role of the boards. Speech given at Westminster Business Forum, London, 3 November 2015

Bonneau T (2005) Regle des 'quatre yeux'. Dr. sociétés, comm. 55

Bournois F, Livian Y-F (1997) Managers, Cadres, Leitende Angestellte: some landmarks about managerial titles and definition. In: Livian Y-F et al (eds) Middle managers in Europe. Routledge, London, pp 25–38

the firm's safety and soundness; 'Key Functions Holders', any person who is responsible for discharging a function which is of specific importance to the sound and prudent management of the firm; 'Material Risk Takers', those individuals whose professional activities have a material impact on the firm's risk profile.

Cabras G (1995) La forma d'impresa. Organizzazione della gestione nelle società di capitali. Giappichelli, Torino
Champaud C (1962) Le pouvoir de concentation de la société par actions. Sirey, Paris
Charreaux G (1997) Les gouvernement des enterprises. Corporate governance: theories et faits. Economica, Paris
Clarke S, Phelan E (2015) Stepping stones to ORSA: looking beyond the preparatory phase of Solvency II. https://it.milliman.com/-/media/Milliman/importedfiles/uploadedFiles/insight/2015/stepping-stones-to-orsa.ashx. Accessed 18 May 2021
Corporate Governance Committee of Borsa Italiana (2020) Codice di *Corporate Governance*. https://www.borsaitaliana.it/comitato-corporate-governance/codice/2020.pdf. Accessed 18 May 2021
Deighton S-P, Dix R-C, Graham J-R, Skinner J-M-E (2009) Governance and risk management in United Kingdom insurance companies. Paper presented at the U.K. Institute of Actuaries, London, 23 March 2009
Dell'Atti S, Sylos Labini S, Di Biase P (2018) The effects of Solvency II on corporate board: a survey on Italian insurance companies. Corp Ownersh Control 16(1):134–144
Dodevska V-P, Nuredini B (2019) Corporate governance in insurance companies - need or trend? Paper presented at UBT International Conference, Prishtina, October 2019
Dreher M (2015) Treatise on Solvency II. Springer, Berlin
EIOPA - European Insurance and Occupational Pensions Authority - (2014) Public consultation on the Set 1 of the Solvency II Guidelines. https://register.eiopa.europa.eu/Pages/Consultations/Public-consultation-on-the-Set-1-of-the-Solvency-II-Guidelines.aspx. Accessed 18 May 2021
EIOPA - European Insurance and Occupational Pensions Authority - (2015) Final Report on Public Consultation No. 14/17 on Guidelines on system of governance. https://register.eiopa.europa.eu/Publications/Consultations/EIOPA_EIOPA-BoS-14-253-Final%20report_Governance.pdf. Accessed 18 May 2021
EIOPA - European Insurance and Occupational Pensions Authority - (2016) Guidelines on System of Governance. https://www.eiopa.europa.eu/content/guidelines-system-governance_en. Accessed 18 May 2021
Fama E, Jensen M (1983) Agency problems and residual claims. J Law Econ 26(2):327–349
Farenga L (2016) Seminari per i dieci anni del codice delle assicurazioni private. In: Quaderno n. 5. I.V.ASS - Istituto Vigilanza per le Assicurazioni - . Available via DIALOG. https://www.ivass.it/pubblicazioni-e-statistiche/pubblicazioni/quaderni/2016/iv5/ivassq0018.pdf. Accessed 18 May 2021
Fleckner A-M, Hopt K-J (2013) Comparative corporate governance. A functional and international analysis. Cambridge University Press, Cambridge
FRC - Financial Reporting Council - (2018a) UK Corporate Governance Code. https://www.frc.org.uk/getattachment/88bd8c45-50ea-4841-95b0-d2f4f48069a2/2018-UK-Corporate-Governance-Code-FINAL.pdf. Accessed 18 May 2021
FRC - Financial Reporting Council - (2018b) Guidance on Board Effectiveness. https://www.frc.org.uk/getattachment/61232f60-a338-471b-ba5a-bfed25219147/2018-Guidance-on-Board-Effectiveness-FINAL.PDF. Accessed 18 May 2021
Goergen M (2018) Corporate governance: a global perspective. Cengage Learning, Andover
Gutiérrez García E (2009) Identificación del alto directivo en la doctrina del TSJ de Madrid (2000-2008). Arz. Social (13)
Henderson MT (2013) Reconceptualizing Corporate Boards. Cato Institute Regulation. Available via DIALOG. https://www.cato.org/sites/cato.org/files/serials/files/regulation/2013/9/regv36n3-5n.pdf. Accessed 18 May 2021
Herbst J, Lovegrove S (2020) Brexit and financial regulation. Oxford University Press, Oxford
I.V.ASS. - Istituto per la Vigilanza sulle Assicurazioni - (2018) Regolamento N. 38 del 3 luglio 2018. (Regulation No. 38 of 3 July 2018). https://www.ivass.it/normativa/nazionale/secondaria-ivass/regolamenti/2018/n38/index.html. Accessed 18 May 2021

Iglesias Prada J-L (1971) Administración y delegación de facultades en la sociedad anonima. Tecnos, Madrid
Juste Mencía J (2000) En torno a la aplicación del régimen de responsabilidad de los administradores al apoderado general. Revista de derecho de sociedades 14:441–458
Juste Mencía J (2006) La posición del equipo directivo en la estructura de gobierno de la sociedad cotizada: la responsabilidad de los Consejeros ejecutivos y miembros de la Alta Dirección. In: Artigas R et al (eds) Derecho de sociedades anónimas cotizadas, vol II. Aranzadi, Madrid, pp 1029–1054
Juste Mencía J (2013) El ámbito subjectivo de la calificación. In: Rojo A et al (eds) La calificación del concurso y la responsabilidad por insolvencia. Aranzadi, Madrid, pp 387–415
Juste Mencía J (2016) Acción social de responsabilidades contra los administradores: nuevos sujetos responsables. In: Artigas R et al (eds) 'Liber Amicorum' Profesor Luis Fernández de la Gándara. Aranzadi, Madrid, pp 433–449
Kakabadse A, Kakabadse N-K, Khan N (2014) The Company Secretary. Building trust through governance. Institute of Chartered Secretaries and Administrators-Henley Business School, University of Reading. Avalaible via DIALOG https://www.icsa.org.uk/knowledge/research/the-company-secretary-report. Accessed 18 May 2021
Koukiadaki A (2009) I *senior managers* nel diritto del lavoro inglese. Dir. rel. ind. (1):17–34
Latorre Chiner N (2013) El apoderado general en la ley concursal. Revista de Derecho Concursal y Paraconcursal 19:65–80
Lener R (2016) La governance delle banche italiane. In: Scritti. Associazione Disiano Preite Bologna. Avalaible via DIALOG. http://www.associazionepreite.it/scritti/lener-la-governance.pdf. Accessed 18 May 2021
Lin L (1996) The effectiveness of outside directors as a corporate governance mechanism: theories and evidence. Northwest Univ Law Rev 90(3):898–930
LMA - Lloyd's Managing Agents - (2019) Guidance for managing agents: Senior Managers & Certification Regime (SM&CR). https://www.lmalloyds.com. Accessed 18 May 2021
Manes P (2017) Corporate governance, the approach to risk and the insurance industry under Solvency II. In: Andenas M et al (eds) Solvency II: a dynamic challenge for the insurance market. Il Mulino, Bologna, pp 93–129
Marino D-M, Cimarelli C (2018) Prima lettura delle novità introdotte dal Regolamento I.V.ASS. sul governo societario delle imprese e dei gruppi assicurativi. In: Diritto bancario. Available via DIALOG. https://www.dirittobancario.it/sites/default/files/allegati/marino_d._e_cimarelli_c._novita_regolamento_ivass_sul_governo_societario_2018.pdf. Accessed 18 May 2021
Marino D-M, Costa S (2015) L'attuazione della direttiva Solvency III: un quadro di sintesi. In: Diritto bancario. Available via DIALOG. http://www.dirittobancario.it/approfondimenti/assicurazioni/l-attuazione-italia-della-direttiva-solvency-ii-un-quadro-di-sintesi. Accessed 18 May 2021
Marly P-G (2015) Nouvelle étape dans la transposition de la directive 'Solvabilité 2'. In: L'Essentiel droit des assurances. Available via DIALOG. http://lext.so/EDAS-615092-61506. Accessed 18 May 2021
Marly P-G (2017a) Précisions sur la gouvernance des organisms d'assurance. In: L'Essentiel droit des assurances. Lextenso. Available via DIALOG. http://lext.so/DAS110f0. Accessed 18 May 2021
Marly P-G (2017b) Dirigeants effectifs et fonction clés. La semaine juridique-Enterprise et affaires 21–22:41–42
Martinez Moreno C (1994) La relación de trabajo especial de alta dirección. Consejo Económico y Social de España, Madrid
Martynova M, Renneboog L (2013) An international corporate governance index. In: Wright M et al (eds) The Oxford handbook of corporate governance. Oxford University Press, Oxford, pp 97–132
Mc Nulty T (2013) Understanding board behavior and effectiveness. In: Wright M et al (eds) The Oxford handbook of corporate governance. Oxford University Press, Oxford, pp 163–176

Menéndez A (2003) Auxiliares del empresario. In: Alonso Garcia R et al (eds) Liber Amicorum. Economia, empresario y trabajo. Homenaje a Manuel Alonso Olea. Civita, Madrid, pp 195–228
Montalenti P (2021) Corporate governance in Europe: a general overview. Assicurazioni 1:9–28
OECD - Organization for Economic Co-operation and Development - (2015) Principles of Corporate Governance. https://www.oecd-ilibrary.org/governance/g20-oecd-principles-of-corporate-governance-2015_9789264236882-en. Accessed 18 May 2021
Pailluseau J (1967) La société anonyme: Technique d'organisation de l'enterprise. Sirey, Paris
Robin Olivier S (2009) I *cadres* nell'ordinamento francese. Dir. rel. Ind. (1):35–46
Rodriguez Artigas F (1971) Notas sober el régimen juridico del director general de la S.A. In: Estudios jurídicos en homenaje a Joaquín Garrigues, vol III. Tecnos, Madrid, pp 113–140
Samin T (2000) Les dirigeants responsables au sens de l'article 17 de la loi bancaire du 24 janvier 1984. Banque et droit. Available via DIALOG. http://www.revue-banque.fr/article/les-dirigeants-responsables-au-sens-article-17-loi. Accessed 18 May 2021
Selleri L (2010) L'impatto di Solvency II sull'organizzazione dell'impresa di assicurazione: verso l'organizzazione per processi? Dir. economia assicur:605–615
Siri M (2017) Corporate governance of insurance firms after Solvency II. In: Marano P et al (eds) Insurance regulation in the European Union. Springer, Berlin, pp 129–177
Siri M (2018) La centralità del governo societario nel sistema di Solvibilità II. In: Quaderno n. 11. I. V.ASS - Istituto Vigilanza per le Assicurazioni - . Available via DIALOG. https://www.ivass.it/pubblicazioni-e-statistiche/pubblicazioni/quaderni/2018/iv11/Quaderno_11.pdf. Accessed 18 May 2021
Sisson K, Marginson P (2003) Management: systems, structures and strategy. In: Edwards P (ed) Industrial relations: theory and practice. Blackwell, Oxford, pp 89–122
Storck M (2016) Le rôle des dirigeants effectifs d'une société de gestion est précisé par la commission des sanctions de l'AMF. Revue de droit bancaire et financier 5:1–2
Tricker R-I (2019) Corporate governance: principles, policies and practices. Oxford University Press, Oxford
Vella F (2014) Banche e assicurazioni: le nuove frontiere della corporate governance. Banca impresa società:289–332
Venuti F et al (2016) The impact of corporate governance on risk taking in European Insurance Industry. World Acad Sci Eng Technol Open Sci J 10(1):188–194
Vicent Chuliá F (2008) Introducción al Derecho Mercantil. Tirant lo Blanch, Valencia
Winter J (2011) The financial crisis: does good corporate governance matter and how to achieve it? Duisenberg School of Finance Policy Paper. Available via DIALOG. https://papers.ssrn.com/sol3/papers.cfm?abstract_id=1972057. Accessed 18 May 2021

The Risk Management System, the Risk Culture and the Duties of the Insurers' Directors

Pierpaolo Marano and Simon Grima

Abstract The risk management system and the risk culture pertain to the organisation of the insurance undertaking and face the risk, which is a multifaceted concept challenging such an organisation. This chapter analyses the perimeter of the risk management system to identify the risks that fall within this system and the persons who, within the insurance undertaking, are responsible for ensuring an effective risk management system to the supervisory authority. The chapter also investigates how corporate bodies can assess the head of the risk management function and the risk management system can incorporate risk culture. Lastly, the chapter illustrates concrete actions the persons with the ultimate responsibility of the risk management system can perform to comply with the task to promote, implement and monitor the risk culture.

1 Introduction

Solvency II, which is considered as one of the most sophisticated insurance regulatory regimes is built around the principles of market consistency which aim is to instil strong risk management, governance and internal control systems within the insurance industry. It proposed to remedy the shortcomings of Solvency I by introducing a sweeping regulatory reform for insurance companies.[1]

[1] See Manes (2017), p. 111 ff.; Van Hulle (2019), p. 38 ff. See also Loguinova (2019) for an assessment of the ideology of Solvency II.

P. Marano (✉)
Department of Legal Studies, Catholic University of the Sacred Heart, Milan, Italy
e-mail: pierpaolo.marano@unicatt.it

S. Grima
University of Malta, Department of Insurance, Msida, Malta
e-mail: simon.grima@um.edu.mt

P. Marano, K. Noussia (eds.), *The Governance of Insurance Undertakings*, AIDA Europe Research Series on Insurance Law and Regulation 6,
https://doi.org/10.1007/978-3-030-85817-9_2

Although Solvency II is mostly known for its risk-based capital requirement calculation, one of the most important elements in this regime is the heavy reliance on robust risk management practices.[2] Thus, an underlying objective for Solvency II is to improve the system of governance within an organisation. As stated in Recital No. 29 of Solvency II, 'some risks may only be properly addressed through governance requirements rather than through the quantitative requirements reflected in the Solvency Capital Requirement. An effective system of governance is therefore essential for the adequate management of the insurance undertaking and the regulatory system'.

This approach is common to the EU regulation on financial services[3] and denotes the willingness of regulators to dominate uncertainty by organising market uncertainty into recognisable categories of quantifiable risks.[4] However, the risk management regulation may facilitate misperceptions about what risk management can and cannot do.[5] The push towards a quantitative risk assessment based on statutory schemes and a fixed pattern to catch it could prevent a true risk culture based on a 'thinking outside of the box' approach.[6] The risk management needs to move from mere calculation to a broader range of activities, including scenario-thinking, war-gaming, playing the devil's advocate.[7]

Solvency II requires insurance undertakings to set up a risk management system and, therefore, enforces risk management to be embedded in the day-to-day activities of insurance undertakings. However, so far, several insurance undertakings have been focusing on improving risk measurement frameworks, rather than taking the opportunity to implement a real cultural change based on an intelligent understanding of the actual risks they are facing.[8] Addressing risks proactively requires that insurance undertakings are aware of the current risk culture within the organisation, the industry and the direct and indirect effect of the wider environment surrounding the industry. It requires an understanding of risk and the tools available to address these risks. Moreover, it requires that directors are fully aware and kept abreast of assumptions about models used to measure and report risks, are involved in and understand the Own Risk Self-Assessment (ORSA), the need for a Risk Register and are involved in the design of and understand the stress tests and reverse stress tests implemented.

However, one should be aware of the concept of risk.[9] Risk classification in insurance markets is the avenue through which insurance undertakings try to be

---

[2] Bernardino (2011), p. 2.

[3] Everson and Vos (2016), p. 139 ff.

[4] Mikes (2011), p. 2.

[5] Enriques and Zetzsche (2013), p. 282 ff.

[6] Manes (2017), p. 110.

[7] Manes (2017), p. 110.

[8] See PricewaterhouseCoopers (PWC) (2019), p. 2.

[9] See Milkau (2017), p. on the different perspectives about risk and culture developed along the historical perspective.

efficient and compete in insurance contracts.[10] Solvency II requests insurers to adopt a forward-looking approach for risks including those of underwriting but not limited to these risks. The intent is to take an enterprise risk-management approach towards capital standards that will provide an integrated solvency framework that covers all significant risk categories and their interdependencies.[11] Every risk management process should be custom made, reflecting the firm's profit goal, existing risk portfolio and risk appetite.[12] Risk is a multifaceted concept, and its identification requires complex approaches that are often misunderstood. The consequence is that decisions are based on limited perception rather than the full value and meaning of what risk is, as a result, the way it is being tackled is incorrect.

Since risk management is concerned with what might happen in the future risk managers are also concerned with creating scenarios by using models to generate: (i) 'stress tests'; this involves evaluating the impact of extreme, but plausible, scenarios that are not considered by value at risk (VaR) or expected shortfall (ES) models and (ii) 'reverse stress tests'[13]—also known as a 'pre-mortem',[14] this is a managerial strategy in which a project team imagines that a project or organisation has failed, and then works backwards to determine what potentially could lead to the failure of the project or organisation. However, these tests are as good as the directors or their advisors. They depend on their experience, skills and knowledge. Therefore, authorising or recruiting the wrong persons can mean that the risk key indicators (red flags) are set and calibrated incorrectly.

Furthermore, Solvency II pushes insurance undertakings to promote a risk culture alongside the setting up of the risk management function. Weaknesses in risk culture are often considered a root cause of the global financial crisis, headline risk and compliance events.[15] A sound risk culture consistently supports appropriate risk awareness, behaviours and judgements about risk-taking within a strong risk governance framework.[16] Thus, risk culture and risk management can be considered as the two sides of the same coin—the risk governance—and the improvement of the risk culture does not affect the performance of financial institutions.[17] However, risk culture can be implemented in different ways. A cognitive risk culture, which focuses on improving the understanding of risk and resolving the problems by addressing their root cause,[18] stands in contrast to compliance-based and defensive risk cultures. The risk culture could be implemented only to demonstrate to the authorities that their request is being fulfiled, or to promote professionally

---

[10] See Croker and Snow (2000), p. 245 ff.

[11] See Klein (2012), p. 186.

[12] See Skipper and Kwon (2007), p. 293.

[13] See Grundke (2011), p. 71 ff.

[14] See Eisenbach et al. (2020), p. 2.

[15] FSB (2014), p. 1.

[16] FSB (2014), p. 1.

[17] Bianchi et al. (2021).

[18] See Agarwal and Kallapur (2018).

sub-optimal or even wrong decisions for the sake of preventing lawsuits and blame.[19]

However, risk culture goes also beyond the regulators.[20] In the current economic environment, companies are looking for opportunities to differentiate themselves from their peers particularly in the area of risk management.[21] Determining and documenting the risk culture, appetite, tolerance and strategy provide credible evidence, which can be used to inform regulators, clients, rating agencies and other stakeholders.[22] By promoting a common language, and structure in which to discuss risk culture and risk management across the undertaking,[23] one can envisage an environment where reporting, communicating and monitoring risk culture is a key part of public disclosures and advertising.[24] However, some organisations still currently lack this focus and consistency.[25]

2 Aim and Research Questions

The introductory remarks outlined the relevance of the risk management system within the governance of the insurance undertakings. A risk culture must be embedded in the governance together with risk management practices. Both the risk management system and the risk culture pertain to the organisation of the company and face the risk. The risk is a multifaceted concept, which challenges the organisation of the insurance undertaking. These remarks allow us to define the aim of this chapter and, ultimately, the research questions.

The preliminary issue concerns the perimeter of the risk management system. The analysis aims to identify the risks that fall within this system and the persons who, within the insurance undertaking, are responsible for ensuring an effective risk management system to the supervisory authority. The risk management system includes the risk management function, but it does not end with the latter. Several people within the company might be deemed responsible by the supervisory authority and/or determine the ultimate responsibility of whoever appointed them as well as of the undertaking. The board of directors is responsible for managing the business (in all its respects) under corporate law. One should understand to what extent individuals bear ultimate responsibility for the functioning of the risk management system, including the head of the risk management function. Thus, corporate bodies

[19] See Agarwal and Kallapur (2018).

[20] See Awrey et al. (2013), p. 217 ff.

[21] See Dobrota (2012), p. 227.

[22] See MFSA (2020).

[23] See Bondesson (2011), p. 58 f.

[24] See International Finance Corporation (IFC) (2015), p. 33.

[25] See Grima and Bezzina (2021) in press.

including staff working within the company fall into the scope of the analysis. While external auditors are outside the scope.

Based on the result of this analysis, our second research question relates to how corporate bodies can assess the performances of the head of the risk management function. Solvency II provides for a list of risks and a questionnaire and is in a sense, at the standardised approach/model level, prescriptive in the methodologies to be used to monitor and quantify the risks, although companies are expected to add-on other risks that the company may face (Pillar II). It is however more flexible when if the undertaking is using an internal model, which can only be used if the undertaking has proven capacity and experience and it is allowed by the regulator. We aim to understand if these lists, questionnaire and models are exhaustive. How can one understand ex-ante if methodologies adopted by the head of the risk management function are adequate?

Understanding risk should be part of the corporate culture. Risk culture defines how a company's management and employees understand risk and manage it to maximise rewards.[26] If the risk management function is part of the risk management system, the risk culture should concern all the operational units that are exposed to the risk considered under the risk management system. Thus, risk culture is a component of the risk management system.[27] Such a culture needs to be promoted, implemented and monitored,[28] and persons are responsible for these processes.[29] With this analysis, we will therefore investigate the third research question, that is, the concrete actions that can be performed by the persons with the ultimate responsibility of the risk management system to comply with the above task.[30]

Based on the above, the next section aims to answer the first research questions and, therefore, will investigate both the perimeter of the risk management system and the legal foundations of the duties imposed on the persons who are responsible for that system to the supervisory authority. In the following two sections we will recommend and suggest solutions to address the other two research questions.

---

[26] Shimpi and Klappach (2013), p. 205.

[27] See Palermo et al. (2017), p. 164 ff., who developed a model of risk culture dynamics.

[28] See Sheedy et al. (2019), who provide the first empirical evidence on how risk compliance is affected by financial incentives and organisational culture.

[29] Shimpi and Klappach (2013), p. 208 f., identifies six important dimensions of an effective risk management culture and outline that leadership is crucial to everyone.

[30] On the internal auditing approaches to risk culture, see Sinha and Arena (2020), p. 81 ff. See also Ring et al. (2013), pp. 364 ff., on the potential use of financial notices as a means of communicating how the regulator interprets the relevance of (risk) culture in an organisation; in particular, the nature of behaviours and actions which might signal what a good or bad (risk) culture looks like.

3 The Perimeter of the Risk Management System and the Persons Who Are Responsible for Its Functioning

Solvency II sets forth that the ‘administrative, management or supervisory body’ (AMSB) of the insurance (or reinsurance) undertaking has the ultimate responsibility for the compliance, by the undertaking concerned, with the laws, regulations and administrative provisions adopted according to Solvency II.[31] Also, Solvency II requires all insurance (and reinsurance) undertakings to have in place an effective system of governance that provides for sound and prudent management of the business.[32] That system must include among other things compliance with the requirements to have in place an effective risk management system comprising strategies, processes and reporting procedures necessary to identify, measure, monitor, manage and report, continuously the risks, at an individual and at an aggregated level, to which they are or could be exposed, and their interdependencies.[33]

The introduction of rules and principles addressed to the corporate bodies of insurance undertakings must consider the absence of a uniform structure of corporate governance in the EU. Solvency II reflects this lack of harmonisation using the generic term ‘administrative, management or supervisory body’ (AMSB) when sets forth rules involving corporate bodies.[34] Although the board structure is a matter of national law, the term AMSB covers both the unitary (one-tier) board structure and the dualistic (two-tier) board structure, which are the recurring board structures in the Member States and regulated by their respective national laws. Where no specific body is specified in national law, the regulatory framework issued under Solvency II provides that the term AMSB means the management body.[35]

The AMSB has the ultimate responsibility of the system of governance comprising the risk management system. Thus, AMSB is responsible for the proper functioning of the risk management system. Consequently, European legislation requires national regulations to identify a corporate body within the AMSB, which is responsible for the system of governance, including the risk management system. Furthermore, the responsibility towards the supervisory authority is established for the whole corporate body as identified by national rules.[36] Thus, it should not be possible to distinguish between the responsibility of the executive and non-executive directors within the management body. European legislation seems to establish their joint responsibility towards the supervisory authority for the compliance to Solvency

[31] See Article 40 of Solvency II.

[32] See Article 41(1) of Solvency II.

[33] See Article 44(1) of Solvency II.

[34] See Van Hulle (2019), p. 402.

[35] See Article 1 (43) Commission Delegated Regulation (EU) 2015/35 of 10 October 2014 supplementing Solvency II.

[36] See EIOPA, Guidelines on system of governance, Guideline No. 17, available at https://www.eiopa.europa.eu/content/guidelines-system-governance_en.

II, including the system of governance/risk management system. This, regardless of what may be provided by national corporate laws.

Being part of the system of governance, the risk management system pursues the same purpose as the first, which is to ensure sound and prudent management of the business.

The meaning of sound and prudent management of the business should be understood, having in mind that the main objective of insurance and reinsurance regulation and supervision in the European Union is the adequate protection of policyholders and beneficiaries.[37] Financial stability and fair and stable markets are other objectives of insurance and reinsurance regulation, and supervision that should also be considered but should not undermine the main objective.[38] Therefore, adequate protection of policyholders has not only a 'passive' meaning consisting of pursuing management of the insurance undertaking that ensures its solvency.

Such protection also has functional significance as clearly expressed by the Directive 2016/97 on insurance distribution (IDD). This Directive sets forth that when carrying out insurance distribution, insurance distributors always act honestly, fairly and professionally in accordance with the best interests of their customers.[39] This principle does not refer only to business conduct but also involves the manufacturing of insurance products.[40] The IDD sets forth product oversight and governance requirements (POG) under which manufacturers must maintain, operate and review a process for the approval of each insurance product to ensure that insurance products meet the needs of the target market.[41] Thus, the sound and prudent management of the business requires insurers not only to ensure their solvency, but also to design products matching the interests and needs of their target market, and to distribute such products to the relevant target market.

Solvency II provides that the risk-management system must cover the risks to be included in the calculation of the Solvency Capital Requirement, as well as the risks which are not or not fully included in the calculation thereof.[42] Some risks may only be properly addressed through governance requirements rather than through the quantitative requirements reflected in the Solvency Capital Requirement. An effective system of governance is therefore essential for the adequate management of the insurance undertaking and the regulatory system.[43] Thus, Solvency II requires insurance undertakings to have in place an effective risk-management system to

[37] See Recital No. 16 of Solvency II, where the term beneficiary is intended to cover any natural or legal person who is entitled to a right under an insurance contract.

[38] See Recital No. 16 of Solvency II.

[39] See Article 17(1) of IDD.

[40] See Joint Position of the European Supervisory Authorities on Manufacturers' Product Oversight & Governance Processes, at point 22. The Joint position is available at https://www.eba.europa.eu/documents/10180/15736/JC-2013-77+%28POG+-+Joint+Position%29.pdf.

[41] See Recital No. 55 of IDD.

[42] See Article 44(2) of Solvency II.

[43] See Recital No. 19 of Solvency II.

identify, measure, monitor, manage and report, continuously, the risks to which they are or could be exposed, and their interdependencies.[44] The IDD complements this provision. The set of rules on POG requests undertakings to manage the risks inherent in poorly designed or improperly distributed products by avoiding the manufacturing and offering of worthless products to customers, and imposing remedial actions in case it happens.[45] POG meets the goal of increasing customer protection by aligning the approach to products with the approach to capital requirements as introduced under Solvency II.[46]

In conclusion, the system of governance comprising the risk management system should be able to address all risks of insurance undertakings, that is, those related to the solvency and the risks inherent to the quality of products and their distribution. The list of risks provided by Solvency II must be complemented with those related to the manufacturing and distribution of the insurance products as arising under the IDD and implementing national laws.[47]

The risk management system must be effective and well-integrated into the organisational structure and in the decision-making processes of the insurance undertaking with proper consideration of the persons who effectively run the undertaking or have other key functions.[48] These persons are the members of the AMSB, taking into account national law, as well as members of the senior management.[49] EIOPA clarified that the AMSB is other than the senior management, which includes persons employed by the undertaking who are responsible for high-level decision making and for implementing the strategies devised and the policies approved by the AMSB.[50]

The AMSB appoints the senior management including the head of the risk management function after a positive fit and proper assessment and is responsible for evaluating reports on risk exposures submitted from the head of the risk management function. Reports and activities will include both the risks to be included in the calculation of the Solvency Capital Requirement as well as the risks which are not or not fully included in the calculation thereof including those related to the manufacturing and distribution of products. These statements introduce the first list of issues outlined earlier concerning how the AMSB can (i) assess the fitness and properness requirements of the head of the risk management function and

[44] See Article 44(1) of Solvency II.

[45] See Marano (2020), p. 65.

[46] See Marano (2020), p. 65.

[47] On the impact of IDD on distribution risk management, Bravo (2020), p. 359 ff.

[48] See Article 44(2) of Solvency II.

[49] EIOPA, Introduction, Guidelines on System of Governance, 2014, at point. 1.21., is available at https://www.eiopa.europa.eu/content/guidelines-system-governance_en.

[50] EIOPA, Introduction, Guidelines on System of Governance, 2014, at point. 1.21. In addition, the following definitions are provided: 'persons having other key functions' which include all persons performing tasks related to a key function, and 'key function holders' who are the persons responsible for a key function as opposed to persons having, carrying out or performing a key function.

(ii) understand ex-ante if methodologies and questionnaires adopted by the head of the risk management function are adequate.

Furthermore, the risk management function is a (key) component of the risk management system as a control function but does not incorporate the whole system which also refers to the business units.

Solvency II does not specifically recognise the 'three lines of defence' model as developed by the Institute of Internal Auditors (IIA) and based on the framework for evaluating internal controls elaborated by COSO.[51] According to the latest version elaborated by the IIA,[52] this model consists of the first line provided by front line staff and operational management, i.e. those providing products/services to clients, where the business units have to anticipate and manage risks at the operating level. The monitoring of risk is the second line, which is provided by the functions of risk management and compliance. These functions provide the oversight and the tools, systems and advice necessary to support the first line in identifying, managing and monitoring risks. Because of the specific nature of insurance, where the liabilities side of the balance sheet is more important, the actuarial function is added to this line.[53] The third line is provided by the internal audit function. This function provides an independent review that the risk management, internal control and actuarial function framework is working as designed.

The three lines model has been challenged promoting four lines of defence, five lines of defence or the integrated lines of defence.[54] An analysis of criticism and a discussion on the most efficient defence model for insurance undertakings is outside the scope of this essay.

Nonetheless, the legal framework introduced under Solvency II sets forth the insurance undertakings must establish information systems that produce complete, reliable, clear, consistent, timely and relevant information concerning the business activities, the commitments assumed and the risks to which the undertaking is exposed,[55] and ensure that all personnel is aware of the procedures for the proper carrying out of their responsibilities.[56] To that end, the risk management function includes the tasks of assisting the AMSB (and other functions in the effective operation of the risk management system)[57] and monitoring the risk management

---

[51] See Van Hulle (2019), p. 408.

[52] IIA, IIA's Three Lines Model. An Update of the Three Lines of Defense, June 2020 available at https://na.theiia.org/about-ia/PublicDocuments/Three-Lines-Model-Updated.pdf.

[53] See Van Hulle (2019), p. 409.

[54] See Borg et al. (2020), p. 303 ff., for further references.

[55] See Article 258(1), let. h), Commission Delegated Regulation (EU) 2015/35 of 10 October 2014 supplementing Solvency II.

[56] See Article 258(1), let. f), Commission Delegated Regulation (EU) 2015/35 of 10 October 2014 supplementing Solvency II.

[57] See Article 269(1) let. a), Commission Delegated Regulation (EU) 2015/35 of 10 October 2014 supplementing Solvency II.

system and the general risk profile of the undertaking as a whole.[58] The AMSB has the ultimate responsibility for ensuring the effectiveness of the risk management system.[59] Such responsibility means ensuring that there is a coordinated and integrated approach to the risk management system and a common 'risk language' with the right tone from the top.[60] Business units are, therefore, the first line of defence within the risk management system introduced under Solvency II. These units are embedded in the risk management system being requested to deal with the risks inherent to their functions. The risk management function must support the business units by providing them with the tools that are pertinent to the management of these risks.

Since the ultimate responsibility of the risk management system lies on the AMSB, the latter should not rely solely on the support provided by the risk management function to the business units. The AMSB must play an active role in promoting and monitoring the implementation of risk culture across the company. This statement is in line with the Insurance Core Principles (ICPs) issued by the International Association of Insurance Supervisors (IAIS). The ICP 8 refers to Risk Management and Internal Controls and provides that the risk management function must be capable of assisting the insurer to promote and sustain a sound risk culture (see Standard 8.1.). The reference to the capability of 'assisting' the insurer should exclude that the risk function has the specific task and the related liability to promote the risk culture. This conclusion opens up the other research question consisting of how the AMSB can assess the performances of the head of the risk management function.

4 Identifying Risk and Managing It

A starting point for addressing risk should be the understanding of what is considered as a risk in the context of the undertaking and the direct and indirect effects over its objectives. Risk is a multifaceted concept, and its identification requires complex approaches that are often misunderstood. The consequence is, that decisions are based on limited perception rather than the full value and meaning of what risk is, as a result, the way it is being tackled is incorrect. Moreover, individuals do not embrace the full multifaceted nature of risk.[61] Regulators impose on directors and individuals, norms and checklists, overuse, or misinterpret the value of models, simulations and templates; thereby reducing responsibility and capability for innovative decision-making. At the same time, the wider use of technology and rules

[58] See Article 269(1) let. b) and c), Commission Delegated Regulation (EU) 2015/35 of 10 October 2014 supplementing Solvency II.

[59] See EIOPA, Guideline No.17, Guidelines on System of Governance, 2014.

[60] See Van Hulle (2019), p. 415.

[61] See Girlando (2021), in press.

reduces the critical thinking of directors and individuals. We advance the automation process by building robots that follow protocols and forget about the part of risk assessment that cannot be programmed. Therefore, before the risk management process can start, one needs to define, understand and communicate the objective, then determine the risks that can affect this objective and identify the controls in place. Regulations and respective guidelines to define this process but forget to address the meaning and context of risk.[62] The framework introduced under Solvency II mentions that we need to address, Market Risk, Settlement Risk, Liquidity Risk, Credit Risk, Interest Rate Risk, Model Risk and any other Business Risk, etc.,[63] and it does go into great detail on how to address these risks and their definition but there is no mention of the definition of risk itself. That is, when risk is a risk or risk is not a risk.[64]

Although there are various definitions of risk, the best working definition is that of 'uncertainty that matters because it can affect one or more objectives'.[65] This can be simplified into two ingredients 'Uncertainty' and 'Materiality'.[66] This should be the main guideline provided by regulators to AMSB.[67] In fact, in risk management, we look at three forms of knowledge and non-knowledge associated with risk, which need to be understood. Known (K) risk, the Unknown (u) risk and the unknowable (U) risk. The first type of risk (K) can be measured, and any disruption forecasted and may be established from prior experience, are understood and appreciated. These events are normally a result of incompetence. The second type (u) are the most commonly encountered situations, but the extent and full implications remain unclear due to the lack of judgment. These events may be quantifiable, but the time of occurrence is unknown. They are events where the location, timing and extent of the event are difficult to quantify. The third type of risk (U) are events that are difficult, if not impossible, to model due to lack of knowledge in hand. To manage unknowable risks, companies should ensure business processes remain flexible, ensuring variable costs, and diversifying across products and markets whenever possible. This type of uncertainty is quantifiable by using simulators that make what is implicit explicit, but there is no availability of data.[68]

Regulations are there to guide and trigger thinking. However, the thinking needs to be done at the level of the undertaking; where it is expected that the personnel and the directors are well equipped with knowledge and experience that enables them to determine objectives and risk-taking that are in line with the appetite and tolerance of the stakeholders/shareholders and that this is communicated appropriately down, up and across the undertaking. Regulators must not do the mistake of micro-managing

---

[62] PricewaterhouseCoopers (PWC) (2019), p. 5.

[63] See, e.g. Article 13, No. 30 to 35 of Solvency II.

[64] See Hillson (2018), p. 6.

[65] See Hillson (2018), p. 6.

[66] See Kruf (2019), pp. 19 ff.

[67] See Hillson (2018), p. 7.

[68] See Higgins and Perera (2018), p. 10.

undertakings by imposing authorisation judgements on who is appropriate or authorised for specific positions, and what and how to address risk. This responsibility should remain the onus of the AMSB.[69]

As noted above regulations require that an insurance undertaking has a risk management function and employs a risk manager or risk team to carry out the day-to-day responsibility of this function on behalf of the directors. Regulations offer a framework through Solvency II and the respective ORSA to address risk in an insurance undertaking, but this is far from solving the problem of ensuring that this responsibility is carried out appropriately. The risk manager is a regulator-approved/ authorised position and in some cases can also fall under the responsibility of a Risk Committee, but the ultimate responsibility is always that of the AMSB. Therefore, the determination of whether the function and the personnel are appropriate is that of the AMSB. However, there is no clear-cut answer to this question, and many a time the reliance is based on the suggestions of advisors built from their understanding of what the regulator would accept as a person's qualifications and experience. Besides, unless on the AMSB there is someone who understands the need for risk management, the function becomes perfunctory and bottom-up, with little feedback and challenge, or on the other hand, it can take the opposite scenario of challenging the wrong things.

The problem is that risk management is not considered as a profession in its own right, and education, experience, associations, institutes and standards are vast. The only common requirement in the case of insurance undertakings is Solvency II and the guidelines and rules that form around it. Regulatory authorisation requirements[70] do not distinguish between qualifications that are focussed mainly on monitoring or setting up policies and procedures, those that are focussed on measurement and statistical models, those that are focussed on monitoring, and those that are focussed on management. That is, a Director who takes on any type of corporate position such as Risk Manager, Internal Auditor, Compliance Officer, MLRO, Valuation Officer, Portfolio Manager, or sits on some committees, needs to obtain authorisation from the regulator—one needs to prepare a Personal Questionnaire and then obtain authorisation by the regulator. This is a requirement of the licence application and ongoing procedure.[71]

A complete risk manager should have all these skills; that is, (1) understanding models and their assumptions, (2) ability to document procedures, standards and policies to ensure they are within the appetite of the undertaking's stakeholders (3) ability to communicate up and down and across the undertaking, (4) ability to understand and advise on risks and (5) ability to lead and manage proactively to ensure continuity.[72]

[69] See Grima (2017), pp. 60 ff.

[70] See Financial Conduct authority (2020), pp. 22 ff.

[71] See European Confederation of Directors' Associations (2015), pp. 16 ff.

[72] See Grima and Bezzina (2018), pp. 12 ff.

To ensure this, the AMSB needs to have a wide-angle scan of these needs and before recruiting ensure that the risk function has players that can offer these assurances or put in a structure that can ensure this is happening within the risk management function. Risk management is not about one person or more taking up that position but about the whole team of employees working together to achieve the objectives. It is about communication and acceptance of objectives and the determination or ‘buy-in’ of everyone to achieve them.

Unfortunately, the absence of this profession and the potential lack of people with this skillset in some Member States leads directors to look at other professions to fill this profession, such as economists, lawyers and accountants who might have taken a short course and a few years of on-the-job training. Even with training, most of the time, their mind-set is either on models and model building or financial or policymaking but lack the management skills and the ability to innovate.[73]

It is important to note this since it explains why the mistake is being done—people with the wrong skillsets are asking and teaching people to have the wrong skillsets. That is, to replicate themselves. That is, ‘what goes in goes out’. One is addressing a new area with the eyes of an old skill/profession, which to such an extent is reactive. If these professions are to understand and address the problem they need to open up to the wider context and think outside their comfort zone or else we will continue to face the same issues we face today—may be a more modern version of the same problems. Similar cases with similar governance issues causing failure or large losses but using more modern techniques.[74]

It should also be noted that the lack of adequate professionalism in risk management is not a matter inherent only to the responsibility of the AMSB towards the supervisory authority of the Member State in which the insurer is based. In the case of cross-border operations, the lack of professionalism of the risk manager could jeopardise compliance with the obligations undertaken by the insurer towards policyholders in the host Member State.

We believe that ultimately, risk management is about character and culture and the AMSB can only fully understand, determine and recognise the fitness and properness of a risk management function if common explicit standards are determining the skillsets of the risk manager by embedding this into a profession. Regulations only talk about the function of the risk manager but forget the skillset or are—as noted above—incorrectly filling this gap with the wrong skillsets.[75] Skillsets that look only at education and forget the other necessary characteristics necessary to reach objectives such as an aligned appetite and tolerance and a common culture. Maybe, this is also, because authorisation/approval, is determined by persons who do not have enough knowledge of what this skillset should be. However, the AMSB does not define and understand what risk is and base their knowledge on regulators, who give them a recipe of what to look out for—so

[73] See Grima and Thalassinos (2020b), pp. 122 ff.

[74] See Grima and Thalassinos (2020a), pp. 4 ff.

[75] See Grima and Bezzina (2021), in press.

they do not use their minds to think but satisfice and do what they are told. However, the regulator himself/herself does not know how to determine risk because s/he does not have the correct skillset to do so and there is no one singled out profession, which can be identifiable in law as a risk profession, similarly to other professions.[76]

It is not surprising that most persons working in a risk function do not know how to define risk, let alone how to manage it.[77] Defining the role of the Risk Manager in law as a separate focussed profession would strengthen the profession, by standardising the training and knowledge requirements, the required responsibilities, and thereby the skillset required, putting them on the same level as other professions even in the eyes of the regulators.

Regulations should be there to reach objectives without hiccups—however if the objectives are incorrect because they are addressing different objectives. Lawyers have one perception of what is risk and what are the objectives, Accountants have another, Economists have another, and they are the people addressing the requirements and drafting regulations—these people are all reactive by nature. Therefore, where is the Risk Managers' skillset in all this, where is the proactivity?[78] You do not address a risk after it happens, because if you know about it because it happened before, you can manage it, and therefore as noted above it is not a risk. For example, the underwriter takes risks he understands a calculated risk to make a profit. The other party who does not want can manage it.[79]

However, Solvency II is driving changes in insurance undertakings, that is, from the AMSB through to wider organisation. For directors, and particularly non-executive directors, this means getting closer to the business. Has the industry (regulators and educators) understood that what was good a few years ago is now day irrelevant? The directors must be simultaneously entrepreneurial and drive the business forward while keeping it under prudent control. Apart from the education, character, experience and charisma of the individual member, one needs to determine how these fit in as a team and this cannot be something determined by regulations or micro-managed by the regulator.[80]

Solvency II makes it clear that the AMSB is not able to delegate its responsibilities, and individual directors[81] must be able to explain the decisions taken by the undertaking. The corollary of their position is that the existence and requirement of having a risk management function demands the board to have risk expertise; therefore, requiring expertise at the board level in every area or function within the undertaking.

These obligations are creating tension and challenges within undertakings, putting a lot of stress on the directors. Therefore, in our opinion, there is a need for a risk

---

[76] See Grima and Bezzina (2018), pp. 3 ff.

[77] See Girlando (2021), in press.

[78] See Grima and Thalassinos (2020b), pp. 121 ff.

[79] See Hillson (2018), p. 7.

[80] See Baldacchino et al. (2020), p. 6.

[81] See Solvency II Wire Data (2011).

management profession and for expanding the directors' skillset. This should compile all standards and frame the understanding of their expected function and skillset as already mentioned above.[82] Without this, the AMSB is at the mercy of the regulators and the knowledge, character and experience of the person leading the risk management function. Whether s/he is fit and proper or not is another question.

5 Importance of Performing and Communicating a Risk Culture Diagnostic

Inappropriate risky behaviour beyond the appetite of stakeholders can destroy the reputation, value and the undertaking.[83] This is why processes and oversight structures to control the level of variability from this appetite is so important. However, unfortunately, regulations and directors forget or ignore the attitudes and behaviour of decision-makers and the reasons why they make specific decisions. Shaping the risk culture, maybe through policies, procedures, standards, and communications ensure that business risks such as reputation and strategy are managed appropriately.[84] Both are important since reputation and following an inappropriate strategy can destroy an undertaking. Regulations do focus on the risk management function on this risk and do point out that these risks need to be addressed appropriately and processes and policies documented and structured appropriately. Regulators, to a certain extent, do micromanage this during onsite visits.[85]

If the AMSB makes risk culture diagnostics a priority, then there is quicker buy-in throughout the undertaking. There needs to be soliciting of views from employees with a message that management believes in the empowerment of all members and that this is a priority. Objectives should be clear and the focus of all. Communication of the risk culture should be a priority on the leadership agenda, and lack of awareness, indifference or disregard for this should not be tolerated.

Humans are very sensitive to signals arising from how an organisation reacts and behaves. If ignoring limits, failure to complete risk reports, or disregard for processes is tolerated and not identified, monitored and corrected, then the undertaking risks perpetuating a cavalier attitude to risk and control throughout the undertaking.[86]

In some cases, it has been difficult to engage with the AMSB on risk management as the focus is often on the technical details around risk measurement. However, the results of the diagnostic should be visual and qualitative, making it easily communicated and, hence, encouraging engagement. That is, to ensure that risk management is not lost in translation and that uncertainties are documented, communicated

---

[82] See Grima and Bezzina (2018), pp. 3ff.

[83] See International Finance Corporation (IFC) (2015), p. 64.

[84] Bonime-Blanc and Ponzi (2016), pp. 16 ff.

[85] See Dalli Gonzi (2019), pp. 113 ff.

[86] See Doff (2008), p. 205 f.

and addressed efficiently and in line with the appetite set at the strategy stage.[87] Benchmarking also provides the context of the results of similar undertakings. The better-informed one is about what others are doing, the better one is at designing a gap analysis for decision-making.[88]

All results, findings and discussions need to be analysed at various levels, depending on data capture, and used to identify 'red flags' needing remedial action whether this is by business unit or function. Tools used for reporting and addressing risk should be user-friendly and enable personnel to engage in understanding risk culture in their part of the undertaking and encourage constructive dialogue on improvement. However, for this to hold, employees must feel secure to answer truthfully and this is best achieved if this is coming from the top and communicated well.[89]

Solvency II, if interpreted well, does promote all this. However, many undertakings are still not recognising the need to improve governance, as this is a change in mentality and may relate to an overhaul of the system of governance, the need to invest, and a change in mentality. Therefore, sometimes even because of the lack of proportionate in the approach and the enforcement of the requirements, Solvency II is seen as a perfunctory function and not as a competitive edge.

Relying on processes and formalised controls will not be enough to give the confidence that an organisation is capable of state-of-the-art risk management. There will always be ways to circumvent the models, systems and controls as we see from some of the cases found in the literature, such as those of Long Term Capital Management, Barings Bank, *Societé General* and many others.[90] It is, therefore, necessary for the AMSB to encourage a strong risk culture where employees are risk-aware, understand the consequences of their decisions, and are confident to raise objections when necessary. Unfortunately, there is no hard and fast rule or fixed methodology to ensure this and the AMSB has the task of putting in measurable and realistic objectives with the help of the risk manager, which recognise uncertainties and ensuring that these are addressed responsibly and with integrity.

That is:

- Objectives must be stated, and achievements measured.
- Information related to the achievement of objectives should accurately present the facts.
- The objectives should be updated regularly, ongoing and sustainable.
- Uncertainty about the future should address both dangers and rewards.
- Being wrong should be acceptable but must be communicated and addressed thoughtfully and rigorously.

[87] Kruf (2019), pp. 24 ff.

[88] Kruf (2019), pp. 27 ff.

[89] See Bondesson (2011), p. 22 f.

[90] Grima and Thalassinos (2020a), pp. 4 ff.

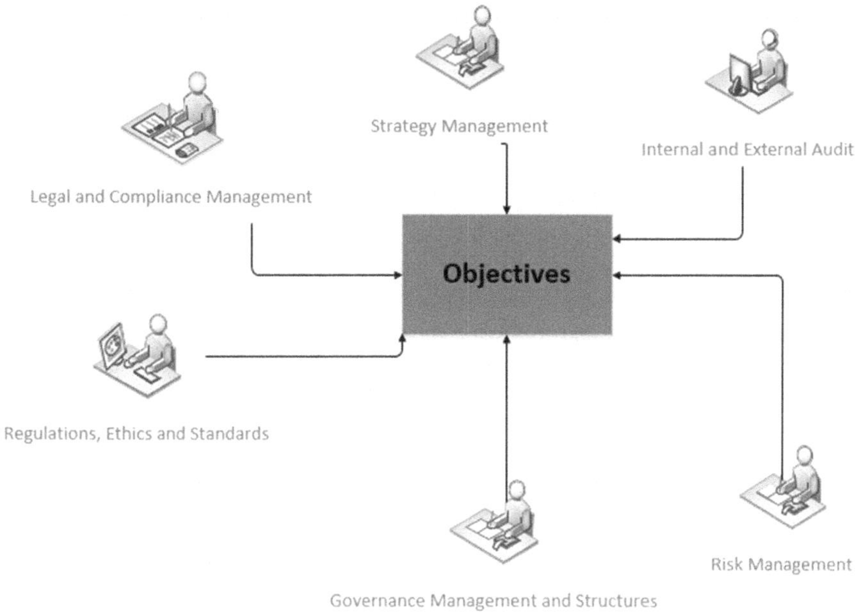

Fig. 1 The risk management system (Source: Authors' own compilation)

- Mandatory and voluntary promises must be maintained, measured, monitored and ensured.[91]

Risk culture is not static and should be actively challenged to encourage continuous improvement. This cycle must be continuously improving by allowing management to benchmark against other undertakings, track own performance over time and provide results at a sufficiently granular level so that remedial action can be applied. Although change does not happen overnight, Solvency II is an opportunity to improve the risk culture within insurance undertakings. However, to do that, insurers need to grasp this opportunity and understand that risk management system is not only one person, but it is a system, that is the result of many other functions working together to reach common objectives with the least hiccups in a sustainable manner[92] (vide Fig. 1).

Moreover, one needs to consider the starting point of the undertaking and proportionality when determining the action to be taken to deciding on how to

[91] See Bondesson (2011), p. 41 f.

[92] See Krivkovich and Cindy (2013), pp. 1ff.

ensure a culture change.[93] This since, although, the above list is generalisable, not all actions may be applicable, and some circumstances might require a different address.[94]

6 Conclusion

Solvency II does provide methodologies, guidelines, and suggestions to measure, monitor, and manage risks. However, these can misguide directors into believing that these are exhaustive, and following these requirements will ensure that we are immune from trouble or danger of loss. As noted above, this is not the case. Far from it, the AMSB needs to understand the risk their undertaking is facing and impose ex-ante adequate and proportional methodologies to mitigate unwanted risks and monitor those risks that they are willing to take.

To do this, the AMSB must understand the culture of the undertaking and its personnel to determine the adequacy to meet objectives. Adequacy in terms of character, education and experience. That is the fitness and properness of the team. Although this task is sometimes delegated to the Human Resource Manager, the AMSB has to have a full view of the delegated task.[95]

Another important task should be that of ensuring that all policies and procedures are documented and reviewed periodically and in line with the strategy of the undertaking. Everything needs to focus on the objectives and appetite and tolerance of the stakeholders and within the mandatory regulatory parameters.

Once these are complete, the communication lines should be addressed to ensure that any risk, variance from the appetite, and tolerance are communicated to the AMSB in a time and through the set communication channels depending on the importance/materiality as decided by the AMSB. Any noise suppressing this communication, such as internal politics should be tackled immediately and stopped.

This shows the importance of having a governance structure with internal controls that are proportional to the size and responsibility of the undertaking, based on the licensable activity it is providing. Although the chosen persons are important and their experience and qualifications are important factors in ensuring the adequacy of the governance structure to meet objectives set, it is the way they fit together and their buy-in to the project and objective to ensure the appropriate communication, integrity, responsibility and sustainability of the set objectives of the undertaking.[96]

The makeup of the AMSB might well need to change with at least one person with risk management and knowledge of internal controls. However, such senior people are in short supply, and it is doubtful there are many of them in some Member

[93] See Grima and Thalassinos (2020b), pp. 120 ff.

[94] See Grima (2019), p. 223.

[95] Micallef et al. (2020), pp. 26 ff.

[96] Kruf (2019), pp. 28 ff.

States, where Risk officers with knowledge and experience on financial modelling, regulations and internal controls within the insurance industry, is less developed and the number of suitably qualified senior staff is low. As noted, this lack of professionalism in one Member State risks spreading to other States in the case of cross-border activity of the insurer concerned.

The solution for having an appropriate and effective AMSB is not something that can be developed overnight just by implementing regulations, but one needs to take a deeper look at the environment and the developments required to arrive at such. Education plays an important part in all this, and regulation needs to push in that direction to ensure that this is brought in line with the new needs; coupled with driving, providing and setting of a European professional status (embedded in the law) for these new skillsets. Moreover, national regulators need to be put in a position to apply the principle of proportionality without fear. Until this is achieved, directors, risk managers and regulators will continue to doubt whether what they are doing is enough and in line with requirements, and fear and confusion will continue to reign.

References

Agarwal R, Kallapur S (2018) Cognitive risk culture and advanced roles of actors in risk governance: a case study. J Risk Finance 19(4):327–342

Awrey D, Blair W, Kershaw D (2013) Between law and market: is there a role for culture and ethics in financial regulation. Del J Corp Law 38:191–245

Baldacchino PJ, Tabone N, Camilleri J, Grima S (2020) An analysis of the board of directors composition: the case of Maltese listed companies. Int J Finance Insur Risk Manag X(1):25–44

Bernardino G (2011) Risk management – a supervisor's approach. Presentation by Gabriel Bernardino, Chairman of EIOPA, at SUERF Annual Lecture in Helsinki, retrieved at https://www.eiopa.europa.eu/content/risk-management-%E2%80%93-supervisor%E2%80%99s-approach

Bianchi N, Carretta A, Farina V, Fiordelisi F (2021) Does espouse risk culture pay? Evidence from European banks. J Bank Finance 122:1–13

Bondesson I (2011) Suitability assessment procedures in solvency II. Outlining suitable processes for own assessment of article 42's fit and proper requirements. UMEA University, pp 17-4, viewed online http://www.diva-portal.org/smash/get/diva2:546867/FULLTEXT01.pdf

Bonime-Blanc A, Ponzi LJ (2016) Understanding reputation risk: the qualitative and quantitative imperative. Corporate Compliance Insights, pp 1–31. https://www.corporatecomplianceinsights.com/wp-content/uploads/2017/11/Understanding-Reputation-Risk-.pdf

Borg G, Baldacchino PJ, Buttigieg S, Botztepe E, Grima S (2020) Challenging the adequacy of the conventional "three lines of defence" model: a case study on Maltese Credit Institutions. In: Grima S, Boztepe E, Baldacchino PJ (eds) Contemporary issues in audit management and forensic accounting, vol 103. Emerald, pp 303–324, chpt. 18

Bravo JM (2020) IDD and distribution risk management. In: Marano P, Noussia K (eds) Insurance distribution directive: a legal analysis. Springer, pp 349–369

Croker KJ, Snow A (2000) The theory of risk classification. In: Dionne G (ed) Handbook of insurance. Kluwer Academic Publishers, pp 245–276

Dalli Gonzi R (2019) In: Grima S (ed) Change and continuity management in the public sector: the DALI model for effective decision making. Emerald Group Publishing Limited, pp 113–123

Dobrota G (2012) Risk management in business – the foundation of performance in economic organizations, risk management - current issues and challenges, Nerija Banaitiene, IntechOpen. Chapter 11, pp 227–252. https://doi.org/10.5772/50706. https://www.intechopen.com/books/risk-management-current-issues-and-challenges/risk-management-in-business-the-foundation-of-performance-in-economic-organizations

Doff R (2008) A critical analysis of the Solvency II proposals. Geneva Pap Risk Insur Issues Pract 33:193–206

Eisenbach TM, Kovner A, Junho Lee M (2020) Cyber risk and the U.S. financial system: a pre-mortem analysis. Federal Reserve Bank of New York. Staff Reports no. 909, January 2020, pp 1–40. https://www.newyorkfed.org/medialibrary/media/research/staff_reports/sr909.pdf

Enriques L, Zetzsche D (2013) The risky business of regulating risk management in listed companies. Eur Company Financ Law Rev 2:272–303

European Confederation of Directors' Associations (2015) A Guide to Corporate Governance Practices in the European Union International Finance Corporation. 2015. World Bank Group, pp 9–24. https://www.ifc.org/wps/wcm/connect/506d49a2-3763-4fe4-a783-5d58e37b8906/CG_Practices_in_EU_Guide.pdf?MOD=AJPERES&CVID=kNmxTtG

Everson M, Vos E (2016) European agencies: what about the institutional balance. In: Research handbook on EU institutional law. Edward Elgar Publishing, Cheltenham. https://doi.org/10.4337/9781782544746.00011

Financial Conduct authority (2020) Corporate Governance of the Financial Conduct authority. Adopted by resolution of the board on 30 January 2020, pp 4–39. Online at: https://www.fca.org.uk/publication/corporate/fca-corporate-governance.pdf

FSB (2014) Guidance on Supervisory Interaction with Financial Institutions on Risk Culture

Girlando A, Grima S, Boztepe E, Seychell S, Rupeika-Apoga R, Romanova I (2021) Individual risk perceptions and behaviour. Emerald Insight. Contemporary studies in Economic and Financial Analysis, vol 106, chapter 23 (in press 2021)

Grima S (2019) Proportionality in the application of insurance solvency requirements: the case of small EU jurisdiction. In: 21st annual conference modern aspects of the legal and regulatory insurance concept. Palic Serbia. 25 to 27 September 2020, pp 222–233

Grima S, Bezzina F (2018) Risk management practices adopted by European Financial Firms with a Mediterranean Connection. Perspectives on Risk, Assessment & Management Paradigms, pp 1–14. IntechOpen. https://kopernio.com/viewer?doi=10.5772/intechopen.80640&token=WzYzMTk0LCIxMC41NzcyL2ludGVjaG9wZW4uODA2NDAiXQ.DyV8CGys17vuNeqzeiHtJP82akc

Grima S, Bezzina F (2021) A study of the effectiveness of corporate governance in EU small states financial services firms. Methods and behavioural tools for decision making in management. Springer Series, Contributions to Management Science (in press, 2021)

Grima S, Thalassinos E (2020a) In: Dalli Gonzi R, Thalassinos I (eds) Financial derivatives: a blessing or a curse? Emerald Group Publishing Limited, pp 1–22

Grima S, Thalassinos E (2020b) In: Dalli Gonzi R, Thalassinos I (eds) Financial derivatives: a blessing or a curse? Emerald Group Publishing Limited, pp 66–172

Grima S, Romanova I, Bezzina F (2017) Misuse of derivatives: considerations for internal control. Contemporary issues in finance: current challenges from across Europe (Series Editor Rupeika-Apoga R, Romanova I, Grima S, Bezzina F), Contemporary studies in economic and financial analysis, vol 98. Emerald Group Publishing Limited, chp 4, pp 49–62

Grundke P (2011) Reverse stress tests with bottom-up approaches. J Risk Model Valid 5(1):71–90

Higgins D, Perera T (2018) Advancing real estate decision making: understanding known, unknown and unknowable risks. Int J Build Pathol Adapt 36(4):6–13

Hillson D (2018) When risk is not a risk? IPMA, pp 6–7, viewed online at https://www.who.int/management/general/risk/WhenRiskNotRisk.pdf

International Finance Corporation (IFC) (2015) Risk culture, risk governance, and balanced incentives. Recommendations for strengthening risk management in emerging market banks. August 2015, pp 1–88. https://www.ifc.org/wps/wcm/connect/fe5f3a6f-1241-46cc-89b9-c4be75e62a7c/IFC+Risk+Culture+Governance+Incentives+report.pdf?MOD=AJPERES&CVID=lw9GOEh

Klein RW (2012) Principles for insurance regulation: an evaluation of current practices and potential reforms, The Geneva Papers on Risk and Insurance-Issues and Practice, 37, 175–199

Krivkovich A, Cindy L (2013) Managing the people side of risk. McKinsey & Company, pp 1–5 online at: https://www.mckinsey.com/business-functions/risk/our-insights/managing-the-people-side-of-risk https://www.mckinsey.com/~/media/McKinsey/Business%20Functions/Risk/Our%20Insights/Managing%20the%20people%20side%20of%20risk/Managing%20the%20people%20side%20of%20risk.pdf?shouldIndex=false

Kruf JP, Grima S, Kzilkaya M, Spiteri J, Slob W, O'Dea J (2019) The PRIMO FORTE framework for good governance in public, private and civic organisations: an analysis on small EU states. Eur Res Stud J XXII(4):15–34

Loguinova K (2019) A critical legal study of the ideology behind Solvency II. Springer

Manes P (2017) Corporate governance, the approach to risk and the insurance industry under Solvency II. In: Andenas M, Avesani RG, Manes P, Vella F, Wood PR (eds) Solvency II: a dynamic challenge for the insurance market. Il Mulino

Marano P (2020) The contribution of Product Oversight and Governance (POG) to the single market: a set of rules on the organization for the business conduct. In: Marano P, Noussia K (eds) Insurance distribution directive: a legal analysis. Springer, pp 55–74

MFSA (2020) MFSA issues risk culture and risk appetite statements positioning risk management at the heart of its strategy. January 29, 2020. https://www.mfsa.mt/publication/mfsa-issues-risk-culture-and-risk-appetite-statements-positioning-risk-management-at-the-heart-of-its-strategy/

Micallef J, Grima S, Seychell S, Rupeika-Apoga R, Zammit ML (2020) A study of the implications of the European Securitisation Regulation 2017/2402 on Malta. Laws 9:1–26

Mikes A (2011) From counting risk to making risk count: boundary-work in risk management. Harvard Business School Working Paper No. 11-069

Milkau U (2017) Risk culture during the last 2000 years-from an aleatory society to the illusion of risk control. Int J Financ Stud 5:31

Palermo T, Power M, Ashby S (2017) J Manag Stud 54(2):154–181

PriceWaterhouseCoopers (PWC) (2019) The future of risk. The insurance risk function of the future. September 2019, pp 1–24. Viewed online at https://www.pwc.co.uk/financial-services/assets/pdf/future-of-risk-in-insurance-report.pdf

Ring PJ, Bryce C, McKinney R, Webb R (2013) Taking notice of risk culture – the regulator's approach. J Risk Res 19(3):364–387

Sheedy E, Zhang L, Ho Tam KC (2019) Incentives and culture in risk compliance. J Bank Finance 107:105611

Shimpi P, Klappach H (2013) Risk culture. In: Kemper C, Flamée M, Yang C, Windels P (eds) Global perspective on insurance today. Palgrave Macmillan

Sinha VK, Arena M (2020) Manifold conceptions of the internal auditing of risk culture in the financial sector. J Bus Ethics 16:81–102

Skipper HD, Kwon WJ (2007) Risk management and insurance. Perspectives in a global economy. Blackwell Publishing

Solvency II Wire Data (2011) Transforming board of directors under Solvency II -Sept 22, 2011. http://siiwdata.solvencyiiwire.com/ https://www.econstor.eu/bitstream/10419/161669/1/888205422.pdf

Van Hulle K (2019) Solvency requirements for EU insurers. Intersentia

The Role of the Compliance Function in the Process of Managing the Risk of Non-Compliance in an Insurance Undertaking

Wojciech Paś

Abstract This chapter is devoted to the role and significance of the compliance function in an insurance undertaking. This chapter presents selected models of compliance functions in European insurance undertakings. The main assumption of the chapter was an attempt to determine the importance of the compliance function in the process of managing the risk of non-compliance by means of the functioning and organisation of this unit within the structures of an insurance undertaking.

1 Introduction

The systematic increase of legal and supervisory requirements imposed on financial institutions, including insurance undertakings, results in a proportionate increase in their exposure to the risk of financial and non-financial losses due to expectations of supervisory bodies and violations of certain legal obligations. The risk of non-compliance in financial institutions should be defined as the risk of failure to comply with applicable law, internal regulations and accepted standards of conduct.[1] The above definition was adopted by the Polish Financial Supervision Authority (KNF) in Resolution No. 258/2011 of 4 October 2011 with regard to the banking sector.[2] However, it seems to have a universal character, applicable also to other financial institutions. In the case of non-compliance, the infringer incurs financial sanctions and can lose its reputation and credibility.

[1]Cichy (2015), pp. 7–8.

[2]Resolution of the Polish Financial Supervision Authority No. 258/2011 of 4 October 2011 on Detailed Principles of Functioning of the Risk Management System and Internal Control System and Detailed Conditions of Internal Capital Assessment by Banks and of Reviewing the Process of Internal Capital Assessment and Maintenance and the Principles of Determining the Policy on Variable Components of Remuneration of Persons Holding Managerial Positions at a Bank.

W. Paś (✉)
University of Wrocław, Faculty of Law, Administration and Economics, Wrocław, Poland

P. Marano, K. Noussia (eds.), *The Governance of Insurance Undertakings*, AIDA Europe Research Series on Insurance Law and Regulation 6,
https://doi.org/10.1007/978-3-030-85817-9_3

Conducting business activity in accordance with applicable laws, internal regulations and supervisory expectations is undoubtedly part of what makes up safe, stable and prudent governance of an insurance undertaking. The legislators qualify the compliance function in the insurance undertaking as a key function which is a part of the insurance undertaking's governance system. There is no doubt that, with an increasing number of regulations, the role and significance of the compliance function in the insurance market will systematically become more prominent, as was the case with more developed areas of the financial market.

The aim of this chapter is to attempt to determine the importance of the compliance function in the process of managing the risk of non-compliance in an insurance undertaking through its functioning and organisation within the structures of insurance undertakings. The chapter was drawn up based on the literature discussing this subject matter and in the light of national and European regulations relating to the compliance function in an insurance undertaking. The chapter also considers the Polish supervisory expectations addressed to financial institutions, especially to in this respect. Considerations devoted to risk management process were also presented taking into account solutions applicable in banks.[3]

2 The Compliance Function in an Insurance Undertaking in the Light of Polish and European Insurance Law and Polish Supervisory Practice

2.1 European Insurance Law

The compliance function in insurance undertakings was separated and shaped because of the entry into force of the Directive of 25 November 2009 on the taking-up and pursuit of the business of Insurance and Reinsurance (Solvency II) (OJ EU L of 17 December 2009).[4] In the Recitals (No. 30) of Solvency II, the European legislator has clearly indicated that an insurance undertaking's governance system includes the risk-management function, the internal audit function, the actuarial function and the compliance function. An effective system of governance is essential for proper management of insurance undertakings.[5] It is worth noting that ineffective internal control systems, of which compliance is an element, were significant fraud factors in banks.[6] In this context, it is worth pointing out that according to the de Larosière High Level Group report on the future of financial

[3]Hull (2011) and Iwanicz-Drozdowska (2017).

[4]Directive 2009/138/EC of the European Parliament and of the Council of 25 November 2009 on the taking-up and pursuit of the business of Insurance and Reinsurance (Solvency II) (OJ EU L of 17 December 2009).

[5]Preamble to Solvency II.

[6]Siri (2017), p. 132 and subsequent.

supervision in the EU, corporate governance was among the most important elements underlying the financial crisis.[7] The management system of the insurance undertaking has been identified as crucial in the light of Solvency II, which states that 'Some risks may only be properly addressed through governance requirements rather than through the quantitative requirements... An effective system of governance is therefore essential for the adequate management of the insurance undertaking and for the regulatory system.'[8] The report by Sharma et al. (2002) identified a causal relationship between undertakings that fail and those that are inherently vulnerable due to 'underlying management weaknesses or operational weaknesses'. Good governance practices and strong risk management are therefore essential aspects of a prudential regulatory framework.[9]

The compliance function in the light of Solvency II is an element of the internal control system, which also includes administrative and accounting procedures, the organisation of internal control, appropriate reporting arrangements at all levels of the insurance undertaking. The compliance function itself, in accordance with Article 46(2) of Solvency II, includes advising the administrative, management or supervisory body on compliance with the laws, regulations and administrative provisions. It also allows for an assessment of the possible impact of any changes in the legal environment on the operations of the undertaking in question as well as the identification and assessment of compliance risk.

The legal provisions and supervisory expectations impacting the shape of the compliance function in insurance undertakings include, most notably:

- Commission Delegated Regulation (EU) 2015/35 of 10 October 2014 supplementing Solvency II
- European Insurance and Occupational Pensions Authority (EIOPA) guidelines on the governance of insurance undertaking
- International standards for the conduct of insurance business activity and principles of insurance supervision, issued by the International Association of Insurance Supervisors (IAIS)
- ISO 19600:2014

The international standards for the conduct of insurance business activity and principles of insurance supervision, issued by the International Association of Insurance Supervisors (IAIS), are among the noteworthy regulations impacting the shape of the compliance function in an insurance undertaking. In Guideline 8.4, the IAIS recommends that insurance undertakings should have an effective compliance system in place which is to support the insurer in meeting its legal and regulatory obligations and promote a culture of compliance. To fulfil the above-mentioned task, the management board should adopt a code of good practice which will serve as a

[7] de Larosière High Level Group (2009), Report on the future of financial supervision in the EU, Brussels.

[8] Siri (2017), p. 132 and subsequent.

[9] Swain and Swallow (2015), p. 145, available at http://www.bankofengland.co.uk/.

reference point for its activities, which are to comply with generally applicable law and accepted ethical standards. The guidelines also refer to the organisation of the compliance function within the structures of the insurance undertaking and the person in charge of that unit (the 'Chief Compliance Officer'). The person appointed to supervise the compliance function should have direct access to the management board in order to keep it informed about:

- the most important compliance risks associated with the business activity of the insurer and the measures taken to combat them
- the assessment of how the various departments and units are meeting the standards and compliance objectives
- personal problems and conflicts of interest
- fines and other disciplinary sanctions imposed by the competent authorities on the insurer or its employees

The ISO 19600:2014 is certainly a benchmark for entrepreneurs who plan to implement the compliance function, including insurance undertakings. This standard specifies general requirements related to the development of compliance. The ISO standard is internationally applied, however in this sense should not be identified as a requirement to be met by entrepreneurs. Its scope includes recommendations related to the implementation, execution and development of the compliance function. It is based on the principles of good governance, proportionality, transparency and sustainability. The standard indicates that having an effective compliance function results in an organisation's possibility to achieve the anticipated business objectives by complying with the law and accepted standards of conduct, as well as ethical standards. The primary task of an organisation in ensuring an effective compliance function is to identify all the requirements associated with its business activity. To that end, it is necessary to perform a self-assessment of the conducted business activity (nature of the activity, services or products provided).

2.2 *Polish Insurance Law and Supervisory Practice*

The compliance function in Polish insurance law has been clearly distinguished and developed in the structure of insurance undertakings following the European Parliament's adoption of Directive 2009/138/EC of 25 November 2009 on the taking-up and pursuit of the business of Insurance and Reinsurance (Solvency II) (OJ EU L of 17 December 2009).[10] This period was certainly a breakthrough for the development of the compliance function in insurance undertakings. Before the adoption of Solvency II, the compliance function was not fully separated and shaped on the

[10] Directive 2009/138/EC of the European Parliament and of the Council of 25 November 2009 on the taking-up and pursuit of the business of Insurance and Reinsurance (Solvency II) (OJ EU L of 17 December 2009).

Polish insurance market. At that time, the tasks of the compliance function were performed by the legal unit, the risk unit or the internal audit unit.[11] This is essential for the proper governance of insurance undertakings.[12]

The separation and shaping of the compliance function in the insurance undertakings took place because of the entry into force of Solvency II. Its final shape, from the perspective of insurance undertakings operating in Poland, was determined by the Act of 11 September 2015 on Insurance and Reinsurance Activity,[13] which implemented Solvency II into Polish law. The above-mentioned regulations introduced an obligation to establish the compliance function in insurance undertakings from 1 January 2016.

The role of the compliance unit is defined in Article 64(2) of the Act on Insurance and Reinsurance Activity. Pursuant to this provision, the compliance function covers:

- advising the undertaking's management and supervisory board on the compliance of conducting insurance or reinsurance business activity with the law
- assessing the possible impact of any changes in the legal status on the undertaking's operations
- identifying and assessing the risk of non-compliance with laws, internal regulations and standards of conduct adopted by the undertaking

At the same time, the compliance function has been qualified as an element of the insurance undertaking's management system, in addition to the risk management function, the internal audit function and the actuarial function, whose combined task is to ensure proper and prudent management of the insurance undertaking. The person supervising the compliance function has been classified as a person playing a key role within the insurance undertaking. Such a qualification determines this person's obligation to meet certain requirements such as:

- having full legal capacity
- having higher education obtained in Poland or obtained in another country, which constitutes higher education within the meaning of the relevant provisions of that country
- not being convicted of an intentional crime or an intentional fiscal offence by way of a final court judgement
- having the professional experience necessary to supervise the key function
- guaranteeing that tasks are performed properly

Of the above-mentioned requirements, the KNF attaches particular importance to the need for the person supervising the compliance function to have the professional experience necessary to perform this function and to guarantee due performance of

[11] Mrozowska-Bartkiewicz and Wnęk (2016), p. 71.

[12] Preamble to Solvency II.

[13] Act of 11 September 2015 on Insurance and Reinsurance Activity (i.e. of 2018 item 999 as amended).

tasks.[14] In the opinion of the supervisory authority, those criteria should be assessed in the light of the principle of proportionality, taking into account the scale and complexity of the activities of the insurance undertaking or the risks to which it is exposed, as well as some kind of projection of the functions of the person in question based on that person's previous professional experience. In particular, an assessment of a person's professional experience acquired hitherto, including any irregularities found in his or her area of responsibility. The supervisor is of the opinion that 'human actions are repetitive and, once a person has committed irregularities, the risk that they will be committed by that person in the future is significantly higher'. The question whether the candidate for the person supervising the compliance function meets the requirements is assessed not only by the statutory bodies of the insurance undertaking, i.e. the management board and the supervisory board, but also on the audit committee. In the opinion of the supervisor, these bodies should not only assess the candidate's technical qualifications, but also determine whether the person in question has the ability to perform the compliance function independently. Each of the above-mentioned bodies of the insurance undertaking should actively assess the candidate and should not limit itself to an automatic acceptance of the candidate based on the management board's recommendations.

At this point it should be noted that the KNF's recommendations do not constitute generally applicable law but are an expression of supervisory expectations directed at insurance or reinsurance undertakings with regard to their activities. Supervisory expectations are also expressed in the form of positions or communications addressed to a specific group of recipients. A supervisory recommendation itself constitutes an indication of what conduct of the insurance or reinsurance undertaking is approved by the supervisory authorities and hence will not be challenged by the KNF.[15] As a consequence, recommendations constitute an expression of the KNF's perception of certain areas of an insurance undertaking's business activity, and actions to the contrary of the supervised entity may, in situations specified in legal regulations, result in the initiation of supervisory activities.[16] However, it should be emphasised that simple non-compliance of an insurance undertaking with a recommendation cannot constitute the basis for imposing supervisory sanctions by the KNF. A circumstance which constitutes grounds for the application of supervisory instruments by the KNF is violation of applicable provisions of law. However, it is possible that a specific recommendation adopts the content of a legal standard.[17] The Corporate Governance Principles for supervised institutions issued by the Polish Financial Supervision Authority should also be mentioned among the most notable provisions of law and supervisory expectations affecting the development of the compliance function in insurance undertakings.

---

[14]Communication of 20 August 2018 on the role and importance of compliance functions by insurance and reinsurance undertakings. Available at: www.knf.gov.pl.

[15]Wojno (2017).

[16]Wojno (2017).

[17]Wojno (2017).

3 Organisation and Tasks of the Compliance Function in the Insurance Undertaking

3.1 Tasks and Structure

The provisions of law do not interfere in a detailed manner in how the compliance function is developed and operated in the organisational structure of the insurance undertaking.[18] The existing legal requirements concerning the compliance function in insurance undertakings concentrate on essential aspects related to the exercise of that function, such as the obligation to establish compliance, a description of the role and tasks of that function and the criteria to be fulfilled by the person who is to supervise the exercising of that function.[19] However, the obligation to establish a compliance function shall not entail the separation of that function from other key functions within the organisational structure of the insurance undertaking in accordance with EIOPA's guidelines on the governance of the insurance undertaking.[20] Nevertheless, considering the tasks and essence of individual key functions, it does not seem that the possible combining of these functions within one organisational structure could contribute to their greater effectiveness. Additionally, it is even impossible to combine some key functions of an insurance company in the light of the third line of defence concept, as in the case with the role of audit function.[21]

The detailed tasks for the compliance function in an insurance undertaking and the manner of their performance are specified in Article 270 of Commission Delegated Regulation (EU) No. 2015/35. In the light of this provision, the compliance function in the insurance undertaking:

- establishes rules and a plan to ensure compliance with provisions of law:
  a) The principles on ensuring compliance specify the tasks, competences and reporting obligations assigned to the compliance function.
  b) The compliance plan describes the planned activities of the compliance function, which cover all relevant areas of insurance and reinsurance undertakings' business activity and their exposure to non-compliance risk.

- assesses the adequacy of measures adopted by the insurance or reinsurance undertaking to prevent non-compliance with provisions of law

An insurance undertaking's failure to establish the compliance function may be sanctioned by the Polish Financial Supervision Authority through supervisory

---

[18] Paś (2018), p. 87.

[19] Paś (2018), p. 87.

[20] Siri (2017), p. 136 and subsequent.

[21] CEIOPS, Advice to the European Commission on the Principle of Proportionality in the Solvency II Framework Directive proposal, CEIOPS-DOC-24/08, May 2008, available at https://eiopa.europa.eu/CEIOPS-Archive/.

measures specified in the Act on Insurance and Reinsurance Activity. The compliance structure of the insurance undertaking itself should be based on an appropriate and clear division of tasks which ensures an effective decision-making process, prevents conflicts of interest and provides an effective information system.[22] At the same time, in line with the principle of proportionality, the compliance system should be adequate to the nature, scale and complexity of the business activity of the insurance undertaking in question. A proportional compliance system should ensure its effective implementation.[23]

When developing the compliance function in an insurance undertaking, it is also worth considering the KNF's position of 20 August 2018 on the role and importance of the implementation of the compliance function by insurance and reinsurance undertakings.[24] In the vision of the compliance function presented by the supervisor, the KNF draws attention to the fact that the core of this function consists in ensuring compliance with the broadly understood legal regulations, including regulations on the prevention of money laundering, personal data protection, as well as ensuring compliance with supervisory recommendations. Implementation of the statutory task of the compliance function, i.e. ensuring compliance with the law, should not interfere with any additional tasks carried out by that function, such as those related to the implementation and application of internal regulations which are in force in the capital group to which the insurance undertaking belongs. In the opinion of the supervisor, establishing a compliance unit in which tasks other than ensuring legal compliance are prioritised is unacceptable. Such prioritisation of tasks by a shareholder may be deemed as an unauthorised influence on the compliance function's autonomy.

The concept of function under Solvency II should be understood as an opportunity to undertake practical tasks.[25] In view of the above, the primary role of the compliance unit is to coordinate non-compliance risk management in a manner ensuring a level of risk acceptable from the perspective of the security of the insurance undertaking. As part of developing the compliance system in an insurance undertaking, consideration should also be given to its model, i.e. whether compliance should be part of the internal control system, as set out in Article 64(1) of the Act on Insurance and Reinsurance Activity, or whether compliance should be understood more broadly as part of the risk management system. In the Act on Insurance and Reinsurance Activity, the Polish legislator adopted the rule of separating the compliance function from the risk management function. However, the compliance function is classified differently by the Polish Financial Supervision Authority, which, in its Corporate Governance Principles for supervised institutions, does not determine whether this function is only an element of the internal control

[22] Leśniak (2017).

[23] Leśniak (2017).

[24] Communication of 20 August 2018 on the role and importance of compliance functions by insurance and reinsurance undertakings. Available at: www.knf.gov.pl.

[25] Leśniak (2017).

system or whether it also includes a risk management system.[26] Thus, it seems that this way it leaves some freedom to financial institutions, including insurance undertakings, in how they choose to organise the compliance function within their internal structures. The above-mentioned concept of understanding the compliance system by financial supervision was also expressed in Resolution No. 258/2011 of the KNF addressed to the banking sector.[27]

On the compliance unit's place in an insurance undertaking's organisational structure, certain supervisory expectations expressed both in the framework of the Corporate Governance Principles for supervised institutions and the positions of the KNF of 16 February 2016 on requirements for the governance system of an insurance/reinsurance undertaking and of 2 August 2018 on the role and importance of the compliance function of insurance and reinsurance undertakings should be mentioned.[28] Pursuant to Article 47 of the Corporate Governance Principles, '1. The supervised institution should develop and implement an effective, efficient and independent function for ensuring the supervised institution's compliance with laws and internal regulations and should take into account supervisory recommendations. 2. The compliance function should be organised in a manner guaranteeing the independent performance of tasks in this respect'. In view of the above, the Polish Financial Supervision Authority expects that financial institutions, including insurance undertakings, will develop the compliance function within their structures in a way ensuring its independence and effectiveness.

The compliance function, as part of an insurance undertaking's governance system, is also subject to a supervisory review by the BION. As part of the assessment of this field, the KNF verifies whether the compliance function implemented by the insurer is adequate to the nature, scale and complexity of the undertaking's business activity and whether the insurer has ensured its integration into the undertaking's organisational structure and decision-making processes. Furthermore, the KNF assesses whether the insurance undertaking carries out mitigation activities in the field of the compliance function, as declared.[29]

It is also worth mentioning that under the Corporate Governance Principles, the status of the head of the compliance unit equals that of the head of the internal audit

[26] Cichy (2015), pp. 7–8.

[27] Resolution of the Polish Financial Supervision Authority No. 258/2011 of 4 October 2011 on Detailed Principles of Functioning of the Risk Management System and Internal Control System and Detailed Conditions of Internal Capital Assessment by Banks and of Reviewing the Process of Internal Capital Assessment and Maintenance and the Principles of Determining the Policy on Variable Components of Remuneration of Persons Holding Managerial Positions at a Bank.

[28] Positions of the Polish Financial Supervision Authority of 16 February 2016 on requirements for the system of governance of an insurance/reinsurance undertaking and of 2 August 2018 on the role and importance of the compliance function exercised by insurance and reinsurance undertakings. Available at: www.knf.gov.pl.

[29] Methodology for the Annual Supervisory Assessment and Examination (BION) for insurance and reinsurance undertakings (assessment for 2019), https://www.knf.gov.pl/knf/pl/komponenty/img/Metodyka_BION_2019_70381.pdf.

unit. At the same time, the aforementioned persons should be able to communicate with the management board, supervisory board and the audit committee directly. Consequently, they should be able to report directly to these bodies. In the light of the Corporate Governance Principles, the KNF expects the head of the compliance unit as well as the head of the internal audit unit to participate in the meetings of the management and supervisory board or audit committee whenever issues related to the internal control system, internal audit function or compliance function are discussed. It should also be emphasised that under the Corporate Governance Principles, the appointment or dismissal of the head of the compliance unit takes place with the approval of the supervisory board or audit committee. In addition, it is worth mentioning that the insurance undertaking is obliged to inform the supervisory authority about changes in the position of the person supervising the compliance function within seven (7) days from the date of such a change. The KNF may also, by way of a decision, prohibit a person from supervising the compliance function if it has been determined that the person in question does not meet the requirements set out in the Act on Insurance and Reinsurance Activity.

The KNF also expects that members of the management board will not combine their functions with supervision of other key functions, i.e. the compliance function, the risk management function, the internal audit function and the actuarial function.[30] The KNF underlines the different nature of the duties imposed on the management board and the duties of the persons supervising other key functions in the insurance undertaking. In the opinion of the supervisory authority, the role of persons supervising other key functions, including the compliance function, is to provide advice and expertise to members of the management board. Similarly, EIOPA sees the role of supervisors with other key functions in line with the guidelines for an insurance company's governance system which indicate that the AMSB interacts with the senior management and key functions holders—including the audit, compliance, actuarial and risk management—'proactively requesting relevant information from them and challenging that information when necessary'.[31]

3.2 *Responsibility for Irregularities of the Compliance Function*

In the light of the KNF's position, irregularities of the compliance function give rise to liability on the part of both the persons supervising the performance of the key function and the president of the management board and other members of the management board. Possible sources of irregularities in the functioning of the

[30] Methodology for the Annual Supervisory Assessment and Examination (BION) for insurance and reinsurance undertakings (assessment for 2019), https://www.knf.gov.pl/knf/pl/komponenty/img/Metodyka_BION_2019_70381.pdf.

[31] Siri (2017), p. 142 and subsequent.

compliance function include an inadequate organisational structure, an inefficiently organised management system, an incorrect organisational and risk management culture, flawed attitudes of the managers in the insurance undertaking or, finally, a lack of independence and objectivity in the functioning of the compliance function.

There should be no doubt that the liability of the person supervising the compliance function, as well as that of the members of the management board of the insurance undertaking in connection with irregularities in the operation of that function is of an administrative and legal nature, which may be based on a breach of certain provisions of the Act on Insurance and Reinsurance Activity. Violation of provisions of law itself is one of the prerequisites for the KNF to apply the supervisory measures referred to in Article 362(1) of the Act on Insurance and Reinsurance Activity in connection with Article 362(2) (1) of the Act on Insurance and Reinsurance Activity. In the light of these provisions, one of the supervisory measures that the KNF is entitled to is the possibility to impose a financial penalty on a member of the management board if an insurance undertaking conducts business in violation of the law.

3.3 Role of the Compliance Function

When creating the compliance unit of an insurance undertaking, the following models can be adopted as a reference (analogous to those existing in banks[32]):

- A central model where responsibility for the entire compliance risk management process lies with the compliance unit, which cooperates with the other units of the insurance undertaking, including in particular business and operational units. It is directly subordinated to the management board of the insurance undertaking.
- A hybrid model in which all units of the insurance undertaking are involved in the process of managing the risk of non-compliance. The compliance unit is in this case responsible for the comprehensive assurance of compliance and the comprehensive process of managing the risk of non-compliance. In particular, it is reflected in the monitoring and verification of business units within the scope of their activities and reporting to the management board and supervisory board.
- A distributed model in which the compliance function is performed by all units of the insurance undertaking. In this model, the compliance unit is only an intermediary in the transmission of information to the management board or even becomes redundant.

The choice of the compliance function model is at the discretion of the insurance undertaking. At the moment, there is no legal requirement for an insurance undertaking to adopt a specific compliance function model. however, when choosing a compliance function model, the insurance undertaking should apply the principle of

[32]Cichy (2015), p. 10.

proportionality. In line with that principle, the choice of the model should be appropriate to the nature, scale and complexity of the business activity of the insurance undertaking in question.

Some guidelines on the model of the compliance function that should be in place in an insurance undertaking have been indicated by the KNF in the Corporate Governance Principles. In the light of Article 47(2) and Article 49 of those Principles, the compliance unit should participate in the process of managing the risk of non-compliance. This role should focus more on coordinating the process itself, reporting to the supervisory board and the management board and providing expertise to these bodies.[33] In this context, it seems that a hybrid model is the supervisor's preferred compliance function model. The above-mentioned position seems to be in line with the so-called three-line defence model adopted in Solvency II, in the line with which the compliance unit is the process owner for managing the risk of non-compliance and business and operational units are the owner of the risk itself. In keeping with the three-line defence model, the compliance function plays an advisory and coordinating role in the process of managing the risk of non-compliance through its monitoring and management. The role of the compliance function itself should not consist in accepting an identified non-compliance risk or in accepting it for the decision-making processes of business units or the Management Board.[34] In this context, the exertion of pressure on the compliance function through existing formal or informal mechanisms for this purpose should be criticised particularly strongly.[35] A key element in guaranteeing the independence of the compliance function is ensuring it is organised in a manner preventing it from influencing its employees with the possibility of having a detrimental effect on their employment situation.[36]

The literature on the subject matter underlines that the compliance function should clearly indicate the boundary conditions which should not be exceeded by business and operational units.[37] At the same time, it should be stipulated that when an insurance undertaking creates the compliance function, the relevant legal requirements and supervisory expectations with respect to that function should be considered. At this point it should be pointed out that while in the case of legal requirements, the insurance undertaking is obliged to comply or otherwise face potential sanctions, in view of the supervisory expectations expressed in the form of positions or recommendations, the undertaking has a certain degree of discretion in their implementation based on the 'comply or explain' principle. Consequently,

[33] Cichy (2015), p. 12.

[34] Communication of 20 August 2018 on the role and importance of compliance functions by insurance and reinsurance undertakings. Available at: www.knf.gov.pl.

[35] Communication of 20 August 2018 on the role and importance of compliance functions by insurance and reinsurance undertakings. Available at: www.knf.gov.pl.

[36] Communication of 20 August 2018 on the role and importance of compliance functions by insurance and reinsurance undertakings. Available at: www.knf.gov.pl.

[37] Rajewski (2018), p. 39.

when establishing the compliance function, an insurance undertaking may, based on the principle of proportionality, decide to organise that function differently than recommended by the supervisory authority, provided that it is justified by the nature, scale and business activity of the undertaking.

In relation to the characteristics of the compliance function, it should be stated that, in the light of Article 64(2) of the Act on Insurance and Reinsurance Activity, all legal regulations, including internal regulations, which affect or may affect the activity of an insurance undertaking should be of interest to that entity. In the context of the scope of the regulations that apply to the business activity of an insurance undertaking, it should be stated that the so-called hybrid model is the most optimal model for the implementation of the compliance function.[38] As indicated above, in this model, the compliance function is performed by all units of the insurance undertaking, and the compliance unit coordinates the compliance process and the process of managing the risk of non-compliance on the systemic level across the insurance undertaking. There is no doubt that the particular focus of an undertaking's compliance unit should lie primarily on the legal provisions strictly governing insurance activity and the regulations, the non-compliance of which generates the greatest risk. On the activity of insurance undertakings, these include the following areas:[39]

- compliance of the undertaking's business activity with the provisions of the Polish and EU law and recommendations of supervisory institutions and other entities which have impact on practices in force on financial markets
- prevention of money laundering, terrorist financing, corruption and other abuses on the part of customers, employees and contractors, safeguarding of legally protected secrets
- protection of confidential information and personal data, supervision of the confidential information flow
- management of conflicts of interest
- assurance that the company's employees will follow the ethical code and relevant market practices
- establishment of principles of ethical conduct when conducting an insurance activity
- advertisement of insurance products
- receipt of reports, investigation procedures, development of standards to protect employees who report irregularities (including whistle-blowers)
- management of operational risk in the compliance area
- contacts with supervisory authorities, including the distribution of the correspondence sent by that authority and replying to its enquiries
- issues related to insurance outsourcing

[38] Rajewski (2018), p. 39.

[39] Mrozowska-Bartkiewicz and Wnęk (2016), p. 77.

- participation in the development of new business models or the creation of new products, taking into account the applicable regulations and appropriate communication
- supervision of the policy related to the receipt and distribution of gifts by employees and the organisation of events participated of customers
- training and information campaigns for employees in the field of compliance culture

3.4 Selected Models of Compliance Functions in European Insurance Undertakings

3.4.1 PZU Group

According to the SFCR report for 2018 published by PZU SA,[40] Compliance Department is responsible for shaping the PZU Group's compliance system while ensuring its consistency across all levels within the PZU Group. PZU's Compliance Department reports to the Company's Management Board and Supervisory Board on all events occurring at the level of both PZU and the subsidiaries with which agreements on cooperation and exchange of information have been entered into. Recommendations issued by the Compliance Department at PZU as part of its activities and compliance analyses are subject to the monitoring process. In each PZU Group company, the compliance function is arranged based on uniform and consistent standards developed at the PZU level in consideration of the 'proportionality principle', that is while taking into account the scale and specific nature of the pertinent PZU Group company. The internal regulations in place delineate the extent and nature of activities of the compliance function, including regular reporting by the subsidiaries' compliance units to PZU's Compliance Department, and then by PZU's Compliance Department to the PZU Management Board and Supervisory Board. This notwithstanding, the subsidiaries' compliance units also report to their own management boards or supervisory boards. The compliance function in PZU Group companies is objective and independent. The most significant powers of PZU's Compliance Department in compliance risk in the PZU Group are as follows:

- analysing and participating in the process of deploying systemic solutions in all functional areas of PZU Group companies and ongoing business processes in terms of compliance risk
- initiating and recommending changes in systemic solutions and analysed processes in place at PZU Group companies ensuing from compliance analyses
- ensuring coordination and uniform solutions in deploying the compliance function and managing compliance risk in the PZU Group

[40] SFCR report for 2018 published by PZU SA, available at: https://www.pzu.pl/relacje-inwestorskie/raporty?queries%5BreportTypes%5D=solvency&queries%5Byear%5D=2019.

- consulting and cooperating with subsidiaries to ensure uniform solutions in deploying the compliance function in the PZU Group, fulfilling reporting obligations arising from the Supplementary Oversight Act and adopting a consistent approach of the PZU Group's regulated subsidiaries to the preparation of responses to inquiries sent by the Polish Financial Supervision Authority systemically to regulated entities
- consulting and exchanging information with subsidiaries to ensure consistency in the process of compliance risk identification and assessment
- conducting systemic compliance analyses in PZU Group companies based on internal regulations, cooperation agreements and policies
- system-level reporting on compliance risk in the PZU Group
- monitoring observance of the standards of conduct, including ethical standards, in consideration of the best practices adopted in PZU Group companies

As part of the exchange of information and cooperation with subsidiaries in the compliance function, the PZU's Compliance Department participates in the deployment, in these companies, of uniform standards and key methodological solutions. The formal basis for cooperation in the compliance function is provided by agreements on cooperation and exchange of information and the provisions of the PZU Group's Compliance Policy which define in detail the rules, extent and nature of such cooperation between PZU and its subsidiaries.

3.4.2 Generali Group

According to the SFCR report for 2018 published by Assicurazioni Generali S.p. A.,[41] the compliance function has the responsibility to advice the Administrative, Management or Supervisory Body on compliance with laws, regulations, and administrative provisions, including those adopted pursuant to the Solvency II Directive for insurance and reinsurance Group companies. The compliance function also advice on other laws, regulations, and administrative provisions, including the Group Code of Conduct and Group policies. Moreover, the compliance function has the responsibility to assess the possible impact of any changes of in the legal environment on the operation of relevant Group company and to identify and assess the compliance risk, including the adequacy of the measures adopted to prevent non-compliance.

Assicurazioni Generali S.p.A., in its capacity as parent company of the Generali Group, has adopted the 'Group Compliance Management System Policy' which includes the fundamental rules on how compliance must be embedded in the daily operations and how the compliance function must be implemented. In this respect,

[41] SFCR report for 2018 published by Assicurazioni Generali S.p.A. available at: https://www.generali.com/investors/reports-and-presentations/report-archive/SFCR-2018-Solvency-and-financial-condition-report.

the above-mentioned policy defines the operating model of the global compliance function across the Group.

In particular, the core processes included under the compliance operating model are the following:

- risk identification
- risk evaluation
- risk mitigation
- risk monitoring
- reporting and planning

The risk identification process is aimed at ensuring that the requirements arising in connection with both the internal and the external regulations are identified and allocated under the responsibility of the relevant operational functions.

The risk evaluation process is aimed at assessing, also under a forward-looking perspective, the risk which each Group company is exposed to and the level of adequacy of the internal control system to achieve its goals. The compliance function, together with the risk management function, performs and supports risk owners in risk assessment activities and ensures that Group methodologies are applied.

The risk mitigation process aims at ensuring the adoption of all necessary for the correct implementation of the requirements set out by the internal and external regulations. In particular, the compliance function ensures that appropriate training programs for all employees are delivered on regular basis, internal regulations and procedures are defined and minimum standard for controls identified, in cooperation with the operational functions.

The risk monitoring process aims at achieving an updated picture on the ability of the Group company to manage compliance risks. Such process consists in the collection and periodical analysis of specific data and indicators that ensure the effective deployment of such risk monitoring

The reporting process aims at ensuring that appropriate information flows towards Senior Management and the Administrative, Management or Supervisory Body of each Group company are in place such a way as to allow these parties to make decisions that consider the level of exposure of the Group company to compliance risks and to assess the adequacy and effectiveness of their internal control systems to manage such risks.

3.4.3 Allianz Group

According to the SFCR report for 2018 published by Allianz Group,[42] key tasks and activities of the compliance function include:

[42] SFCR report for 2018 published by Allianz, available at: https://www.allianz.com/en/investor_relations/results-reports/sfcr.html.

- Advising the Board of Management on compliance with laws, regulations, and regulatory requirements applicable to the Allianz Group (external requirements) as well as on the potential impact of material changes in the legal environment
- Identifying and assessing compliance risk (risk of legal or regulatory sanctions, material financial losses, and/or reputational damages that Allianz SE or the Allianz Group might sustain as a result of non-compliance with external requirements
- Monitoring of appropriate and effective internal procedures to ensure compliance with material external requirements applicable to the Allianz Group
- Observing and analysing developments in the legal environment and evaluating the potential impact of material changes to the legal environment on the Allianz Group

The compliance function reports to the Board of Management on current compliance issues as and when required, but at least once a year.

The compliance function is a core component of the Allianz Group's Internal Control System. Fulfilment of the compliance function's duties is ensured by the compliance department of Allianz SE (Group Compliance).

4 Management of the Risk of Non-Compliance in an Insurance Undertaking on the Example of Solutions Existing in Poland

In the light of Article 50(2) of the Corporate Governance Principles issued by the Polish Financial Supervision Authority, the process of risk management in financial institutions consists of individual, interrelated activities. Similarly, the process was regulated in the Regulation of the Minister of Development and Finance of 6 March 2017 on the risk management system and internal control system, remuneration policy and detailed estimation of internal capital in banks (Journal of Laws of 2017, item 637). At the same time, attention should be paid to supervisory expectations concerning the process of managing the risk of non-compliance in banks expressed in Recommendation H on the internal control system in banks. While these regulations and supervisory expectations are addressed to banks, they can provide a reference point for illustrating the model of the process of managing the non-compliance risk that may occur in insurance undertakings. In the light of Article 37 (4)-(8) of the above-mentioned Regulations, responsibilities of the compliance unit include:

- identification of the risk of non-compliance, in particular through the analysis of legal regulations, the bank's internal regulations, market standards and the results of internal investigation procedures conducted by the compliance unit
- assessment of the risk of non-compliance by measuring or estimating that risk

- development and implementation of mechanisms for controlling the risk of non-compliance based on an assessment of the risk of non-compliance
- monitoring of the extent and profile of the risk of non-compliance following the application of mechanisms for controlling the risk of non-compliance
- the periodic submission of reports on non-compliance risk to the management and supervisory board or audit committee, if the latter has been appointed

4.1 Identification of the Risk of Non-Compliance

The first component of the process of managing the risk of non-compliance is its identification. The purpose of this activity is to identify areas where the risk of non-compliance may occur. For this purpose, the compliance unit should have guaranteed access to relevant sources of information on the business activity and operational activities of the insurance undertaking. Only in this way will the compliance function be able to perform its tasks independently and objectively.[43] This may be achieved, for example, through the participation of the compliance unit in the work on the implementation or modification of products offered by the insurance undertaking. In addition, the participation of the compliance unit in this process is required by the Polish Financial Supervision Authority in the light of the recommendations on the product management system. In line with Recommendation 11, 'the Undertaking should carry out detailed analyses of products before they are placed on the market and each time when there are changes in the target customer group or significant changes in products'. As part of product analyses, the insurance undertaking should carry out a qualitative analysis consisting of an assessment of compliance with the applicable laws, guidelines and recommendations of the supervisory authority and the internal regulations adopted by the Undertaking, an analysis of whether clauses that have been considered as prohibited contractual or analogous clauses are present in the products, as well as an analysis of potential risks associated with the product, including those relating to inadequacy of the premium offered by the undertaking. However, the process involved in changing or implementing the products offered by the undertaking should not be the only source of information on potential risks of non-compliance. In its Recommendation H on the internal control system in banks, the Polish Financial Supervision Authority also distinguishes the following basic sources of information which should be used in the identification of risk of non-compliance (in line with Recommendation 15.2):

- changes in provisions of law, internal regulations and market standards
- registers and documentation maintained by the bank (e.g. register of operational risk losses)

[43] Cichy (2015), p. 21.

- information obtained from other organisational units as part of the performance of their duties, including in particular as part of their independent monitoring process
- findings of the compliance unit made in connection with the ongoing verification and testing carried out by that unit
- results of internal investigation procedures conducted by the compliance unit or other organisational units of the bank
- irregularities identified by the bank in all three lines of defence
- information from an anonymous infringement notification channel
- arrangements resulting from supervisory activities performed by authorised institutions (e.g. the KNF) and activities performed by other authorised institutions (e.g. Consumer Protection and Competition Office, Financial Ombudsman)

4.2 Assessment of the Risk of Non-Compliance

The second component of the process of managing the risk of non-compliance is risk assessment, also called risk analysis, measurement or estimation. Risk assessment is performed once a risk has been identified and consists in risk estimation.[44] Nevertheless, the risk of non-compliance is a risk that is difficult to measure. Qualitative methods, consisting of expert risk measurement carried out by compliance officers, are crucial in risk assessment. This assessment results in the determination of the level of the identified risk (e.g. high, medium or low) based on an established procedure or methodology. In this sense, the assessment of the risk of non-compliance may consist in an estimation of the amount of financial and non-financial losses that an insurance undertaking may incur as a result of failure to meet those risks. These losses may result from fines imposed by regulators such as the Consumer Protection and Competition Office or the Polish Financial Supervision Authority. For example, in the case of an identified risk of non-compliance consisting in a potential breach of the collective interests of consumers, the amount of the penalty that the President of the Consumer Protection and Competition Office may impose if that risk occurs amounts to 10% of the turnover achieved in the financial year preceding the year in which the penalty is imposed. The above does not include to the losses that may arise from litigation with particular clients, as well as losses resulting from the loss of credibility among clients. The following methods should be distinguished as part of the assessment of the risk of non-compliance (in line with the KNF's Recommendation 16.2 on the internal control system in banks):

- self-assessment of risk
- scenario analyses

[44] Cichy (2015), p. 21.

- analyses of regulatory gaps
- indicators of the risk of non-compliance

4.3 Control of the Risk of Non-Compliance

The use of risk mitigation mechanisms is the next step in the process of managing the risk of non-compliance. They have a preventive function. The purpose of the control mechanisms is to minimise the risk of non-compliance.[45] In the light of Article 36 (1) of the Regulation of the Minister of Development and Finance of 6 March 2017 on the risk management system and internal control system, remuneration policy and detailed estimation of internal capital in banks, the following types of control mechanisms should be distinguished:

- procedures
- division of responsibilities
- authorisation, in particular the authorisation of financial and economic operations
- access control
- physical inspection
- process of recording financial and economic operations in accounting, reporting and operational systems
- stocktaking
- documentation of derogations
- performance indicators
- training

The risk control mechanisms defined by the KNF in Recommendation H on the internal control system (Recommendation 7.2.) are also noteworthy:

- analysis of new products and services introduced to the bank's offer
- analysis of modifications to these products and services and analysis of the sales processes of these products and services, in terms of compliance with provisions of law, internal regulations and market standards
- issuance of detailed guidelines by the compliance unit
- coordination of the process of informing about changes in laws, internal regulations and market standards
- participation in key implementation projects, in the context of ensuring compliance with the provisions of law, internal regulations and market standards (provided that the independence of the compliance unit in the testing process is not affected)

[45] Cichy (2015), p. 21.

- performance or commissioning of training to the extent indicated by the compliance unit
- determination of non-compliance risk indicators

4.4 *Risk Monitoring*

Monitoring of the identified and assessed risk of non-compliance aims to determine whether the applied risk mitigation mechanisms have reduced the risk likelihood and to determine whether the level of that risk is acceptable from the perspective of the adopted risk management strategy of the insurance undertaking. Risk monitoring should also be perceived as a control of prior stages of the process of managing the risk of non-compliance. The purpose of this activity is also to demonstrate to the management and supervisory board whether the level of risk of non-compliance is acceptable. The instruments for risk monitoring include the following:[46]

- compliance tests
- surveys, including self-assessment surveys
- evaluation of the maturity of the compliance model
- performance indicators (e.g. the percentage of trained employees, processed customer complaints and requests, the pace of implementation and performance of internal recommendations and post-inspection recommendations of the supervisor)

4.5 *Reporting to the Management Board and the Supervisory Board*

Reporting constitutes the final element of the process of managing the risk of non-compliance. As part of this activity, the compliance unit should inform the management and supervisory board on a regular basis (monthly, quarterly and annually) and on an ad hoc basis (e.g. internal investigation procedures) of the level and profile of the risk of non-compliance within the insurance undertaking. At the same time, the reports should contain information on individual components of the process of managing the risk of non-compliance, including the identified risks of non-compliance, their assessment, the applied control mechanisms and the results of monitoring of those risks. To ensure transparency, it seems that cyclical reports should be provided to both the management and the supervisory board.

[46]Cichy (2015), p. 22.

5 Conclusions

The main assumption of the chapter was an attempt to determine the importance of the compliance function in the process of managing the risk of non-compliance by means of the functioning and organisation of this unit within the structures of an insurance undertaking. The aim of the compliance unit as well as of the process of managing the risk of non-compliance itself should be to reduce the risk by ensuring adequate mitigation actions. In this context, the role of compliance should be perceived not as a restriction of business development, but as an opportunity to prevent significant financial losses resulting from the materialisation of the risk of non-compliance. Effective implementation of the compliance function allows both operating and business units to make informed decisions on risk acceptance. This is of particular importance in an era of systematic growth of legal and supervisory requirements applicable to financial institutions, including the risks associated with the conduct of business and relationships with customers (conduct risk). This results in a proportionate increase in an insurance undertakings' exposure to the risk of incurring significant financial and non-financial losses due to their violation of specific obligations.

Given the above, it should be concluded that ensuring the compliance of an insurance undertaking's business activity with applicable laws, internal regulations and supervisory expectations is undoubtedly part of safe, stable and prudent management of an insurance undertaking. Conscious managing of the risk of non-compliance also helps to reduce reputational risk, which is particularly important for financial institutions which are to enjoy public trust. The organisation of compliance units is a matter of interest to the Polish Financial Supervision Authority, which draws attention to the fact that irregularities with regard to that function give rise to liability on the part of the person supervising that function as well as the members of the management board of the insurance undertaking. There is no doubt that, with increasing regulation, the role and importance of the compliance function in the insurance market will continue to increase systematically, as is the case with more developed fields of the financial market.

References

Cichy Ł (2015) Funkcja compliance w bankach, CEDUR, Komisja Nadzoru Finansowego, Warszawa 2015

Hull JC (2011) Zarządzanie ryzykiem instytucji finansowych, Wydawnictwo Naukowe PWN, Warszawa 2011

Iwanicz-Drozdowska M (2017) Zarządzanie ryzykiem bankowym, red. Iwanicz-Drozdowska M., Poltex, Warszawa

Leśniak D (2017) Komentarz do art. 45 ustawy o działalności ubezpieczeniowej i reasekuracyjnej, w: M. Szczepańska oraz P. Wajda (red.), Ustawa o działalności ubezpieczeniowej i reasekuracyjnej. Commentary. Warsaw

Mrozowska-Bartkiewicz B, Wnęk A (2016) Funkcja compliance w zakładzie ubezpieczeń, "Prawo Asekuracyjne" nr 1/2016
Paś W (2018) Rola funkcji compliance w zarządzaniu ryzykiem braku zgodności w zakładzie ubezpieczeń, "Wiadomości Ubezpieczeniowe" nr 3/2018
Rajewski K (2018) Funkcja compliance w strukturze organizacyjnej zakładu ubezpieczeń – wyzwania i aspekty praktyczne, "Prawo Asekuracyjne" nr 3/2018
Siri M (2017) Corporate governance of insurance firms after Solvency II. In: Marano P, Siri M (eds) Insurance regulation in the European Union. Solvency II and beyond. Palgrave Macmillan, p 132 and subsequent
Swain R, Swallow D (2015) The prudential regulation of insurers under Solvency II, Bank of England, Quarterly Bulletin 2015 Q2
Wojno B (2017) Komentarz do art. 365 ustawy o działalności ubezpieczeniowej i reasekuracyjnej, (w:) M. Szczepańska oraz P. Wajda (red.), Ustawa o działalności ubezpieczeniowej i reasekuracyjnej. Commentary. Warsaw

List of Documents

Commission Delegated Regulation (EU) 2015/35 of 10 October 2014 supplementing Solvency II
Communication of 20 August 2018 on the role and importance of compliance functions by insurance and reinsurance undertakings. Available at: www.knf.gov.pl
De Larosière High Level Group (2009), Report on the future of financial supervision in the EU, Brussels
Directive 2009/138/EC of the European Parliament and of the Council of 25 November 2009 on the taking-up and pursuit of the business of Insurance and Reinsurance (Solvency II) (OJ EU L of 17 December 2009), Act of 11 September 2015 on Insurance and Reinsurance Activity (i.e. of 2018 item 999 as amended)
European Insurance and Occupational Pensions Authority (EIOPA) guidelines on the governance of insurance undertaking
International standards for the conduct of insurance business activity and principles of insurance supervision, issued by the International Association of Insurance Supervisors (IAIS)
ISO 19600:2014
KNF.GOV.PL, *KNF.GOV.PL*, KNF (2012)
Methodology for the Annual Supervisory Assessment and Examination (BION) for insurance and reinsurance undertakings (assessment for 2019)
CEIOPS, Advice to the European Commission on the Principle of Proportionality in the Solvency II Framework Directive proposal, CEIOPS-DOC-24/08, May 2008., available at https://eiopa.europa.eu/CEIOPS-Archive/
Positions of the Polish Financial Supervision Authority of 16 February 2016 on requirements for the system of governance of an insurance/reinsurance undertaking and of 2 August 2018 on the role and importance of the compliance function exercised by insurance and reinsurance undertakings. Available at: www.knf.gov.pl
Regulation of the Minister of Development and Finance of 6 March 2017 on the risk management system and internal control system, remuneration policy and detailed estimation of internal capital in banks (Journal of Laws of 2017, item 637)

Recommendation H on the internal control system in banks issued by the Polish Financial Supervision Authority
Resolution of the Polish Financial Supervision Authority No. 258/2011 of 4 October 2011 on Detailed Principles of Functioning of the Risk Management System and Internal Control System and Detailed Conditions of Internal Capital Assessment by Banks and of Reviewing the Process of Internal Capital Assessment and Maintenance and the Principles of Determining the Policy on Variable Components of Remuneration of Persons Holding Managerial Positions at a Bank
SFCR report for 2018 published by PZU SA, available at: https://www.pzu.pl/relacje-inwes-torskie/raporty?queries%5BreportTypes%5D=solvency&queries%5Byear%5D=2019
SFCR report for 2018 published by Assicurazioni Generali S.p.A. available at: https://www.generali.com/investors/reports-and-presentations/report-archive/SFCR-2018-Solvency-and-financial-condition-report

Insurance Outsourcing: A Legal Analysis

Monika Szaraniec

Abstract Outsourcing plays an important role in the operation of insurance and reinsurance companies. This article aims to define the legal conditions of insurance outsourcing and their evaluation by the author. The example of limiting the scope of outsourcing in the activities of insurance and reinsurance companies in the Polish law shows its specificity compared to other outsourcing in business. This specificity lies primarily in the need to control insurance outsourcing by the EU and national supervisory authorities. There is a tendency in the law to extend the regulations related to insurance outsourcing to the further performance of a process, service or activity by insurance companies, particularly in the field of cooperation of traditional distributors with *Insurtech*. The lack of legal regulations forces EIOPA to look for appropriate and effective legal solutions in the field of supervision over insurance outsourcing. This process is mainly based on self-regulation of the market through 'soft law'—this practice sets new tasks for the EU and national regulators.

1 Introduction

Despite certain legal restrictions of the objective scope of outsourced activities and liability of the insurance undertaking for the data provided within the framework of an outsourcing contract, such undertakings decide to outsource to external entities an increasing amount of activities. The EU legislator strives to adjust legislation to the evolving business reality, which is evident in the increasingly precise legal regimes of outsourcing, especially in EIOPA Guidelines. A major role in the process of concluding outsourcing agreements is played by supervisory authorities, which monitor the outsourcing process and anticipate possible negative results.

M. Szaraniec (✉)
Cracow University of Economics, College of Economy, Finance and Law, Institute of Law, Cracow, Poland
e-mail: monika.szaraniec@uek.krakow.pl

P. Marano, K. Noussia (eds.), *The Governance of Insurance Undertakings*, AIDA Europe Research Series on Insurance Law and Regulation 6,
https://doi.org/10.1007/978-3-030-85817-9_4

This study is a contribution intended to further investigations on outsourcing as well as subsequent research and discussion. It must be pointed out that many practically important questions, such as the relation between outsourcing and the regime of insurance secrecy or personal data protection, fall beyond the scope of this chapter.

2 Definitions of Outsourcing

The name outsourcing is a contraction of three English words: 'outside resource using'—meaning the use of external resources.[1] This is an institution very gladly used in the processes of managing enterprises and human resources, and in those areas it is generally understood as business strategy through which a part of work of a given organisation is delegated to external entities.[2] For that purpose, there are exceptionally numerous publications on outsourcing in the area of management. I could not omit that thread, and many definitions which I present below were developed in sciences relating to management.

In the European Union legislation, one can encounter legal definitions of the term 'outsourcing'. However, the Commission Directive 2006/73/EC of 10 August 2006 implementing Directive 2004/39/EC of the European Parliament and of the Council as regards organisational requirements and operating conditions for investment firms and defined terms for the purposes of that Directive[3] and the Directive 2009/138/EC of the European Parliament and of the Council of 25 November 2009 on the taking-up and pursuit of the business of Insurance and Reinsurance (Solvency II),[4] which handle that issue, limit the objective scope of their definitions of outsourcing exclusively to contracts in which one of the parties is respectively: investment firm or insurance undertaking or reinsurance undertaking. Because of the clearly limited subjective scope of the definitions of outsourcing offered in the abovementioned legislative acts and their clearly sectional nature, defining the term 'outsourcing' only for the purpose of a specific regime, in this part of the considerations, I would like to point to a more universal definition of outsourcing, relating to business activity in general.

Similarly, in the Polish legal system, there is no general definition of the term 'outsourcing' even though that term appears on several occasions. In the Act on insurance and reinsurance activities, we can find a provision under which outsourcing means a 'a contract between the insurance undertaking or reinsurance undertaking and the service provider under which the service provider performs a process, service or activity which would be otherwise performed by the insurance

[1]Trocki (2001), p. 13; Juchno and Kaszubski (2001), p. 5.

[2]Śliwa (2015), p. 39.

[3]Dz.U.UE.L.2006.241.26.

[4]Dz.U.UE.L.2009.335.1.

undertaking or reinsurance undertaking, including contracts under which the service provider delegates the performance of such process, service or activity to other entities through which the service provider performs the given process, service or activity'.[5] It can be easily noticed that the definition was drafted similarly to the abovementioned examples from European Union law and applies only to a narrow scope covered by the statutory framework of the Act. Consequently, it may not be treated as a general definition of outsourcing in the Polish legal system.[6]

There is no single universal definition of outsourcing, therefore it seems necessary to outline its conceptions as developed in the literature of the subject (mainly economic sciences).[7] Certain authors define outsourcing as taking advantage by an organisation—recipient of services—of services of an external service provider, from outside the ordering firm's organisational structure. Such services are to consist in performance by the service provider of the ordering firm's tasks on the latter's behalf.[8] Other researchers are of the opinion that outsourcing means delegation, on contractual basis, of material, human or technological resources to another entity along with the transfer to that entity of decision-making competences corresponding to the delegated means.[9]

In the widest sense, outsourcing is viewed as a restructuring project intended to bring more flexibility in the operation of an organisation by reducing the organisational structure through cutting down on the number of units, organisational positions or management levels, which relates to the *lean management* conception.[10]

Outsourcing may be approached as manifestation of business management. As a result of the development, progress and changes in market economy, entrepreneurs are searching for new management applications to increase their competitiveness, since competitiveness is a necessary precondition to the existence and development of businesses. Outsourcing is also a consequence of the progressing globalisation, whose scope covers all countries and societies and, directly or indirectly, relates to economic operators. An effect of the ongoing globalisation processes is a growth of competitiveness, more efficient operation of markets and improvement of consumers' position.[11] Enterprises approach the institution of outsourcing as a tool for the optimisation of their activities intended to achieve their strategic goals. In the light of the above, when an entrepreneur concentrates on its principal activity, in which it has a market advantage, the areas amounting to the entrepreneur's auxiliary

[5] Art. 2(1) item 27 of the Act of 11 September 2015 on insurance and reinsurance activities (Dz. U. 2020, poz. 895, 1180).

[6] Nowak (2008), pp. 357–358.

[7] So, e.g. Domberger (1998) or Greaver (1999).

[8] So, e.g. Dominguez (2013), p. 27; Lei and Hitt (1995), p. 836; Grossmann and Helpman (2002), p. 115.

[9] Greaver Jr (1999), p. 3.

[10] Nadolna (2007), p. 200; Trocki (1999).

[11] Kowalski (2008), p. 14.

or incidental objects are delegated outside. The rule of thumb is that the strong points of an enterprise must always remain within its organisation.[12]

When discussing insurance outsourcing, it is worth paying attention to offshoring (offshore outsourcing, international outsourcing). From the perspective of theory and practice of management, it consists in delegation of a part of services for rendition by foreign entities—in countries where labour costs are lower or intellectual capital resources are richer. In literature, it is indicated that this relates predominantly to business, IT and research and development services.[13] In this respect, in the case of internationally operating insurance conglomerates, international outsourcing may apply.

In insurance practice, there is sometimes a specific type of cooperation between insurers known as fronting. This is nothing more than full reinsurance, associated with the transfer of the entire insurance risk to the reinsurer. In practice, this means that the insurer only acts as a distributor of such insurance, while remaining a party to the concluded insurance contract and usually handling such insurance normally; however, the insurance risk is borne entirely by the reinsurer in a given case.[14]

3 Outsourcing Types

According to the type of connections, we can distinguish capital and contractual outsourcing. In case of capital outsourcing, there are capital links between corporate partners. Capital outsourcing is one of possible methods of creating capital groups, consisting in severance from the parent company of a part of its activities and establishment a subsidiary with a view to its pursuance. On the other hand, contractual outsourcing is the case when the ordering party and the service provider are not related in capital terms but are separate entities bound by a contract for the performance of specific activities.[15]

Outsourcing may also be divided according to its significance to the company. If the delegated activity provides benefits in a longer time perspective and its nature is of key importance to the enterprise, we can speak of strategic outsourcing. Decisions about its launch are made by top management, considering the critical success factors of the strategy's implementation. If the timeframe is shorter and/or the significance of the delegated activities is lower, we have to do with tactical outsourcing.[16]

Another criterion of outsourcing's division is the distinction according to the scope of the severed business function. On that basis, three types of activity may be

[12] Kłos (2009), p. 33.

[13] Ciesielska (2009), p. 21.

[14] Czublun (2016), p. 5. See also: Jovanovic (2013), pp. 44–45.

[15] Trocki (1999), p. 37.

[16] Trocki (1999), p. 59.

distinguished: (1) core business, constituting the essence of an enterprise's operation. This is an area, within a company, which decides about the company's competitive advantage and may be identified with the conception of key competences; (2) auxiliary activities (core related business) comprising strategically essential functions which are not of key importance to the organisation; (3) incidental activities (non-core related business), that is functions of little or minimum strategic importance. In commercial practice, the most commonly delegated functions are incidental and, to an increasing degree, auxiliary activities, which are not the company's key asset.[17]

In the 80s of the twentieth century, a rapid development of outsourcing started from delegating IT services to external entities. IT services were treated as support processes and most outsourcing contracts related to processes supporting the core activities: administration, logistics, purchases, etc. It was relatively late that business processes became implemented with the use of external entities. Following such sectoral division, one can distinguish between Information Technology Outsourcing (ITO) (St. Armant, 2010), consisting in the development of applications, maintenance of IT systems, manufacturing support, etc. The second rapidly growing type of outsourcing is Business Process Outsourcing (BPO) covering the operation of call-centres, management of human resources, accountancy, etc. (Deloite, 2013). From the technological point of view, outsourcing of technologies. In the opinion of Tower Group and FDIC (Federal Deposit Insurance Corporation, 2004), there are four different outsourcing models: direct captive (subsidiary company), joint venture, direct service provider, indirect service provider (sub-outsourcer).[18]

Outsourcing may also be divided according to the scope of the delegated functions. Partial or selective outsourcing principally boils down to severance of a narrow area of the enterprise, leaving the rest inside the organisation. On the other hand, full or total outsourcing means that most areas of the enterprise organisation's activity are outsourced to one or more providers for a period specified in the contract.[19]

According to the option of using external entities' services home or abroad, national outsourcing and cross-border outsourcing can be distinguished. Cross-border outsourcing (transnational outsourcing, offshore outsourcing) is usually used by companies from highly developed countries and consists in the establishment of outsourcing cooperation with foreign economic organisations in developing countries which, due to lower costs, make attractive business partners.[20]

[17] Kopczyński (2010), p. 14.

[18] Gołąb (2017), p. 164.

[19] Malarewicz-Jakubów and Tanajewska (2014), p. 236.

[20] Kłos (2009), p. 56.

4 Outsourcing Management

Outsourcing is a complex conception and the discussion of the essence of that phenomenon on the borderline of economy and management calls for its wider presentation, allowing for multiple aspects, especially the following reasons for using outsourcing: (1) the ordering party's decision whether to make or buy, (2) analysing on each occasion the main reasons for the outsourcing, (3) decision about the form of cooperation with a specific outsourcing partner.[21]

Introduction of outsourcing as institution in economic practice calls for a dynamic, extended over time and procedural approach, allowing to take account of different conditions, particularly in management, economy and law, enabling to achieve the intended effects of reaching for external services.[22]

When analysing particular stages of implementing outsourcing as an organisational solution in an enterprise, attention should be drawn to the fact that, as such, it is an interdisciplinary process, since its efficient implementation requires the use of different techniques and skills as well as different areas of expertise in law, organisation and management. Introduction of outsourcing is a strategic change for the enterprise, which is why outsourcing directly affects: strategy, organisational structure, economic and social conditions within the enterprise. Implementation of outsourcing in an enterprise allows to distinguish key phases and stages of the outsourcing process.[23] Management of the outsourcing process comprises at least the following stages:

(1) designing (planning) outsourcing
(2) choice of the outsourcing partner and signing the appropriate outsourcing agreement
(3) management of performance of the outsourcing agreement and relations with the outsourcing partner until the end of cooperation[24]

The first stage involves a preliminary analysis of the strategic conditions and assessment of liability of the enterprise's specific areas to severance. This stage must include: the definition of the specific purposes of the outsourcing, analysis of costs and advantages of implementing that institution, analysis of chances and risks relating to the implementation of outsourcing. This phase relates to the enterprise's strategic goals. It is also necessary to specify the scope of outsourcing and its role.

The second phase is the phase of introducing the outsourcing, involving the stages of selecting and acquiring the appropriate partner and signing the agreement. The purpose of that phase is to guarantee internal order during the implementation of the outsourcing by preparing an implementation schedule. At this stage, the agreement is finally signed, governing: the organisation, rights and obligations of the

[21] Juchno and Kaszubski (2001), p. 5.
[22] Kopczyński (2010), p. 14.
[23] Matejun (2015), pp. 93–99.
[24] Byrski (2018), p. 10.

parties and all other cooperation areas. Such agreement is the outsourcing contract. When preparing and signing that type of document, it must be remembered that often the success of an external servicing process depends both on the construction, scope and specificity of its clauses. Provisions of each outsourcing agreement should be specifically negotiated and cover all legal aspects. In the process of preparing outsourcing agreements, an enterprise may hire external consultants.[25] The last phase of implementation is the operative stage, in which organisational relations taking place in the enterprise are subject to modification, and cooperation is established with the external service provider. The operative process should also cover, in the first place, control and monitoring of the contract's performance, the aim of which must be to ensure that the actual activities performed as a part of external servicing are in line with the planned activities.

5 Legal Aspects of the Outsourcing Contract

Presentation of the legal framework of outsourcing is not an easy task. The basic difficulty follows from the fact that, in truth, it is difficult to talk about the 'outsourcing contract' even though the term is in widespread use. A closer analysis of both outsourcing practice and literature of that subject points to the conclusion that outsourcing means, in the first place, a certain method of organising business activity, consisting in the discussed 'delegation outside' of a part of the enterprise's activities. Therefore, outsourcing is more of a mechanism in economy and management than any specific legal construction. This type of mechanism may use diverse legal instruments.[26]

Outsourcing consists in the conclusion of a contract under which the ordering party delegates, as a part of the ordering party's enterprise, specific services relating to the operation of the enterprise to an external entity, and the party undertaking to perform the services pledges to render them in exchange for remuneration.

The contract which forms the legal basis for outsourcing is a commercial contract *sensu stricto* (business-to-business) since both contractual parties are entrepreneurs. By its nature, it is a consensual, bilaterally binding, non-gratuitous and mutual agreement. Its parties may be referred to as the delegating party and the outsourcer.[27]

In principle, the outsourcing contract does not require any specific form, however, the need for its written documentation may arise under the provisions on accounting or tax legislation.

The outsourcing agreement belongs to the category of empirical contracts. These contracts are formed as a result of mass conclusion of agreements of similar, analogous content and usually have specific names reflecting their general nature.

[25] Sobińska (2001), p. 35.

[26] Robaczyński (2018), p. 396.

[27] Robaczyński (2018), p. 397.

Such contracts are governed directly by the norms on the general question of performing obligations and possibly, by *analogia legis,* by specific obligational law norms on nominate contracts insofar as one can speak of their similarity with those contracts. Currently, the operation of innominate contracts is a universal legal phenomenon.[28] This means that it is possible to establish a legal construction of a contract which does not correspond to any of the statutory contract types, whose obligational framework may lead to effective performance of the contract's subject. The possibility of forming such contracts strictly relates to the principle of free formation of contracts.[29] The outsourcing contract (excluding, e.g., insurance outsourcing, as will be discussed in a further part of this study) is formed under the principle of the freedom of contract, which means that the parties concluding the contract may define the legal relationship in their discretion as far as its content or purpose is not contrary to the nature of the relationship, the law or the principles of social coexistence.

From the point of view of the classical civil law classification, the outsourcing contract may assume different nature. As such, this construction fits into the group of contracts for the provision of services. In certain situations, this may be a mandate contract, however, more frequently it may be a contract for the provision of services otherwise not regulated. Generally, when we have to do with multiple services rendered by the outsourcer, the purposes of outsourcing may also be achieved by applying the construction of a contract for a specific work, just as the agency, carriage, forwarding or storage contracts. In practice, complex economic relations force the formation of complex mixed contracts, comprising elements of different legal relationships.[30]

In the context of the above, one must agree with the opinion of academic authors recognising outsourcing as a mechanism in the field of economy and economic processes, such as: business stimulation, optimum employment strategy, etc. On the other hand, it does not give rise or directly attach to any specific legal construction. In the preparation of outsourcing agreements, contracting parties use different obligational constructions to optimally adjust the legal terms to the economic requirements.[31]

Since it is impossible to unambiguously indicate the contract type forming the basis for outsourcing, the final spectrum of the parties' rights and obligations will depend on the final shape of the contract and understanding between the parties. Unless otherwise provided in the agreement, the rules on specific contracts type will come into play. The fact that, in a particular case, a given contract type becomes the basis for outsourcing has no principal importance from the point of view of the abovementioned rights and obligations. The principles of good faith and trust may,

---

[28] In Polish law, the term innominate contract refers to contracts without a legal regime, which may be concluded according to the principle of free contract conclusion.

[29] Malarewicz-Jakubów and Tanajewska (2014), p. 237.

[30] Kłos (2009), p. 74.

[31] Robaczyński (2018), p. 398.

however, affect the performance of the parties' obligations if they have both contemplated that a specific contractual agreement has the economic purpose of outsourcing.[32]

Based on the analysis of outsourcing contracts concluded in the ordinary course of trade, one can distinguish the principal elements of that contract, i.e.: specification of the scope of works, agreement as to the level of the rendered service, remuneration, term of the agreement, terms of managing the process, rules on intellectual property, sectoral provisions, terms of terminating the contract, rules on subcontractors and court jurisdiction to resolve disputes.[33]

In the outsourcing practice, an essential legal problem is protection of business secrets. In response to that question, it must be concluded that there are no specific rules governing outsourcing from that point of view. Consequently, the general rules on the protection of business secrets should apply. It must be reminded that business secrets may be protected by: (1) the duty of so-called professional secrecy; (2) rules on combatting unfair competition; (3) special contractual clauses.[34]

An essential element of the outsourcing regulation is the supervision exercised over the phenomenon. The possibility of outsourcing tasks to another entity may, therefore, be subject to restrictions following from the legal regimes of pursuing certain types of activity. This problem is especially evident in the context of insurance activities.

6 Outsourcing in Insurance Activities

Under the abovementioned Solvency II Directive, specific rules were introduced in the insurance law system on the entrusting by insurance and reinsurance undertakings of their own activities to external contractors, including requirements relating to the contents of contracts under which the outsourced activities are performed. Insurance undertakings, as public trust institutions, should perform their tasks properly and safely to customers, which is why requirements in respect of outsourcing of specific activities and functions constitute a material element of the system of governance in an insurance undertaking. Moreover, insurance outsourcing is subject to disclosure obligations and supervision by the Polish Financial Supervision Authority (KNF).

[32] Sobińska (2008), p. 89.

[33] Malarewicz-Jakubów and Tanajewska (2014), p. 238.

[34] Spyra and Włodyka (2018), p. 24.

6.1 The Legal Regime and the Scope of Financial Outsourcing Under the Solvency II Directive

Under Art. 13(28) of the Solvency II Directive, 'outsourcing' means an arrangement of any form between an insurance or reinsurance undertaking and a service provider, whether a supervised entity or not, by which that service provider performs a process, a service or an activity, whether directly or by sub-outsourcing, which would otherwise be performed by the insurance or reinsurance undertaking itself.

Moreover, the EU legislator indicated, in Recital (37) of the Solvency II Directive, that: '[i]n order to ensure effective supervision of outsourced functions or activities, it is essential that the supervisory authorities of the outsourcing insurance or reinsurance undertaking have access to all relevant data held by the outsourcing service provider, regardless of whether the latter is a regulated or unregulated entity, as well as the right to conduct on-site inspections. To take account of market developments and to ensure that the conditions for outsourcing continue to be complied with, the supervisory authorities should be informed prior to the outsourcing of critical or important functions or activities', which means that the role and importance of outsourcing was recognised for the proper management of an insurance undertaking.

The EU legal regime under the abovementioned Directive imposes the requirement of minimum harmonisation. Minimum harmonisation is the case when a directive imposes a set of minimum requirements to be implemented by EU Member States, which is often a consequence of recognising the fact that legal systems in certain EU Member States already provide for more stringent requirements. This allows Member States to introduce more far-reaching provisions than set out in the Directive.

Outsourcing of critical or important operational functions or activities may not be undertaken to: (1) materially deteriorate the quality of the governance system in a given undertaking; (2) excessively increase the operating risk; (3) impede the supervisory authority's ability to monitor the compliance by the insurance undertaking with its obligations; (4) impair the provision of continuous and satisfactory services to policyholders.

Therefore, it is the duty of Member States to ensure that insurance undertakings and reinsurance undertakings assume full liability for the performance of all their obligations under the Directive in case of outsourcing their operational functions or insurance or reinsurance activities.[35]

The Directive does not introduce any express prohibition of limiting liability for damages caused to an insurance undertaking's customers because of non-performance or improper performance of the contract by the outsourcing service provider. However, more restrictive solutions in this regard may be introduced in the

[35] Art. 49 Solvency II.

provisions implementing the rules of the Solvency II Directive into Member States' legal systems.

The obligations of insurance undertakings include the preparation in writing—beside risk management terms, rules of internal control and internal audit—also of the operating terms of outsourcing—such terms are to be reviewed at least once a year and should be approved in advance by the supervisory authority. Insurance undertakings and reinsurance undertakings are obliged to notify the supervisory authority in good time about outsourcing of critical or important functions or activities and about all later significant changes to such functions or activities.

For that purpose, Member States of the EU should ensure that insurance undertakings and reinsurance undertakings entering into an outsourcing agreement with regard to a given function or insurance or reinsurance activity take necessary steps to guarantee the following conditions: (1) the outsourcing service provider must cooperate with the authorities supervising the insurance undertaking or reinsurance undertaking in relation to the outsourced function or activity; (2) insurance undertakings and reinsurance undertakings, their statutory auditors and supervision authorities must have an actual access to the data relating to the outsourced functions or activities; (3) supervisory authorities must have an actual access to the premises of the outsourcing service provider and must be able to enforce such access rights.

Additionally, the authorities supervising an insurance undertaking or reinsurance undertaking should be entitled to carry out—independently or through parties designated by such authorities—on-site inspections at the service provider's premises. In case of cross-border outsourcing services being rendered in the EU, the competent supervisory authority of the home state of the insurance undertaking or reinsurance undertaking must notify the appropriate authority in the Member State of the outsourcing service provider before carrying out the on-site inspection. The Solvency II Directive requires as well that the supervisory entitlements relating to the right to information about the insurance undertaking's situation or the right to impose administrative penalties that may be imposed on insurance undertakings and reinsurance undertakings should apply also in relation to the activities outsourced by insurance undertakings or reinsurance undertakings.[36]

Provisions of the Solvency II Directive are indistinct or constitute mere guidelines—indicating the goal that should be achieved by transposing specific provisions into national legal systems, which is characteristic of many directives. In this context, it is also worth pointing to the Commission Delegated Regulation (EU) 2015/35 of 10 October 2014 supplementing Directive 2009/138/EC of the European Parliament and of the Council on the taking-up and pursuit of the business of Insurance and Reinsurance (Solvency II)[37] or EIOPA Guidelines on system of governance.[38]

[36] Czublun (2010), p. 32.

[37] OJ L 12/1, 17.01.2015; hereinafter: Delegated Regulation.

[38] EIOPA Guidelines on system of governance No. EIOPA BoS-14/253 PL, https://eiopa.europa.eu/GuidelinesSII/EIOPA_Guidelines_on_System_of_Governance_PL.pdf.

6.2 *Outsourcing Rules Applicable to Insurance Undertakings Under the Delegated Regulation*

An insurance undertaking or reinsurance undertaking outsourcing or planning to outsource insurance or reinsurance functions or activities to a service provider, must introduce, in writing, the rules of outsourcing, taking into account the outsourcing's impact on the activities of the undertaking and solutions in the area of reporting and monitoring, which should be implemented in case of the decision to outsource. The undertaking must guarantee compliance of the outsourcing agreement's terms with the obligations of the undertaking under Art. 49 of the Directive Solvency II.

If the insurance undertaking or reinsurance undertaking and the outsourcing service provider belong to the same group, the undertaking outsourcing its critical or important operational functions or activities is obliged to consider the scope in which it controls the service provider or can influence the latter's actions. When selecting the service provider mentioned above with regard to critical or important operational functions or activities, the administering, managing or supervising body must ensure: (a) a thorough analysis to guarantee that the potential service provider has the skills, capacities and, possibly, authorisations required under legal provisions, enabling the service provider to duly perform the outsourced functions or activities, taking into consideration the undertaking's objects and needs; (b) taking by the outsourcing service provider of all measures to ensure that the fulfilment of the outsourcing undertaking's needs is not threatened by any actual or potential conflict of interest; (c) conclusion between the insurance undertaking or reinsurance undertaking and the service provider of a written agreement specifying expressly the respective rights and obligations of the undertaking and of the service provider; (d) clarifying in intelligible terms the conditions of the outsourcing agreement to the administering, managing or supervising body and their approval by such body; (e) non-violation of law, especially provisions on data protection, in connection with the outsourcing; (f) subordination of the service provider to the same rules on information security and confidentiality relating to the insurance undertaking or reinsurance undertaking, their policyholders or beneficiaries, as applicable to the insurance undertaking or reinsurance undertaking.[39]

In addition, the Delegated Regulation specifies the requirements that must be met by an outsourcing contract concluded by an insurance undertaking or reinsurance undertaking. Under that provision, the written agreement to be concluded between the insurance undertaking or reinsurance undertaking and service provider must specifically include the following express contents: (a) the duties and responsibilities of both parties involved; (b) the service provider's commitment to comply with all applicable laws, regulatory requirements and guidelines as well as policies approved by the insurance or reinsurance undertaking and to cooperate with the undertaking's supervisory authority with regard to the outsourced function or activity; (c) the

[39] Art. 274 (1)–(3) of the Delegated Regulation.

service provider's obligation to disclose any development which may have a material impact on its ability to carry out the outsourced functions and activities effectively and in compliance with applicable laws and regulatory requirements; (d) a notice period for the termination of the contract by the service provider which is long enough to enable the insurance or reinsurance undertaking to find an alternative solution; (e) that the insurance or reinsurance undertaking is able to terminate the arrangement for outsourcing where necessary without detriment to the continuity and quality of its provision of services to policyholders; (f) that the insurance or reinsurance undertaking reserves the right to be informed about the outsourced functions and activities and their performance by the services provider as well as a right to issue general guidelines and individual instructions at the address of the service provider, as to what must be considered when performing the outsourced functions or activities; (g) that the service provider shall protect any confidential information relating to the insurance or reinsurance undertaking and its policyholders, beneficiaries, employees, contracting parties and all other persons; (h) that the insurance or reinsurance undertaking, its external auditor and the supervisory authority have effective access to all information relating to the outsourced functions and activities including carrying out on-site inspections of the business premises of the service provider; (i) that, where appropriate and necessary for the purposes of supervision, the supervisory authority may address questions directly to the service provider to which the service provider shall reply; (j) that the insurance or reinsurance undertaking may obtain information about the outsourced activities and may issue instructions concerning the outsourced activities and functions; (k) the terms and conditions, where applicable, under which the service provider may sub-outsource any of the outsourced functions and activities; (l) that the service provider's duties and responsibilities deriving from its agreement with the insurance or reinsurance undertaking shall remain unaffected by any sub-outsourcing taking place according to point (k).[40]

[40] Art. 274(4) of the Delegated Regulation.

6.3 *EIOPA[41] Guidelines on System of Governance[42]*

An important source in the context of guidelines delivered by supervisory authorities in respect of the organisation of outsourcing are EIOPA Guidelines on system of governance. EIOPA Guidelines are not a source of law, but mere recommendations addressed to national supervisors, suggesting a direction for the implementation of operating principles in the areas subject to supervision; however, they provide essential information about the desired direction of operating solutions in such areas.

In case of delivery of guidelines by EIOPA to national supervisory authorities or directly to financial institutions, it must be emphasised that the national supervisory authority or financial institution is obliged to notify (within two months of the delivery of the guideline or recommendation) if it will comply or intends to comply with the given guideline or recommendation. If the national supervisory authority or the financial institution does not comply with the respective instrument or does not intend to do so, the national supervisory authority or financial institution is obliged to notify that fact to EIOPA, providing justification. As such, *soft law* instruments delivered by EIOPA are not legally binding on the national supervisory authorities, however, those authorities are obliged to answer EIOPA's guidelines and recommendations addressed to them. Furthermore, EIOPA is obliged to publish information that a national supervisory authority does not comply or does not intend to comply with a given guideline or recommendation. EIOPA may also, in a specific situation, decide to publish the justification of non-compliance with a given guideline or recommendation, as provided by the respective national supervision authority. The national supervisory authority is notified in advance about such publication.[43]

And so, in Guideline 1.7, it was laid down who, within the governance system of an insurance undertaking, may be considered the person responsible, performing a key function: 'The notification requirements only apply to persons who effectively run the undertaking or are key function holders as opposed to persons who have or perform a key function. In case of outsourcing of a key function or outsourcing of a part of a function where this part is regarded as key, the person responsible is

[41] Under Art. 16 of the Regulation (EU) No 1094/2010 of the European Parliament and of the Council of 24 November 2010 establishing a European Supervisory Authority (European Insurance and Occupational Pensions Authority), amending Decision No 716/2009/EC and repealing Commission Decision 2009/79/EC (OJ L 331,15.12.2010, p. 48), EIOPA has the right to deliver guidelines and recommendations addressed to national supervisory authorities or directly to financial institutions.

[42] EIOPA Guidelines on system of governance No. EIOPA BoS-14/253 PL, https://eiopa.europa.eu/GuidelinesSII/EIOPA_Guidelines_on_System_of_Governance_PL.pdf; and the Final Report on Public Consultation No. 14/017 on Guidelines on system of governance.

[43] So: Szaraniec (2020), pp. 36–60. See also: Art. 16(3) of the Regulation (EU) No. 1094/2010. Moreover, if the guideline or recommendation so requires, the financial institution shall clearly and specifically notify if it complies with the guideline or recommendation.

considered to be the one who has the oversight over the outsourcing at the undertaking'.

According to EIOPA Guideline 14, on outsourcing of key functions, the insurance undertaking should implement competence and reputation assessment procedures in relation to persons engaged by the service provider or sub-provider for purposes relating to the performance of the outsourced key functions. The undertaking should designate, out of its personnel, a person generally responsible for the outsourced key functions, who must have sufficient competences and reputation and have sufficient expertise and experience regarding the outsourced key function to be capable of verifying the level of its performance and the results achieved by the service provider. The designated person is deemed to be responsible for the key function and, as such, must be notified to the supervisory authority.[44]

6.4 *Insurance Outsourcing in Polish Law*

The Act of 11 September 2015 on insurance and reinsurance activities (hereinafter: Polish Insurance Activities Act) includes provisions on outsourcing in insurance and reinsurance activities. Those provisions were adopted because of the need to implement the Solvency II Directive into the national legal system.

Under the legal definition expressed in Art. 3(1) item 27 of the Polish Insurance Activities Act, for the purposes of that act, the term outsourcing means: 'a contract between the insurance undertaking or reinsurance undertaking and the service provider under which the service provider performs a process, service or activity which would be otherwise performed by the insurance undertaking or reinsurance undertaking, including contracts under which the service provider delegates the performance of such process, service or activity to other entities through which the service provider performs the given process, service or activity'.

The source of outsourcing in the understanding of the Polish Insurance Activities Act may be any contract, either nominate or innominate, as long as it relates to performance of a process, service or activity which would be otherwise performed by the insurance undertaking or reinsurance undertaking.[45]

The possibility of entering into outsourcing contracts by insurance distributors in Poland will relate only to insurance or reinsurance undertakings since only such solution was provided for in the Polish Act on insurance and reinsurance activities.[46] Under Art. 3(1) item 27 of that Act, the Polish legislator introduced a broad definition of the outsourcing contract to subsequently narrow down the contract's scope under Art. 73 only to certain insurance activities and to so-called functions

[44] Mrozowska-Bartkiewicz and Wnęk (2016), pp. 11–12.

[45] Machulak and Ziemba (2018), p. 3 et seq.

[46] See: Arts. 73–76 of the Act of 15 September 2015 on insurance and reinsurance activities (Dz.U. z 2019 r. poz. 381).

within the governance system, whereby, in listed situations, outsourcing contractors are exempt from insurance secrecy.[47] Under Art. 73 of that Act:

(1) the insurance undertaking may, by way of outsourcing, entrust in writing performance of the insurance activities referred to in Art. 4(7) item 3 and Art. 4(8) and (9)[48] of the Polish Insurance Activities Act
(2) the insurance undertaking or reinsurance undertaking may, by way of outsourcing, entrust in writing performance of the activities referred to in Art. 4(2) item 2 and 4 and in Art 4(5)[49]
(3) the insurance undertaking or reinsurance undertaking may, by way of outsourcing, entrust in writing to other entities the performance of functions belonging to the governance system[50]

In addition, the Polish Insurance Activities Act does not preclude the possibility of subcontracting by the service provider of the undertaking's activities or functions to another party (sub-outsourcer).[51]

Under Art. 274(4) of the Delegated Regulation, a contract between the insurance undertaking or reinsurance undertaking and the external provider should specify the terms under which the provider may sub-outsource the outsourced functions and activities. The agreement should also include an obligation of the external provider under which the latter's obligations and tasks under the contract with the insurance (reinsurance) undertaking should remain intact in case of possible sub-outsourcing. EIOPA also draws attention to the fact that if the sub-outsourcing involves further delegation of critical or important functions, this should be approved by the insurance undertaking or reinsurance undertaking.[52]

[47] So: Art. 35(2) item 26 of the Polish Insurance Activities Act.

[48] By way of example, this will be the following activities: making declarations of intention in matters relating to claims for compensation or other benefits under insurance contracts, insurance guarantee contracts, or entrusting their conclusion to authorised insurance intermediaries, as well as reinsurance contracts' conclusion; payment of compensations or other benefits under the said contracts; determining the causes and circumstances of fortuitous events; determining the amount of damage or compensation or other benefits payable to the entitled parties under insurance contracts or insurance guarantee contracts.

[49] By way of example, this will be the following activities: making declarations of intention in matters relating to claims for compensation or other benefits under inward reinsurance contracts or retrocession contracts; exercising control over assignors' compliance with contractual terms; acts directly relating to reinsurance activities, especially acts performed in the area of statistical advice, actuarial consulting, risk analysis, research for customers, investing reinsurance undertaking's assets, or activities of preventing or mitigating the consequences of insurance accidents or financing of such activities from the provident fund.

[50] By 'governance system', one should understand, according to Art. 3(1) item 46 of the Polish Insurance Activities Act, a system covering the function of risk management, function of legal compliance, function of internal audit and actuarial function, ensuring due and prudent management of the insurance undertaking or reinsurance undertaking.

[51] Such situation is admissible, e.g., in banking activities. For more on that, see: Byrski (2018), p. 90 et seq.

[52] Machulak and Ziemba (2018), p. 14.

The provision of Art. 73 of the Polish Insurance Activities Act lays down an exhaustive list of activities and functions that may be entrusted by an insurance undertaking to a service provider under an outsourcing contract. In that context, it is excluded that an insurance undertaking might entrust to a service provider, under an outsourcing contract, performance of any activities or functions other than expressly and directly listed in Art. 73 of that Act[53] (more on that in section 6 of this article).

Another crucial obligation is the requirement, provided in Art. 75(2) of the Polish Insurance Activities Act, to notify the supervisory authority at least 30 days ahead of the implementation of outsourcing in respect of functions belonging to the governance system or critical or important activities, and of any essential change to the outsourcing of such functions or activities. In the context of such notification, one should consider the EIOPA Guidelines.[54] It seems that the obligation to notify the supervisory authority about an essential change to the outsourcing covers not only planned changes in the contract with the external service provider. EIOPA points out that the notification obligation should also cover such situations as, for example, non-compliance by the external service provider with applicable legislation or material problems with access to data or information.[55] However, in such instances, the insurance (reinsurance) undertaking could not usually make the notification in advance. Therefore, it would be reasonable to assume that the obligation materialises only upon detection by the insurance undertaking of the existing irregularities possibly qualifying as an essential change to the outsourcing.[56]

Art. 76 of the Polish Insurance Activities Act introduces a prohibition of any exclusion or limitation of the insurance undertaking's liability for damages caused respectively to policyholders, insured parties or beneficiaries under insurance contracts.[57] Such liability may not be excluded or limited even if the insurer cannot be assigned *culpa in eligendo*. Also, the liability of an undertaking for damages caused to assignors in consequence of non-performance or improper performance of outsourcing may not be excluded or limited.[58]

[53] Wajda (2016), p. 376; Kozłowska (2016), p. 196; otherwise: Machulak and Ziemba (2018), p. 6.

[54] See Guideline 64. In its written notification of outsourcing, the insurance (reinsurance) undertaking should include a description of the scope and the rationale for the outsourcing and the service provider's name. When outsourcing concerns a key function, the information should also include the name of the person in charge of the outsourced function or activities at the service provider.

[55] Final Report on Public Consultation No. 14/017 on Guidelines on system of governance, p. 100.

[56] Machulak and Ziemba (2018), p. 13.

[57] In literature, based on the example of the banking market, it is indicated that such an absolute prohibition does not satisfy the test of legal proportionality. The author is of the opinion that a provision should be adopted obligating payment service providers to implement an adequate and effective solution securing the coverage of possible costs relating to the payment of compensation under customer claims for damages caused by non-performance or improper performance of a contract, e.g., by such outsourcing partner's civil liability insurance. So: Byrski (2018), pp. 466–467.

[58] Mrozowska-Bartkiewicz and Wnęk (2016), p. 11.

6.5 Outsourcing and Insurance Intermediation

Neither the Solvency II Directive nor the Directive (EU) 2016/97 of the European Parliament and of the Council of 20 January 2016 on insurance distribution (IDD)[59] relates its provisions on outsourcing to the conclusion of legal acts by insurance intermediaries. In the discussed Guidelines, EIOPA postulates the principle that the competent national supervisory authorities should make sure that in case of an insurance intermediary, other than the undertaking's employee, given authority to underwrite business or settle claims in the name and on account of an undertaking, the undertaking ensures that the activity of such intermediary is subject to the outsourcing requirements.[60]

EIOPA's Guidelines refer to situations in which the insurance intermediary renders to the insurance undertaking an entire service package, e.g., claim settlement, payment of benefits under contracts concluded both through that intermediary and other distributors, including directly with the insurance undertaking, services involving the intermediary's possibility of independent assessment and assumption of insurance risk and not mere execution of the insurance undertaking's instructions under the power of attorney to render insurance intermediation services.[61]

Thus, it must be concluded that situations in which the insurance intermediary assuming the risk uses tools provided by the insurance undertaking are not examples of outsourcing.

On the other hand, in situations when the insurance intermediary, during insurance intermediation, uses his own tools intended for the assessment and acceptance of risk, one might speak of such activity's outsourcing by the insurance undertaking and, in such event, this should be both reflected in the provisions of contracts concluded with such intermediary and allowed for in the outsourcing policy of the insurance undertaking. It must be noted that on such occasions the insurance undertaking is not exempt from its obligations relating to the outsourcer's proper supervision, as discussed above.[62]

[59] OJ L 26/19, 2 February 2016.

[60] See EIOPA Guideline 61: *When an insurance intermediary, who is not an employee of the undertaking, is given authority to underwrite business or settle claims in the name and on account of an undertaking, the undertaking should ensure that the activity of this intermediary is subject to the outsourcing requirements.*

[61] Mrozowska-Bartkiewicz and Wnęk (2016), pp. 12–13.

[62] Mrozowska-Bartkiewicz and Wnęk (2016), pp. 12–13.

7 EIOPA Guidelines on Outsourcing to Cloud Service Providers[63]—Note

On 6 February 2020, EIOPA published 'Guidelines on outsourcing to cloud service providers'. Those are guidelines addressed to insurance undertakings and reinsurance undertakings concerning the application by such undertakings of the provisions on outsourcing of the Solvency II Directive and Commission delegated regulations in relation to outsourcing to cloud service providers. The Guidelines apply on the level of insurance or reinsurance undertaking and of a group. Insurance and reinsurance undertakings are required to 'make every effort to comply' with the Guidelines and to follow them in accordance with the regulatory framework.

Undertakings should revise and update their internal policies and processes within 1 January 2021 to adjust them to the said Guidelines.[64] The Guidelines apply to any arrangements relating to cloud outsourcing made by insurance and reinsurance undertakings; however, special emphasis is put on the outsourcing of critical or important operational functions or activities to cloud providers.

The critical matters relating to the adaptation of insurance undertakings to the discussed EIOPA Guidelines will be:

(1) Documentation requirements (Guideline 5)—in this context, insurance undertakings and reinsurance undertakings should maintain a special register of their cloud outsourcing arrangements. The register should be regularly updated and provided to the supervisory authority upon the latter's request. Moreover, insurance and reinsurance undertakings must ensure updates of all their internal outsourcing policies and procedures to reflect the new Guidelines.
(2) Risk assessment of cloud outsourcing (Guideline 8), which should involve an approach proportional to the nature, scope and complexity of the risks inherent in the services outsourced to cloud service providers as incurred by insurance or reinsurance undertakings. This includes assessment of the potential impact of the cloud outsourcing on the undertaking's operational and reputational risk.
(3) Due diligence on cloud service provider (Guideline 9)—meaning that insurance and reinsurance undertakings should ensure, in their selection and evaluation processes, that the service provider is adequate according to the criteria specified in their written outsourcing policies. Due diligence concerning the cloud service provider's choice must be carried out prior to outsourcing any operational function or activity.

[63] https://eiopa.europa.eu/Pages/News/EIOPA-consults-on-guidelines-on-outsourcing-to-cloud-service-providers.aspx.

[64] Arrangements on cloud outsourcing should be concluded by insurance or reinsurance undertakings from 1 January 2021. By the end of 2022 such undertakings should adjust their existing cloud outsourcing agreements relating to contracts involving critical or important operational functions or activities concluded before that date to the Guidelines or explain to supervisory authorities why they have not done so or provide a plan for handling the situation.

(4) Contractual requirements (Guideline 10)—this Guideline introduces certain clauses to be included in every outsourcing agreement covering critical or important cloud-based operational functions or activities concluded between the insurance or reinsurance undertaking and the cloud service provider.
(5) Sub-outsourcing of critical or important cloud-based operational functions or activities (Guideline 13)—requirement imposed on cloud service providers to notify their customers of any planned significant changes to the subcontractor's services. Customers of cloud service providers have the right to express their consent or object to such changes.
(6) Termination rights (Guideline 15)—clear definition of exit strategies necessary to enable termination of contracts without detriment to the continuity or quality of services rendered to policyholders (insurance undertakings' customers).[65]

In addition, insurance undertakings and reinsurance undertakings must grant supervisory authorities the rights of access and audit of their CSPs (including the right of access to data centres, etc.).

A large part of the Guidelines concentrates on questions of safety and organisation and, on this occasion, it is necessary to engage governance/compliance teams and panels responsible for safety. In the context of the requirement to ensure information security, an interesting—and apparently having potentially significant practical impact—element are comments of the supervisory authorities on encryption and disclosure of information. As a rule, all data processed in cloud are to be encrypted in transit and at rest. Supervised entities may derogate from that rule when encryption is technically impossible or economically groundless.

8 Final Conclusions

The above investigations revealed that outsourcing means, in the first place, a certain method of organising business activities, consisting in the abovementioned 'delegation' of a part of the undertaking's activities outside. Consequently, outsourcing is treated more as mechanism in economy and management than any specific legal construction. In fact, this type of mechanism may use different legal instruments.[66] The problems of outsourcing are of major importance for the operation of insurance undertakings and reinsurance undertakings. Therefore, it is extremely crucial to specify the legal framework for outsourcing because, in practice, almost every contract concluded by an insurance undertaking or reinsurance undertaking with an external provider should be analysed in the context of the abovementioned legal provisions.

[65] https://www.williamfry.com/newsandinsights/news-article/2020/09/07/how-do-the-eiopa-guidelines-on-cloud-outsourcing-impact-insurers-and-reinsurers.
[66] Robaczyński (2018), p. 481.

The definition of outsourcing as included in the Solvency II Directive contains requirements and restrictions provided for activities of critical nature or important for the operation of a given insurance (reinsurance) undertaking or pertaining to functions of the governance system. Moreover, Solvency II creates a specific concept of insurance outsourcing, which shows features that distinguish it from the general approach to the outsourcing process. The minimal nature of the Directive allows Member States to specify such activities in national law. In Polish law the object of outsourcing may only be the activities indicated in Art. 73 of the Polish Insurance Activities Act. This means that insurance and reinsurance undertakings may not outsource any activities other than those expressly listed in the discussed provisions. As a result, it must be concluded that the applicable legislation imposes on insurance and reinsurance undertakings a restriction of the freedom to conclude contracts in respect of outsourcing.[67] In Polish law, the objective scope of regulation of the outsourcing contract is much wider in the banking market than in the insurance market since the Polish legislator allows payment institutions to outsource much more banking functions to the outsourcing contractor,[68] and introduces a prohibition of restricting or excluding its liability vis-a-vis the payment service provider. The legislator also introduced an exemption from the payment outsourcing regime in respect of services rendered by technical service providers as long as they do not enter into possession of the funds subject to the payment transaction.[69]

There is a clear trend of expanding the insurance outsourcing regime to further performance of a process, service or activity by an insurance undertaking—an example is the EIOPA Guidelines on outsourcing to cloud service providers. Soon, one should expect expansion of the insurance outsourcing regime in respect of establishing cooperation between Insurtech companies and traditional insurance distributors. IDD does not point to the problem of outsourcing in its provisions. However, development of new technologies gives rise to the need for the legal regulation of outsourcing, especially in respect of regularising and harmonising the relevant legal regime in the entire internal financial market of the European Union. On the payment services market, tendencies may be observed of controlling the cooperation between payment institutions and Fintech companies—as evidenced by EBA Guidelines in this regard.[70]

[67] There are also such views in the literature that insurance outsourcing can be performed without restrictions. Moreover, it seems that, formulated in Art. 49 sec. 2 lit. a–d of the Solvency II Directive, the list of negative requirements relating to outsourcing of essential or important functions or operational activities is closed, which means that it is not possible to set other restrictions in this respect. See: Machulak and Ziemba (2018), p. 13.

[68] See: Arts. 6a and 6b of the Act of 29 August 1997—Banking Law (Dz.U. 2018, item 2187), or Arts. 9a-9g of the Act of 5 November 2009 on cooperative savings and credit unions (Dz.U. 2018, item 2386).

[69] So: Art. 6 item 10 of the Act of 19 August 2011 on payment services (Dz.U. 2017, item 2003). For more on that, see: Byrski (2018), p. 307.

[70] https://eba.europa.eu/documents/10180/2761380/EBA+revised+Guidelines+on+outsourcing_PL.pdf/7551b1c5-534d-44aa-b524-61eb8929154d.

The absence of legislation on the EU level forces ESAs to search for appropriate and effective supervisory instruments in the solutions adopted in other countries of the world and in Europe for the development of Insurtech companies and their cooperation with traditional insurance distributors. New technologies pose new challenges to supervisory authorities, most serious ones after the global financial crisis of 2008. Finally, it would be impossible not to notice that the introduction of new technologies on the insurance market is based mainly on the market's self-regulation through 'soft law' (guidelines and recommendations). An analysis of the current construction of guidelines and recommendations under the applicable EU legislation gives rise to the thesis that the legislator 'reinforced' the performance of such guidelines and recommendations by their addressees. They are binding on the addressees as far as fulfilment of their objectives is concerned, and non-binding in terms of the means leading to such ends. A disciplinary instrument in this construction is the possibility of disclosing (publishing) by the supervisory authority the received information relating to the refusal to adjust by the supervised entity to the issued guideline or recommendation. Due to all those solutions, introduction of new technologies on the insurance market may be based on the delivery of guidelines and recommendations, however, there is a need for appropriate legislative solutions in this regard on the European Union level. The construction of uniform insurance market of the EU implies that any activities in this regard should be compulsory, harmonised and consistent for the entire market and for particular Member States.[71]

References

Byrski J (2018) Outsourcing w działalności dostawców usług płatniczych, Warszawa

Ciesielska D (2009) Offshoring usług. Wpływ na rozwój przedsiębiorstwa, Warszawa

Czublun P (2010) Outsourcing według dyrektywy, Miesięcznik Ubezpieczeniowy no 4

Czublun P (2016) In: Czublun P (ed) Ustawa o działalności ubezpieczeniowej i reasekuracyjne. Komentarz, Warszawa

Domberger S (1998) The contracting organisation. A structural approach to outsourcing decisions and initiatives, New York

Dominguez L (2013) Outsourcing krok po kroku dla menedżerów, Warszawa

Gołąb P (2017) Outsourcing w działalności ubezpieczeniowej. In: Nowak A, Nowak S, Jagodziński J (eds) Polski obszar europejskich rynków finansowo-ubezpieczeniowych, Warszawa

Greaver MF Jr (1999) Strategic outsourcing. A structured approach to outsourcing decisions and initiatives, New York

Grossmann GM, Helpman E (2002) Integration versus outsourcing in industry equilibrium. Q J Econ 117(1)

Jovanovic M (2013) Fronting insurance and its impact on the development of insurance in Serbia, European insurance law revive, no 3

Juchno R, Kaszubski RW (2001) Outsourcing w działalności bankowej, Glosa no 6

Kłos M (2009) Outsourcing w polskich przedsiębiorstwach, Warszawa

Kopczyński T (2010) Outsourcing w zarządzaniu przedsiębiorstwami, Warszawa

[71] Szaraniec (2020), pp. 36–60.

Kowalski T (2008) Stan i prognozy rozwoju gospodarczego i ich wpływ na działania przedsiębiorstw w Polsce. In: Mruk H (ed) Nowoczesne sposoby konkurowania w biznesie, Poznań
Kozłowska M (2016) In: Czublun P (ed) Ustawa o działalności ubezpieczeniowej i reasekuracyjnej. Komentarz, C. H. Beck, Warszawa
Lei D, Hitt MA (1995) Strategic restructuring and outsourcing: the effect of mergers and acquisitions and LBOs on building firm skills and capabilities. J Manag 21(5)
Machulak P, Ziemba J (2018) Outsourcing w działalności ubezpieczeniowej i reasekuracyjnej -zagadnienia prawne, Wiadomości Ubezpieczeniowe no 4
Malarewicz-Jakubów A, Tanajewska R (2014) Prawne i ekonomiczne aspekty outsourcingu, Optimum Studia Ekonomiczne no 4 (70)
Matejun M (2015) Outsourcing. In: Szymańska K (ed) Kompendium metod i technik zarządzania. Teoria i ćwiczenia. Warszawa
Mrozowska-Bartkiewicz B, Wnęk A (2016) Reżim prawny outsourcingu ubezpieczeniowego, Prawo Asekuracyjne no 3
Nadolna B (2007) In: Czubakowska K (ed) Od auditingu do sponsoringu, Warszawa
Nowak P (2008) Outsourcing – próba odnalezienia definicji pojęcia na gruncie polskiego prawa pracy, Roczniki Admistracji i Prawa nr XVIII no 1
Robaczyński W (2018) In: Katner W (ed) System Prawa Prywatnego, t. 9, Prawo zobowiązań – umowy nienazwane, C.H. Beck, Warszawa
Śliwa N (2015) Bilans outsourcingu – najważniejsze korzyści i straty z wydzielenia działalności, [w:] S. Wawak, M. Sołtysik (red.), Współczesne trendy w outsourcingu, Kraków
Sobińska M (2001) Kryteria i proces doboru konsultanta do tworzenia projektu i wdrażania outsourcingu systemu informatycznego. In: Nowicki A, Unolda J (eds) Aspekty społeczne doskonalenia systemów informacyjno-decyzyjnych, Wrocław
Sobińska M (2008) Zarządzanie outsourcingiem informatycznym, Wrocław
Spyra M, Włodyka S (2018) Zastosowanie umów w zarządzaniu przedsiębiorstwem. Outsourcing. In: Stec M (ed) System Prawa Handlowego tom 5, Warszawa
Szaraniec M (2020) Regulatory gaps concerning the introduction of new technologies in insurance distribution – the new role and activities of supervisory authorities. Outline of the background of the problem, Prawo Asekuracyjne No. 2
Trocki M (1999) Outsourcing jako metoda restrukturyzacji przedsiębiorstw. Gospodarka materiałowa i Logistyka, no 9
Trocki M (2001) Outsourcing, Warszawa
Wajda P (2016) In: Szczepańska M, Wajda P (eds) Ustawa o działalności ubezpieczeniowej i reasekuracyjnej. Komentarz, Warszawa

Remuneration Policies of Insurance Undertakings in Europe: Principles for a Deeply Heterogeneous Reality

Covadonga Díaz Llavona

Abstract The provisions on remuneration policies and practices under the Solvency II framework have been recently supplemented by an Opinion published by the European Insurance and Occupational Pensions Authority. The lack of any high-level standard in this respect in the Directive and the open character of most of the principles and orientations entailed in these instruments have led to a landscape of different national implementation rules, which also need to be connected to the different corporate governance provisions of each Member State.

This chapter aims to analyse the European provisions about remuneration in the insurance industry and connect them first to those provided for the banking sector, and then to the Member States regimes that arise from both the implementation of the EU policies and the international rules, with the purpose of pointing out the weaker aspects of the existing regulation and proposing some possible ways for improvement.

1 Introduction

On 1 January 2016, the Directive 2009/138/EC of the European Parliament and of the Council on the taking-up and pursuit of the business of Insurance and Reinsurance (Solvency II Directive) entered into force.[1]

In relation to the present chapter, the provisions of Solvency II Directive were supplemented by the Commission Delegated Regulation (EU) 2015/35, and more recently, by an Opinion of the European Insurance and Occupational Pensions

[1] Although the Solvency II framework is working well, the Directive itself foresaw a review of its provisions at the latest by 1 January 2021 to improve the existing regulation based on the experience during the past years of application and to consider the changes in the economic context. References to this review will be made later.

C. Díaz Llavona (✉)
University of Oviedo, Commercial Law Department, Oviedo, Spain
e-mail: cdllavona@uniovi.es

P. Marano, K. Noussia (eds.), *The Governance of Insurance Undertakings*, AIDA Europe Research Series on Insurance Law and Regulation 6,
https://doi.org/10.1007/978-3-030-85817-9_5

Authority (EIOPA) on the supervision of remuneration principles in the insurance and reinsurance sector (EIOPA -BoS-20-040, 31 January 2020).

While the guidelines are few and apparently clear, the way in which the European Institutions have incorporated the new remuneration provisions via delegated act, without including an express mention in the Directive itself, entails many problems that are addressed in the chapter. As will be shown, the poor structure of the insurance sector provisions is in contrast to the much better constructed regime of the remuneration provisions included in the CRD III and CRD IV package for the banking sector. A comparison of both schemes can reveal some means for improvement in the insurance sector. As it gets analysed in the latter part of the chapter, the insurance market shows a complex situation regarding remuneration policies, arising mainly from two factors: on the one hand, the European insurance industry presents a wide range of organisational structures and business models, especially regarding size and risk profile. These differences demand a flexible application of the rules and, in some cases, the taking into account of the proportionality principle. On the other hand, the application of these special rules to insurance undertakings does not prevent these undertakings from also being subject to the company law of their country of origin. It is a known fact that the structure of the governing bodies of the companies and the legal regime applicable to them vary greatly between Member States, which makes it more difficult to determine the scope and application of provisions contained in the above-mentioned insurance industry's specific rules on remuneration policies.

The chapter aims to analyse the European provisions about remuneration in the insurance industry and connect them first to those provided for the banking sector, and then to the Member States regimes that arise from both the implementation of the EU policies and the international rules, with the aim of pointing out the weaker aspects of the existing regulation and proposing some possible ways for improvement.

2 European Regulatory and Supervisory Framework for Remuneration Policies in Insurance Undertakings

The introduction of Solvency II regime involved a complete transformation of the prudential framework for insurance firms in the European Union. The new risk-based approach was achieved by the Directive and the delegated acts that followed through a three-pillar structure: quantitative requirements (Pillar I), governance of the undertaking and supervisory activity (Pillar II) and supervisory reporting and public disclosure (Pillar III). The issues addressed in this study fall under the second pillar, which sets out requirements for risk management, governance and process of supervision.

The Directive itself does not include specific remuneration provisions, but it does dedicate the whole Section 2 of Chapter IV to the system of governance of insurance and reinsurance undertakings. Articles 41 to 50 set out some high-level principles that apply to all aspects of the system of governance of the firms and, therefore, also to their remuneration system. At this respect, among those principles, as provisions connected in certain way to the remuneration system of undertakings, one can refer to the need of a transparent organisational structure with clear allocation and appropriate segregation of responsibilities (Art. 41), the fit and proper requirements for persons who effectively run the undertaking or have other key functions (qualification and experience, and persons of good repute) (Arts. 42–43), or with a clearer link to remuneration, the need to implement an effective risk-management system to identify, measure, monitor, manage and report on a continuous basis the risks to which the undertaking could be exposed (Arts. 44–45), or the need for an internal control system with four control functions: risk-management, compliance, internal audit, actuarial and risk-management (Arts. 46–49, 246).[2] The connection with remuneration is, in any case, indirect, as there is no specific provision on compensation of staff in the Directive.

Following the Lamfalussy process, the principles entailed in the Directive were further developed by the Commission Delegated Regulation (EU) 2015/35 of 10 October 2014. On the governance system, Chapter IX of the Regulation includes detailed provisions in five aspects: Elements of the system of governance, Functions, Fit and proper requirements, Outsourcing, and Remuneration policy. As said, remuneration is the only element not expressly mentioned in the higher standard, but it is considered as a key issue for risk management in the Delegated Regulation. As expressed in Recital 102 of the Regulation, 'remuneration policies and practices which provide incentives to take risks that exceed the approved risk tolerance limits of insurance and reinsurance undertakings can undermine the effective risk management of such undertakings. It is therefore necessary to provide for requirements on remuneration for the purposes of the sound and prudent management of the business and in order to prevent remuneration arrangements which encourage excessive risk-taking'.

As a general requirement for the system of governance, Article 258.1.l) calls for a written remuneration policy, even when the Directive does not include it among the other areas in which a written policy is required.[3] The approval process of this written policy should follow the same requirements as the other policies expressly mentioned in the Directive and, therefore, on the one hand, it should be approved by the administrative, management or supervisory body of the insurance or reinsurance undertaking (41.3 Directive)[4] and, on the other hand, the remuneration policy shall

[2] As will be shown, the EC Regulation, which does include for the first time specific requirements on remuneration of staff in insurance undertakings, sets the link with the Directive via the need of a sound and prudent management of the business.

[3] The inclusion of remuneration in Article 41.3 of the Directive is one of the proposals included by EIOPA in its Opinion on the 2020 review of Solvency II—EIOPA-BoS-20/749, 17 December 2020, paragraph 8.47.

[4] As will be shown, this acts as a minimum requirement often exceeded by stricter measures at national level.

be reviewed at least annually and in the case of any significant change in the system or area concerned.

2.1 European Principles Relating Remuneration Policy and Practices in the Insurance Sector

As is the case with the Directive, the Regulation sets out nothing but principles to be observed by companies in shaping their remuneration policies. Article 275 includes seven main principles and another eight that specify the way in which the part of remuneration connected with tasks and performance of some members of the staff should be designed by the undertaking.

These following can be highlighted as the main principles:

- Alignment between remuneration policy and practices and the risk management strategy of the undertaking and the long-term business and its performance as a whole
- Respect of the risk tolerance limits of the undertaking
- Consideration of the tasks and performance of the administrative, management or supervisory body (AMSB), persons who run the undertaking or have other key functions, or other categories of staff whose professional activities have a material impact on the undertaking's risk profile
- Responsibility of the AMSB for the oversight of the remuneration policy's implementation
- Need of an effective governance on remuneration
- Need of an independent remuneration committee to support the AMSB in the oversight, implementation and operation of the remuneration policies and practices, if appropriate, in relation to the significance of the undertaking (size and internal organisation)
- Disclosure of the remuneration policy to all members of the staff

Risks arise mainly from the variable part of remunerations, and this part is usually connected with the performance of the remunerated person. As said, in turn, the third principle referred to the consideration of the tasks and performance of those persons who run the company or have key functions in it is developed in other eight ones:

- Need for balance between the fixed and variable components of the remuneration schemes and for the fixed component to represent a sufficiently high proportion of the total remuneration. The objective is to avoid that an excessive dependence of a performance-related remuneration could artificially alter individuals' behaviour and, conversely, that a decision of not paying the variable remuneration considering the situation of the undertaking could be made without excessively affecting the remuneration received.

- In case of performance-related variable remuneration, the principle of connection between the total amount and the performance, not only of the individual, but also of his/her business unit and the overall result of the undertaking or of the group.
- Need for a substantial deferred component of the variable remuneration to connect it with the mid and long-term results of the undertaking. The deferral period shall not be less than three years.
- Consideration of both financial and non-financial criteria when assessing an individual's performance.
- Inclusion of a downwards adjustment for exposure to current and future risks in the measurement of performance.
- Relation between termination payments and performance achieved over the whole period of activity without rewarding failure.
- Commitment of persons subject to the remuneration policy to not use hedging strategies or insurances that could undermine the risk alignment effects of their remuneration arrangement.
- Independence of the variable part of remuneration of staff engaged in the four key functions (risk management, compliance, internal audit and actuarial) from the performance of the units and areas submitted to their control.

As this is the first level of regulation for the remuneration principles,[5] there are many concepts that remain quite open and need further accuracy. That is the case with the sufficiently high proportion of the fixed component of the remuneration, or with the substantial deferred component of the variable remuneration. This lack of definition led in the first years of implementation of the Directive and the Regulation to divergent practices across the European Union, and that is why the European Insurance and Occupational Pensions Authority (EIOPA) released the *Opinion on the supervision of remuneration principles in the insurance and reinsurance sector*, in April 2020 (EIOPA-BoS-20-040, 31 January 2020).

2.2 EIOPA's Perspective on Remuneration in the Insurance Industry

The Opinion looks for a more consistent approach and convergence of national supervisory practices on the implementation of remuneration principles in the insurance sector. As it is known, opinions are non-binding instruments and therefore this one does not prevent the Supervisory Authorities to consider stricter criteria when appropriate or, reversely, to adopt a more flexible approach in supervision of low-risk undertakings. Despite this non-binding character, the Opinion acts as a very valuable tool of convergence through a better definition of the open concepts

[5] As will be shown in Sect. 3 of this chapter, it would be preferable that the Directive itself included at least some high-level principles on remuneration policies and practices of staff in insurance undertakings, in line with the structure followed by the European institutions in the banking sector.

mentioned in the Regulation. Nevertheless, the selection of an instrument like the opinion, non-compulsory and less detailed than other tools available for EIOPA, could restrict its future scope. As it will be pointed out, there are many questions that remain unsolved. Even when probably the need for an in-depth regulation is higher in the banking sector, a framework like the one existing for banks—including the Guidelines of the European Banking Authority (EBA) on sound remuneration policies[6]—could have led to a more finished result.[7] This idea will be approached again later in the text.

2.2.1 Scope

As pointed out, risk arising from the compensation policy of the undertaking appears mostly in connection with the variable part of the remuneration and on remunerations of the highest paid employees. Hence, the instrument narrows its scope of application according to two cumulative criteria:

- Category of staff member: only AMSB members, other executive directors who effectively run the undertaking, key function holders (in the sense of the key functions already seen), or other categories of staff whose activities have material impact on the undertakings' risk profile.
- Minimum amount of the variable component of the annual remuneration: over EUR 50,000 provided it represents more than 1/3 of the staff member's total annual remuneration.

2.2.2 Developed Aspects

The Opinion addresses the four more indeterminate and open principles of the Regulation by establishing several benchmarks for the evaluation of the remuneration policies and practices at national level.

- On the need for balance between fixed and variable components of remuneration and for the fixed part to represent a sufficiently high proportion of the total amount, the text establishes a threshold of 1:1 ratio, i.e. the amount of the variable component should not exceed that of the fixed one.
- On the portion of variable remuneration that must be deferred, EIOPA sets the benchmark in the 40% of the total variable amount. Even when it is only an

[6]Guidelines on sound remuneration policies under Articles 74(3) and 75(2) of Directive 2013/36/EU and disclosures under Article 450 of Regulation (EU) No 575/2013, EBA/GL/2015/22, 21 December 2015.

[7]About the need for more detailed provisions in the insurance sector, as is the case with the banking activity, vid. Butera and Montemaggiori (2018), p. 41 et seq.

indicative threshold, it helps in defining the open expression 'substantial portion' used in the Regulation.

If the 1:1 ratio of variable remuneration is not observed (a deviation could be considered justified by the supervisory authority in view of the risk profile of the undertaking), then the proportion of the deferred component should also be higher.

- The text also refines the principle of consideration of both financial and non-financial criteria when assessing an individual's performance. These criteria refer to the quantitative and qualitative requirements set out in the remuneration policy for the pay-out of the variable remuneration. Criteria must include achievable objectives and measures as well as consequences of the non-compliance, and the assessment should consider a multi-year framework.
- Quantitative and qualitative requirements should be balanced too, but at this point, the Opinion does not set out any specific ratio. It does cite a distribution of 80% financial and 20% non-financial as a potentially not balanced division, which could lead to the conclusion that in this respect, there is no need of a 1:1 ratio, as is the case with variable and fixed components of the remuneration. A higher proportion of quantitative requirements seems to be acceptable, provided that it does not reach such a high percentage.[8]
- The principle of inclusion of a downwards adjustment for exposure to current and future risks in the measurement of performance also gets the attention of EIOPA. This mechanism should adjust remuneration not only when individuals do not meet their personal objectives, but also when their business units or the undertaking as a whole fail to do so. The downward adjustment inserted in the remuneration policy must include examples of how it would work and the rationale behind its dynamic. The Opinion's approach at this point is rather superficial and although it refers to all kind of adjustments—even with an express reference to clawback clauses—it does not go into any further analysis.
- Last point addressed refers to the principle of connection between termination payments and performance achieved over the whole period of activity. At this respect, the text distinguishes between those termination payments which are generally considered as variable remuneration and those which generally do not have this qualification. According to this general consideration of the payments, outside the concept of variable remuneration fall all mandatory payments (labour law, settled in a court decision), those that respond to a predefined generic formula, and those connected to a non-competition clause, but only, in this latter case, up to the amount of the fixed remuneration which would have been paid if staff where still employed.

  As generally considered variable remuneration, the text refers to any payment that arose from a termination because of a failure of the undertaking or because of a material reduction of the undertakings' activities in which the staff was active,

[8] In this respect, vid. Esquerra Resa (2020), p. 11 et seq.

or finally, to payments that arose from a settlement between the undertaking and the staff member in case of a labour dispute.

One finds here again a completely open formula[9] that leaves room for very different interpretations, starting with what is considered variable remuneration as it is expressed in terms of what is generally understood as such.

As shown, although the Opinion represents a significant step forward for the interpretation of the principles included in the Regulation, some provisions yet remain very undetermined and leave a very broad margin of assessment to undertakings and to the supervisory dialogue with them. This may be aligned with the different risk profiles of undertakings but can also lead to deep differences in treatment between Member States, and even to an undesirable situation of legal uncertainty in the insurance sector.

3 Regulatory Framework of Remuneration Policies and Practices in the Banking Sector: Means for Improvement in the Insurance and Reinsurance Sector

The legal treatment of remuneration policies and practices in the banking sector received the attention of the European legislator years earlier than in the insurance sector.

Following the financial crisis of 2008, several reports outlined that, while failures in the governance system have not been the main cause of the crisis, they did have played certain role.[10] A better bank governance would without any doubt contribute to reduce the likelihood of new bank crisis situations.

Among the identified failures in the governance system, the danger of certain incentives for directors and senior staff was frequently pointed out.[11] While some of these remuneration policies turned out to be inadequate for any firm, they showed particularly harmful effects in the banking sector. The variable and equity-based compensations stimulated dangerous behaviours consisting of generating short term earnings while taking on high long-term risks.

[9]Much more open than the provisions included in point 9.3 of the EBA's Guidelines.

[10]See in this respect the so-known *Larosière Report* of 25 February 2009, of the High-level Group of Financial Supervision in the EU. Among other causes of the financial crisis, it mentions, as a corporate governance failure, in paragraph 24 'the remuneration and incentive schemes within financial institutions (that) contributed to excessive risk-taking by rewarding short-term expansion of the volume of (risky) trades rather than the long-term profitability of investments'.

[11]Basel Committee on Banking Supervision, Compensation Principles and Standards Assessment Methodology, January 2010, mainly principle 4.

These policies affected not only directors' remuneration, but also senior managers', the latter going completely unnoticed by supervisors and legislators for a long time.[12]

As the banking sector showed slightly less resistance to the crisis than the insurance sector, some initiatives and studies addressed the remuneration issue focusing only on credit institutions.[13] Most of them, however, adopted a global approach proposing measures for all financial institutions.

Even though there are significant differences between banks and insurance undertakings in terms of their activity and the type of risks they are exposed to, they have also many elements in common. They are both regulated sectors subject to a strong legal and supervisory system, in both risk is an inherent element of their activity, and in both the directors, when managing the company, must consider not only the shareholders' interest, but also the interest of the debtholders or the policyholders, respectively.

As pointed out, after the financial crisis the main trend has been to tackle the problems and come up with solutions in remuneration policies in the financial sector as a whole (without making any difference between banks and insurance undertakings). That is the case with the Commission Recommendation of 30 April 2009, on remuneration policies in the financial services sector,[14] the FSB Principles for Sound Compensation Practices of 25 September 2009, or the European Commission's Green Paper on Corporate Governance in Financial Institutions and Remuneration policies, of 2 June 2010.[15] While this joint treatment was the trend among non-compulsory instruments, the binding regulations of both financial sectors have followed separate paths so far (regarding the instruments used and the level of detail of the provisions rather than the content itself. As it can be observed most of the provisions envisaged for insurance undertakings since 2015 clearly follow those established for credit institutions in previous years).

As said, the central position of banks in the crisis led the European Legislator to focus their concern about remuneration issues in these financial institutions first. At this respect, CRD III Package included for the first time specific remuneration requirements. According to Recital 3 of Directive 2010/76/EU,[16] 'in order to address the potentially detrimental effect of poorly designed remuneration structures on the sound management of risk and control of risk-taking behaviour by individuals, the requirements of Directive 2006/48/EC should be supplemented by an express obligation for credit institutions and investment firms to establish and maintain, for

[12] Hopt (2013), p. 13.

[13] Basel Committee on Banking Supervision, op. cit.

[14] 2009/384/EC. In a non-binding way, the Recommendation includes already most of the principles that years later will be introduce in the CRD Framework.

[15] COM (2010) 284 final. Vid. also Commission Feedback Statement on Corporate Governance in Financial Institutions, of 11 November 2010.

[16] Directive 2010/76/EU, of the European Parliament and of the Council of 24 November 2010 amending Directives 2006/48/EC and 2006/49/EC as regards capital requirements for the trading book and for re-securitisations, and the supervisory review of remuneration.

categories of staff whose professional activities have a material impact on their risk profile, remuneration policies and practices that are consistent with effective risk management'.

The Directive included some express provisions in the main text and added one new section (11) on remuneration policies to Annex V of Directive 2006/48/EC (CRD I), where it already set out some basic principles, most of them coming from the previously cited soft-law instruments. Article 1.3.4 of the Directive 2010/76/EU itself required CEBS[17] to issue guidelines on sound remuneration policies which complied with the principles included in the amended Annex V of CRD I. These guidelines got published in December 2010.

The revision process launched in 2010 continued to progress with the CRD IV reform. Thus, Directive 2013/36/EU included a more complete regime on remuneration policies in the main text of the Directive (Articles 92 et seq.). Following the Lamfalussy scheme, these first level provisions were also developed through Regulation (EU) 604/2014,[18] which aimed to fix the criteria to identify those categories of staff whose professional activities have a material impact on an institutions' risk profile,[19] and Regulation (EU) 575/2013, Article 450 of which set out disclosure requirements for the remuneration policies of credit institutions. Two other three level instruments completed this regulatory structure: first, the EBA Opinion on the use of allowances,[20] and later the EBA guidelines[21] of 21 December 2015.[22]

[17] Committee of European Banking Supervisors. On 1 January 2011, the European Banking Authority (EBA) was established, taking over CEBS' ongoing tasks and responsibilities.

[18] Commission Delegated Regulation (EU) No 604/2014 of 4 March 2014 supplementing Directive 2013/36/EU of the European Parliament and of the Council with regard to regulatory technical standards with respect to qualitative and appropriate quantitative criteria to identify categories of staff whose professional activities have a material impact on an institution's risk profile. It is a very useful instrument that does not exist for insurance undertakings' staff.

[19] The EBA recently published a draft for the revision of provisions included in Regulation 604/2014 that can be found under the reference EBA/RTS/2020/05, 18 June 2020.

[20] EBA/Op/2014/10, 15 October 2014, Opinion of the European Banking Authority on the application of Directive 2013/36/EU (Capital Requirements Directive) regarding the principles on remuneration policies of credit institutions and investment firms and the use of allowances.

[21] EBA/GL/2015/22, 21 December 2015, Guidelines on sound remuneration policies under Articles 74(3) and 75(2) of Directive 2013/36/EU and disclosures under Article 450 of Regulation (EU) No 575/2013.

[22] EBA proposed to revise the guidelines on sound remuneration policies in light of the amendments introduced by the fifth Capital Requirements Directive (CRD V); mainly, the gender-neutral requirement for remuneration policies. The consultation period ended on 29 January 29 2021, and the final guideline is expected to be published in the first half of 2021.

3.1 *Means for Improvement in the Insurance Sector*

As previously shown, the regulatory framework on remuneration policies and practices for insurance undertakings did not follow such a well-constructed structure as in the banking sector. Directive 2009/138/EC did not include any specific provision on this matter and, even though it has been already amended in the following years (mainly through Directive 2014/51/EU) no requirements were added so far in this regard. As mentioned, Regulation 2015/35 is a delegated act (level 2 of the Lamfalussy scheme) with a very weak connection with the Directive, considering that there are no high-level principles on remuneration for insurance undertakings. The link between both instruments, Directive and Regulation, is only indirect, and must be made through Articles 41 to 50 of the Directive, which relate to the system of governance of insurance and reinsurance undertakings, with no special reference to any remuneration requirement.[23]

The release of the EIOPA's Opinion *on the supervision of remuneration principles in the insurance and reinsurance sector* in 2020 did not solve the problem at all and left many loose ends in capital questions, as it has been showed. Whether a non-compulsory instrument like guidelines or an opinion can be found justified in the banking sector where there are already several level 1 and 2 provisions with quite detailed principles, the situation is not the same in the insurance field. Here, there is a need to amend Directive 2009/138/EU to include high level principles on remuneration policies. As it was mentioned in footnote 3, EIOPA's *Opinion on the 2020 review of Solvency II* proposes already an amendment in this respect, but only to include the remuneration policy within the policies that need to be written and periodically reviewed. In any event, the reform should be wider, considering the inclusion of an express reference to most of the remuneration principles laid out now in Regulation 2015/35. The reform would also require certain development via regulatory technical standards (RTS) to clarify concepts used in the Directive and the Regulation, as is the case with the concept of the staff whose professional activities have a material impact on the undertaking's risk profile. Same situation exists relating distinction between fixed and variable remuneration. Provisions in the insurance sector have a lack on determination at both aspects that cannot be found in the banking provisions, where those concepts are precisely defined and where any

[23] A reference must be made to the Memo of the European Commission, 'Capital Requirements – CRD IV/CRR: Frequently Asked Questions', 16 July 2013, section 11, p. 28: '(...) for the sake of consistency and in order to avoid regulatory arbitrage between sectors, it will be necessary to review the existing legislation in other sectors (Solvency II, UCITS Directive) to align it, when necessary, to the outcome of the final text of the CRD IV package. Nevertheless, the specificities of each sector should be considered, and the rules should not necessarily be identical for banks, insurance companies and investment funds'. The revision of Solvency ii was not carried out regarding the amendments on remuneration policies included in the CRD IV.

compensation that falls outside the concept of fixed part of remuneration shall be considered variable with no room for a *tertium genus.*[24]

3.2 A Forward-Looking Approach to Supervision in the Financial Sector as a Whole

The convenience of the inclusion of specific first-level provisions on remuneration policies and practices for the insurance sector is a minimum requirement and is the only feasible one now. A brief mention to another forward-looking approach should however be made.

The financial market shows how in the last decades the boundaries between banking, insurance and securities have become increasingly blurred and how many of these activities are carried out now by financial conglomerates which get subject to different sectoral regulations and supervisory authorities depending on the type of transaction involved. Bearing that in mind, it should be questioned if there is still a point in having completely separate provisions for the banking and the insurance sector when in many cases, requirements set for both sectors are essentially the same, and in those cases where provisions differ considerably, this separate treatment does not always respond to an actual difference in the market.[25]

The forward-looking approach of cross-sectoral supervisory legislation for financial institutions also poses the question of the convenience of a new European financial supervisory model. As it is known, while the EU follows the sectoral supervisory model with three different supervisory authorities (ESAs) for banking (EBA), insurance (EIOPA) and securities (ESMA), some Member States, considering the above-mentioned blurring of lines between financial sub-sectors, have moved to either a single supervisory model or to the so-called twin peaks model.[26] According to the single supervisory model, there is only one supervisory authority in charge of the three financial sub-sectors (with some supervisory role of the Central Bank in some countries) as is the case in Germany, Poland or Sweden. The twin peaks model[27] divides the supervision into two separate authorities. One is in charge

[24] It may be recalled here that provisions included in the EIOPA's Opinion in this respect are merely for guidance purpose and distinguish between termination payments generally considered as variable remuneration and those which generally do not have this qualification.

[25] Vid. Al-Darwish et al. (2011), p. 40 et seq. See also footnote 23.

[26] Colaert (2015), p. 1586 et seq.

[27] This model was pointed out as the desirable system to evolve to in the so-known *Larosière Report* of 25 February 2009, of the High-level Group of Financial Supervision in the EU, section V, pp. 216 and 217 (P. 216: There may be merit, over time, in evolving towards a system which would rely on only two Authorities: The first would be responsible for banking and insurance issues, as well as any other issue which is relevant for financial stability (e.g. systemically important hedge funds, systemically important financial infrastructures). The second Authority would be responsible for conduct of business and market issues, across the three main financial sectors. Combining

of prudential supervision whereas the other supervises markets and conduct of business. This is the supervisory structure followed in Belgium, France, the Netherlands, or Portugal.[28] Among these, it is worth to refer expressly to the Netherlands regime. Differences arise there not only from the twin peaks supervisory model (adopted already in 2002), but also from the particular approach taken in the implementation of the CRD IV. The Dutch Act on Remuneration Policies of Financial Undertakings, February 2015 (*Wet beloningsbeleid financiële ondernemingen*), looking for the above-mentioned cross-sectoral supervisory legislation approach, broadened the scope of the Directive extending its provisions to all financial undertakings, including banks, insurers, investment firms, payment services providers, or premium pensions institutions. The Dutch case is also unique because the Legislator also carried out some 'gold-plating' amendments when transposing the remuneration requirements of the CRD IV. As key measures in this respect one can refer briefly to the bonus ceiling of 20% of the fixed salary of the employee—much more restricted than in the original European provision—the severance payment ceiling of one year's salary of directors, or the express inclusion of bonus clawback if circumstances require so.[29]

Even when a complete revision of the supervisory model would be neither possible nor appropriate now at the European level, one cannot ignore that this is the direction of any long-term evolution of the supervisory structures in the financial sector.

4 Implementation of European Provisions: Interplay with National Corporate Law

As pointed out in the introduction of this chapter, the application of the analysed special rules to insurance undertakings does not prevent these undertakings from being subject to general directives in corporate governance and to the company law of their country of origin.

In this respect, it must be distinguished between non-listed undertakings and those with shares admitted to trading on regulated markets on the one hand. On the other hand, differences arise from the varied board structures and what is considered

banking and insurance supervisory issues in the same Authority could result in more effective supervision of financial conglomerates and contribute to a simplification of the current extremely complex institutional landscape).

[28] A deeper analysis of the differences in the supervision structures of each Member state can be found in: Schoenmaker and Véron (2017), p. 1 et seq. The text of this policy contribution will be published as a chapter of Godwin and Schmulow (2021).

[29] For a deeper analysis, see Van Loopik and Ter Haar (2016), p. 389.

as key staff of the undertakings and the legal regime applicable to them at national level.[30]

All this leads frequently to difficulties in determining the scope and application of provisions contained in the above-mentioned insurance industry specific rules on remuneration policies.

As will be shown, national provisions also entail differences in the way in which remuneration principles of the Regulation and provisions of EIOPA's Opinion have been implemented (beyond what have been already exposed about supervisory models in the different Member States).

4.1 Listed Insurance Companies

Insurance undertakings with shares admitted to trading on a regulated market are subject to Directive (EU) 2017/828 of the European Parliament and of the Council of 17 May 2017, amending Directive 2007/36/EC as regards the encouragement of long-term shareholder engagement.

Approval of the general remuneration policy by the AMSB body of the undertaking as required in Article 35.5 of the Solvency II Directive must be completed here with the vote of the policy at the general meeting as regards directors' remuneration. This vote is in principle binding, but Member States may provide for it to be merely advisory. In any case, submission to vote must be done at every material change and at least every four years (Article 9a of Directive (UE) 2017/828).

Difference is therefore significant and requires clarification of who should be considered directors, in order to submit their remuneration policy to the prior approval or control by the general meeting. According to Article 2.i) Directive (UE) 2017/828 'director' means: (i) any member of the AMSB of a company; (ii) where they are not members of the AMSB of a company, the chief executive officer and, if such function exists in a company, the deputy chief executive officer;[31] and (iii) where so determined by a Member State, other persons who perform functions similar to those performed under point (i) or (ii).

Again, there is room for national interpretation and, as will be shown, supervisory criteria and legal provisions show significant differences in this respect.

---

[30] As Recital 28 of Directive (UE) 2017/828 points out.

[31] If CEOs are named among the members of the AMSB, they remain considered as directors, but under point (i) of the classification.

4.2 National Corporate Law and Implementation Measurements of the Specific Insurance Provisions Towards Remuneration

The remuneration policy must apply to the undertaking as a whole but include specific provisions considering the tasks and performance of the AMSB, persons who effectively run the undertaking or have other key functions, and other categories of staff whose professional activities have a material impact on the undertakings' risk profile (Article 275.1.c) Solvency II Directive). Further, provisions included in the EIOPA's Opinion apply only to AMSB members, other executive persons who effectively run the undertaking, key function holders and other categories of staff whose professional activities have a material impact on the undertakings' risk profile.

The application of these general rules to the corporate structure of each undertaking usually poses many questions about their scope and their application (or not) to some functions and individuals and receives frequently attention in guidelines prepared by the national supervisory authorities with quite different approaches in each case.

On the following paragraphs the chapter analyses the legal regime and criteria of some of the European Member States with more particularities in this respect, pointing out the differences among them. As one can observed, there are many aspects in which the supervision and the corporate governance requirements vary notably among Member States, with all the potential risk and legal uncertainty that this situation entails.

4.2.1 Belgium

Generally, Belgium allows both the monistic and the dualistic system of board structure (Article 7:85 et seq. of the *Code des sociétés et des associations*[32]). According to the first one, *le conseil d'administration* can carry out all acts needed for the fulfilling of the company purpose. Following a dualistic system, board is organized in two bodies: *le conseil d'surveillance* and *le conseil de direction*. Here, *le conseil de surveillance* develops the general policies and the strategy of the company, and the daily management belongs to *le comité de direction*.

Compared to the general rule, according to the Belgian Insurance Supervision Act,[33] insurance undertakings must use a special dualist model with two bodies: *le conseil d'administration* and *le comité de direction* with two main differences with the general dualistic system. On the one hand, powers of *le comité de direction* arise

[32] Loi du 23 mars 2019 introduisant le Code des sociétés et des associations et portant des dispositions diverses (M.B. 4 abril 2019, pp. 33239 et seq.).

[33] Loi du 13 mars 2016 relative au statut et au contrôle des entreprises d'assurance et de réassurance.

from a delegation of *le conseil d'administration*. On the other hand, at least three members of the *comité* are also members of *le conseil d'adminsitration* (in the pure dualistic models both bodies have completely different members).[34]

In this case, according to the *Circulaire 2016_31 relative aux attentes prudentielles de la Banque nationale de Belgique en matière de système de gouvernance pour le secteur de l'assurance et de la réassurance (version révisée en mai 2020)*[35] (point 8.1), both bodies, the supervisory and the management one, are subject to the provisions of the EU Regulation and the EIOPA's opinion.

Apart from listed companies, remuneration policies of insurance undertakings do not have to be submitted to the general meeting except in cases when that policy includes a notice period and a severance pay for non-executive members of *le conseil d'administration* (point 8.2 *Circulaire*, and its footnote 42).

The Belgian system entails very detailed provisions on insurance corporate governance supervision. The *Circulaire* embraces all proposals included in the EIOPA's Opinion and converses most of them into binding provisions requiring the undertakings for explanation to the supervisor (The National Bank of Belgium) when they do not comply with the provided benchmarks.

4.2.2 Germany

Remuneration policies of insurance undertakings are covered here by the *Aktiengesetz* (the German company law, mainly in Articles 87 and 113) and the *Versicherungsaufsichtsgesetz* (the insurance supervision law, mainly in Articles 33 and 189).

The governance structure is dualistic for all kinds of companies—included insurance undertakings—and is split into two bodies: *Aufsichtsrat* (supervisory board) and *Vorstand* (management board), whose members are completely different from each other.

While remuneration of the *Aufsichtsrat* must be included in the by-laws or approved by the general meeting, that of the *Vorstand* needs only the *Aufsichtsrat*'s approval.

Regarding insurance companies, the German Supervisor (BaFin[36]) has published two resolutions: The Decision *Aspekte der Vergütung (Art. 275 DVO (EU) 2015/35)*,[37] and the Circular 2/2017.[38] According to those provisions, even when remuneration principles included in the Delegated Regulation (EU) 2015/35 shall apply to the undertaking as a whole, restrictions considered in Article 275 of the Regulation

[34] Strypstein (2020), p. 59 et seq.

[35] Vid. Chhor (2020), p. 165 et seq.

[36] Bundesanstalt für Finanzdienstleistungsaufischt.

[37] VA 52-I 2510-2016/0006, 20 December 2016.

[38] Rundschreiben 2/2017 (VA)-Mindestanforderungen an die Geschäftsorganisation von Versicherungsunternehmen (MaGo), 25 Januar 2017.

and provisions included in the EIOPA's Opinion only get development with respect to the members of the management board, persons who run the undertaking or have other key functions, or other categories of staff whose professional activities have a material impact on the undertaking's risk profile. Considering that the Regulation refers to the administrative, management or supervisory body and that the Opinion focuses on the AMSB members and other executive directors, one can understand that both, supervisory and management boards in case they are split should be subjected to those provisions.[39] It must be considered that according to point G-18 of the German Corporate Governance Code[40] supervisory board remuneration should be fixed remuneration (in that case, provisions included in EIOPA's Opinion would not have impact in such policies). Nevertheless, it is only a recommendation and only applicable to listed companies, and in any case, it also bears the possibility of providing performance-related remuneration (thus, variable) to the members of the supervisory board (if so, that component should be geared to the long-term development of the company).

The German provisions towards insurance undertakings remuneration are otherwise very complete and include specific benchmarks regarding some of the principles included in the EU Delegated Regulation. With respect to the sufficiently high proportion of the total remuneration the BaFin's Decision recommends a minimum percentage of 40 for staff under the *Vorstand*, and a minimum of 60% in the case of members of that management board. Even when those provisions were foreseen in 2019, before EIOPA's Opinion, there is no contradiction in this respect considering that the Opinion allows supervisors to raise that threshold.

4.2.3 Italy

Remuneration provisions for insurance companies are found in the *Codice Civile*[41] (the Italian Civil Code, where these questions are addressed in Articles 2325 et seq.) and the *Codice delle assicurazioni private*[42] (the Insurance Code), and two resolutions of the Italian insurance supervisor, the IVASS:[43]: the Regulation 38/2018 of 3 July[44] and the Letter to the Market of 5 July 2018.[45]

[39] In this same direction vid. Scheidl (2019), p. 67.

[40] Corporate Governance Kodex, *Regierungskommission Deutscher Corporate Governance Kodex*, version of 16 December 2019.

[41] Royal Decree 16 March 1942, n°262, last updated with the Legislative Decree of 16 July 2020, n°76, and the Legislative Decree of 8 April 2020, n° 23, transformed in Law of 5 July 2020, n°40.

[42] Legislative Decree of 7 September 2005 n° 209, last updated with Legislative Decree of 17 March 2020, n° 18.

[43] *Istituto per la Vigilanza sulle Assicurazioni.*

[44] *Regolamento IVASS n. 38 del 3 luglio 2018.*

[45] *Lettera al Mercato, 5 luglio 2018.*

Insurance undertakings can adopt here the three governance systems admitted in the Civil Code since 2003:[46] traditional, monistic, and dualistic. Among these, in the insurance sector, one finds mainly the traditional and the dualistic structures. According to the first one, there are two bodies in charge of the management and the supervision respectively: the *consiglio d'amministrazione* and the *collegio sindicale* (2380 *Codice Civile*). The general meeting chooses the members of both and fixes their remuneration. The management body can appoint delegated members or establish an executive committee.

According to the dualistic model (2409 bis *Codice Civile*), the governance structure is organized in a supervisory and a management board, but in this case the general meeting nominates only the members of the supervisory one (*consiglio di sorveglianza*) and is this body who chooses the components of the management board (*consiglio di gestion*). Pursuant to the general provisions of the Civil Code, the general meeting only decides the remuneration of the supervisory board. Under this structure, there is room for the designation of delegated members of the management board, but not for an executive committee.

On insurance undertakings, the IVASS Regulation (Articles 39 et seq.) follows the general regime and allows both systems, traditional and dualistic. The general meeting determines the retribution of the members of the bodies designed by it (*consiglio d'amministrazione* and *collegio sindacale* in the traditional model, and *consiglio di sorveglianza* in the dualistic one) and approves the remuneration policy prepared by the *consiglio di sorveglianza* for the management board (*consiglio di gestion*). Hence, the general meeting has a say in any case.

The remuneration of the supervisory boards—*collegio sindacale* and *consiglio di sorveglianza*—is limited in its variable components, and it shall not include compensation linked to results or based on financial instruments.

The Italian Supervisor establishes three governance systems (*rafforzato, ordinario and semplificato*) for insurance undertakings depending mainly on the level of life technical provisions and non-life insurance premiums. The Supervisor only envisages specific provisions developing remuneration principles of the EU Regulation in companies which require the reinforced—*rafforzato*—system (those with life technical provisions over 10 billion € or non-life premiums over 1 billion €). In that case, where Article 275 EU Regulation its applied, 50% of the variable component of the remuneration should consist of shares or other connected instruments,[47] and 40% of the total variable amount should be deferred not less than 3–5 years. If the proportion of variable components of the whole remuneration is especially high, then not less than the 60% of it should be deferred.

As shown, these limits do not apply when the governance system of the undertaking is ordinary or simplified, i.e. it does not come into play for companies with levels of technical provisions of 10 billion or less, or non-life premiums of one

[46] Vid. *Indagine conoscitiva: La Corporate Governance di Banche e Compagnie di Assicurazioni – IC36*, Autorità garante della concorrenza e del mercato, Roma, 2009.

[47] A new parameter not required at a European level.

billion or less. In these cases, provisions of the EU regulation and the EIOPA's opinion apply with no further interpretation.

4.2.4 Spain

The Spanish corporate law[48] follows a monistic system in the configuration of the governance structure of companies, and the situation remains unchanged when it comes to insurance undertakings.

In the governance structure, next to the general meeting one only finds another body: the *consejo de administración* (management board) whose members are appointed by the general meeting. The *consejo* itself can name one or several delegated executive administrators or appoint an executive committee. In that case, the *consejo* plays a supervisory role, even though there are some competences that cannot be subject of delegation (Article 249 bis TRLSC).

Over the last years, authors and case-law have argued about the scope of the power of the general meeting on remuneration of the *consejo de administración*. In particular, the terms used by the national legislator in Articles 216 et seq. have given rise to doubts about the competence of the general meeting for determining not only the remuneration of the *consejo de administración* itself, but also the compensations owed to the executive delegates or to the members of the executive commission.[49] In this respect, in the last two years, the Supreme Court (Ruling 494/2018[50]) and the Central Economic-Administrative Court (Resolution 3156/2019[51]) have solved the question considering that the powers of the general meeting on the remuneration of the *consejo de administración* must also reach the remuneration of the executive delegated members and of the members of the executive committee.

The Spanish insurance supervisor (DGSFP[52]) has reproduced[53] the orientations of EIOPA with no gold-plating measures and leaving, therefore, a wide margin for insurance undertakings to establish their policies.

[48] Real Decreto Legislativo 1/2010, de 2 de julio, por el que se aprueba el texto refundido de la Ley de Sociedades de Capital (TRLSC).

[49] In favour of that broader scope, as the most representative work vid. Fernández Del Pozo (2015), pp. 199–248. Against this extended interpretation, among others, vid. Paz-Ares (2018), full issue.

[50] Sentencia del Tribunal Supremo 494/2018, de 26 de febrero, Roj: STS 494/2018 - ECLI: ES: TS:2018:494.

[51] Resolución del Tribunal Económico-Administrativo Central, de 17 de julio de 2020, R.G. 3156/ 2019.

[52] Dirección General de Seguros y Fondos de Pensiones.

[53] Nota en relación con la aplicación de la Opinión y de las recomendaciones de la Autoridad Europea de Seguros y Pensiones de jubilación sobre las políticas de remuneración variable, DGSFP, 30 de junio de 2020.

5 Conclusion

The legal treatment of remuneration policies and practices in the insurance sector received attention of the European Legislator years later than in the banking sector and only, so far, through second level provisions in the Lamfalussy scheme. The remuneration principles appear in the Commission Delegated Regulation (EU) 2015/35, but no changes in the Solvency II Directive have been made with this aim.

As a short-term way for improvement of the insurance sector regime, an amendment of the text of the Solvency II Directive should be made as soon as possible, with inclusion of an express reference to most of the remuneration principles laid out now in Regulation 2015/35, in order to give consistency and clarity to the supervisory legal framework.

The use of a non-compulsory instrument to develop the remuneration principles as is the case of the EIOPA's Opinion *on the supervision of remuneration principles in the insurance and reinsurance sector* does not appear to be the most appropriate solution, especially when there are no first level provisions in this respect. Following the better constructed structure of the remuneration provisions in the banking sector would certainly solve much of the problems arisen from the inadequate insurance scheme.

As a forward-looking approach, considering that in the last decades the boundaries between banking, insurance and securities have become increasingly blurred, it should be questioned if there is still a point in having completely separate provisions for the banking and the insurance sector and if there would be convenient to evolve to a greater convergence in the financial supervision regulation, with hardly any difference between financial sub-sectors or, at least, with more similar schemes. As Larosière Report pointed out in 2009, it could also be desirable to change the European sectoral supervisory model to a twin peaks model because this is not a short-term evolution but a far future possible orientation of the supervisory structures in Europe.

In addition to problems resulting from the inadequate structure of the remuneration provisions at European level, the insurance market shows a complex situation regarding remuneration policies, arising mainly from two factors: on the one hand, the European insurance industry presents a wide range of organisational structures and business models, especially regarding size and risk profile. These differences demand a flexible application of the rules and, in some cases, the taking into account of the proportionality principle. On the other hand, the application of these special rules to insurance undertakings does not prevent these undertakings from also being subject to the company law of their country of origin. It is a known fact that the structure of the governing bodies of the companies and the legal regime applicable to them vary greatly between Member States, which makes it more difficult to determine the scope and application of provisions contained in the above-mentioned insurance industry specific rules on remuneration policies. Even when the aim is not the full harmonisation, the truth is that there are very deep differences between national regimes, in particular, relating aspects like the power of the general meeting to approve directors' remuneration policies.

The current supervisory system on remuneration policies and practices in the insurance sector shows, in short, many areas for improvement, as previously shown in this chapter.

References

Al-Darwish, Hafeman, Impavido, Kemp, O'malley (2011) Possible unintended consequences of Basel III and Solvency II. IMF Working Paper WP/11/187

Butera S, Montemaggiori F (2018) La governance delle imprese di assicurazione secondo il principio di proporzionalitá. Fondamenti internazionali europei e regole nazionale. Rivista Assicurazioni, Giappichelli Editore, Numero único: 41–90

Chhor LC (2020) Fonctions de contrôle indépendantes Instruments au service de la bonne gouvernance. Bulletin des Assurances, Wolters Kluwer 25:143–176

Colaert V (2015) European banking, securities and insurance law: cutting through sectoral lines? Common Mark Law Rev, Wolters Kluwer 52:1579–1616

Esquerra Resa L (2020) La remuneración de los Administradores y Directivos en el sector asegurador. Comentario al Dictamen (Opinión) de la EIOPA sobre los principios de remuneración (EIOPA-BoS-20/040)(1). Revista de Derecho del Mercado de Valores, Wolters Kluwer 26:11 et seq

Fernández Del Pozo L (2015) El misterio de la remuneración de los administradores de las sociedades no cotizadas. Las carencias regulatorias de la reforma. Revista de Derecho Mercantil, Aranzadi 297:199–248

Godwin A, Schmulow A (eds) (2021) The Cambridge handbook of twin peaks financial regulation. Cambridge University Press

Hopt KJ (2013) Better governance of financial institutions. European Corporate Governance Institute, Law Working Paper, n°207/2013

Paz-Ares C (2018) Perseverare diabolicum (A propósito de la STS 26-II-2018 y la retribución de los consejeros ejecutivos). InDret 2:1–52

Scheidl F (2019) Corporate Governance von Versicherungsunternehmen: eine theoretische, regulatorische und empirische Analyse, Doktor Dissertation, Universität der Bundeswehr München, at p 6, also in Scheidl F (2019) Corporate Governance und Wertschöpfung bei Versicherungsunternehmen – Eine qualitativ-empirische Analyse. Zetischrift für die gesamte Versicherungswissenschaft 108:255–274

Schoenmaker D, Véron N (2017) A twin-peaks vision for Europe. Policy Contribution, Bruegel 30

Strypstein N (2020) Attentes prudentielles en matière de gouvernance des entreprises d'assurance et de réassurance: impacts du CSA et autres évolutions. Bulletin des Assurances, Wolters Kluwer 25:43–72

Van Loopik M, Ter Haar M (2016) Chapter 26 of the banking regulation review, 7th edn. Jan Putnis, Law Business Research

Corporate Governance Standards for Insurers in Singapore

Christopher Chen

Abstract This chapter examines the corporate governance regime for insurers in Singapore. Singapore aims to be a global hub for insurance and reinsurance in the Asia Pacific region, and as an international financial centre it currently hosts a mixture of local and international insurers and reinsurers serving different market sectors. However, the domestic insurance market is small, and insurers registered in Singapore come from many countries and provide products and services to many businesses and individuals outside the city-state. This presents challenges to the sole financial regulator, the Monetary Authority of Singapore (MAS), in implementing and enforcing corporate governance standards on various (re)insurers, many of which are part of larger overseas insurance groups. What should be the way to impose corporate governance standards on various types of (re)insurers? This chapter addresses these questions in the context of Singapore. The general regulatory concerns over corporate governance standards and Singapore's corporate governance regimes for insurers are first introduced. Specific corporate governance issues are then examined, including the implementation of standards for non-domestic insurers or a branch or subsidiary of a larger insurance group from overseas, and the governance of captive insurers and reinsurers. Singapore's approach is then discussed and the effectiveness of corporate governance regulations for insurers is assessed. Empirical evidence is presented when data are available.

1 Introduction: Unique Challenges to Singapore

Corporate governance is an important tool for effectively regulating insurers and insurance intermediaries. In this chapter, Singapore's corporate governance regime for insurers is examined. In particular, this chapter examines corporate governance of insurers from the perspective of regulatory compliance in addition to the need to control of agency costs. The rules are examined in the context of Singapore as an

C. Chen (✉)
College of Law, National Chengchi University, Taipei, Taiwan

P. Marano, K. Noussia (eds.), *The Governance of Insurance Undertakings*, AIDA Europe Research Series on Insurance Law and Regulation 6,
https://doi.org/10.1007/978-3-030-85817-9_6

international financial hub with multiple tiers of insurers and reinsurers serving different market segments.

First, like many financial businesses, insurance companies may suffer from agency problems.[1] In a principal-agent relationship, managers (i.e. agents) of an insurance company may not pursue the best interest of the company and its shareholders (i.e. the principal). This is the so-called agency problem that implies that companies might incur some costs to monitor the management. Those costs are generally considered 'agency costs'.[2] As is the case for listed companies in the stock market, corporate governance aims at to improve management quality and reduce 'tunnelling'.[3]

Second, insurers are, like banks, heavily regulated as they collect large sums (as premiums) from customers to provide insurance and thus have much influence on the financial market. Therefore, they must be governed properly through appropriate corporate governance. As Sect. 2 below demonstrates, the board and senior management are expected to play significant roles in complying with the various regulatory requirements. Thus, corporate governance in insurers' regulatory compliance should be examined.

Hence, one argues that 'the effectiveness of insurer governance should also include a reduction in governance risk and compliance risks…'[4] However, the role of corporate governance in addressing agency costs and regulatory compliance for insurance companies requires further investigation. What corporate governance standards are appropriate for insurers? In particular, this chapter considers whether the corporate governance tools used for listed companies in the stock market can be applied, and if they are suitable for achieving better regulatory compliance.

Singapore is selected as a case study for investigating the corporate governance of insurers, as it presents some unique challenges. As a city-state, the domestic market for life and general insurance is limited to a population of about six million. Singapore's advantages, in terms of being a financial centre and insurance hub, mainly benefit reinsurance and non-retail insurance offerings.[5] Only a few large domestic direct insurers operate in the competitive market of Singapore. In contrast, many foreign insurers have offices, branches or subsidiaries in Singapore that underwrite or provide negotiable insurance coverage, for risks incurred not only in Singapore but also regionally or globally. Many captive insurers are also registered in the city.

[1] See Jensen and Meckling (1976), p. 305.

[2] Jensen and Meckling (1976), p. 308.

[3] In general, tunnelling refers to the 'transfer of assets and profits out of firms for the benefit of those who control them'. Johnson et al. (2000), p. 22.

[4] Li et al. (2017), p. 3.

[5] 'Singapore as a Global Insurance Marketplace'—Keynote Address by Mr Ravi Menon, Managing Director, Monetary Authority of Singapore, at the 12th Singapore International Reinsurance Conference on 6 November 2013, retrieved from the website of Monetary Authority of Singapore https://www.mas.gov.sg/news/speeches/2013/singapore-as-a-global-insurance-marketplace (last accessed on 20 July 2020).

These features of the Singapore market raise further questions. What are the optimal corporate governance regimes, considering the various types of insurers in the market? Some may be extremely concerned about agency costs, but others may not. The effects of corporate governance on regulatory compliance may also vary depending on the size and nature of the business. Thus, is the current approach sufficient to address the demand for regulatory compliance? If not, what should the regulatory approach be? Ensuring regulations are effective but that foreign insurers with limited involvement in the domestic market are not over-burdened is a delicate balancing act for regulators when aiming to make Singapore a global insurance hub.

In Sect. 2 of this chapter, the function of good corporate governance in addressing agency problems and in regulatory compliance will be examined, with Singapore law used as examples of the latter. The corporate governance rules for insurers issued by the Monetary Authority of Singapore (MAS), the single financial regulator in the market, are then introduced. Based on the discussion in Sect. 2, Sect. 3 will first offer empirical evidence in the form of corporate governance statistics on selected insurers in Singapore. We then examine Singapore's approach to corporate governance standards for insurers and the effectiveness of corporate governance rules in promoting regulatory compliance. Section 4 concludes the chapter.

2 Corporate Governance Regimes for Insurers in Singapore: The Two Perspectives

Why does corporate governance matter? In this part, key areas in which the board and/or senior management are expected to play important roles in ensuring regulatory compliance are identified. The key corporate governance standards under Singapore law are then introduced.

2.1 Corporate Governance and Agency Costs for Insurers

Many studies have examined the rationale of good corporate governance and its effect on the proper management of a company, along with its role in reducing agency costs, by focusing on firms listed for trading on the stock market. Insurance companies also suffer from the agency problem.

A phenomenon recognised in modern corporations is the separation of ownership from control.[6] The management of a company does not necessarily consist of shareholders (i.e. equity owners). Thus, the agency problem arises. The agents (management) may not be motivated to effectively manage the company, as their incentives are capped by their remuneration. Managers may also divert company

[6]Berle and Means (1932).

resources to their own pockets. This is referred to as 'tunnelling'.[7] In both instances, the agent's conduct may not serve the best interests of the company (i.e. the principal). Hence, agency problem may arise. A company may incur some monitoring costs to control the agent's conduct, thus reducing the efficiency of the organisation.[8]

The severity of the agency problem for insurance companies can depend on many factors. The ownership structure of an insurer can affect the degree of separation and control. Insurance companies that are publicly listed for trading on stock exchanges (e.g. Prudential in London or AIA in Hong Kong) may have thousands of investors and shareholders (often throughout the world), who can be individual or institutional investors (e.g. private equity funds). These firms exhibit a high degree of separation between ownership and control, and thus may incur higher agency costs. Other insurers are wholly owned by a parent holding company (e.g. HSBC Insurance (Singapore) Pte Ltd as part of the HSBC group). These firms have only one ultimate owner, and senior managers are most likely not shareholders. Some may not even have a controlling shareholder (i.e. widely held firms).[9] Thus, the interactions between the management and the owner differ from those in a publicly traded company. These subsidiaries may well incur agency costs and the management may not serve the best interests of the shareholders, but the severity of the costs and the effectiveness of ownership control will differ from those of an insurer listed for trading. Thus, while most insurers will incur some agency costs, the extent will depend on the ownership and management structure.

Corporate governance for insurers thus has an important function, as it can improve management performance through requirements regarding board and senior management remuneration, and reduce tunnelling through board independence and auditing requirements.[10] The same is also true for pension funds.[11]

2.2 *Corporate Governance and Regulatory Compliance*

Corporate governance is also an important regulatory tool as it can ensure good regulatory compliance by insurers. The argument that '[a] risk management function that has an independent, autonomous, and credible status in a firm with unalloyed

[7] See above n 3.

[8] Jensen and Meckling (1976), p. 308.

[9] For example, the largest shareholder of Prudential plc, one of the largest insurers in the UK, held barely more than 5% of voting shares (with the runner-up holding just short of 5%) pursuant to the company's 2019 annual report. See the 2019 annual report of Prudential plc, p. 400, at https://www.prudentialplc.com/~/media/Files/P/Prudential-V3/reports/2019/prudential-plc-ar-2019.pdf (last accessed 21 July 2020).

[10] See Sect. 2.3 below for a more detailed discussion of Singapore law.

[11] Kowalewski (2012), p. 14.

access to the board can limit tail exposure preceding and during a market crisis'[12] is obviously persuasive. Strong corporate governance by the senior management and the board's leadership can reduce the risk posed by a siloed risk management structure inside a firm.[13] Principal-agent conflicts that can undermine the effectiveness of risk management may also be reduced by good corporate governance,[14] which can thus be regarded as essential for full regulatory compliance. In Singapore, the regulator clearly recognises the key role of the board, stating that it is the 'basic tenet of the [regulator's] risk-based supervisory approach'.[15]

The role of the board in complying with rules and regulations issued by the financial regulator, the Monetary Authority of Singapore (MAS), can be illustrated through various examples in Singapore law.

First, the board of directors of an insurer is ultimately responsible for its sound and prudent management.[16] Singapore largely followed the corporate governance principles adopted by the Organization for Economic Cooperation (OECD) that largely followed the corporate governance framework developed in the US and UK.[17] In particular, the board of directors play the instrumental role in the governance and management structure of company. The board should therefore supervise the senior management of an insurer. The board is thus central to establishing the policies, procedures and processes of internal controls.[18] 'The internal audit function should also have appropriate independence with reporting lines to the institution's Board or to an audit committee of the Board (the "Audit Committee")'.[19] The board of directors, especially independent directors, also play a key role in vetting related party transactions.[20]

Second, the board has a supervisory role in prudential regulation compliance. For example, when calculating their risk-based capital, the board and the senior management should oversee the governance and the use of the internal credit rating process for unrated debt securities[21] or investments containing non-linear payouts.[22] Reporting regularly to the board and senior management should be a requirement.[23]

---

[12] Dill (2019), p. 168.

[13] Dill (2019), pp. 167–168.

[14] Dill (2019), pp. 168–169.

[15] MAS, Guidelines on Corporate Governance, para. [7].

[16] MAS, Guidelines on Risk Management Practices for Insurance Business, para 2.2.2.

[17] Chen et al. (2018), p. 988.

[18] MAS, Guidelines on Risk Management Practices – Internal Controls, para 1.1.2.

[19] MAS, Guidelines on Risk Management Practices – Internal Controls, para 2.6.2.

[20] See Enriques et al. (2009).

[21] MAS, Notice on Valuation and Capital Framework for Insurers (Notice 133), Annex 4E para 1 & 2.

[22] MAS, Guidelines on Use of Internal Models for Liability and Capital Requirements for Life Insurance Products Containing Investment Guarantees with Non-Linear Payouts (ID 01/13), para 2.3.1 & 3.1.4.

[23] MAS, Notice on Valuation and Capital Framework for Insurers (Notice 133), Annex 4E para 3.

In terms of investment decisions, the board of directors has the duty to approve and review the investment policy of an insurer,[24] and to conduct additional oversight to ensure that the interests and rights of policy owners are not compromised.[25] An appointed actuary should provide written recommendations for the allocation of insurance funds[26] to the board, and alert board members about any issues that need attention.[27] This can help the board and senior management make appropriate management decisions. In terms of reinsurance management, the board should also ensure there is a sound and prudent reinsurance management strategy in addition to operational policies.[28]

The board is also ultimately responsible for approving risk management strategies and policies concerning insurers' core insurance activities[29] and their 'own risk and solvency assessment' (ORSA).[30] The board should also oversee an insurer's technology risk management through a sound and robust framework,[31] be involved in key IT decisions[32] and regularly review the fraud management strategy.[33] Maintaining effective oversight and governance of outsourcing arrangements is also under the board's remit.[34]

Third, the board also has responsibility for ensuring that the business complies with business conduct regulations. Under Singapore law, '[a]n institution should have clear written policies, approved by the Board or senior management, on issues relating to dealings with customers and risk disclosures'.[35] For a financial adviser, an insurer or insurance broker recommends new life insurance products to customers, and each member of the board is expected to be personally satisfied that the product is suitable for the target customer segment.[36]

The board and senior management are responsible for setting the right tone when conducting marketing and distribution activities for customers, ensuring these activities are responsible and professional[37] and that safeguards required by law

---

[24] MAS, Notice on Investment of Insurers (Notice 125), para 8, 12 and 18.

[25] MAS, Notice on Investment of Insurers (Notice 125), para 8.

[26] Insurance (Actuaries) Regulations reg 7(1).

[27] Insurance (Actuaries) Regulations reg 10(1).

[28] MAS, Reinsurance Management (Notice 114), para 7 & 9.

[29] MAS, Guidelines on Risk Management Practices for Insurance Business, para 2.2.2; MAS, Guidelines on Risk Management Practices – Market Risk, para 3.1.1.

[30] MAS, Guidance on Insurers' Own Risk and Solvency Assessments, para 3.1; MAS, Enterprise Risk Management ("ERM") for Insurers (Notice 126), para 33.

[31] MAS, Technology Risk Management Guidelines, para 3.0.2 and 3.1.1.

[32] MAS, Technology Risk Management Guidelines, para 3.1.1.

[33] MAS, Insurance Business – Insurance Fraud Risk, 2.1.3.

[34] MAS, Guidelines on Outsourcing, para 5.2.

[35] MAS, Guidelines on Risk Management Practices – Internal Controls, para 3.1.1.

[36] Financial Advisers Regulations, reg 18B.

[37] MAS, Guidelines on Standards of Conduct for Marketing and Distribution Activities, para 1.1.

(e.g. call-backs or mystery shopping) are incorporated into the relevant policies and processes.[38]

Finally, the board has various administrative duties. For example, the directors must sign off the annual returns submitted to the MAS.[39] The board has the responsibility to ensure that sound risk management and controls are in place in terms of anti-money laundering and the countering of financing of terrorism (AML \CFT) practices.[40] The quality of board and senior management oversight is an important assessment benchmark.[41]

The boards of insurers are expected to shoulder far more responsibility than those of non-financial institutions. Thus, good corporate governance should directly affect how the board and senior management can fulfil their roles in terms of regulatory compliance. Strengthening the corporate governance standards of insurers thus represents an important regulatory tool that is central to insurance regulations.

2.3 Corporate Governance Standards for Insurers Under Singapore Law

As in the general corporate governance regimes of listed companies, the independence of the board, the separation of the role of the chairman and the chief executive officer and the creation of sub-committees at the board level all help to improve and ensure standards of corporate governance. Regulators also control the appointment of key positions in insurance firms. Good corporate governance may be a condition for acquiring a licence as an insurer or reinsurer, which can include ensuring that 'fit and proper' criteria are satisfied.

Corporate governance standards for insurers in Singapore are mainly regulated by the Insurance (Corporate Governance) Regulations 2013 (ICGR), first published in April 2013, and only amended once in 2018. The ICGR generally follows the corporate governance mechanisms stated in the Code of Corporate Governance (the 'Code') issued by the Monetary Authority of Singapore (MAS) for listed companies in the Singapore Exchange (SGX). However, the Code is to some extent modified in the ICGR.

First, the ICGR applies different standards depending on the size of the insurer. Larger firms are subject to a higher degree of regulation. The ICGR divides insurers into Tier 1 and Tier 2 insurers. A direct life insurer in Tier 1 has a minimum of S$5 million in total assets, while a direct general insurer has a minimum of S$500 million

[38] MAS, Guidelines on Standards of Conduct for Marketing and Distribution Activities, para 1.2.

[39] E.g. Insurance (Approved Marine, Aviation and Transit Insurers) Regulations, Second Schedule; Insurance (Authorised Reinsurers) Regulations reg 9.

[40] AML\CFT Guidelines, para 3.2.

[41] MAS, Guidelines to MAS Notice 314 on Prevention of Money Laundering and Countering the Financing of Terrorism, para 1–3.

(about US$ 360 million),[42] unless otherwise approved by the MAS.[43] Tier 2 insurers include all those not in Tier 1.

Second, regardless of the type of insurer, the independence of the board of directors represents the essential corporate governance regime. In principle, a Tier 1 insurer should have a majority of directors who are independent, but the threshold for a Tier 2 insurer is one third of the board.[44] However, where a Tier 1 insurer has a single shareholder who holds 50% or more of the share capital or voting power (i.e. has majority control), it only needs more than one-third of the board to be independent, but the majority of the board must be independent from management and business relationships (although not from substantial shareholders).[45] In this situation, in which a single shareholder has majority control, failing to meet the minimum standards may result in criminal sanctions.[46] Compliance with the ICGR is therefore mandatory rather than in the form of 'comply or explain', as is the case for the general Code of Corporate Governance.[47]

An independent director is not involved in any management and business relationship with the insurer or any substantial shareholder of the insurer, and has served on the board for less than nine years.[48] In addition, neither the director nor his immediate family can have any management or business relationships with the insurer's subsidiaries.[49] Independence from the substantial shareholders also means that a director cannot be a substantial shareholder (who holds at least 5% of the insurer's shares) or be connected to a substantial shareholder (such as through employment or as an executive).[50]

Third, the ICGR also requires the separation of the roles of the chairman of the board and executives.[51] This represents an attempt to avoid the situation of chairman-chief executive officer (CEO) duality, in which the same person is the chairman and the top executive. Separating the roles should mean that the board is more likely to be effective in monitoring senior management and making proper decisions. The rule also means that the chairman of an insurer must be a non-executive (although not necessarily independent) director, as the chairman cannot be an executive director.

Fourth, specialised board committees can strengthen corporate governance. A Tier 1 insurer is required to have more committees at the board level, such as

[42] ICGR Reg 4(1)(a).

[43] ICGR Reg 4(3).

[44] ICGR Reg 6(1).

[45] ICGR Reg 5(2).

[46] ICGR Reg 5(6) to (8).

[47] MAS, Code of Corporate Governance (2018), paras. [6]–[9].

[48] ICGR Reg 2.

[49] ICGR Reg 5.

[50] ICGR Reg 6.

[51] ICGR Reg 8(1).

nominating, remuneration, audit and risk management committees.[52] Tier 1 insurers can also have an executive committee, again subject to the independence standards.[53] However, the requirement to have nominating, remuneration and risk management committees may be waived if the insurer is a subsidiary of a bank or another insurer whose board performs the function of these committees, subject to the notification of the regulator.[54]

These committees (other than the executive committee) should comprise at least three directors. A majority of the members of the nominating, remuneration and audit committees must be independent directors.[55] Board independence is thus also enforced at the committee level. The audit committee must include at least three directors who have no management and business relationships with the Tier 1 insurer.[56] However, the requirement is lower for risk management committees, in which a majority of members must be non-executive directors (who may or may not be independent).[57] Members of these committees require unfettered access to the firm's information so that they can do their jobs effectively.[58]

The responsibilities of the nominating committee are to nominate and review directors and the principal officer, actuary, chief financial officer and chief risk officer.[59] The primary function of the remuneration committee is to recommend a framework to determine the remuneration (including bonuses) of directors and executive officers of Tier 1 insurers.[60] The audit committee oversees internal and external audits and accounts, which can include related party transactions.[61] The risk management committee is responsible for an enterprise-wide independent risk management system and for monitoring its effectiveness.[62]

The standards are more relaxed for a Tier 2 insurer. The functions of the abovementioned committees are mainly delegated to the board of directors.[63] The board of a Tier 2 insurer can of course delegate to a sub-committee, although the ICGR does not make this mandatory.

Fifth, as is common in financial institutions, the appointment of nominated committee members, the chief financial officer and the chief risk officer must be approved by the MAS beforehand.[64] This is in addition to the general rule that an

[52] ICGR Reg 10(1).

[53] ICGR Reg 9.

[54] ICGR Reg 10(3).

[55] ICGR Reg 11(1) and 16(1).

[56] ICGR Reg 17(1).

[57] ICGR Reg 18(1).

[58] ICGR Reg 10(2).

[59] ICGR Reg 12(1).

[60] ICGR Reg 15(3).

[61] ICGR Reg 17(2).

[62] ICGR Reg 18(2).

[63] ICGR Reg 21 to 27.

[64] ICGR Reg 19(1).

insurer's chief executive officer and appointed actuaries must be approved by the MAS before their appointment.[65] An insurer should ensure that its board assesses whether any directors or key executives have any conflicts of interest that prevent them from discharging their duties before requesting approval from the MAS.[66]

Finally, although not stated in the ICGR, key insurer or insurance broker personnel in Singapore must be deemed 'fit and proper'. These personnel include the firm's chief executive officer (CEO), directors, approved or certifying actuaries, brokering staff, substantial shareholders and anyone with effective control of the insurer.[67] An insurer should also have a policy approved by the board to ascertain whether these key personnel are fit and proper.[68]

The three general standards in the 'fit and proper' criteria are (a) honesty, integrity and reputation; (b) competence and capability; and (c) financial soundness.[69] These are designed to reduce the likelihood of the misuse of funds. The standards are not elaborated further in this chapter.[70]

In summary, the key features of corporate governance regimes for insurers under Singapore law are as follows. First, the MAS imposes higher standards on larger insurers (i.e. the Tier 1 insurers) but the rules are more relaxed for smaller firms. Second, the corporate governance standards are mandatory for insurers, rather than 'comply or explain' for listed companies in the stock market. Third, the basic requirements include the independence of the board of directors and the creation of board committees for larger insurers, thus ensuring the proper appointment of board members and senior management. Creating remuneration incentives that align personal interests with the firm's interests, conducting proper audits of the company's accounts and maintaining appropriate risk management strategies are also important. The regime is strengthened by the 'fit and proper' requirements of board of directors. A licensed insurer also has an obligation to disclose 'key features of its corporate governance framework and management controls'[71] to the public, thus improving transparency.

3 Reflection: Challenges to Singapore as an Insurance Hub

One key question is how the agency cost and regulatory compliance perspectives can be reconciled when designing corporate governance regimes for insurers. Regulators should also avoid imposing over-burdening costs. This part first examines corporate

---

[65] Insurance Act s 31(5).

[66] MAS, Appointment of Director, Chairman and Key Executive Person (Notice 106), para 7.

[67] MAS, Guidelines on Fit and Proper Criteria (FSG-G01), para 6. (Fit and Proper Criteria).

[68] MAS, Appointment of Director, Chairman and Key Executive Person (Notice 106), para 10.

[69] Fit and Proper Criteria, para 8.

[70] See Fit and Proper Criteria, para 9 to 15.

[71] MAS, Public Disclosure Requirements (Notice 124), para 9(a).

governance practices of selected insurers in Singapore, based on public information, to provide an overview of such practices. Then, the chapter investigates corporate governance regime for insurers in Singapore from two perspectives. First, the chapter considers whether Singapore's regulations are sufficiently flexible to meet different types of insurance services providers in the Singapore market. Second, the chapter assesses the effectiveness of key corporate governance regimes in improving the ability of boards to make proper management decisions, supervising senior management teams and ensuring compliance with insurance regulation.

3.1 Corporate Governance Practices of Selected Insurers in Singapore

How do insurers in Singapore respond to the corporate governance regulations identified? Market practices must be examined to better understand corporate governance among insurers in Singapore.

However, extracting precise data for all insurers registered with the MAS is extremely difficult. Information on the corporate governance practices of insurers registered in Singapore is surprisingly lacking in the public sphere. The annual returns submitted by insurers to the regulator[72] do not contain any information regarding the board of directors and senior management. However, many insurers are either branches or wholly owned subsidiaries of other firms. They may be incorporated as private companies, and thus their information is not required to be made in public as their shares are not traded publicly in the stock market. Information for captive insurers is even scarcer, as they are subject to less regulatory requirements. Thus, acquiring a full picture of the corporate governance practices of all insurers in the market is challenging.

Table 1 provides limited data from public reports by some insurers in Singapore.

The list of financial institutions available on the website of the MAS indicates that at end of May 2020, there were 17 direct life insurers, 51 general direct insurers and 8 composite insurers registered in Singapore, in addition to 35 reinsurers (including life, general and composite reinsurers) and 77 captive insurers (of all kinds).[73] The number of direct insurers that can be successfully identified as providing corporate governance information in the public sphere from the total (as shown in Table 1) is very limited.

Based on this limited sample of information, we make the following observations. First, there is obviously room to improve the transparency of corporate governance data, given the importance of corporate governance in terms of agency problems and regulatory compliance. The MAS publishes annual returns submitted by insurers on

[72] MAS website: https://www.mas.gov.sg/statistics/insurance-statistics/insurance-company-returns (last accessed 24 July 2020).

[73] See MAS website: https://eservices.mas.gov.sg/fid (last accessed 24 July 2020).

Table 1 Corporate governance benchmarks for some direct insurers in Singapore based on their latest annual reports

Insurer	Board size	Number of independent directors	Number of executive directors	Chairman-CEO duality
Great Eastern Life Assurance (2019)[a]	10	6	1	No
NTUC Income Insurance Cooperative Ltd (2018)[b]	10	8	0	No
Prudential Assurance Company Singapore Pte Ltd (2019)[c]	5	3	2	No
Tokio Marine Life Insurance Singapore Ltd (2020)[d]	5	3	0	No
SingLife (2020)[e]	5	2	1	No
Aviva Ltd (Singapore) (2020)[f]	5	2	1	No
China Taiping Insurance (Singapore) Pte Ltd (2018)[g]	3	1	2	No
Tokio Marine Insurance Pte Ltd (2020)[h]	5	NA	2	No
QBE Insurance (Singapore) Pte Ltd (2020)[i]	5	2	NA	No
United Overseas Insurance Ltd (2019)[j]	9	4	1	No
MS First Capital Insurance Ltd (2020)[k]	9	NA	NA	No

The table is produced by the author
[a]See https://www.greateasternlife.com/content/dam/great-eastern/sg/homepage/about-us/investor-relations/annual-reports/2019-annual-report.pdf (last accessed 24 July 2020)
[b]See https://www.income.com.sg/annual-report/2018/index.html (last accessed 24 July 2020)
[c]See https://www.prudential.com.sg/annual-reports (last accessed 24 July 2020)
[d]See https://www.tokiomarine.com/sg/en/about-us/life-insurance/management-team.html (last accessed 24 July 2020)
[e]See https://singlife.com/about-us/shareholders-and-board-of-directors/ (last accessed 24 July 2020)
[f]See https://www.aviva.com.sg/en/about-us/corporate-governance/ (last accessed 24 July 2020)
[g]See https://www.sg.cntaiping.com/images/document/08AnnualReports/2018_CNTPAnnualReport.pdf?format=pdf (last accessed 24 July 2020)
[h]See https://www.tokiomarine.com/sg/en/about-us/general-insurance/management-team.html (last accessed 24 July 2020)
[i]See qbe.com/sg/about-qbe/corporate-governance (last accessed 24 July 2020)
[j]See https://www.uoi.com.sg/uoi/assets/pdfs/annual-report-2019.pdf (last accessed 24 July 2020)
[k]See https://www.msfirstcapital.com.sg/board_directors.html (last accessed 24 July 2020)

its website, and therefore basic information on the financial conditions of these insurers is already in the public space. Further basic information (such as a list of board members) on insurers' corporate governance practices could be disclosed on the same platform. If an insurer is already compelled to disclose financial information about its insurance business and funds, it should have no valid grounds to reject the disclosure of its basic corporate governance practices.

Thus, it is suggested that the regulator request insurers to submit additional information about board composition, independence and other critical governance benchmarks. Even if an insurer is a wholly owned subsidiary of a parent insurer, there are still advantages to improving transparency as it serves many customers in the local market. Although concerns over agency costs for such subsidiaries may be reduced, the proper management of insurance funds and regulatory compliance can still be an issue.

Second, the companies in the limited sample all appear to generally comply with the minimum board independence requirements and the rule against chairman-CEO duality. However, one interesting pattern observed in the limited data is that insurers that are public companies (e.g. Great Eastern Life or NTUC Income) tend to have larger boards and more independent directors than those incorporated as private companies (indicating that they are subsidiaries of another financial holding company or an overseas insurer).

The differences in terms of compliance strategies (if the limited data represent the whole population of insurers registered in Singapore) are understandable. If an insurer is a wholly owned subsidiary of another foreign insurer, the board of the subsidiary is likely to have less management power when most important decisions are probably determined by the board of the parent company. Thus, there is no need for a larger board in the subsidiary insurer in terms of making management decisions. Large boards also increase operational costs.

However, insurers that are public companies (sometimes listed for trading on the stock exchange) may face more scrutiny from other shareholders and the market. If the insurer is not a subsidiary, the board is expected to play a more significant role in making management decisions. Thus, it is understandable that they have larger boards of directors, and consequently more independent directors. One study in 2016 has shown that the average number of independent directors on the board of the top 50 companies listed in the Singapore Exchange was about 5.7 persons.[74] The number of independent directors in Great Eastern and NTUC Income (the first companies in Table 1) are comparable with other large companies listed in Singapore's stock market.

The question for regulators is to determine the optimal size of the board and the level of board independence. Although there may be less concern over agency costs if an insurer is a wholly owned subsidiary of a parent insurer, the board must still play its role in regulatory compliance. Thus, would a small board serve its purpose in terms of regulatory compliance? This question is addressed in the following two sections.

[74] Chen (2016), p. 341.

3.2 Reflection on the Corporate Governance Standards

There are pros and cons on how regulators should impose corporate governance standards. One common approach is that regulators would apply a uniform approach to request insurers to follow certain minimum standards. A uniform approach for the corporate governance of insurers has both pros and cons. Uniformity may facilitate more effective supervision, as a common benchmark can make it easier for regulators and the market to evaluate and assess corporate governance standards in the same market. Equal treatment may also be beneficial, as a smaller insurer is still susceptible to agency costs and the possibility of business mismanagement, so minimum standards should still apply.

However, a uniform approach to insurers' corporate governance standards may have some disadvantages. First, given the diversity of insurers in the market, a uniform requirement applicable to all kinds of insurers may not be the most efficient as it invariably must ignore the variety of firm characteristics. For example, some insurers may be publicly listed companies with thousands of shareholders and prospective investors in the capital market, and others may be wholly owned subsidiaries of parent insurers or captive insurers for an industrial group. In terms of agency costs, higher standards may be more appropriate for the former than the latter. However, a uniform approach does not capture the difference in terms of ownership structure (or other characteristics). Therefore, there is a possibility that regulators impose requirements that are unfit for certain insurers.

Second, the impact of compliance resources differs depending on the type and size of the insurer. Smaller insurers may not be able to compete with larger competitors in attracting suitable board member candidates as the costs may be too high.[75] Hence, a uniform approach may be more advantageous for larger insurers if the compliance costs are too high. Over-regulation may increase compliance costs and might lead to some insurers setting up businesses in other countries. This could damage Singapore's competitive advantage in terms of being a global insurance hub. In contrast, under-regulation may cause ineffective corporate governance. Regulators need to carefully balance the costs and benefits to make the most optimal requirement.

Singapore, as an international financial centre, faces challenges in implementing corporate governance standards to insurers. First, the retail and wholesale markets in Singapore are distinct. Some insurers serve local customers, regardless of whether they are individuals or businesses. However, many insurers, reinsurers or brokers conduct, negotiate and offer risk protection at a wholesale level. The management and regulatory compliance of local insurers thus directly affect domestic customers. Imposing higher standards on insurers serving retail customers may therefore be preferable.

In contrast, there should be less need to overly regulate insurers in the wholesale market. As they do not deal directly with retail customers, there are fewer prudential

[75] Chen (2019), pp. 358–359.

and consumer protection concerns. In the small world of reinsurance, the market may be able to deal with specific concerns (e.g. agency problems) without more intrusive regulations. A more flexible approach in the wholesale market may also help Singapore become an insurance risk trading centre without creating unnecessary regulatory burdens.

Moreover, some insurers are registered as local companies while others are registered abroad. Locally registered insurers may be purely local firms (e.g. MS First Capital Insurance) or part of a local financial group (e.g. Great Eastern Life Assurance as part of the OCBC Group, or UOB Overseas Insurance as part of the UOB group). Others may be local wholly owned subsidiaries of a foreign insurer (e.g. Chubb Insurance Singapore or MSIG Insurance (Singapore)). However, some foreign insurers prefer to set up branches (Allianz Global Corporate & Speciality SE, Singapore Branch, or Aetna Insurance Company Ltd, Singapore Branch) rather than create subsidiaries to conduct business in the city-state.

From the perspective corporate governance, being a local firm or a branch can make a huge difference. Regardless of the ultimate owner, a locally registered company must follow Singapore's company law and MAS regulations in terms of corporate governance. A locally incorporated company must be governed by a separate board, although many insurers (particularly wholly owned subsidiaries of foreign insurers) may choose not to make public information about the board and senior management. In contrast, if the commercial presence of a foreign insurer is through a branch, the insurer remains a foreign-incorporated company and there is no need to have a separate board of directors for the Singapore business. In addition, the power of the MAS to enforce rules against the board of a foreign company is more limited as the MAS in principle cannot exercise its regulatory power in another country. Thus, enforcing corporate governance standards on foreign firms with branches in Singapore will be more challenging.

Last, Singapore is also home to many captive insurers. These are insurance companies set up by another company or industry group to underwrite the risk of the owner or the group. They are typically set up in offshore tax havens, but Singapore is one of the largest centres of captive insurers in Asia. Various exemptions are provided in Singapore law to attract them. For example, captive insurers are not subject to the same capital requirements as other direct insurers provided they meet the minimum paid-up capital requirement.[76] The fund solvency requirement is also more relaxed.[77] The MAS exempts captive insurers from some reporting requirements, although this measure reduces transparency in the captive sector. Nevertheless, the nature of captive insurers means that there are limitations on their ability to underwrite non-in-house risk.[78]

[76] Insurance (General Provisions and Exemptions for Captive Insurers) Regulations 2018 reg 3.

[77] Insurance (General Provisions and Exemptions for Captive Insurers) Regulations 2018 reg 4 and 5.

[78] MAS, Captive Insurance – Writing of In-House and Non In-House Risks (Notice 121), para 7.

Captive insurers typically underwrite risks only from the same industry group, so there may be a lower demand for regulatory compliance. If a captive insurer is wholly owned by its parent company, there is less concern over agency costs. Thus, captive insurers may not need to be subject to the same corporate governance requirements as other direct insurers or re-insurers.

The current state of Singapore's corporate governance regime can thus be considered in light of the challenges faced from the diversity of insurers.[79] As discussed in Sect. 2.3, this regime is in general a uniform approach consisting of minimum requirements. The minimum requirements are largely in line with the common requirement for listed companies in the stock market. Hence, the minimum corporate governance requirements should not cause too much over-burden on insurers if the requirements are also commonly complied with by firms in the capital market.

However, the MAS also made some adjustments for some degrees of differential treatment. The application of corporate governance rules by the MAS differ according to the size of the business. A larger insurer (presumably serving more customers) is subject to a higher standard, and smaller insurers receive more leniency. If a larger insurer is majority owned by another insurer, the threshold for board independence is also lowered to one third (rather than half the board).[80] In addition, insurers that are subsidiaries of other insurers may also be exempt from the requirement to have particular committees at the board level.

A further question is whether Singapore's approach effectively allays concerns from having a uniform approach with some degrees of differential treatment. From the agency cost perspective, granting exemptions for insurers that are wholly subsidiaries should have addressed some concerns discussed above. Most insurers registered with the MAS are within the Tier 2 category and thus are subject to lower corporate governance requirements.

However, size may not be a suitable benchmark if viewed from the perspective of regulatory compliance. Imposing higher requirements for larger insurers (i.e. Tier 1 insurers) is understandable, as any lapse in compliance is likely to affect a larger number of customers. However, the argument that smaller insurers should enjoy lower regulatory compliance is not convincing. After all, any lapse in compliance or occurrence of corporate scandals still hurt retail customers and a small insurer's shareholders.

The MAS regulations currently require a Tier 1 insurer to ensure that at least half the board are independent directors, but the threshold drops to one third for Tier 2 (i.e. smaller) insurers. The one-third threshold is the same as the minimum requirement for other listed companies, as prescribed by the Code of Corporate Governance.[81]

---

[79] See above Sect. 2.3.

[80] See Sect. 2.3 above.

[81] MAS, Code of Corporate Governance, Provision 2.1; and SGX Listing Rule 210(5)(c) (effective from 1 January 2022).

Thus, the lower threshold of board independence for Tier 2 insurers is arguably compatible with the general corporate governance standards for non-financial firms, and therefore lowing corporate governance standards for smaller insurers should not cause a concern, even if a smaller insurer is a public company that has many shareholders under the current corporate governance framework in Singapore.

However, the general Code of Corporate Governance requires a firm to have at least half of the board as independent directors under some circumstances (e.g. when the chairman and chief executive are the same person).[82] This requirement is also stated in the *Guidelines on Corporate Governance for Financial Holding Companies, Banks, Direct Insurers, Reinsurer and Captive Insurers which are Incorporated in Singapore*,[83] but not in the ICGR, which was issued in the same year. The guidelines have not been updated in the Code of Corporate Governance for listed companies, which was revised in 2018. In addition, the guidelines only apply to insurers incorporated in Singapore, and do not apply to branches of a foreign insurer. Thus, there may be gaps in terms of board independence requirements.

In addition, it is not clear why a large insurer that is a subsidiary of a bank or another insurer may be exempted from having some board-level committees. Compliance costs may be saved if the function of the committees (e.g. nomination) is accomplished by the parent company's board of directors. If the insurer is large, arguably it should still be subject to the full set of corporate governance requirements, even if it is a wholly owned subsidiary of another bank or insurer, to ensure better regulatory compliance for prudential or business conduct reasons. The MAS could consider this in future.

3.3 *Effectiveness of Corporate Governance Regimes in Regulatory Compliance*

The board of directors is the ultimate decision-maker for major corporate decisions and supervises the senior management team, but it also takes responsibility for numerous regulatory compliance issues, ranging from prudent regulations and risk management to the conduct of business and AML/CFT.[84] The effectiveness of corporate governance requirements in Singapore in terms of compliance with insurance regulations should thus be investigated. General issues are raised in this section, which may apply not only to the Singapore market, but also to those of other countries.

Current corporate governance regimes in Singapore could be open to some general criticism in terms of regulatory compliance. One general question is whether board independence regime is sufficient to support and improve the quality of

[82] MAS, Code of Corporate Governance, Provision 2.2.

[83] MAS, Guidelines on Corporate Governance (2013), p. 7.

[84] See Sect. 2.3 above.

regulatory compliance by an insurer. The concept of board independence and some other commonly seen corporate governance regimes (such as audit and remuneration committees) are closely linked to address the agency problem and corporate scandals (such as accounting frauds). Having more outsiders on the board may provide more diverse views, and an outsider may also be more willing to speak up and less likely to collude with the management. Therefore, the regime could improve the monitoring of the management and reduce agency costs.

However, whether corporate governance regimes based on the concept of board independence is much less explored. One study of banks in Tunisia also shows that board independence plays an important roles in enhancing credit quality of loans.[85] Another research shows that financial performance of banks were better during the financial crisis for financial institutions with more independent directors on audit and risk committees.[86] Therefore, there are evidence suggesting that having some independent directors on the board should also improve the board's monitoring function and thus help to achieve better regulatory compliance.

In addition, the ability of the board to monitor and ensure the quality of regulatory compliance is also supported by other regulatory requirements. For example, under Singapore law, the appointment of a director on the board and some key persons (including substantial shareholders, chief executive officer, or actuaries) might require prior regulatory approval.[87] In addition, directors and key persons of an insurer need to satisfy the 'fit and proper' criteria.[88] In other words, directors (no matter they are independent or not) need to possess the quality of 'honesty, integrity, and reputation', 'competence and capability', and 'financial soundness'.[89] In particular, the competence and capability requirements, combined with prior regulatory approval process, could ensure that the board and top management of an insurer should possess sufficient knowledge, experience and expertise to complete their function of supervising internal control system and ensuring compliance with regulations.

However, there are also counter arguments. First, whether the board can be effective in supervising the internal control system and various regulatory compliance functions partly depends on the information the board (and particularly independent directors) can acquire. Ideally, the board and individual directors should be able to acquire the information they need to make a judgment. However, it does not necessarily mean that information must be provided to the board without being requested. Thus, proper information flow is essential to the success of corporate

[85] Moussa (2019), p. 640.

[86] Yeh et al. (2011), p. 437.

[87] See Sect. 2.3 above.

[88] See Sect. 2.3 above.

[89] Fit and Proper Criteria, para 8.

governance regimes.[90] For example, directors could actively review and examine the role of compliance officer and front-desk supervisors based on their own initiative to ensure that salespersons would behave properly when promoting an insurance product to a client. Naturally, the board should be able to request information on sales practice generally or regarding an individual case to consider whether the existing regime is sufficient to meet regulatory requirements. However, when a misselling incident occurs, the board is only made aware of the incident when they are informed. Hence, there could be an information gap between what the board actually knows and what happens in practice. Such gap could undermine the board of directors to exercise their function effectively.

Second, to fully accomplish the regulatory compliance requirements imposed on the board, directors (independent or otherwise) must possess sufficient expertise not only in terms of insurance-specific issues but also in a broad range of topics such as risk management,[91] sales practices, anti-money laundering and even IT outsourcing.[92] Hence, knowledge and understanding of financial models is essential.[93] A board also has the responsibility to ensure that senior management have the appropriate skills to manage the risks posed by internal models and that the company has clear and comprehensive policies regarding the use of such models.[94] One survey in the US conducted a decade ago shows that most directors of public companies at the time were doubtful on the company's ability to monitor a risk management plan.[95] Thus, there could be real concerns over the board's ability and capacity in supervising the internal control and compliance systems in a specialised business like insurance.

From this perspective, board independence alone cannot address the ability of the board to handle a wide range of compliance matters. Independence may mean that directors are less likely to collude with management in terms of internal control and compliance, but board members with diverse backgrounds can also be beneficial (e.g. finance, law, accounting, etc.). One study in South Africa finds that higher board independence is actually detrimental to efficiency of life insurers in the country.[96] However, whether the same finding could be replicated in Singapore or other countries is subject to further studies.

---

[90] *G20/OECD Principles of Corporate Governance* (2015), http://www.oecd-ilibrary.org/governance/g20-oecd-principles-of-corporate-governance-2015_9789264236882-en (last accessed 24 July 2020), pp. 5–6.

[91] For example, MAS, Enterprise Risk Management ('ERM') for Insurers (Notice 126), para 56.

[92] MAS, Technology Risk Management Guidelines, para 5.1.1.

[93] MAS, Guidelines on Use of Internal Models for Liability and Capital Requirements for Life Insurance Products Containing Investment Guarantees with Non-Linear Payouts (ID 01/13), para 3.1.

[94] MAS, Guidelines on Use of Internal Models for Liability and Capital Requirements for Life Insurance Products Containing Investment Guarantees with Non-Linear Payouts (ID 01/13), para 3.1.2 and 3.1.3, and 3.2 *et seq*.

[95] Bamberger (2020), p. 711.

[96] Alhassan and Boakye (2020), p. 217.

However, in Singapore the focus of the corporate governance requirement is on board independence. While this may satisfy the need to contain agency costs, there is no clear effort to ensure that the board has sufficient expertise in terms of regulatory compliance. Although directors must be 'fit and proper' and have proper competence and capacity, it does not necessarily warrant that appointed directors must possess sufficient knowledge or experiences review and supervise a wide range of regulatory compliance issues especially when specific knowledge (e.g. risk management for investment) is required.

Moreover, to measure 'competence and capacity' of a director or chief executive officer, the MAS in Singapore relies on general benchmarks such as 'past performance or expertise' or 'satisfactory educational qualification or experience, relevant skills and knowledge'.[97] Nevertheless, the looping question is what the necessary knowledge and experienced required for a wide range of compliance issues and how to keep a balanced composition of the board to strengthen its ability to oversee an insurer's regulatory compliance. In theory, a nomination committee could select suitable candidates based on the professional knowledge of the committee members, but whether this is always true in practice should be investigated further.

Third, an over-reliance on independent directors may cause other issues. They may become overloaded, thus increasing their legal risk and reducing the possibility of hiring good candidates in the future. As Sect. 3.1 shows, insurers that are public companies in Singapore appear to have larger boards and more independent directors, while those that are wholly owned subsidiaries of another insurance or banking group tend to have smaller boards and fewer (often only two or three) independent directors. These few independent directors will then carry the full responsibility of overseeing regulatory compliance and internal processes, in addition to other corporate governance functions (e.g. reviewing related party transactions). This likelihood should be considered further by regulators in the current corporate governance requirements.

4 Conclusion

Singapore presents a challenge to setting appropriate corporate governance standards for insurers. The market consists of multiple layers of direct insurers and reinsurers with various ownership structures and business focuses. In this chapter, it is argued that Singapore could improve transparency, notably for direct insurers and in terms of agency costs and regulatory compliance. The general approach adopted in Singapore is a uniform approach with minimum requirements and some different treatments. Large insurers are subject to a higher standard while smaller ones enjoy lower requirements. Given that the regulatory standards are minimum requirements and are compatible with the general corporate governance requirements for

[97] Fit and Proper Criteria, para 14.

companies in the stock market, having a lower standard for smaller insurers and large insurers that are majority owned by another insurer is acceptable, as agency costs are not necessarily increased. However, regulators should also rethink and evaluate the reliance on board independence and having a more balanced composition of directors to ensure regulatory compliance and internal governance functions in addition to existing corporate governance and 'fit and proper' requirements. Regulators could rather seek to improve board diversity (in terms of expertise), the role of nomination committee and selection process of board members, and internal information flow, to help the board to make proper decisions regarding compliance of insurance regulations.

References

Alhassan AL, Boakye M-AA (2020) Board characteristics and life insurance efficiency in South Africa. Pac Account Rev 32(2):217–237

Bamberger KA (2020) Technologies of compliance: risk and regulation in a digital age. Texas Law Rev 88(4):669–739. https://web-b-ebscohost-com.libproxy.smu.edu.sg/ehost/detail/detail?vid=0&sid=3fa13b4c-a4c4-4df4-bc73-d398854a4e72%40pdc-v-sessmgr05&bdata=JnNpdGU9ZWhvc3QtbGl2ZSZzY29wZT1zaXRl#AN=48969651&db=bsu

Berle Jr AA, Means GC (1932) The modern corporation and private property

Chen C (2016) Solving the puzzle of corporate governance of state-owned enterprises: the path of the Temasek model in Singapore and lessons for China. Northwest J Int Law Bus 36 (2):303–370

Chen C (2019) A one-size-fits-all approach to corporate governance codes and compliance by smaller listed firms: an examination of companies listed in Hong Kong and Singapore. Berkeley Bus Law J 15(2):337–364

Chen C, Wan WY, Zhang W (2018) Board independence as a Panacea to tunneling? An empirical study of related party transactions in Hong Kong and Singapore. J Empir Leg Stud 15 (4):987–1020

Dill A (2019) The role of corporate governance in macro-prudential regulation of systemic risk. In: Bank regulation, risk management, and compliance: theory, practice, and key problem areas. Routledge, pp 159–192

Enriques L, Hertig G, Kanda H (2009) Related party transactions. In: The anatomy of corporate law – a comparative and functional approach, 2nd edn. Oxford University Press, Oxford, pp 153–182

Jensen MC, Meckling WH (1976) Theory of the firm: managerial behavior, agency costs and ownership structure. J Financ Econ 3(4):305–360

Johnson S, La Porta R, Lopez de Silanes F, Shleifer A (2000) Tunneling. Am Econ Rev 90 (2):22–27. http://www.nber.org/papers/W7523.pdf%5Cnpapers3://publication/uuid/666B592F-7513-4BF5-914F-109E82074A9C

Kowalewski O (2012) Corporate governance and pension fund performance. Contemp Econ 6 (1):14–97

Li H, Zhang H, Tsai S-B, Qiu A (2017) China's insurance regulatory reform, corporate governance behavior and insurers' governance effectiveness. Int J Environ Res Public Health 14(10):1238

Moussa FB (2019) The influence of internal corporate governance on bank credit risk: an empirical analysis for Tunisia. Article Glob Bus Rev 20:640

Yeh Y-H, Chung H, Liu C-L (2011) Committee independence and financial institution performance during the 2007-08 credit crunch: evidence from a multi-country study. Corp Gov: Int Rev 19 (5):437–458

Statutes and Regulations in Singapore

Insurance Act (Cap 142)
Insurance (Actuaries) Regulations
Insurance (Approved Marine, Aviation and Transit Insurers) Regulations
Insurance (Authorised Reinsurers) Regulations
Insurance (Corporate Governance) Regulations 2013
Insurance (General Provisions and Exemptions for Captive Insurers) Regulations 2018
Financial Advisers Regulations
MAS, Appointment of Director, Chairman and Key Executive Person
MAS, Captive Insurance – Writing of In-House and Non In-House Risks (Notice 121)
MAS, Code of Corporate Governance
MAS, Enterprise Risk Management ("ERM") for Insurers (Notice 126)
MAS, Guidance on Insurers' Own Risk and Solvency Assessments
MAS, Guidelines on Corporate Governance
MAS, Guidelines on Fit and Proper Criteria (FSG-G01)
MAS, Guidelines on Outsourcing
MAS, Guidelines on Risk Management Practices – Internal Controls
MAS, Guidelines on Risk Management Practices – Market Risk
MAS, Guidelines on Risk Management Practices for Insurance Business
MAS, Guidelines on Standards of Conduct for Marketing and Distribution Activities
MAS, Guidelines on Use of Internal Models for Liability and Capital Requirements for Life Insurance Products Containing Investment Guarantees with Non-Linear Payouts (ID 01/13)
MAS, Guidelines to MAS Notice 314 on Prevention of Money Laundering and Countering the Financing of Terrorism
MAS, Insurance Business – Insurance Fraud Risk
MAS, Notice on Investment of Insurers (Notice 125)
MAS, Notice on Valuation and Capital Framework for Insurers (Notice 133)
MAS, Public Disclosure Requirements (Notice 124)
MAS, Reinsurance Management (Notice 114)
MAS, Technology Risk Management Guidelines

Part II
Insurance Business and Corporate Law

Recovery and Resolution of Insurance Companies and Director's Duties

Michele Siri and Arthur Van den Hurk

Abstract In this chapter, largely finalised before the presentation of a legislative proposal for a European Insurance Recovery and Resolution Directive, on September 2021, recovery and resolution frameworks of insurance companies and insurance groups are discussed. Currently, the insurance regulatory framework at the European level (Solvency II) does not contain a fully developed framework with respect to recovery and (orderly) resolution such as the Bank Recovery & Resolution Directive and the Single Resolution Mechanism. Recent developments at the international level on the initiative of the Financial Stability Board and International Association of Insurance Supervisors are discussed. It is the expectation that the Solvency II 2020 review will introduce minimum harmonising regulatory standards at the European level with respect to the recovery and resolution of insurers. In this chapter, the assumption is made that the legislative proposal of the European Commission will be based on the technical advice, provided by EIOPA in the context of the Solvency II 2020 review. Therefore, this chapter discusses this technical advice in some detail. Recovery and resolution frameworks, particularly ex-ante planning, requires insurance companies and insurance groups to expand their focus from the regular going concern focus to adverse circumstances, including the ability to recover and to be resolved in orderly manner. The chapter assesses the consequences this change of focus might have on the governance of insurance companies and groups.

M. Siri (✉)
Jean Monnet Professor of European Union Financial and Insurance Markets Regulation, Department of Law, University of Genoa, Genoa, Italy
e-mail: michele.siri@unige.it

A. Van den Hurk (✉)
Financial Law Centre, Radboud University, Nijmegen, The Netherlands

Aegon, The Hague, The Netherlands
e-mail: arthur.vandenhurk@jur.ru.nl

P. Marano, K. Noussia (eds.), *The Governance of Insurance Undertakings*, AIDA Europe Research Series on Insurance Law and Regulation 6,
https://doi.org/10.1007/978-3-030-85817-9_7

1 Introduction

The governance of insurance companies and insurance groups is significantly more regulated and subject to supervisory scrutiny than the governance of companies outside the financial sector. Insurance regulatory frameworks, such as in the European Solvency II framework, include extensive requirements with respect to the system of governance. In the Solvency II framework these requirements form part of Pillar 2, within the 3 Pillar design of the Solvency II framework.[1] These requirements are, to a large extent, based on the assumption that insurance companies and insurance groups are operating and continue to operate on a going concern basis. Insurance supervision (going concern) has a similar key focus.

In particular, since the financial crisis of 2008–2009, supervision of the financial sector has increasingly focused on more adverse circumstances that financial undertakings, including insurance companies, could be faced with, such as a (threatening) breach of solvency requirements and the ability of insurance companies to recover from such as breach or threatening breach.

Furthermore, increasing attention is also paid to circumstances in which financial institutions, such as banks, central counterparties, as well as insurance companies, despite efforts to turn the situation around, are unable to recover by themselves, fail and consequently should be either liquidated in bankruptcy or resolved in an alternative manner. Although regulation and supervision aim to prevent the failure of financial institutions, these mechanisms are not equipped nor designed to prevent failures of financial institutions altogether.[2] Clearly, additional prudence increases costs and makes financial products such as insurance products more expensive.[3]

In both liquidation and resolution, supervisory authorities, dedicated resolution authorities, as well as trustees in bankruptcy, aim to ensure that losses to creditors, in particular the clients of financial institutions, such as insurance policyholders and beneficiaries, are limited to the minimum. Resolution should provide for an alternative to liquidation in bankruptcy, mainly to provide a better outcome than liquidation in bankruptcy would provide.

[1] Pillar 1 consists of the quantitative requirements, such as valuation, the calculation of technical provisions, investments, capital requirements and own fund requirements, Pillar 2 consists of the system of governance, risk management and internal controls, qualitative aspects of the prudent person principle, outsourcing and remuneration, the own risk and solvency assessment (ORSA) and supervisory review process (SRP) and Pillar 3 consists of regulatory reporting and public disclosure requirements.

[2] Solvency II (the Solvency Capital Requirement or SCR) is calibrated to 99.5% of the value at risk (VaR) over a one-year time horizon, the chance of a failure of 0.5% on that time horizon. Solvency II is therefore not a zero-failure regime.

[3] See also van Hulle (2019), pp. 236–237. The author is critical of the fact that some supervisors still carry on supervision with the objective or preventing all insurance failures by requiring a solvency ratio that is well above 100% of the SCR ratio, which is not necessarily in the interest of policyholders and beneficiaries, because it makes insurance more expensive.

Resolution regimes intend to provide an additional layer of protection to policyholders and beneficiaries, in addition to the protection that is already offered by 'regular' (primarily 'going concern') insurance regulation and supervision. While recovery frameworks aim to improve the chances of insurance companies to continue operating on a going concern basis, and can be considered part of regular supervision, resolution measures aim to reduce losses, once an insurance company has failed or is likely to fail. Recovery and resolution requirements are closely linked, and are therefore often part of a single regulatory package.

The development of a recovery and resolution regime can be characterised as the addition of a 4th pillar to the Three-Pillar structure, a pillar focused on recovery and resolution, including ensuring preparedness for such eventualities through ex-ante planning of recovery and resolution measures. The need to further develop crisis prevention and resolution mechanisms for insurers, comparable to those that have been in place at the European level for several years for banks and certain investment firms, became even more apparent last year, against the backdrop of the COVID-19 pandemic. This global event has made the need for reform of the insurance regulatory framework increasingly clear.[4] The crisis has led to greater supervisory scrutiny of corporate recovery and liquidation plans, with a particular focus on clear decision-making processes, early warning indicators, credible management actions to address financial difficulties and robust stress scenarios that test the recovery indicators and management actions identified by the insurer.

Both recovery and resolution measures can have a significant impact on the governance of insurance companies and insurance groups. This is most clear when insurance companies or insurance groups actually fail and management and oversight of the company are taken over by resolution authorities or by a trustee in bankruptcy, but measures can also impact the governance of the company at an earlier stage, when the company is still solvent and is operating on a going concern basis. As part of ex-ante recovery and resolution planning, companies might be forced by supervisory authorities or resolution authorities to take decisions that impact or even interfere with and be considered sub-optimal to the day-to-day management and corporate structure of the insurance company or insurance group.[5] Some arrangements (such as pooling of critical services in a group) may make perfect sense in a going concern situation, but because such services might need to be disentangled in a resolution scenario, could provide an additional challenge for a resolution authority.[6]

---

[4]EIOPA, *Background document on the opinion on the opinion on the 2020 review of Solvency II - Impact assessment*, EIOPA-BoS-20/751, 17 December 2020.

[5]For example, instructions by resolution authorities to remove material impediments that could prevent the orderly resolution of the company.

[6]Clearly, this requires a proportionate approach and balancing between a sustainable and efficient operating model in going concern, while limiting potential material impediments to orderly resolution.

2 State of Play in Insurance

Currently, the European insurance regulatory framework only provides for limited requirements with respect to recovery and does not include requirements for the resolution of insurance and reinsurance companies. In other words, in contrast to European banks and investment firms, European insurance regulation currently does not provide for an equivalent to the European Bank Recovery & Resolution Directive (BRRD) and/or the Single Resolution Mechanism (SRM). As part of the Solvency II 2020 review, this is expected to change. Together with the formal proposal of the European Commission for amendments to the Solvency II framework, which was published on September 22, 2021, a separate legislative proposal was published to introduce a recovery and resolution framework for insurers and reinsurers, on a minimum harmonisation basis, a proposal for a European Insurance Recovery & Resolution Directive, which we will refer to in this chapter as the IRRD-proposal. In fact, this is one of the most important material changes in the 2020 review of Solvency II.[7]

At the same time, several European countries have already introduced recovery and resolution regimes for insurance and reinsurance companies at the Member State level. Based on information from an EIOPA survey, conducted in the first quarter of 2016, three EU Member States (The Netherlands, France and Romania) had recently reinforced their national recovery and resolution frameworks. Similarly, the European landscape with respect to resolution funding and insurance guarantee schemes is based on national laws and consequently diverse.

3 International and European Context

At the international level, work on recovery and resolution of insurers and reinsurers is being undertaken by both the Financial Stability Board (FSB) and, as referred to above, by the International Association of Insurance Supervisors (IAIS).

[7]ECB, *The new EU framework for financial crisis management and resolution*, July 2011 and EIOPA, *Background document on the opinion on the 2020 review of Solvency II – analysis*, EIOPA-BoS-20/750, 17 December 2020. A legislative proposal for a European Insurance Recovery and Resolution Directive was published in September 2022 after the finalisation of this chapter. See European Commission, Proposal for a Directive of the European Parliament and of the Council establishing a framework for the recovery and resolution of insurance and reinsurance undertakings and amending Directives 2002/47/EC, 2004/25/EC, 2009/138/EC, (EU) 2017/1132 and Regulations (EU) No 1094/2010 and (EU) No 648/2012, COM/2021/582 final.

3.1 Financial Stability Board

In 2011, the FSB adopted the so-called FSB Key Attributes of Effective Resolution Regimes for Financial Institutions, which were adopted by the G20 in October 2011 at their Cannes meeting as the international standard for resolution regimes.[8] The 2011 FSB Key Attributes were supplemented in 2014 with additional guidance for specific types of financial institutions, including insurers. Annex II of the updated FSB Key Attributes[9] provides guidance on the implementation of the Key Attributes in relation to resolution regimes for insurers. It supplements the Key Attributes by indicating how particular KAs, or elements of particular KAs, should be interpreted when applied to resolution regimes for insurers. According to the FSB, while the general assumption is that traditional insurance activities and even some non-traditional insurance activities that are no longer viable will typically be resolved through run-off and portfolio transfer procedures, it may not be possible, however, to rely on these tools in all circumstances, and particularly in those cases in which the business model is complex or there is no corresponding market for portfolio transfers.[10] The objective of an effective resolution regime is to make the resolution of financial institutions feasible without severe systemic disruption and without exposing taxpayers to losses, while protecting vital economic functions through mechanisms which make it possible for shareholders and unsecured and uninsured creditors to absorb losses in a manner that respects the hierarchy of claims in liquidation.[11] Specifically for insurers, the protection of policyholders and beneficiaries is identified as an objective of a resolution regime.

3.2 International Association of Insurance Supervisors

The International Association of Insurance Supervisors (IAIS) is the international standard-setting body responsible for developing and assisting in the implementation of supervisory and supporting material for insurance supervision. As part of its

[8] It should be noted that the FSB Key Attributes state that any financial institution *that could be systemically significant or critical* if it fails should be subject to a resolution regime consistent with the Key Attributes. Therefore, it does not explicitly set expectations with respect to resolution regimes that are more generally applicable.

[9] Financial Stability Board, Key Attributes of Effective Resolution Regimes for Financial Institutions, 15 October 2014, https://www.fsb.org/wp-content/uploads/r_141015.pdf.

[10] Financial Stability Board, Key Attributes of Effective Resolution Regimes for Financial Institutions, 15 October 2014, https://www.fsb.org/wp-content/uploads/r_141015.pdf, p. 75. However, it should be noted that a run-off or a portfolio transfer is likely to be, in many cases, to be an appropriate resolution tool (either a solvent or insolvent run-off, or supplemented by other resolution tools (such as e.g. the transfer of an insurance portfolio to a bridge institution, restructuring of liabilities in resolution and/or suspension of policyholders' surrender rights).

[11] Financial Stability Board, Key Attributes of Effective Resolution Regimes for Financial Institutions, 15 October 2014, https://www.fsb.org/wp-content/uploads/r_141015.pdf, preamble, p. 3.

mission, it has issued the Insurance Core Principles (ICPs) as a globally accepted framework for insurance supervision. The ICPs seek to encourage the maintenance of consistently high supervisory standards in IAIS member jurisdictions. The latest updated version of the ICPs dates as of November 2019. The document also includes the Common Framework for the Supervision of Internationally Active Insurance Groups, adopted as per the same date.

IAIS has developed various principles that relate to both recovery and resolution. In particular, Insurance Core Principle (ICP) 12 (Exit from the Market and Resolution), ICP 25 (Supervisory Cooperation and Coordination) can be mentioned in relation to resolution, as well as the related ComFrame standards and guidance.[12] In terms of recovery planning, reference can be made to ICP 16 (Enterprise Risk Management for Solvency Purposes), ICP 23 (Group Wide Supervisor) and ICP 25, mentioned above, as well as the related ComFrame materials for IAIGs. The IAIS has also developed an Application Paper on recovery planning[13] and is in the process of developing an application paper on resolution powers and resolution planning.[14]

ICP 12 covers both the voluntary exit of insurers from the market and the resolution of insurers that are no longer viable or are likely to be no longer viable, and have no reasonable prospect of returning to viability. Contrary to the IAIS Glossary, 'Resolution' in the meaning of ICP 12 also includes 'liquidation.' We will not discuss the content of ICP 12 separately, as the content of ICP 12 is largely reflected in the EIOPA Opinion on the 2020 review of Solvency II that will be discussed later. Where appropriate, we will refer to the ICPs in that context.

ICP 16 (Enterprise Risk Management for Solvency Purposes) is also relevant in the context of recovery and resolution, given the links between enterprise risk management, the ORSA and recovery and resolution planning, and the specific reference in 16.15 to recovery planning in a group context. Lastly, ICP 23 (The Group-wide Supervisor) and ICP 25 (Supervisory Cooperation and Coordination) are also relevant in this context, due to the role of the group-wide supervisor particularly in recovery.

In addition to the relevant Insurance Core Principles, the IAIS has also developed an application paper on recovery planning,[15] and is in the process of developing an Application Paper on Resolution Powers and Planning.[16]

[12]ComFrame is the IAIS Common Framework for Internationally Active Insurance Groups (IAIGs), which provides standards and guidance in addition to the ICPs that apply to all insurance companies and groups, specifically for IAIGs. The latest version of the ICPs as well as the ComFrame material was adopted by the IAIS in its Annual General Meeting in November 2019.

[13]IAIS Application Paper on recovery planning, November 18, 2019, https://www.iaisweb.org/page/supervisory-material/application-papers//file/87519/application-paper-on-recovery-planning.

[14]IAIS, Draft Application Paper on Resolution Powers and Planning, November 9, 2020, https://www.iaisweb.org/page/consultations/closed-consultations/2021/application-paper-on-resolution-powers-and-planning.

[15]IAIS, Application Paper on Recovery Planning, November 18, 2019, https://www.iaisweb.org/page/supervisory-material/application-papers//file/87519/application-paper-on-recovery-planning.

[16]IAIS, Public consultation on draft Application Paper on Resolution Powers and Planning. A public consultation on this draft paper was held between November 9, 2020 and February 5, 2021,

According to the IAIS Glossary, 'resolution' means the following: Actions taken by a resolution authority towards an insurer that is no longer viable, or is likely to be no longer viable, and has no reasonable prospect of returning to viability.[17] The alternative to resolution for a failing insurance entity is typically 'liquidation': A process to terminate operations and corporate existence of the entity through which the remaining assets of the insurer will be distributed to its creditors and shareholders according to the liquidation claims hierarchy. Branches can also be put into liquidation, separately from the insurance legal entity they belong to.[18]

Furthermore, for completeness sake, it is also useful to mention the definitions of 'recovery plan': 'A plan developed by an insurer that identifies in advance options to restore its financial condition and viability under severe stress' and 'resolution plan': 'A plan that identifies in advance options for resolving all or part(s) of an insurer to maximise the likelihood of an orderly resolution, the development of which is led by the supervisor and/or resolution authority in consultation with the insurer in advance of any circumstances warranting resolution.'

Lastly, while the IAIS does not provide for a definition of insurance guarantee scheme or policyholder protection scheme (PPS), the latter term is referred to in the IAIS Insurance Core Principles and discussed in more detail in an IAIS issues paper.[19] A PPS intends to provide a minimum layer of protection to policyholders in the event that the safeguards within the supervisory regime are not sufficient, i.e. beyond the safeguards that the Solvency II regime provides.

PPSs are designed to protect policyholders and beneficiaries in the case of the insolvency of an insurer, serving as backstops against claims. Whilst PPSs' objectives focus on providing a minimum level of protection to policyholders, where the design of the PPS includes such functions, they can also contribute to the objectives of resolution regimes by: (i) facilitating the continuation of insurance; (ii) providing financial support to an insolvent insurer and/or an entity which intends to purchase an insolvent insurer or to which insurance policies will be transferred from an insolvent insurer; (iii) aiding in portfolio transfers; (iv) working as a bridge institution where no immediate purchaser of an insolvent insurer can be found.[20] Therefore, PPSs can play a relevant role in both the resolution and in the liquidation of insurers.

Arguably, the design and in particular the harmonisation of recovery and resolution frameworks, resolution funding and insurance guarantee schemes across the European Union is even more complex as it is or has been for banks. At the same

https://www.iaisweb.org/page/consultations/closed-consultations/2021/application-paper-on-resolution-powers-and-planning.

[17] IAIS Glossary.

[18] IAIS Glossary.

[19] IAIS, Issues Paper on policyholder protection schemes, October 2013, https://www.iaisweb.org/page/supervisory-material/issues-papers//file/34547/issues-paper-on-policyholder-protection-schemes.

[20] IAIS, Issues Paper on policyholder protection schemes, pp. 4–5.

time, the urgency and need for harmonisation may be perceived differently for the insurance sector than for banks. The dynamics of the failure and/or the resolution of an insurer is different from bank failures and resolution and many jurisdictions appear to have dealt with insurance failures or near-failures in many cases, even without a dedicated recovery and resolution regime.

It should be mentioned that, while currently only a few Member States have a specific recovery and resolution regime for insurers in place, many—if not all—Member States have dealt with failures or near-failures of insurance companies. Despite the absence of recovery and resolution frameworks, failures or near-failures do not appear to have led in all cases to significant detriment to policyholders/beneficiaries and the local insurance markets seem to have been able to absorb such failures in practice, with or without the presence of a PPS and/or resolution regime. At the same time, insurers' failures regularly involve insurers that operate on a cross-border basis, which creates additional challenges in regular supervision as well as in the case of failures of insurance companies and their liquidation or resolution.

At the international level, work on recovery and resolution of insurers and reinsurers is being undertaken by both the Financial Stability Board (FSB) and, as referred to above, by the International Association of Insurance Supervisors (IAIS).

3.3 European Context

Pursuant to, inter alia, Article 242(2) of the Solvency II Directive, the harmonisation of recovery and resolution and insurance guarantee schemes, at the European level, forms part of the Solvency II 2020 review. In that context, the European Commission has requested EIOPA for technical advice, to be provided to the European Commission by 30 June 2020.

Before this, on 5 July 2017, EIOPA had published an opinion to the institutions of the European Union on the harmonisation of recovery and resolution frameworks for (re)insurers across the Member States.[21] In this opinion, EIOPA argues that a minimum degree of harmonisation in the field of recovery and resolution of insurers would contribute to achieving policyholder protection, as well as maintaining financial stability in the EU.

EIOPA clarifies that 'minimum harmonisation' entails: 'the definition of a common approach to the fundamental elements of recovery and resolution (objectives for resolution and resolution powers) which national frameworks should address, while leaving room for Member States to adopt additional measures at national level, subject to these measures being compatible with the principles and objectives set at

[21] EIOPA Opinion to Institutions of the European Union on Harmonisation of recovery and resolution frameworks for (re) insurers across the Member States, EIOPA-BoS/17-148, 5 July 2017, https://eiopa.europa.eu/Publications/Opinions/EIOPA-BoS-17-148_Opinion_on_recovery_and_resolution_for_(re)insurers.pdf.

the EU level. These additional measures at the national level might be required in order to better address the specificities of the national markets'.[22]

On 30 July 2018, EIOPA published a discussion paper on resolution funding and national insurance guarantee schemes. EIOPA positions this discussion paper as a follow-up to the EIOPA Opinion on the harmonisation of recovery and resolution frameworks for (re)insurers across the Member States that EIOPA published in 2017. EIOPA considers resolution funding and IGSs as essential elements for the resolution of failing insurers. In the discussion paper, EIOPA distinguishes between resolution funding and insurance guarantee schemes. With respect to resolution funding EIOPA distinguishes between three sources of resolution funding: (i) the assets and liabilities of the failing insurers itself, (ii) national resolution funds and (iii) national IGSs or other policyholder protection schemes. EIOPA considers the primary function of IGSs to compensate policyholders for their losses in the event of insurance insolvency. At the same time, EIOPA recognises that some schemes have additional functions relating to the resolution framework. Some insurance guarantee schemes may also be used to fund resolution actions, such as the transfer of insurance policies to a third party or may function as a bridge institution. EIOPA has subsequently published a consultation paper on harmonisation of national insurance guarantee schemes on 9 July 2019,[23] in the context of the Solvency II 2020 review, building on its earlier work in this area,[24] and has recently dedicated a chapter of the EIOPA Opinion on the 2020 review of Solvency II on insurance guarantee schemes. In that opinion, EIOPA appears to have departed from the viewpoint that the primary function of an insurance guarantee scheme should be the compensation of policyholders and beneficiaries for their losses when an insurer becomes insolvent, and instead places the continuation of insurance policies on equal footing to compensation, given that they both meet the primary purpose to protect policyholders.[25]

In addition to the EIOPA work on recovery and resolution and on insurance guarantee schemes, EIOPA has published a series of three papers on systemic risk and macro-prudential policy in insurance in the period 2017–2018. In its first

---

[22] EIOPA Opinion to Institutions of the European Union on Harmonisation of recovery and resolution frameworks for (re) insurers across the Member States, EIOPA-BoS/17-148, 5 July 2017, p. 4, https://eiopa.europa.eu/Publications/Opinions/EIOPA-BoS-17-148_Opinion_on_recovery_and_resolution_for_(re)insurers.pdf.

[23] EIOPA, Consultation Paper on Proposals for Solvency II 2020 Review Harmonisation of National Insurance Guarantee Schemes, EIOPA-BoS-19-259, https://eiopa.europa.eu/Publications/Consultations/EIOPA-BoS-19-259_Consultation%20paper%20on%20Harmonisation%20of%20IGSs.pdf.

[24] EIOPA Discussion paper on resolution funding and national insurance guarantee schemes, EIOPA-CP-18-003, 9 July 2018, https://eiopa.europa.eu/Publications/Consultations/EIOPA-CP-18-003_Discussion_paper_on_resolution_funding%20and.pdf.

[25] EIOPA Opinion, paragraph 13.4.

paper,[26] EIOPA aims to identify and analyse the sources of systemic risk in insurance from a conceptual point of view, independent of the policy measures developed at the international level by the IAIS. The second paper[27] focuses on Solvency II tools with a macroprudential impact. While the Solvency II framework is designed to be a microprudential regime for the EU insurance sector, it contains elements as well that may have financial stability impact. In particular, reference is made in the paper to long-term guarantee measures[28] and measures on equity risk. In addition, while this is not a specific measure for the insurance sector, the measure that allows supervisory authorities to prohibit or restrict certain types of financial activities is considered in the paper. While these measures primarily serve their intended micro-prudential purpose[29]—according to EIOPA—they also contribute to limiting pro-cyclicality. Lastly, while not examined further in the paper, the prudent person principle, the own risk and solvency assessment and capital add-ons in specific circumstances are also mentioned. The third paper[30] explores potential new instruments and measures that could be included in a macroprudential framework, grouped in the following blocks: capital and reserving based tools, liquidity-based tools, exposure-based tools and pre-emptive planning. In the context of recovery and resolution, in particular pre-emptive planning (recovery and resolution planning), as well as capital surcharges,[31] and temporary freezes of redemption rights of policyholders are explored. Based on the work at international level, the EIOPA papers on systemic risk and macro-prudential policy, as well as the EIOPA Opinion on the 2020 Review of Solvency II, discussed in the subsequent paragraph, the European Commission has included several proposals to include macro-prudential tools in the formal proposal to amend the Solvency II Directive, which has been published on 22 September 2021.

3.4 EIOPA Opinion on the 2020 Review of Solvency II

On 17 December 2020, EIOPA has published its opinion on the 2020 review of Solvency II. The Solvency framework, which became applicable in EU Member States on 1 January 2016, provided that certain areas of the framework would need to

[26] EIOPA, Systemic risk and macroprudential policy in insurance, Publications office of the European Union, Luxembourg, 2017, also available on the EIOPA website.

[27] EIOPA, Solvency II tools with macroprudential impact, Publications office of the European Union, Luxembourg, 2018, also available on the EIOPA website.

[28] EIOPA, Solvency II tools with macroprudential impact, Publications office of the European Union, Luxembourg, 2018, also available on the EIOPA website.

[29] Ensuring sufficient loss absorbing capacity and reserving.

[30] EIOPA, Other potential macroprudential tools and measures to enhance the current framework, Publications office of the European Union, Luxembourg, 2017, also available on the EIOPA website.

[31] E.g. for systemic risk, such as higher loss-absorbing (HLA) capacity.

be reviewed by the European Commission at the latest by 1 January 2021. In that context, the European Commission has requested for EIOPA technical advice on the Solvency II 2020 review in February 2019 on nineteen main topics, including recovery and resolution, insurance guarantee schemes and on macro-prudential issues. With respect to these themes, the technical advice also builds on the earlier work of EIOPA, described above. The original deadline for the advice was the end of June 2020. However, the COVID-19 crisis has led to an extension of the response time to a holistic impact assessment that was undertaken by EIOPA in the context of the draft technical advice. Furthermore, to allow for an assessment of the COVID-19 crisis on the Solvency II review, the deadline for the technical advice was extended to the end of 2020. Evidently, the further development of a European framework on insurance recovery and resolution will depend on the European Commission's and co-legislators' willingness to consider the EIOPA advice. It is clear from the European Commission's proposals, published on 22 September 2021, that the European Commission, in line with the EIOPA advice, intends to proceed with a legislative proposal with respect to minimum harmonisation of insurance recovery and resolution. In addition, the European Commission has considered a minimum framework for Insurance Guarantee Schemes at the European level, but considers this not appropriate at this point in time, given the uncertainties created by the COVID-19 pandemic, and the need to focus on economic recovery. According to the European Commission, the introduction of such a framework could entail important implementation costs for insurers, in particular in member states that do not have such a scheme yet.

The EIOPA Opinion,[32] as well as the earlier papers of EIOPA on recovery and resolution have clearly taken the model that has been developed for the banking sector as a starting point: recovery and resolution planning requirements for banking and investment firms have evolved since the Bank Recovery and Resolution Directive (BRRD) and Single Resolution Mechanism Regulation (SRMR) came into effect in 2014. Subsequent guidance, technical standards and opinions issued by the European Banking Authority (EBA), European Central Bank (ECB), and European Commission have resulted in a mature regulatory landscape for Recovery Planning in particular. EIOPA and IAIS have, in recent years, published papers in respect of pre-emptive recovery planning, while the European Systemic Risk Board (ESRB) and Financial Stability Board (FSB) have also placed emphasis on the importance of recovery and resolution planning for insurers.

Under the BRRD framework, early intervention is described as supervisory measures in an early stage to address unsafe and unsound practices or activities that could pose risks to banks or to the banking system.[33] These early supervisory actions can range from supervisory measures that encompass moral suasion to more corrective sanctions, which are triggered when banks are deemed to be in danger of

[32] EIOPA, *Opinion on the 2020 review of Solvency II*, EIOPA–Bos-20/749, 17 December 2020.

[33] Article 27 of the BRRD. See also Recital 1 and 19 of the BRRD.

failing. On one hand, the use of early supervisory measures is part of the supervisory review process and is guided by forward-looking assessments, risk and impact frameworks and by the work of specialist supervisory teams. On the other hand, intervention is also undertaken using, as *ultimum remedium,* sanctions, often referred to as prompt corrective actions, which are needed to minimise the impact that an insolvent bank would have on deposit insurance schemes.

Through such forward-looking assessments, the areas of greatest concern regarding the bank's various business lines and risks, its associated strategies and the quality of its governance, management and internal controls are identified. The supervisory focus is directed to these areas to allow the supervisor to identify and address weaknesses at an early stage. Therefore, while appropriate methodologies and good sources of information are important, supervisory judgment will almost always be needed to interpret the information and assess the financial health of a bank.

Early intervention actions taken, therefore are not exclusively prompted by a formal early intervention/recovery framework that prescribes action, but are also taken as part of ongoing supervisory monitoring.[34]

Due to the sectorial nature of EU legislation, insurance companies do not fall under the scope of the BRRD. However, in light of the Solvency II 2020 Review, it is necessary to assess if the principles and rationale that informed the introduction of recovery and resolution planning for banks and investment firms subject to the BRRD also guide the choices and design of the future European recovery and resolution regime for insurers. In addition, it is necessary to ask whether the provisions of the BRRD are fit for the purpose to be used in the insurance regulatory framework.

According to the recitals of the BRRD there are at least two key factors that have led to the need to prepare a common set of rules for the recovery phase of a crisis and for management of the insolvency of banks: the need to preserve systemically important functions of institutions, subject to the BRRD[35] and the increased cross-

[34] Georgosouli (2013), pp. 209–220: '[. . .] judgement is based on hard, observable facts as opposed to the degree to which it is based on a view as to what might happen in the future'. In that sense, he concludes, 'judgement-led regulation equals to "forward-looking" regulation'. [. . .] scope of discretion for regulators and presupposes that regulators have the capacity and the willingness to use that discretion. Early intervention is arguably another key aspect of judgement-led regulation, rely on discretion, focus on outcomes and, at least in principle, secure an increased level of flexibility for regulators and regulatees alike'.

[35] Recital 1 BRRD: The financial crisis has shown that there is a significant lack of adequate tools at Union level to deal effectively with unsound or failing credit institutions and investment firms ('institutions'). Such tools are needed, in particular, to prevent insolvency or, when insolvency occurs, to minimise negative repercussions by preserving the systemically important functions of the institution concerned. During the crisis, those challenges were a major factor that forced Member States to save institutions using taxpayers' money. The objective of a credible recovery and resolution framework is to obviate the need for such action to the greatest extent possible.

border operations and interconnectedness of institutions.[36] While avoiding the term 'systemic importance' it is clear that insurers do provide important societal and economic functions and are increasingly active on cross-border basis. However, these critical functions consist exclusively of the prudent execution of the insurance business and activities, including most prominently the protection of the rights of policyholders and beneficiaries, as well as safeguarding the provision of specific forms of insurance cover. Other roles, such as the role that insurers play as e.g. institutional investor, are of course relevant as well, but should in our view not be considered critical functions in the same manner as for instance the responsibilities that banks bear for e.g. maintaining payment systems and payment infrastructure.

The BRRD introduced recovery and resolution planning, as well as specific tools and powers to resolution authorities allowing for failing institutions to be resolved instead of being liquidated, applying normal insolvency procedures. The preventive line undertaken by the BRRD is therefore based on three components: crisis preparation (with recovery and resolution plans), early intervention and resolution.[37]

In our view, resolution funding cannot be seen as separate from insurance guarantee schemes, to the extent the purpose of an insurance guarantee scheme is to facilitate a run-off/insurance portfolio transfer as an alternative to liquidation in ordinary bankruptcy proceedings. Therefore, the purpose of an insurance guarantee scheme does not necessarily have to ensure direct compensation of policyholders/ beneficiaries, such as is generally the case with deposit guarantee schemes in a banking context.

4 A European Recovery and Resolution Framework

In 2017 EIOPA published its opinion on the harmonisation of recovery and resolution frameworks for insurers across the European Union and, more recently, in 2019, issued a consultation paper on the review of Solvency II in 2020, including recovery and resolution planning considerations. In 2018 the IAIS issued a draft application

[36] Recital 3 BRRD: Union financial markets are highly integrated and interconnected with many institutions operating extensively beyond national borders. The failure of a cross-border institution is likely to affect the stability of financial markets in the different Member States in which it operates. The inability of Member States to seize control of a failing institution and resolve it in a way that effectively prevents broader systemic damage can undermine Member States' mutual trust and the credibility of the internal market in the field of financial services. The stability of financial markets is, therefore, an essential condition for the establishment and functioning of the internal market.

[37] EBA, *Discussion Paper - Application of early intervention measures in the European Union according to Articles 27-29 of the BRRD*, EBA/DP/2020/02, 26 June 2020, p. 4. See also: FSI, *FSI Insight - Early intervention regimes for weak banks,* April 2018; GOV.UK, *Bank Recovery and Resolution Directive (BRRD) implementation*, 3 November 2016; Basel Committee on Banking Supervision, Frameworks for early supervisory intervention, March 2018.

paper on Recovery Planning before issuing a final application paper on Recovery Planning in November 2019. The EIOPA and IAIS publications provide industry with a clear steer on the future expectations relating to recovery and resolution planning.[38]

If the EU legislator already in 2009 had noted the need to prepare a stronger protection apparatus in the insurance market with a view to the stability and solidity of the company with the introduction of a three-pillar system and which is divided into capital, risk control and market information, today, also in the light of a comparative look with the adjacent banking sector, this system seems to move towards the contingency of a fourth pillar such as that of forecasting and planning the crisis and insolvency. Prevention is other to the other goals of supervision, which include ensuring stability, solidity, and transparency.

In fact, the introduction of recovery and resolution plans, on the model of what has already happened for credit institutions and recipients of the BRRD directive, is one of the most important points of attention in the revision of Solvency II.[39]

The rest of this paper will take as an assumption that, following the EIOPA technical advice for the Solvency II 2020 review, the European Commission's forthcoming proposal for changes to the Solvency II framework, will include a certain level of harmonisation of recovery and resolution frameworks in the European Union, based on minimum harmonisation. EIOPA clarifies, as stated in its earlier publications, that 'minimum harmonisation' entails 'the definition of a common approach to the fundamental elements of recovery and resolution (objectives for resolution and resolution powers) which national frameworks should address, while leaving room for Member States to adopt additional measures at the national level, subject to these measures being compatible with the principles and objectives set at the EU level. These additional measures at the national level might be required to better address the specificities of the national markets'.

EIOPA observes that while Solvency II has improved insurance supervision, the risk of failures and near-failures still exists,[40] and in the absence of a harmonised framework at the EU level, the current landscape is fragmented, with some Member States having adopted frameworks at the national level, but the majority of Member

[38] IAIS, *IAIS Stakeholder Teleconference on Resolution*, 21 April 2020: The International Association of Insurance Supervisors (IAIS) is a voluntary membership organisation of insurance supervisors and regulators from more than 200 jurisdictions (p. 2) [. . .] (p. 4) The planned Application Paper on Resolution Powers and Planning will aim to provide guidance on supervisory practises related to resolution, which is defined in the IAIS Glossary1 as 'actions taken by a resolution authority towards an insurer that is no longer viable, or is likely to be no longer viable, and has no reasonable prospect of returning to viability' (p. 4). [. . .] Resolution can be seen as a final step taken by the supervisor and/or resolution authority, after all other preventive or corrective measures have proven to be insufficient to preserve or restore an insurer's viability (p. 7).

[39] ECB, *The new EU framework for financial crisis management and resolution*, July 2011 and EIOPA, *Background document on the opinion on the 2020 review of Solvency II – analysis*, EIOPA-BoS-20/750, 17 December 2020.

[40] Paragraph 12.40 of the EIOPA Opinion.

States have not.[41] As mentioned, it has not been the intention of Solvency II to take away the risk of failures or near-failures of insurers altogether.

According to EIOPA, the level of minimum harmonisation it envisages includes a framework consisting of four elements: (i) preparation and planning, (ii) early intervention, (iii) resolution and (iv) cross-border cooperation. In line with the EIOPA advice, these four elements also form key elements in the European Commission's IRRD proposal. For completeness' sake, we will discuss all four elements in this chapter: the first three are primarily relevant in terms of the governance of insurance undertakings and groups, while cross-border cooperation profile is of common significance and inherent to the principles fundamental to the EU internal market. Some bankruptcies of large insurers operating under the freedom to provide services, after obtaining authorisation in their home member state, have evidenced that the single market can only function properly if supervision is coordinated and the risk of regulatory arbitrage is mitigated.[42] The IRRD proposal should be seen as an extension and reinforcement of the Solvency II framework, which provides for a robust prudential framework for insurers and reinsurers in Europe, reducing the likelihood of failures and enhancing the resilience of the insurance and reinsurance sector. The IRRD proposal aims to provide authorities with a credible set of resolution tools to intervene sufficiently and quickly if insurers are failing or are likely to fail to ensure a better outcome for policyholders, while minimising the impact on the economy, the financial system, and any recourse to taxpayers' money.[43] The scope of application of the IRRD proposal (Article 1) is aligned with the scope of the Solvency II Directive (insurance and reinsurance undertakings established in the European Union and falling within the scope of Article 2 of the Solvency II Directive) and additionally includes a group dimension to the recovery and resolution framework (Articles 67–71). A novelty envisaged by the IRRD proposal is the requirement for member states to establish a resolution authority (Article 3). This could either be a dedicated and independent resolution authority or be function within a pre-existing authority, including a national central bank or supervisory authority. If the latter is the case, adequate structures should be in place to avoid conflicts of interests that might arise with the other functions conducted by such an authority. In addition, the resolution authority is required to be operationally independent, which includes having separate staff, reporting lines, and decision-making processes, from any supervisory or other functions of that authority. The introduction of this new category of authorities will require amendments to the EIOPA (EU) Regulation no. 1094/2010 to also include, where appropriate, references to these authorities (in particular in Articles 83–88). In the final provisions of the IRRD proposal (Title VII), amendments are proposed to the Solvency II Directive, which underlines the notion that the IRRD should reinforce Solvency II and be

[41] 12.41. This is obvious, as the Solvency II framework, as any other regulatory framework, has not been designed to provide a zero-failure framework.

[42] Impact Assessment, p. 11.

[43] Explanatory memorandum to the IRRD proposal, p. 1.

aligned with the prudential framework for insurers and reinsurers in Europe and complement the existing intervention powers of the Solvency II framework. The amendments to the Solvency II Directive consist in particular of a clarification of the concept of supervisory powers in deteriorating financial conditions (Article 141 of the Solvency II Directive) and proposals that suggest amending company law provisions and other national rules that could pose obstacles in the effective use of the resolution tools in the IRRD proposal.

4.1 Preparatory Measures and Corporate Governance Rules

Preparatory measures can be distinguished in measures, aimed to facilitate the recovery under the responsibility of the insurer to restore its financial position and viability in the event the insurer comes under severe stress, and measures that should enable the resolution actions of the resolution authority towards an insurer that is no longer viable, or is likely to be no longer viable, and has no reasonable prospect of returning to viability. The key differences between these two phases are the objectives (recovery versus resolution) and who is in charge of the process (the insurance company and its corporate bodies or the resolution authorities). The IRRD proposal provides that at least 80% of the insurance market of member states should be subject to recovery planning. Low-risk profile undertakings should be excluded. 70% of the insurance market should be subject to resolution planning. Again, low-risk profile undertakings should be excluded.

4.1.1 Pre-emptive Measures with Respect to Recovery

Pre-emptive measures with respect to recovery generally focus on the preparation of an ex-ante or pre-emptive recovery plan. According to the IAIS, the objective of such a recovery plan is twofold: (a) to aid the insurer in understanding its own risks from severe stress scenarios, and (b) to be better prepared to provide an effective response.

The focus of a recovery plan is on situations that pose a serious risk to the viability of the insurer or any material part of its business.[44]

Pre-emptive recovery planning is different from a recovery plan, referred to in Article 138 of the Solvency II Directive, which insurers are required to develop within two months after a breach of the SCR. However, it is expected that pre-emptive recovery planning will allow insurers to make better informed and timely decisions in times of crisis. Through the process of pre-emptive recovery planning, insurers will have already identified and assessed a range of recovery measures expected to be available to them in times of crisis, which should make the

[44]IAIS, Application Paper on Recovery Planning, November 2019, paragraph 2.

development of the recovery plan in accordance with Article 138 of the Solvency II Directive more efficient.[45]

The preparation of an ex-ante recovery plan is the responsibility of the insurance undertaking and/or the insurance group, subject to supervisory scrutiny. Therefore, it is the undertaking itself that assesses, describes and determines how it intends to recover from severe stress scenarios without failing and triggering the withdrawal of its insurance license (in case of the recovery of a licensed insurance company). In terms of governance actions, the supervisory authorities will assess if the scenarios and described recovery measures can be considered realistic and are expected to be achievable in stress scenarios. As an example, suppose the insurance company relies on external reinsurance or access to capital markets in a recovery scenario, are the assumptions that the undertaking has access to such facilities in a stress scenario realistic, has it already made preparatory arrangements—if needed—to ensure access to such facilities? As part of a future recovery framework, it is reasonable to expect that supervisory authorities will have the ability to take supervisory action if a recovery plan is not realistic and instruct the company to amend the plan. Conceptually, such supervisory action is expected to be largely in line with regular expectations of the supervised entity. Although views might differ between the supervisory authorities and the corporate bodies of the undertaking, the undertaking remains in charge of the development of the plan and the objectives of the undertaking are aligned, namely, to continue the undertaking as a going-concern enterprise. The IRRD proposal introduces explicit requirements with respect to ex ante recovery planning, subject to proportionality. 'Low-risk profile undertakings', a concept introduced through the Solvency II proposals, can benefit from proportionate application of Solvency II requirements. The IRRD proposal contains a provision that allows for simplified obligations for certain undertakings (Article 4 of the IRRD proposal). Simplified obligations will apply in any case to 'low-risk profile undertakings' in the meaning of the Solvency II proposals, which will take account of the nature of these undertakings, and avoid unnecessary administrative burdens (see Article 5(3) of the IRRD proposal). National authorities will be obliged to report annually to EIOPA on application of Article 4.

4.1.2 Pre-emptive Resolution Planning

Pre-emptive resolution planning consists of two elements: the development of resolution plans and of resolvability assessments. Resolvability assessments are part of the resolution planning process and aim to identify any impediments to the resolvability of undertakings.[46] A resolution plan is developed by the resolution

[45] EIOPA Analysis, pp. 638–639.

[46] EIOPA Analysis, p. 653.

authority, not by the undertaking itself, nor by the supervisory authority.[47] As mentioned, a resolution plan is, according to the IAIS Glossary, a plan that identifies in advance options for resolving all or part(s) of an insurer to maximise the likelihood of an orderly resolution, the development of which is led by the supervisor and/or resolution authority in consultation with the insurer in advance of any circumstances warranting resolution. Interestingly, the IAIS leaves open the possibility that a resolution plan is developed by the supervisory authority, rather than a resolution authority. In general, we believe it is advisable that the development of a resolution plan is dealt with by a separate authority or a department within the supervisory authority that is operationally independent from regular supervision. The objectives of going concern supervision and gone concern resolution differ, which could lead to different choices and potentially conflicts of interests.

In itself, the development of a resolution plan does not impact the insurance undertaking or the insurance group. It is not up to the undertaking 'to rule over its grave' and to decide how the undertaking will be resolved. However, a resolution plan will require close cooperation between the resolution authority and the undertaking (and with the supervisory authority), and the impact of the resolution plan may be felt by the undertaking in going concern as well, mainly due to the resolvability assessment by the resolution authority. Through resolution planning, the resolution authority intends to ensure that the undertaking is resolvable in an orderly manner. This will involve the identification of potential impediments to resolution. In case the resolution authority identifies the presence of material impediments to resolution, it may have to adapt the resolution strategy or require such impediments to be removed by the insurance undertaking ex-ante. This will require close cooperation with the supervisory authorities and the undertaking itself and a thorough assessment if the ex-ante removal of such impediments is in fact necessary. Impediments to resolution (gone concern) might well be efficiencies on a going concern basis (e.g. shared services within a group) and the ex-ante intervention by a resolution authority may be disproportionate if other solutions are also feasible (such as the continuation of such services during resolution).[48]

Both the process of ex-ante recovery planning, particularly ex-ante resolution planning, can have a significant impact on insurers. Where insurers are generally focused on running their operations on a going concern business, both recovery and resolution planning are aimed at the situation where this is no longer the case. To be prepared for such circumstances may require different choices than if the focus is strictly on the going concern circumstances of the operations.

[47] The resolution authority and supervisory authority can be part of the same authority or be entirely separate. If combined in the same authority, they are usually operationally independent from the supervisory authority, given the different tasks of the resolution authority.

[48] Continuation of essential services might be realised as well by proper internal documentation of such services through service-level agreements or other internal outsourcing agreements. Resolution authorities are expected to have the power to ensure the continuity of essential services by requiring other entities to continue to provide such services (see EIOPA Opinion, paragraph 12.18).

The IRRD proposal provides resolution authorities with powers to require the insurer to remove, *ex ante*, substantive impediments to resolution. However, the IRRD proposal currently uses inconsistent terminology (material impediments, substantive impediments, impediments) to indicate the impediments may need to be removed upon the instruction of the resolution authority. It should be clear that these powers only relate to 'substantive' impediments, due to the potential intrusive nature of this power to the going concern operations of the insurer. Furthermore, we believe this power should be limited to the continuity of critical functions. The IRRD proposal includes, in addition to the concept of critical functions, references to core business lines (Article 9(6) c and the requirement, as part of the resolution plan, to demonstrate how core business lines (in addition to critical functions) can be separated. We doubt if the reference to core business lines is relevant and suggest that this should be removed. Safeguarding core business lines should not be an objective of resolution, but only the preservation and continuity of critical functions. The inclusion of core business lines might have been inspired by the BRRD framework, where the emphasis of resolution is on the preservation of the bank and/or the entities in the group. The key concern for resolution authorities in the insurance sector should not be the preservation and continuity of the insurer or the insurance group, but instead safeguarding the rights of policyholders and beneficiaries, which might well be affected without the preservation of the group or entities in the group (e.g. by portfolio transfers and run-offs).

5 Triggers to Place an Insurer or Reinsurer in Resolution and Director's Duties

A crucial component of a resolution framework is the trigger for entry into resolution. This is the moment on which the insurer transitions from 'going concern' to 'gone concern'.[49] After this point, the insurer no longer forms part of the regular commercial economic circumstances. At this point, the resolution authority typically takes full control of the insurer. Therefore, this moment is also crucial for the corporate bodies of the insurer, as well as for the investors/shareholders. Clearly, such a decision should not be taken lightly and therefore the conditions for taking such a decision should be as clear as possible.

According to the FSB Key Attributes, resolution should be initiated when an undertaking is no longer viable or likely to be no longer viable and has no reasonable prospect of becoming so. The resolution regime should provide for timely and early entry into resolution before a firm is balance sheet insolvent and before all equity has been fully wiped out. There should be clear standards or suitable indicators of

[49] EIOPA, background document on the opinion of the 2020 review of Solvency II, analysis, EIOPA-BoS-20/750, 17 December 2020, page 629.

non-viability to help guide decisions on whether firms meet the conditions for entry into resolution.[50]

The FSB uses the term 'non-viability' to identify the transition from going concern to gone concern (i.e. from recovery to resolution). This means that all possible recovery measures must have been exhausted and failed or ruled out.

In accordance with the FSB Key Attributes, EIOPA proposes to set—at the EU level—triggers for entry into resolution as follows:

a. The undertaking is no longer viable or likely to be no longer viable and has no reasonable prospect of becoming so.
b. Possible recovery measures have been exhausted—either tried and failed or ruled out as implausible to return the undertaking to viability—or cannot be implemented in a timely manner.
c. A resolution action is necessary in the public interest.[51]

According to EIOPA, the triggers should be judgment-based and allow for sufficient discretion to assess the situation and decide on the need for resolution actions.[52]

According to EIOPA, an undertaking could be considered to be no longer viable or likely to be no longer viable based on the following, non-exhaustive set of criteria:

- The undertaking is in breach or likely to be in breach of the MCR and there is no reasonable prospect of compliance being restored.
- The undertaking is in breach or likely to be in breach of other prudential requirements (e.g. requirements on assets backing technical provisions), there is no reasonable prospect of compliance being restored and such non-compliance will likely lead to balance sheet or cash flow insolvency.
- There is a strong likelihood that policyholders and/or creditors will not receive payments as they fall due.[53]

It is our impression that the first, and part of the second condition, are likely to be the most relevant conditions to determine the (expected) non-viability of licensed insurance and reinsurance entities.[54] Furthermore, there appears to be some overlap

---

[50] FSB Key Attributes of Effective Resolution Regimes for Financial Institutions, 15 October 2014, paragraph 3.1.

[51] EIOPA Opinion, paragraph 12.3.3.

[52] EIOPA Opinion, paragraph 12.31.

[53] EIOPA, background document on the opinion of the 2020 review of Solvency II, analysis, EIOPA-BoS-20/750, 17 December 2020, page 670.

[54] The FSB makes a distinction between 'insurer', which refers to an insurance company or a holding company and an 'insurance company', which means any legal entity (including its branches) that assumes insurance risks in exchange for a premium payment and is licensed under a jurisdiction's legal framework as an insurance company for any type of insurance product (for example, reinsurance, life insurance, non-life insurance, etc.): FSB, Key Attributes Assessment Methodology for the Insurance Sector Methodology for Assessing the Implementation of the Key Attributes of Effective Resolution Regimes for Financial Institutions in the Insurance Sector, 25 August 2020, page 5.

between cash-flow insolvency in the second condition and the likelihood that policyholders will not receive payments as they fall due in the third condition. Lastly, we believe the balance sheet is mainly relevant to determine if other entities (non-insurance companies, such as holding companies or service companies) in a group have failed or are likely to fail. In our view, it would be more appropriate to split the second condition into two separate conditions and combine one part with the first condition. The third condition could be limited to creditors in general[55] as this condition is likely to be relevant to for the resolution of non-insurance entities (e.g. holding companies, service-companies) in the context of the resolution of an insurance or reinsurance entity.

- The undertaking is in breach or likely to be in breach of the MCR, and/or in breach or likely to be in breach of other prudential requirements (e.g. requirements on assets backing technical provisions), there is no reasonable prospect of compliance being restored in such a manner that there are objective indications that this would justify a withdrawal of the insurance or reinsurance license in the near future.
- The liabilities of the undertaking exceed the assets of the undertaking or there are objective indications that the liabilities will exceed the assets of the undertaking in the near future that this will lead to balance-sheet insolvency.
- There are objective indications that creditors will not receive payments as they fall due.

When reworded in this manner, the first condition is focused on the non-viability of licensed insurance and reinsurance entities (and linked to the intervention ladder of Solvency II)[56] and the second and third condition are focused on the non-viability of other entities in an insurance group in the context of the resolution of an insurance or reinsurance entity (balance-sheet insolvency[57] and cash-flow insolvency[58]), which appear to be less relevant to determine the non-viability of a licensed insurance entity. The IRRD-proposal offers, with slightly different wording, the same criteria as EIOPA suggests.

Furthermore, as indicated, EIOPA advises to introduce 'judgment-based' triggers for the entry into resolution, as opposed to 'rules-based' triggers. We doubt if the distinction between judgment-based and rules-based triggers is useful as it could unnecessarily create uncertainty with respect to moment at which resolution can be triggered. The criterion 'failure or likely to fail' already inherently provides for a judgment-based trigger that requires supervisory discretion and is not necessarily an automatic, mechanic trigger.[59]

---

[55] Although not excluding policyholders/beneficiaries.

[56] Whereby in particular an irreparable breach of the MCR will lead to the withdrawal of an insurance license.

[57] Second condition.

[58] Third condition.

[59] EIOPA suggests that rules-based triggers are inflexible. As explained, we doubt if this is truly the case.

It is our impression that the European Commission does not follow EIOPA's advice for 'judgement-based triggers'. Resolution actions, in accordance with the IRRD proposal, can be taken only when cumulatively a number of conditions have been met (Article 19 IRRD proposal). These conditions each allow for discretion, which means that these triggers are, to a certain level, still 'judgement-based', but not to the extent as proposed by EIOPA.

A related issue is that EIOPA suggests to define triggers for resolution in such a way that they allow for resolution before an undertaking is balance sheet or cash-flow insolvent and before all equity has been wiped out.[60] As explained before, we believe the criterion related to balance-sheet insolvency is relevant in particular for the possibility of including other—non-insurance—entities in the resolution of an insurance entity and we do not see a justification for triggering the resolution of such entities before the resolution of an insurance or reinsurance entity is triggered. In the context of the resolution of a licensed insurance entity the criterion 'before all equity has been wiped out' does not have much added value. The relevant intervention level should be related to the coverage of the MCR and the impossibility of the insurance company itself to avoid an irreparable breach of the MCR.

Furthermore, EIOPA suggests that the resolution authority should have the authority to withdraw the license of the insurer.[61] We doubt if this authority should indeed be granted to the resolution authority, or instead should be left with the supervisory authority that has granted the license and might be best positioned to withdraw the license as well, obviously in close consultation with the resolution authority. The EIOPA Opinion is silent on the withdrawal of the insurance license, if the insurer would enter into ordinary bankruptcy proceedings.

5.1 *Triggers for the Entry Into Recovery and Preventive Measures*

EIOPA advises maintaining the current triggers for the entry into recovery that are currently already included in the Solvency II Directive.[62] Apart from informing the supervisory authorities, the entry into recovery implies the preparation and

[60] Paragraph 12.176 Background Document. In the same sense: IAIS, draft Application Paper on Resolution Powers and Planning, 9 November 2020, paragraph 24: 'The resolution regime should have a forward-looking trigger that would provide for entry into resolution before an insurer is balance sheet insolvent or is unable to pay its obligations as they come due.' It should be noted that 'insurer', in the IAIS terminology, means 'insurance legal entity or insurance group' (IAIS Glossary, November 2019, page 6) and is therefore intended to have a broader scope than only licensed insurance entities.

[61] Paragraph 12.18 of the EIOPA Opinion.

[62] Non-compliance with the SCR or a risk of non-compliance in the following three months. It should be noted that EIOPA, in the EIOPA Opinion, only refers to non-compliance with the SCR, but we assume that this is meant to include a risk of non-compliance in the subsequent three months as well, as currently worded in the Solvency II Directive.

submission, within two months, of a realistic recovery plan to the supervisory authorities. This recovery plan should lead to the re-establishment of a sufficient level of own funds to cover the SCR. In addition, supervisory authorities have the power to prohibit the free disposal of assets located within their territory when recovery is triggered.[63]

5.2 *Preventive Measures*

In addition, notwithstanding the obligation to submit a recovery plan, where the solvency position of the undertaking continues to deteriorate, supervisory authorities have the power to take all measures necessary to safeguard the interests of policyholders in the case of insurance contracts or the obligations arising out of reinsurance contracts. These measures should be proportionate.[64] These preventive measures are already included in the current Solvency II framework.[65] However, EIOPA proposes to articulate such measures more explicitly under the heading 'preventive measures' and to introduce appropriate 'triggers' at the EU level for the use of preventive measures.[66] Currently, EIOPA observes divergent approaches by national competent authorities which it considers not be in line with the principle of supervisory convergence and raises concerns about the level playing field in insurance.[67]

EIOPA suggests to introduce the following set of measures used in Solvency II: (a) Require more intensive dialogue with the undertakings, scheduling regular meetings with the company's management in order to better understand the strategy of the company, recent technical and financial results, recent changes in insurance products and investment and their impact on the solvency position as well as to have up to date information on measures taken or measures to be taken by the company in order to improve the SCR coverage ratio (e.g. conservative dividend policy, increase of own funds, de-risking), including any recent dialogue between the undertakings and its qualifying shareholders/owners on the possibility of capital support; (b) Require additional or more frequent reporting; (c) Require the administrative, management, or supervisory body of the undertaking to take preventive measures within a specific timeframe in case of concrete risk of progressive and structural deterioration of its capital position that may put the undertaking under stress and the undertaking's inaction leads to an increased risk to policyholders. This could also include a requirement to update the pre-emptive recovery plan when assumptions set

[63] Article 140 Solvency II Directive.

[64] Article 141 Solvency II Directive.

[65] Article 141 of the Solvency II Directive. ICP 10.2 also refers to preventive measures if the insurer seems likely to operate in a manner that is inconsistent with regulatory requirements.

[66] EIOPA Opinion, paragraph 12.25.

[67] EIOPA Analysis, p. 649.

out in the initial plan do not appear realistic, and to take the measures set out in the updated plan; (d) Require the undertaking to limit variable remuneration and bonuses.[68]

EIOPA suggests that, similar to the resolution triggers, triggers for the application of preventive measures should be 'judgment-based' and allow for sufficient supervisory discretion, contain relevant qualitative and quantitative factors, but should not result in a new pre-defined intervention level.[69] According to EIOPA, relevant factors that would need to be taken into consideration by NSAs in their assessment for intervening preventively include, for instance: (1) Solvency ratio and historical volatility of the SCR ratio; (2) Trends in the financial statement figures; (3) Business plan, including information about the products, risk mitigation techniques, investment plan and dividend policy; (4) The possibility and likelihood for the undertaking to raise additional capital; (5) ORSA, particularly, the three year projection of the SCR and MCR coverage ratios, the change in risk appetite and risk tolerance and the change in the investment strategy—business plan; (6) Financial plans and strategy of the company, including recent changes in them that could cause risk of non-compliance with capital requirements; (7) Impact of the sensitivity analysis on the SCR trigger and MCR trigger; (8) Conclusions from inspections and meetings with the Administrative, Management or Supervisory Body (AMSB); (9) Other issues or aspects (market triggers), such as interest rate volatility and the widening of the credit spread.[70]

It is clear from the wording used by EIOPA[71] and the factors mentioned that it envisages a high level of discretion and flexibility for supervisory authorities for the application of preventive measures. The question can be raised if these factors truly result in the EU-level triggers. We doubt if such a degree of flexibility will effectively prevent the observed divergence of national approaches.[72]

As mentioned, the IAIS refers to preventive measures if the insurer seems likely to operate in a manner that is inconsistent with regulatory requirements. The way EIOPA articulates preventive measures seems to allow for a broader application of preventive measures.

Furthermore, a preliminary question may be raised as well: The use of preventive measures is presented by EIOPA as a supervisory tool of national competent authorities in deteriorating financial conditions. This means the supervisory power, in deteriorating financial conditions, to take all measures necessary to safeguard the

[68] EIOPA Opinion, paragraph 12.8.

[69] EIOPA Opinion, paragraphs 12.26 and 12.27. EIOPA refers to 'soft triggers', allowing for a sufficient degree of supervisory judgment and discretion according to different products and national market specificities, EIOPA, background document on the opinion of the 2020 review of Solvency II, analysis, EIOPA-BoS-20/750, 17 December 2020, page 667.

[70] EIOPA, background document on the opinion of the 2020 review of Solvency II, analysis, EIOPA-BoS-20/750, 17 December 2020, page 667.

[71] E.g. 'judgment-based', 'soft triggers', 'supervisory judgment and discretion', 'for instance.'

[72] EIOPA, background document on the opinion of the 2020 review of Solvency II, analysis, EIOPA-BoS-20/750, 17 December 2020, paragraph 12.156.

interests of policyholders, notwithstanding the power of supervisory authorities to require a short-term financing plan or recovery plan.[73] In accordance with Article 136 of the Solvency II Directive, undertakings should have procedures in place to identify deteriorating financial conditions and notify the supervisory authorities when such deterioration occurs.[74] This provision appears to assume the primary responsibility of the undertaking and its corporate bodies to determine when deteriorating financial conditions occur, not of the supervisory authority.[75] These procedures are obviously subject to supervision by the national competent authorities.

The question is how the proposal of EIOPA to introduce adequate triggers at the EU level for the use of preventive measures relates to the own responsibility of insurers (and their governance arrangements) to have procedures in place to identify deteriorating financial conditions? Are the factors mentioned by EIOPA intended to be factors to be considered for the procedures to be maintained by undertakings (and therefore subject to ex-ante supervision) or is it the intention of EIOPA that supervisory authorities have the discretion to intervene in deteriorating financial conditions if they come to the conclusion that the undertaking is facing deteriorating financial conditions, independent from the internal procedures of the undertaking pursuant to Article 136 of the Solvency II Directive? We believe the use of preventive measures by supervisory authorities should be linked to the internal procedures of the undertaking to identify deteriorating financial conditions, subject to ex-ante supervisory oversight. This contributes to the predictability of the use of supervisory measures (i.e. when the undertaking has identified such deteriorating financial conditions) and leaves the primary responsibility of the undertaking in deteriorating financial conditions, when the undertaking is still operating on a going concern basis, with the undertaking.

It should be borne in mind that it is likely that, when deteriorating financial conditions are observed and notified to the supervisory authorities, it is likely that the insurance company is also taking action or will soon take action by means of the preparation and execution of a recovery plan or short-term financing plan. It should be avoided that measures taken by supervisory authorities in deteriorating financial conditions interfere with the execution of the recovery plan.

6 Resolution Objectives

EIOPA proposes that Solvency II should clearly set out the objectives for resolution, without an ex-ante predefined ranking.[76] This proposal is also included in the IRRD-proposal, in article 18. These objectives are the following: (a) To protect

---

[73] Article 141 of the Solvency II Directive.

[74] Article 136 of the Solvency II Directive.

[75] Or potentially in exceptional circumstances, where the undertaking fails to observe and/or notify such conditions to the supervisory authority.

[76] EIOPA Opinion, paragraph 12.11.

policyholders, beneficiaries and claimants; (b) To maintain financial stability, in particular, by preventing contagion and by maintaining market discipline; (c) To ensure the continuity of functions of undertakings whose disruption could harm the financial stability and/or real economy; (d) To protect public funds.

The question may be raised, what is meant by EIOPA with the notion 'without an ex-ante predefined ranking'. We consider resolution to be an alternative to liquidation[77] that should be considered and applied when the objectives mentioned above cannot be achieved in a similar way in ordinary bankruptcy proceedings. This is also the intention of the IRRD proposal. However, in the IRRD proposal the choice between resolution and bankruptcy proceedings is placed in the context of the public interest test. In our view, these objectives should always include the protection of policyholders, beneficiaries, and claimants, possibly together with one of the other objectives.[78] However, it should be recalled that the critical functions that insurers fulfill consist (only) of the prudent exercise of their insurance business, which suggests that objective (a) and (c) overlap to a large extent and the added value of objective (b) is limited. Financial stability is only at stake when policyholder rights are threatened (a), which likely coincides with a critical function (c). Therefore, as well as in accordance with Recital 16 of the Solvency II Directive,[79] the emphasis should always be on policyholder protection and/or the protection of specific types of insurance cover, which implies in our view a predefined ranking with respect to this objective.

7 Bail-in Tool in Insurance

Probably the most intrusive and painful resolution powers, as suggested by EIOPA, is the power to restructure, limit or write down liabilities, including (re)insurance liabilities and allocate losses to shareholders, creditors and policyholders.

According to EIOPA, the exercise of the resolution powers should be subject to adequate safeguards:

---

[77] E.g. an alternative to ordinary bankruptcy proceedings. According to the IAIS is liquidation a process to terminate operations and corporate existence of the entity through which the remaining assets of the insurer will be distributed to its creditors and shareholders according to the liquidation claims hierarchy.

[78] See for example also Article 3A:85 of the Dutch Financial Supervision Act that adopts this ranking of objectives.

[79] Recital 16 reads as follows: 'The main objective of insurance and reinsurance regulation and supervision is the adequate protection of policy holders and beneficiaries. The term beneficiary is intended to cover any natural or legal person who is entitled to a right under an insurance contract. *Financial stability and fair and stable markets are other objectives of insurance and reinsurance regulation and supervision which should also be taken into account but should not undermine the main objective.*' (italics added).

i. The hierarchy of claims should be respected, while providing the flexibility to depart from the general principle of equal (*pari passu*) treatment of creditors of the same class.
ii. Creditors, including policyholders, should not incur a loss greater than they would have incurred in a winding-up under normal insolvency proceedings (the 'no creditor worse off than in liquidation' (NCWOL) principle).[80]

Furthermore, when allocating losses to policyholders, resolution authorities should consider the following safeguards:

a) The allocation of losses to policyholders should only take place as a last resort option, i.e. all other feasible measures and options that could have averted (further) losses for policyholders have been exhausted or have been deemed unlikely to be successful.
b) The exercise of the power is deemed necessary for other powers to be effective (for instance, to enable a portfolio transfer) and, hence, to limit the losses for policyholders.
c) Policyholders who are covered by IGSs or other mechanisms should be compensated to the extent possible.[81]

It is clear that the allocation of losses to policyholders and beneficiaries should only take place as a last resort measure when all other measures have failed. However, in case of insurance failures, it might be unavoidable to resort to this tool to effect resolution tools such as a portfolio or share transfer to another insurer or to effectuate a run-off. A bail-in of policyholders might be more beneficial to policyholders than a liquidation in bankruptcy proceedings, in which losses to policyholders might be worse. An important safeguard for policyholders in this respect is the respect of the NCWOL-principle, as referred to above. To determine if the NCWOL-principle is respected is complex, as it will require a reliable calculation of the entitlements of policyholders and beneficiaries in liquidation. This will determine the level of the possible bail-in of policyholders and beneficiaries.

The EIOPA Opinion does not cover the valuation of insurance liabilities in insolvency. We believe it is essential that this point is also addressed in the EU framework, as it is crucial to determine if the insurer fails or is likely to fails, the extent to which bail-in can be applied to insurance liabilities and the need to additionally rely on resolution funding and/or entitlements may exist on an insurance guarantee scheme, if such a scheme is available in Member States. Lessons could potentially be learned from existing resolution frameworks, such as has been developed in the Netherlands, where valuation principles have been developed in the

[80] EIOPA Opinion, paragraph 12.20.

[81] EIOPA, Background Document on the Opinion on the 2020 review of Solvency II, box 12.5 on p. 663, EIOPA-BoS-20/750, 17 December 2020.

Dutch Act and lower legislation,[82] as well as good practices have been developed by the insurance industry.[83] Furthermore, in the Dutch resolution framework, a mechanism has been developed whereby a provisional insolvency valuation is being undertaken at or close to the moment the insurance entity fails or is likely to fail, followed by a final valuation when the resolution process or liquidation is finalised. The provisional valuation serves as the basis for the potential for bail-in and to determine if provisional payments to policyholders can continue to be made during the resolution process. These provisions are supported by a backstop-facility in the form of resolution funding on an ex-post basis by the insurance industry that provides a safeguard against breaches of the NCOWL-principle. The IRRD-proposal seems to be largely in line with the Dutch framework, in terms of valuation (chapter VII), with nuanced differences. According to the IRRD-proposal, a first valuation is done before the insurer is placed in resolution. This valuation serves to determine if the conditions for resolution (failing or likely to fail) have been met. A second valuation takes place after the the insurer is placed in resolution. This (provisional) valuation forms the basis for the resolution action to be taken, which includes the extent to which the bail-in tool can be applied, while respecting the NCWOL-principle. These provisional valuations are followed by a 'definitive valuation' (article 24(5)), which will still be based on estimates of the treatment of creditors in ordinary bankruptcy proceedings and which does not prejudice the final valuation, referred to in article 54, which takes place at the end of the resolution process. A safeguard for shareholders and creditors in case of a breach of the NCWOL-principle is included in article 55. However, it is not specified in the IRRD-proposal to whom creditors and shareholders have such entitlement.

8 Concluding Remarks

Based on the current regulatory framework above described, which does not fully consider the IRRD-proposal in all respects, multiples challenges might occur from the expectation that insurance companies and groups should ensure they are recoverable and resolvable in the context of directors' duties, which have a focus on running the company on a going concern basis.

While in ordinary times the directors must always consider and balance the interests of shareholders and policyholders, on the contrary, in deteriorating financial conditions, one could say that the balance shifts more towards the protection of policyholders, but that is already more or less inherent to the subordinate position of

[82] Article 3A:89-3A:91 of the Dutch Financial Supervision Act, Decree Valuation Insurance Liabilities in bankruptcy, 10 July 2019.

[83] Dutch Association of Insurers, Good practice calculation bankruptcy value https://www.verzekeraars.nl/media/7925/good-practice-berekenen-faillissementswaarde.pdf.

shareholders/privileged position of policyholders (shareholders bear losses first, policyholders last).

In the context of recovery and resolution, it is appropriate to ask whether the 'regular' director duty of care is suitable to inform decisions by that are needed in adverse financial circumstances as well as to inform preparatory decisions such as with respect to ex-ante recovery planning and ex-ante removal of impediments to resolution. An interesting point is how to judge the preparation for resolution (ex-ante removal of impediments to resolution). This might happen when the company is still running on a going concern basis and the decisions that need to be taken do not necessarily make sense from a going concern perspective: making an insurance company resolvable might make it less efficient than when you would only consider the going concern.

References

Basel Committee on Banking Supervision, *Frameworks for early supervisory intervention*, March 2018

Communication from the Commission to the European Parliament and the Council on the review of the EU prudential framework for insurers and reinsurers in the context of the EU's post pandemic recovery, https://ec.europa.eu, https://ec.europa.eu/info/publications/210922-solvency-2-communication_en (2021)

Commission Staff Working Document accompanying the documents Proposal for a Directive of the European Parliament and of the Council amending Directive 2009/138/EC as regards proportionality, quality of supervision, reporting, long-term guarantee measures, macro-prudential tools, sustainability risks, group and cross-border supervision and Proposal for a Directive of the European Parliament and of the Council establishing a framework for the recovery and resolution of insurance and reinsurance undertakings and amending Directives 2002/47/EC, 2004/25/EC, 2009/138/EC, (EU) 2017/1132 and Regulations (EU) No 1094/2010 and (EU) No 648/2012 SWD/2021/260 final Assessment Report, https://eur-lex.europa.eu/legal-content/EN/TXT/?uri=CELEX:52021SC0260 (2021)

Dutch Association of Insurers, *Good practice calculation bankruptcy value* https://www.verzekeraars.nl/media/7925/good-practice-berekenen-faillissementswaarde.pdf

EBA, *Discussion Paper - Application of early intervention measures in the European Union according to Articles 27-29 of the BRRD*, EBA/DP/2020/02, 26 June 2020

ECB, *The new EU framework for financial crisis management and resolution*, July 2011 and EIOPA, *Background document on the opinion on the 2020 review of Solvency II – analysis*, EIOPA-BoS-20/750, 17 December 2020

EIOPA, *Background document on the opinion on the opinion on the 2020 review of Solvency II - Impact assessment*, EIOPA-BoS-20/751, 17 December 2020a

EIOPA, *Consultation Paper on Proposals for Solvency II 2020 Review Harmonisation of National Insurance Guarantee Schemes*, EIOPA-BoS-19-259, https://eiopa.europa.eu/Publications/Consultations/EIOPA-BoS-19-259_Consultation%20paper%20on%20Harmonisation%20of%20IGSs.pdf

EIOPA, *Discussion paper on resolution funding and national insurance guarantee schemes*, EIOPA-CP-18-003, 9 July 2018., https://eiopa.europa.eu/Publications/Consultations/EIOPA-CP-18-003_Discussion_paper_on_resolution_funding%20and.pdf

EIOPA, *Opinion on the 2020 review of Solvency II*, EIOPA–Bos-20/749, 17 December 2020b

EIOPA, *Opinion to Institutions of the European Union on Harmonisation of recovery and resolution frameworks for (re)insurers across the member states*, EIOPA-BoS/17-148, 5 July 2017., https://eiopa.europa.eu/Publications/Opinions/EIOPA-BoS-17-148_Opinion_on_recovery_and_resolution_for_(re)insurers.pdf
EIOPA, *Other potential macroprudential tools and measures to enhance the current framework*, Publications office of the European Union, Luxembourg, 2017, also available on the EIOPA website
EIOPA, *Solvency II tools with macroprudential impact*, Publications office of the European Union, Luxembourg, 2018, also available on the EIOPA website
EIOPA, *Systemic risk and macroprudential policy in insurance*, Publications office of the European Union, Luxembourg, 2017, also available on the EIOPA website
European Commission, Proposal for a Directive of the European Parliament and of the Council establishing a framework for the recovery and resolution of insurance and reinsurance undertakings and amending Directives 2002/47/EC, 2004/25/EC, 2009/138/EC, (EU) 2017/1132 and Regulations (EU) No 1094/2010 and (EU) No 648/2012, COM/2021/582 final
Financial Stability Board, *Key Attributes Assessment Methodology for the Insurance Sector Methodology for Assessing the Implementation of the Key Attributes of Effective Resolution Regimes for Financial Institutions in the Insurance Sector*, 25 August 2020
Financial Stability Board, *Key Attributes of Effective Resolution Regimes for Financial Institutions*, 15 October 2014., https://www.fsb.org/wp-content/uploads/r_141015.pdf
FSI, *FSI Insight - Early intervention regimes for weak banks,* April 2018
Georgosouli A (2013) Judgement-led regulation: reflections on data and discretion. J Bank Regul 14:209–220
GOV.UK, *Bank Recovery and Resolution Directive (BRRD) implementation*, 3 November 2016
IAIS, *Application Paper on recovery planning*, 18 November 2019., https://www.iaisweb.org/page/supervisory-material/application-papers//file/87519/application-paper-on-recovery-planning
IAIS, *Draft Application Paper on Resolution Powers and Planning*, 9 November 2020., https://www.iaisweb.org/page/consultations/closed-consultations/2021/application-paper-on-resolution-powers-and-planning
IAIS, *IAIS Stakeholder Teleconference on Resolution*, 21 April 2020
IAIS, *Issues Paper on policyholder protection schemes*, October 2013., https://www.iaisweb.org/page/supervisory-material/issues-papers//file/34547/issues-paper-on-policyholder-protection-schemes
IAIS, *Public consultation on draft Application Paper on Resolution Powers and Planning*. https://www.iaisweb.org/page/consultations/closed-consultations/2021/application-paper-on-resolution-powers-and-planning
Van Hulle K (2019) Solvency II requirements for EU insurers, Solvency II is good for you. Intersentia, Cambridge, Antwerp, Chicago

Restructuring, Winding-Up & Portfolio Transfer of Insurance Companies in Distress

Kyriaki Noussia, Peter Underwood, and Stergios Frastanlis

Abstract Insurance companies often need to go through restructuring for various reasons. Such restructuring can happen in company law through the mechanism of M&A, or under EU legislation via portfolio transfer (see e.g. Article 14 of Directive 2002/83/EC and Article 12 of Directive 92/49/EEC in the field of non-life insurance). This chapter discusses reorganising, restructuring and winding-up of insurance companies, as well as insurance portfolio transfers by means of company law mechanisms (M&A) and under the Cross-Border Mergers Directive, as well as under the Solvency II Directive. It then goes on to discuss the position under Greek law, and uses as a case study the winding-up of Aspis Pronia in 2009 and the transfer of the insurance undertakings' portfolios. The analysis will allow us to identify that the level of insurance portfolio transfers harmonisation in the EU is not as high as expected, and that a common framework and harmonisation is needed.

1 Introduction

Due to extenuating facts, insurance companies are often forced to change their activity, abandon product lines, restructure a group's business or simply exit the insurance market completely. Such occurrences may affect the situation and protection of the policyholder. The implementation of the Third Generation Insurance Directive aimed to not only deregulate the EU insurance markets, but to also enhance

K. Noussia (✉)
University of Reading, School of Law, Reading, UK
e-mail: k.p.noussia@reading.ac.uk

P. Underwood
University of Exeter, School of Law, Exeter, UK
e-mail: p.d.underwood@exeter.ac.uk

S. Frastanlis
S.A. Papadimitriou and Partners Law Firm, Athens, Greece
e-mail: sgf@saplegal.gr

P. Marano, K. Noussia (eds.), *The Governance of Insurance Undertakings*, AIDA Europe Research Series on Insurance Law and Regulation 6,
https://doi.org/10.1007/978-3-030-85817-9_8

market efficiency and consumer choice. When an exit of an insurance company is forced, any such market exit may take place either through voluntary or involuntary withdrawals (run-off) or insolvency or via M&As. The transfer of all or part of an insurance undertaking's portfolios is governed by Article 14 of Directive 2002/83/EC in the field of life insurance and by Article 12 of Directive 92/49/EEC in the field of non-life insurance. According to these articles, each Member State is obliged under the conditions laid down by national law, to authorise insurance undertaking with head offices within its territory to transfer all or part of their portfolios of contracts, concluded under either the right of establishment or the freedom to provide services, to an accepting office established within the Community. Any such transfer is subject to certification by the competent authorities of the home Member State of the accepting office that the latter possesses the necessary solvency margin. Whenever a transfer of portfolio is authorised under the law, the transfer becomes immediately effective for policyholders and beneficiaries, and as a result of portfolio transfer one or more lines of business from one insurance company are transferred to another to allow additional capital to be released and transferred. Furthermore, portfolio transfers act as an effective tool for managing discontinued business. The same applies as per Directive 2009/138/EC (recast) Solvency II, Art. 39. The Solvency II Directive introduced EU-wide prudential rules and created, for the first time, a fully harmonised regime for the prudential regulation of insurance and reinsurance businesses in Europe, with the aim of encouraging the development of a properly integrated insurance market. It aimed at introducing in all Member States a modern, economic and risk-based regime of prudential supervision for insurance and reinsurance undertakings and for groups. Notwithstanding the Solvency II regime, insurance portfolio transfers are often made by means of company law mechanisms (e.g. via the merger and acquisition of the company).

This chapter discusses reorganising, restructuring and winding-up of insurance companies, as well as insurance portfolio transfers by means of company law mechanisms (M&A) and under the Cross-Border Mergers Directive, as well as under the Solvency II Directive. It then goes on to discuss the position under Greek law and uses as a case study the winding-up of Aspis Pronoia in 2009, and the transfer of the insurance undertakings' portfolios. The analysis will allow us to identify that the level of insurance portfolio transfers harmonisation in the EU is not as high as expected, and that a common framework and harmonisation is needed.

2 Restructuring of Insurance Companies Under Company Law

This section will review the tools available to insurance companies under company law provisions whilst in distress. It will proceed as follows; first it will evaluate mergers and acquisitions, including the consideration of asset sales, contractual offers, and schemes of arrangements. It will then evaluate the role of cross-border mergers, considering how the directive operates and how this has been implemented into the United Kingdom's jurisdiction. It will then consider the role of Brexit briefly and discuss the likely effects of Brexit on cross-border mergers. Then it will move to assess other options such as liquidation and administration which could be applicable for insurance companies in distress. It will then consider some of the wider concepts within company law, such as the duties directors must adhere too when undertaking reorganisation and restructuring.[1]

2.1 Mergers and Acquisitions & Schemes of Arrangement

There are three principal ways of restricting companies within the domestic market, and in addition to these domestic options there is also the cross-border merger. This section will consider the three domestic methods of domestic structure, and the subsequent section will evaluate the cross-border merger provisions following the implementation of an EU directive.

2.1.1 The Contractual Basis for Reorganisation

The first deal structure available to insurance companies is the asset sale, this is where all or part of an undertaking's assets are purchased. This occurs where one company purchases the assets from another and upon the sale, title will be transferred to the acquirer. This transfer is no different than the sale of a company's products to its consumers, it can, however, be substantially more complex given the volume of assets. The sale of each asset will be required to adhere to the relevant formality requirement provisions to execute that sale. In the context of land, rights in rem may need to be considered and the relevant formalities complied with in accordance with the Land Registration Act 2002 to facilitate the sale.

One key advantage when compared with other deal structures is that the liabilities can be left with the target company. However, there remain significant challenges in relation to an asset sale, the need to comply with formalities, and rights for each individual asset can be disproportionately time consuming. Kershaw claims that because of this, asset sales are more common in smaller private companies than in publicly traded companies in which they are very rare.[2] Moreover, whilst the asset sale does permit the ability not to take on liabilities, there are statutory measures where the buyer must assume certain liabilities, and such is the case with employees. Whilst asset sales may therefore present themselves as initially appealing, the burden of complying with each formality, and risk of potential breach for not complying becomes inherently more difficult. Furthermore, merely purchasing assets alone will not necessarily result in a cheaper outcome. There remains the cost of the

[1] Milman (2014), pp. 1–5.

[2] Kershaw (2016), p. 32; Fama and Jensen (1983), p. 301; Habersack (2018), p. 1; Kershaw (2007), p. 267.

transactions, and the price adjustment for the assets being sold. The directors will be under a duty to ensure a fair price is achieved for the assets being sold and will also need to ensure that the corporate constitution allows for such sales. Therefore, given the size and complexity insurance companies operate in, the formality arrangements may outweigh benefits which often come with the asset sale component of restructuring.

In addition to the sale of assets, there is the contractual offer or the sale of shares which provides another avenue for corporate restructuring. Then contractual offer involves an offer which is made to shareholders directly to purchase their shareholding. The contractual nature of the transaction may require approval if there are restrictions in the articles of association or in a shareholders' agreement. This is more common in a smaller private company as public companies are subject to the Takeover code[3] where there is no such negotiation, but an offer to purchase shares subject to specific terms. The shareholders dispensing of their shares can therefore be considered no different than the sale of any other property. The term 'tender offer' is also used to describe a contractual offer and they are often referred to as takeovers. Kershaw highlights that this method is the most common for companies seeking to take control of another.[4] Given the strict separate legal nature of a company,[5] the company will remain unaffected when a share sale is exercised. If the offeror is seeking to gain complete control[6] but is unable to negotiate a purchase, then section 979 of the Companies Act 2006 may provide some additional assistance in the form of 'squeeze out'. This provision allows the offeror to acquire 100% providing they follow the squeeze out procedure. In this regard, the offeror is required to obtain 90% of the shares offered to force a purchase. Importantly, this 90% is not the total number of shares required but of the offer they are making.[7] If the offeror already controlled 90% of the shareholding, then the requirement would be that they acquire 90% of the 10% not possessed. Once this threshold is met, the offeror is bound to purchase all the shares on the terms offered.[8]

2.1.2 Schemes of Arrangement

Having evaluated the two methods of organisation which are premised on a contractual basis, this section will now proceed to consider the schemes of arrangement which can be used to implement a share transfer scheme or a merger scheme. Most jurisdictions provide for a specific statutory merger; however, in the UK, this is not

[3] A detailed analysis of the Take-Over code is beyond the scope of this chapter, for a detailed analysis of this, see Kershaw (2016).

[4] Kershaw (2016), p. 38.

[5] Lim (2013), p. 480.

[6] 100% of the shareholding.

[7] Companies Act 2006, s 979 (5).

[8] Ibid, s 981.

provided for and is instead dealt with under a scheme of arrangement. The closest the UK has come to forming a statutory footing for mergers is under The Companies (Cross-Border Mergers) Regulations 2007 which sets out the procedure for the merging of a UK company with an EEA company. A more detailed analysis of cross-border mergers will follow in the subsequent paragraphs. The benefit of this scheme of arrangement is that it is capable of dealing with more than just mergers, it can also be used to implement a share sale for control. One significant difference in respect of mergers and the preceding analysis on share sale and asset sales is that on completion of a merger one company is automatically wound-up. Whilst a company following an asset sale or share sale may be wound up shortly after the completion of the transaction, it is not a result of the transaction, whereas a merger is.

The statutory basis for a scheme of arrangement is found within Parts 26 and 26A of the Companies Act 2006 'arrangements and reconstructions'. Part 26 deals with general arrangements and reconstructions whilst Part 26A provides additional requirements for companies which are in financial difficulty. The basic structure, irrespective of which part is utilised, is that there is a court order to consider the compromise or arrangement,[9] court sanctioning and registration.[10] The benefits of the scheme of arrangement for companies in distress is that it can be utilised to restructure a company's debt. Part 26A will apply where a company has encountered or is likely to encounter financial difficulties which may affect its ability to continue to operate as a going concern.[11] Additionally, the arrangement must be between creditors of a class, or members with the purpose to reduce the financial difficulties. Moreover, an arrangement in under this part can include a reorganisation of the company's share capital which may release funds to redress financial distress. The ability to be able to restructure both share structures for control and debt via credit affords insurance companies in distress with wider options than a merger scheme would typically provide for.

The process for a scheme of arrangement pursuant to Parts 26 and 26A will now be set out. The first requirement is that there is meeting of creditors or members which is ordered by the court. An application for such an order for companies in distress can not only be brought by the company itself, but it can also be brought by a member or a creditor of the company. Moreover, for companies in distress the liquidator or administrator is also able to apply for a court ordered meeting.[12] The requirement from the meeting is that each member or creditor who will be affected will be permitted to participate in the ordered meeting. If the scheme will only effect one class, then there is no requirement for a meeting for the class unaffected.[13] Given that the arrangement is between the company and either the creditor, the consent of the company must be provided, and as such this process is unlikely to be utilised to

[9] Ibid, ss 896 and 901C.

[10] Ibid, ss 899 and 901F.

[11] Ibid, s 901A.

[12] Ibid, s 901C.

[13] Re British & Commonwealth Holdings Plc (No 3) [1992] 1 WLR 672.

commence a hostile takeover.[14] However, shareholders may be permitted through the articles or statutory provisions[15] to call a general meeting where special resolutions could form the basis for approval. In addition to the court order for a meeting, there is the requirement for a statement to be circulated or made available.[16] This statement is of significance because it must set out the compromise or arrangements effect. It is noteworthy that directors remain under a duty to provide information, and a default in relation to this is an offence and liable for a fine.

Once the court ordered meeting has the requisite approvals, a court sanction must be applied to sanction the scheme.[17] For the court to sanction this, there is a minimum requirement of consent from the corresponding members or creditors. A minimum of 75% approval is required[18] from the class of shareholders or creditors to which the scheme affects. Once the agreement is sanctioned it is binding on all creditors or members irrespective of whether they voted in favour of the scheme or not.[19] For companies where a debt restructuring may affect a pension scheme there is the additional requirement for a notice to be sent to the pensions' regulator in addition to the creditor,[20] for insurance companies dealing with restructuring of pension debts this is an additional requirement to overcome to attain a scheme of arrangement.

The procedure for restructuring debt or share structure is, therefore, one requiring three fundamental elements: a court ordering of a meeting, the court sanction of the scheme, and then the registration. As alluded above, the scheme of arrangement can be used widely to cover more than just share sales, such as a reorganisation of debt. Given the wide interpretation of scheme of arrangement, there is the capacity for a merger to fall within the remit of a scheme. The Companies Act provides the court with the power to amalgamate companies.[21] This amalgamation is essentially a merger and allows the courts to transfer both assets and liabilities, and further allows for the dissolution of the transferee company following a completion of transfer to the transferor. Part 27 of the Companies Act adapts the scheme of arrangement to specific types of merging public companies as defined by section 904.[22] These are merger by absorption and merger by formation. The merger by absorption is whereby a proposed transfer under a scheme by one or more public companies is transferred to an existing company. Conversely, the merger by formation is where two or more public companies are proposing a transfer under a scheme into a new company. Upon successful transfer, the transferee companies will be dissolved

[14] *Re Savoy Hotel [1981] Ch. 351.*

[15] Companies Act 2006, s 303.

[16] Ibid, s 901D.

[17] Ibid, s 901F.

[18] Ibid, s 901F.

[19] Ibid, s 901F (5).

[20] Ibid, s 901I.

[21] Ibid, s 900 & 901I.

[22] Companies Act 2006.

without the need for liquidation. The avoidance of liquidation in favour of transfer and dissolution could be more attractive because of the significant costs involved with liquidation.

The procedure under Part 27[23] is analogous to Part 26;[24] however, Part 27 provides that a scheme under Part 26 must not be sanctioned unless Part 27 has been complied with respect to public companies' requirements. The consequence of falling into Part 27 is that additional requirements need to be complied with. The significant additional terms are as follows: there must be draft terms of the scheme prepared,[25] these terms must then be published.[26] Additionally, there is the requirement for both a director's explanatory report[27] alongside an expert's report.[28] One advantage of Part 27 is in relation to ownership of the merging companies. If there is a requisite ownership or approval of 90% or more, than the requirement of a meeting is not required which can expediate and reduce the costs of the scheme.

Therefore, it can be ascertained that schemes of arrangement for an insurance company in distress can be utilised to facilitate numerous restructuring methods,[29] including restructuring of finance, mergers, and acquisitions.[30] This restructuring requires court sanctioning and approval from the members or creditors, and for companies in distress additional provisions are required to be complied with to ensure protection of wider stakeholders. This section has evaluated and outlined the options available within the UK from a company law perspective on restructuring for insurance companies.[31] The subsequent section will evaluate the role of cross-border mergers and their application to UK based insurance companies.

2.2 *Cross-Border Mergers*

This section will evaluate the options available to insurance companies where the proposed merger, acquisition or scheme extends further than domestic companies. Part 26[32] is only available where the company or companies are domestic; where they are not Part 26 cannot be used to facilitate a scheme. In an effort to provide for mergers within the European Economic Area (EEA) the European Union has

[23] Ibid.

[24] Ibid.

[25] Ibid, s 905.

[26] Ibid, s 906.

[27] Ibid, s 908.

[28] Ibid, s 909.

[29] For a further discussion, see Morse and Worthington (2010), Ch 12.

[30] Hostile takeovers have not been considered and are beyond the scope, for a detailed analysis of this as a method of control, see Kershaw (2016).

[31] McCormack (2020), pp. 11–22.

[32] Companies Act 2006.

provided a directive[33] to facilitate this. This has been implemented in the UK by The Companies (Cross-Border Mergers) Regulations 2007 (No. 2974) (hereafter 'the regulations'). This section will first outline the applicability and procedure of the directive before considering the application specifically in relation to the UK.

2.2.1 The Directive on Cross-Border Mergers of Limited Liability Companies

The Directive aims to facilitate the cross-border merger of limited liability companies where at least two of the companies have their principal place of business governed by different Member States.[34] The company which is subject to cross-border merger will still be required to comply with the provisions and formalities of the Member State's national law.[35] A merger under the directive includes the transfer of all assets and liabilities, the merger by absorption as has already been described, and a merger by formation, whereby two or more companies are dissolved and all assets transferred to the new company.

Given the larger scope of cross-border mergers, there are additional requirements which need to be complied with to facilitate a merger. The draft terms of the merger must be published before a general meeting for each of the merging companies one month before.[36] In addition to this, depending on the requirements within a Member State, these particulars of the merger must be published in the national gazette of the Member State in which the relevant company operates. Much like the merging of public companies under Part 27[37] there are reports which are required to be compiled and publicised. There is the requirement for a management or administrators report,[38] alongside the report of an independent expert report.[39] Once these reports have been presented to the members, they are able to be voted upon and gain approval at the general meeting. Following the approval by members, a pre-merger certificate needs to be obtained from the courts of the relevant competent authority. Before the completion of the merger, the courts will scrutinise the legality of the merger to ensure compliance. Following this approval, the law of each Member State in respect of registration will apply, and the relevant documents for the merger will be filed accordingly. The effect of a cross-border merger is similar to

[33] Directive 2005/56/EC of the European Parliament and of the Council of 26 October 2005 on cross-border mergers of limited liability companies. Subsequently repealed and codified under Directive 2017/1132.

[34] Directive (EU) 2017/1132 of the European Parliament and of the Council of 14 June 2017 relating to certain aspects of company law, Art. 118.

[35] Ibid, Art. 121.

[36] Ibid, Art. 123 (1).

[37] The Companies Act 2006.

[38] Directive (EU) 2017/1132 of the European Parliament and of the Council of 14 June 2017 relating to certain aspects of company law, Art. 124.

[39] Ibid, Art. 125.

a domestic one in that liabilities and assets are transferred into either the new company by formation or the transferee company absorbing the companies subject to the merger. The transferor companies will cease to exist following a successful merger.[40] Where companies are related through pre-existing share structures, there are simplified formalities, such as there being no requirement for members' approval.[41]

This consolidated framework provides the minimum formalities upon which Member States should seek to apply domestic law to cross-border mergers. It reverts back largely to domestic law for guidance in respect of cross-border mergers.[42] This may be in part due to the earlier directive in 2005 having largely been applied throughout the EEA Member States. This section has outlined the framework within the most recent directive relating to cross-border mergers. This directive provides clarity as to which domestic laws apply but often reverts back to domestic and local provisions. The next section will address how cross-border mergers are dealt within the UK and how the articles in the directives have been applied in a domestic context.

2.2.2 The Companies (Cross-Border Mergers) Regulations 2007 (No. 2974)

This section will analyse the application of the directive on cross-border mergers and how they apply in the UK context when a domestic company is merged with an EEA company. The procedure on cross-border mergers was adopted into UK law following the 2005 EU directive. It provides for a merger where one of the companies subject to the merger is not a domestic company. The regulations provide for a merger without the need for the previously analysed scheme of arrangement.

The regulations define a cross-border merger as one by absorption; absorption of wholly owned subsidiary or by formation of a new company.[43] The procedure outlined under this mechanism is procedurally similar to that outlined in Part 26.[44] Where a UK merging company wishes to merge, they must first seek court approval of the pre-merger requirements outlined in Part 2.[45] Within this application there is the requirement for all the terms and effects of the merger to be clearly outlined. In a similar manner to both Parts 27[46] and the directive[47] a directors' report alongside,

[40] Ibid, Art. 131 (2)(c).

[41] Ibid, Art. 132 (1).

[42] Mukwiri (2019) accessed 17.4.2021.

[43] The Companies (Cross-Border Mergers) Regulations 2007, ss 2 (2)–(4).

[44] The Companies Act 2006.

[45] The Companies (Cross-Border Mergers) Regulations 2007, Part 2.

[46] Companies Act 2006.

[47] Directive (EU) 2017/1132 of the European Parliament and of the Council of 14 June 2017 relating to certain aspects of company law.

and independent experts report is required. Once the requisite disclosures and publications have been complied with, then the subsequent vote from the members, and creditors if required, which requires a 75% approval for the merger to be accepted.[48] These formality requirements do not apply where a company is seeking to absorb a wholly owned subsidiary. Once the required formalities and votes have been complied with then the court may approve the cross-border merger.[49] The consequences are similar to the domestic scheme of arrangement whereby the assets and liabilities are transferred, and the transferor companies are dissolved.

2.2.3 The Effect of Brexit

The effect of the UK's withdrawal of the EU is likely to have a significant impact on the functioning of cross-border mergers within the UK and across the wider EEA Member States. The regulations governing the cross-border mergers have been revoked pending the UK's withdrawal.[50] The result of this is that from the relevant 'exit day',[51] i.e. 1 January 2021 the cross-border mergers have ceased to be an option for insurance companies wishing to complete a merger with a company outside of the UK. The timeframe for completion of a cross-border merger requires that all pending mergers must also be complete by the exit day for the formalities to be met.

Solvency II created, for the first time, a fully harmonised regime for the prudential regulation of insurance and reinsurance businesses in Europe.[52]

Looking specifically at Solvency II, post Brexit, the UK needs to domesticate the elements of the regime that are currently entrenched in EU legislation, and because the UK will also no longer be under any obligation to apply Solvency II standards to UK (re) insurers, the PRA may make further changes to the UK rules. As post-implementation period, the UK is treated as a third country and UK (re)insurers are subject to rules established by the Directive for third country (re)insurance undertakings in the same way as other non-EEA firms wishing to carry on insurance business in the EEA. In addition, as the Withdrawal Act preserves a very high proportion of this corpus of law as 'retained EU law' the interpretation of retained EU law will be a matter of law. The approach, as stated above, is to treat EEA states and EEA firms consistently with other third countries and firms. This includes the possible assessment of the EU regime as equivalent to the new, domestic or domesticated legal with temporary divergence so as to minimise disruption and

[48] The Companies (Cross-Border Mergers) Regulations 2007, ss 13 (1) and 14.

[49] Ibid, s 16.

[50] The Companies, Limited Liability Partnerships and Partnerships (Amendment etc.) (EU Exit) Regulations 2019, s 5.

[51] The European Union (Withdrawal) Act 2018 (Exit Day) (Amendment) (No. 3) Regulations 2019, s 20.

[52] Maddock and Matthews (2020), pp. 1–41.

avoid material unintended consequences for the continuity of financial services provision.[53]

The procedure for insurance companies wishing to merge either domestically or with another EEA company is a court governed proceed with varying degrees of formality requirements attached depending on the type of company. The benefit of the cross-border regulations and directive is that it permits two or more companies to merge from different jurisdictions and with different registration requirements. The removal of these regulations from an UK perspective reduces the options available to insurance companies in distress as they will not be able to restructure from outside the UK. The domestic scheme of arrangement is a flexible tool which not only allows for mergers and acquisitions but also allows for debt restructuring which could be a valuable tool for insurance companies in distress. This section has considered the options available on both a domestic and European level to insurance companies in distress with respect to restructuring. The following section will evaluate additional considerations which companies in distress need to take into account when considering options to restructure.

2.3 Further Considerations

This section will propose some further considerations that companies and their respective corporate managers should evaluate when considering restructuring. It will consider the options of winding-up alongside administration as alternative options to mergers and acquisitions. It will then highlight the importance of the fiduciary duties attached to corporate managers when restructuring.

2.3.1 Administration

The purpose of administration is to rescue the company, this can be viewed differently from winding-up. Rescue may not be considered due to the decisions of the members or the financial position the company may find itself in. The benefit of administration is that whilst the primary aim is to rescue the company as a going concern, wider conceptions of rescuing property or elements of the company may also be considered.[54]

Administration can be entered into by court order or without one. The main benefit of administration is the Moratorium which prevents creditors enforcing claims against the company[55] which allows greater time for insurance companies in distress to evaluate options. The formal appointment of a licenced administrator is

[53] Ibid, 30–41.

[54] Ibid, Schedule B1.; Davis (2004), pp. 124–126.

[55] Ibid, Schedule B1, 42 and 43.

required to manage the company and take control of the process.[56] Another benefit of administration is the availability of pre-packs.[57] This is where trade deals and negotiations are carried out prior to entering administration, with an agreement to buy the company or part of the company once the administration process is entered into.[58] The great advantage of this mechanism is that it can reduce the impact that insolvency proceedings have, and allow successful elements of the company to be sold whilst certain liabilities can remain with the insolvent company to enter into liquidation. Therefore, despite the substantial regulation surrounding, the availability of the ability to pre-package elements of the company for sale is likely to be advantageous for companies in distress. Moreover, the ability for pre-pack administration allows for quick resolution which could avoid negative publicity for larger insurance companies. Given that insurers will be selling a product to cover a period of time, coverage of insurance companies at risk could further exacerbate the distress the insurance company is in. The pre-pack administration allows for a procedure whereby this could be avoided or minimised. Furthermore, this allows the insurance company to seek to rescue the company in its entirety or its profitable elements.

2.3.2 Winding-Up

Although winding-up may not fall into the strict remit of reorganisation, it is worth consideration for insurance companies in distress.[59] Under the Insolvency provisions, a company which is subject to a member's voluntary liquidation may empower its liquidator by special resolution to transfer the whole or part of the business or property to another company in return for shares.[60] Insurance companies which form part of a larger corporate group may upon consideration seek to liquidate one of their related companies as opposed to merging or acquiring.

The process for winding-up is that assets of the company are collected and realised, the liabilities are discharged, and the surplus returned to persons entitled. A benefit of winding-up is that it can be carried out either whilst solvent or insolvent. The members of a company are free to propose this winding-up.[61] Similarly to the procedure under mergers, there remains the requirement to engage with the court for winding-up. A petition must be presented, followed by an advertisement and a subsequent hearing to make a winding-up order. The effect of the winding-up order results in a liquidator taking control of the company[62] to facilitate the

[56] Ibid, Schedule B1, Paragraph 6.

[57] Ibid, Schedule B1, Paragraph 59.

[58] For a more detailed account of pre-packs, see: Umfreville (2018), pp. 58–63; Astle (2015), p. 72; Finch (2006), p. 568.

[59] For a comprehensive analysis of corporate insolvency, see Van Zwieten (2018).

[60] Insolvency Act 1986, ss 110–111.

[61] Ibid, s 90.

[62] Ibid, ss 135–140.

winding-up of the company and the distribution of assets. In this regard, for insurance companies in distress, winding-up procedures could assist in the dissolution of the company where restructuring may not be of economic benefit.

2.3.3 Director's Duties

Director's Duties do not operate in a vacuum and are not a restructuring method or rescue procedure as per the preceding sections. The duties are a further consideration for directors or corporate managers for companies who are in distress and seeking to restructure, trade through or wind up. Director's duties are fiduciary in origin and most jurisdictions now have their own statutory basis.[63] Within the UK the duties are found in the Companies Act[64] which outlines the general duties and standards which directors need to uphold.[65]

In the context of companies in distress, directors and corporate managers should ensure that they are exercising these duties in accordance with due care and diligence requirements.[66] Two specific considerations are relevant to dealing with corporate rescue when companies are in distress.[67] The first is wrongful trading,[68] while the second is fraudulent trading. Continuing to trade through and failing to recognise the need for restructuring or rescue could result in director disqualification[69] or an order for contribution for losses.[70] To be liable, the director needs to have known or ought to have known that insolvent liquidation was unavoidable.[71] This relates to a standard of behaviours which can be linked to the director's duties provisions in the Companies Act. This is of significance as if the directors are considering pre-pack administration or a scheme of arrangement then they ought to consider the impact of their delay to action this, ensuring that this is carried out before rescue is possible.[72] Moreover, fraudulent trading can constitute a criminal offence[73] that is wider than wrongful trading as it will include any persons who were knowingly contributing to continuing to trade with intent to defraud.[74] Therefore, given the civil and criminal consequences which can be attached to corporate managers of

[63] For a more detailed analysis and discussion on directors' duties, see Omar (2018).

[64] Companies Act ss 170–182.

[65] See Keay (2011), p. 138; Arden (2010), p. 1.

[66] Ibid, s 174.

[67] Gustafsson (2017), p. 239.

[68] Insolvency Act s 214.

[69] Company Directors Disqualification Act 1986, s 10.

[70] Insolvency Act s 214.

[71] Ibid, s 214 (2)(b).

[72] Keay (2002), p. 379.

[73] Companies Act 2006, s 993.

[74] For a more comprehensive discussion, see R v Smith [1996] 2 BCLC 109.

companies in distress, mitigation and consideration of these principles should be borne in mind when evaluating rescue stories.

This section has evaluated the ways in which goals to restructure whilst in distress can be attained through the tools available from company law. It has assessed the availability of mergers and acquisitions alongside cross-border mergers to ascertain how attractive these tools may be to an insurance company in distress. Moreover, it has emphasised the challenges to cross-border mergers to companies based in the United Kingdom following the withdrawal from the European Union. Additionally, the scheme of arrangement for domestic purposes allows for a broad use to encompass debt restructuring. The following section will consider the restructuring of insurance companies through insurance law, including an evaluation of the insurance portfolio transfer and the tools available through the Solvency II Directive.

3 Restructuring of Insurance Companies Under Insurance Law

3.1 Insurance Portfolio Transfers

The process of insurance portfolio transfers in the EU was set by the Third Non-Life Directive,[75] the Consolidated Life Directive[76] and the Reinsurance Directive,[77] all of which set the legal and regulatory framework for the procedures, enabling a single official authorisation granted by the competent authorities of the country of company's head office, allowing it to be also recognised in other EU Member States. The consent of the policyholder was not regarded as essential and was not needed and the latter was to be notified only after the transfer has already been authorised.[78] The company accepting the portfolio had to abide with the solvency requirements in its home country and with those of the country of the branch, if a branch is transferred. The Directives establish a basic unified framework to limit jurisdictional discrepancies.[79] Of the starkest differences in portfolio transfers regulation are the ones noted in civil and common law countries[80] regarding the body responsible for

[75] Council Directive 92/49/EEC of 18 June 1992 on the coordination of laws, regulations and administrative provisions relating to direct insurance other than life assurance and amending Directives 73/239/EEC and 88/357/EEC (third nonlife insurance Directive), OJ L 228/1.

[76] Directive 2002/83/EC of The European Parliament and of The Council of 5 November 2002 concerning life assurance (Life Directive), OJ L 345/1.

[77] Directive 2005/68/EC of the European Parliament and of the Council of 16 November 2005 on reinsurance and amending Council Directives 73/239/EEC, 92/49/EEC as well as Directives 98/78/EC and 2002/83/EC, OJ L 323/1.

[78] Third Non-Life Directive, Art. 12(6); Life Directive, Art. 14(5).

[79] Bugden (2005), p. 5.

[80] Tsagas (2019), pp. 282–303.

the transfer authorisation, i.e. the courts, in the latter case, and the supervisory authorities in the former case.

Such discrepancies result in problems as in common law countries, courts may authorise the transfer of portfolio and any accompanying contracts, whereas the civil law supervisory authority can only decide on the transfer of portfolio itself, leaving the rest to negotiations, hence the need for a discussion of the transfer with reinsurers whose contracts are being transferred so as to have their prior consent, so as to ensure the continuation of coverage.[81]

3.2 *Insurance Portfolio Transfers (Solvency II)*

Article 39 of Solvency II replaces the regime of Article 14 of Directive 2002/83/EC of 5 November 2002 allowing in effect an insurance undertaking to transfer a portfolio of contracts to an insurance undertaking established in a Member State after it has received the authorisation of the supervisory authority of its home Member State. As per Article 39 of Solvency II, it is stipulated that under the conditions laid down by national law, Member States can authorise insurance and reinsurance undertakings with head offices within their territory to transfer all or part of their portfolios of contracts, concluded either under the right of establishment or the freedom to provide services, to an accepting undertaking established within the EU. The prerequisites for such an authorisation are that the competent authority of the home Member State of the accepting undertaking certifies that this undertaking possesses the necessary eligible own funds to cover the Solvency Capital Requirement, to cover the Solvency Capital Requirement as per Solvency II Article 100, after taking the transfer into account. It is up to the supervisory authorities of the home Member State of the transferring insurance undertaking to authorise the transfer after obtaining the agreement of the authorities of the Member States where the contracts were concluded, either under the right of establishment or the freedom to provide services. In addition, the competent authorities of the Member States where the contracts were concluded have consented or did not oppose within a period of three months after receiving a request for consultation.

Post Brexit and post the expiry of the transition period, UK insurers and reinsurers who may want to pursue the option of a portfolio transfer will not be able to conduct such a transfer under Art. 39 of Solvency II, as the provision does not apply to third-country insurers and reinsurers. It is questionable if the specific portfolio-transfer rules will apply to portfolio transfers of UK insurers after the expiry of the transition period.[82]

---

[81] Khomenko (2017), pp. 36–39, 46–48.

[82] Dentons LLP (2021) accessed 5.4.2021.

3.3 Winding-Up (Solvency II)

This section will analyse the rules for winding-up insurance companies under Directive 2009/138/EC. Regulation on winding-up of insurance companies under insurance law are set out specifically in Solvency II under the Title IV 'reorganisation and winding-up of insurance undertakings'.[83] The directive does not harmonise national legislation but provides a framework for mutual understanding for Member States on the process of winding-up of an insurance company. The directive limits the definition of winding-up to the collective proceedings which involving the realisation of the assets of an insurance undertaking and distributing among the creditors.[84] The purpose of winding-up is therefore to liquidate and realise assets and distribute the proceeds to the creditors in the order of priority as identified by the directive.

Chapter III[85] sets out the procedure to be followed for winding-up. The competent authorities of the home Member States are the only parties entitled to make a decision concerning the opening of winding-up proceedings.[86] 'Competent authorities' are the administrative or judicial authorities of the Member States which are competent for the purposes of reorganisation methods or winding-up proceedings.[87] The decision to commence winding-up proceedings of insurance undertaking shall be governed by the applicable law in the home Member State unless otherwise provided in Articles 285–292.[88] The law of the home Member State will therefore govern the proceedings unless this contradicts the provisions in Articles 285–292. In this regard, the directive is not providing harmonisation, but providing that the relevant jurisdiction to oversee the winding-up will be that of the home Member State. Article 274 provides a list of what the law of the home Member State must determine, notably including the assets which form part of the state, the role of the liquidator, the effects of proceedings on current insurance contracts, the rules governing claims, and ascertaining who bears the cost of winding-up.

In relation to insurance claims, Member States are required to ensure that insurance claims take precedence over other claims except for employee's rights, tax systems and rights in rem.[89] Under Article 276, insurance undertakings are also required to keep a special register of all calculated special provisions. Once winding-up provisions have commenced, this register may not be amended except with for the very limited reason of clerical error.

---

[83] Directive 2009/138/EC of the European Parliament and of the Council of 25 November 2009 on the taking-up and pursuit of the business of Insurance and Reinsurance (Solvency II).

[84] Ibid, Art. 268 (1) (d).

[85] Ibid.

[86] Ibid, Art. 273 (1).

[87] Ibid, Art. 268 (1) (a).

[88] Ibid, Art. 274.

[89] Ibid, Arts. 275 – 1 (b).

Chapter IV contains the common provisions which provide additional provisions notwithstanding the position of the law from the home Member State. Article 285 by way of derogation introduces some additional guidance. Employment contracts are to be governed exclusively by the law of the Member States applicable to the employment contract or employment relationship. Contracts conferring the right to make use of or acquire immovable property are to be governed where the property is situated. With regards to insurance over immovable property, a ship or aircraft subject to registration in a public register, this is to be governed by the law of the Member State in which the register is kept.[90] The rights in rem will not be affected in respect of tangible or intangible, movable or immovable objects, both specific and indefinite assets, for which Article 286 provides additional guidance as to the remit this includes. The same is true of goods or property subject to retention of title and set off, winding-up proceedings will not affect the application of these principles.

The directive in relation to winding-up therefore prescribes very little in addition to that of the home Member State of the insurance undertaking. When an insurance company becomes insolvent[91] the decision to wind up the company is made by competent authorities in the EU country in which the insurance company is registered. The directive provides that with exception of some express provisions, outlined above, the law of the home Member State will function to wind up the insurance undertaking. Therefore, the directive is more facilitative in providing a framework outlining the circumstances in which Member State law applies.[92] However, the home Member State must have a supervisory authority which must inform their counterparts in the EU countries about the decisions of the winding-up procedure and any implications.[93] This has been applied since with Advocate General Hogan providing the opinion that it is up for the home Member State to decide upon how winding-up proceedings are undertaken. In this regard, Solvency II, whilst providing clarity on jurisdictional application of the law, in terms of which jurisdiction prevails, does little to amend substantive winding-up procedures for insurance undertaking within their home Member State.

If an insurance company becomes insolvent, the decision to reorganise or wind up the company is made by the relevant authorities in the EU country where the insurance company is registered. The supervisory authorities must tell their counterparts in all other EU countries about the decision, including any practical implications. Winding-up proceedings apply to all EU branches of the insurance company. Creditors must all be informed and treated in the same way, regardless of the EU country they are based in. The Solvency II Directive gives EU countries different options for dealing with insurance claims when winding-up an insurer. They can either give insurance claims absolute priority over all other claims on the

[90] Ibid, Art. 285.

[91] Depending on the definition set out by the home Member State.

[92] Khomenko (2017), p. 20.

[93] Directive 2009/138/EC of the European Parliament and of the Council of 25 November 2009 on the taking-up and pursuit of the business of Insurance and Reinsurance (Solvency II), Article 284.

insurer, give insurance claims priority but allow claims on salaries, social security, taxes and assets to take precedence over insurance claims, or decide that the costs of winding-up the insurer take priority over insurance claims.[94]

3.4 *Reorganisation Measures (Solvency II)*

Similar considerations apply to the rules dealing with reorganisation measures (Title IV, Chapter II, Articles 269–272 of the Directive 2009/138/EC). The directive establishes coordination rules to ensure that the reorganisation measures adopted by the competent authority of a Member State to preserve or restore the financial soundness of an insurance undertaking produce full effects throughout the Community, in compliance with the law of the home Member State. The reorganisation measures referred to in the directive concern measures involving any intervention by the competent authorities which are intended to preserve or restore the financial situation of an insurance undertaking, and which affect pre-existing rights of parties other than the insurance undertaking itself, including but not limited to measures involving the possibility of a suspension of payments, suspension of enforcement measures or reduction of claims.[95] Other reorganisation measures such as the portfolio transfers of insurance companies or the appointment of an administrator to perform specific actions against the financial distress may also apply.

According to the directive, the reorganisation measures shall not preclude the opening of winding-up proceedings by the home Member State. Also, the reorganisation measures taken in accordance with the legislation of the home Member State shall be fully effective throughout the Community without any further formalities, including against third parties in other Member States, even where the legislation of those other Member States does not provide for such reorganisation measures or alternatively makes their implementation subject to conditions which are not fulfilled. Such measures shall be effective throughout the Community once they become effective in the home Member State.[96] To achieve mutual recognition of the reorganisation measures throughout the Community, it is necessary for the competent supervisory authorities of the Member States to cooperate and to coordinate their actions.

The *lex concursus* rule, which stipulates that the reorganisation measures shall be governed by the laws, regulations and procedures applicable in the home Member State is not absolute. There are some deviations from this rule, which are provided in in Articles 285 to 292 of the directive.

---

[94]European Commission, 'Winding-up of insurance undertakings Rules on reorganising and winding-up insurance companies'. <https://ec.europa.eu/info/business-economy-euro/banking-and-finance/insurance-and-pensions/winding-insurance-undertakings_en> accessed 5.4.2021.

[95]Directive 2009/138/EC (Solvency II), Art. 268 (c).

[96]Directive 2009/138/EC (Solvency II), Art. 269.

The purpose of the directive does not seem to be the harmonisation of the national laws of the Member States in respect of the reorganisation measures for insurance undertakings that apply in each Member State, but rather to enhance the cooperation between the various Member States in such cases. Therefore, the directive aims to have binding force on all Member States to which it is addressed only in respect of the result it seeks to obtain, while it allows Member States freedom of choice on the means that can be applied to achieve the result, in matters in which national deviations and peculiarities need to be considered. In this respect, it seeks to establish coordination rules so that decisions by other Member States on the adoption of reorganisation measures can be fully effective in other Member States as soon as they take effect in the home Member State.[97]

The coordination of the competent authorities in respect of the adoption of reorganisation measures is addressed through a combination of the principles of unity, universality and coordination. The principle of unity is expressed through the exclusive competence that each Member State grants to its competent authorities to take decisions on reorganisation measures concerning a particular insurance undertaking, including its branches. It is only the home Member State's supervisory authority of the insurance undertaking in distress that may adopt the relevant reorganisation measures and hold sole responsibility for them.

The principle of universality is expressed through the following rules:[98]

(a) Recognition of the sole jurisdiction of the competent authority in respect of the reorganisation measures that are adopted in accordance with the law of the home Member State.
(b) The application of a single system of law, the law in force in the home Member State (*lex concursus*).
(c) The automatic recognition of the reorganisation measures adopted by the competent authority of the home Member State in accordance with the law if this Member State in all the other Member States.

This automatic and mutual recognition of reorganisation measures in all EU Member States plays a decisive role in the coordination of decisions concerning reorganisation measures for insurance undertakings before they find themselves in financial distress.

The coordination of the Member States on ensuring that the effects of decisions on reorganisation measures are produced throughout the European Union is achieved through the provision of relevant information to the supervisory authorities. In this respect, the competent authorities of the home Member State shall inform as a matter of urgency the supervisory authorities of that Member State of their decision on any reorganisation measure, where possible before the adoption of such a measure and failing that immediately thereafter. Then, the supervisory authorities of the home Member State shall inform as a matter of urgency the supervisory

[97] Directive 2009/138/EC (Solvency II), Art. 269 par. 5.

[98] On the principle of universality, see Perakis (2004), p. 754.

authorities of all other Member States of the decision to adopt reorganisation measures including the possible practical effects of such measures.[99]

All insurance companies can face difficulties for various reasons. When such difficulties occur, it is to ensure that these are managed in a manner that minimises the impact on financial stability, policyholders and beneficiaries in all Member States involved.[100] In this respect, it is important that there is a legal framework in place providing the insurers with the appropriate tools and means to prevent or reserve a deteriorating financial situation of an insurance undertaking. As a general comment, it is to consider that a legal framework cannot solve financial problems of a company in distress but can be of help in terms of facilitating a restructuring process and enabling a smooth implementation of the restructuring measures taken from the competent authority on behalf of the company in distress.[101] Therefore, even if an efficient legal framework is in place, some companies in distress may recover but other may fail. However, it is important to achieve at the EU level a minimum harmonisation of national laws of the Member States in this respect by introducing general principles relating to recovery and resolution frameworks (i.e. appropriate preventive measures and pre-emptive recovery planning) for insurance undertakings to apply in a proportionate way, while at the same time leaving room for Member States to adopt additional measures at national level being compatible with the above general principles and requirements set at the EU level.[102]

4 Greek Case Study: Aspis Pronia

4.1 The Legal Framework

In 2008, the supervision of insurance companies was passed from the Ministry of Trade to a legal entity namely the Private Insurance Supervisory Committee (PISC),[103] and in a short period thereafter it was further passed to the Bank of Greece which became the sole regulator of the private insurance sector.[104] The state supervision of the Greek private insurance and reinsurance industry is mainly governed by Law 4364/2016, which introduced in Greece the Solvency II Directive

[99] Directive 2009/138/EC (Solvency II), Art. 270.

[100] Central Bank of Ireland (2020), pp. 3, 4.

[101] See Baird (2010), p. 256: 'Legal rules cannot cure nonlegal problems. Legal rules cannot make the imprudent wise and the unlucky fortunate. [. . .] Bankruptcy law cannot work miracles, and more harm than good comes from seeking that which cannot be had'.

[102] See Opinion on the 2020 Review of Solvency II (Chapter 12), EIOPA-BoS 20/749, 17 December 2020; Central Bank of Ireland (2020), pp. 3–4.

[103] The PISC took over the supervision of insurance companies on 01.01.2008 by virtue of Art. 1 of Law 3229/2004.

[104] The Bank of Greece took over the supervision of insurance companies on 01.12.2010 by virtue of Art. 1 par. 1 of Law 3867/2010.

(2009/138/EC), Articles 2 and 8 of Directive 2014/51/EU and Article 4 of Directive 2011/89/EU. The insurance intermediaries' conduct of business is governed by Law 4583/2018 (implementing the Insurance Distribution Directive (IDD)). Insurers and reinsurers must conduct their business in a fit and proper manner and comply with the regulatory obligations that have been set to safeguard their soundness. These obligations are also compliant with the provisions of the EU Solvency II legislative framework enacted in Greece in 2016 (Law 4364/2016). On capital requirements, each insurance and reinsurance company is obliged to comply with the Solvency II regulatory requirements. For reinsurance companies, the minimum solvency margin should amount to at least 3 million Euros pursuant to Article 267 of Law 4364/2016. Insurance and reinsurance companies are placed under compulsory winding-up proceedings if their licence has been revoked on the grounds of failing to abide by solvency requirements, or if the regulator has frozen their assets pursuant to Law 4364/2016. The proceedings have immediate effect in all EU and EEA Member States where the insurer is established. The liquidator is appointed by the country's regulator and has the duty to notify all persons who are entitled to insurance compensation and domiciled in other EU and EEA Member States about the proceedings and the procedure to notify their claims. Claims arising from compulsory third-party liability insurance are covered by the Auxiliary Fund. Claims arising from life assurance are handled by the Private Insurance Guarantee Fund (established by Law 3867/2010).[105]

4.2 *The Case of Aspis Pronia*

Aspis Pronia General Insurances S.A., a member of Aspis Group of Companies, was a Greece-based insurance company providing insurance plans for pension and investment programs, medical, family, individual and child coverage, as well as property and casualty insurance for over 1 million citizens in Greece, all of which—as a result of the company's license having been revoked since 2009 because of Aspis Pronia's inefficiency to cover its large financial deficit that exceeded EUR 500 million, had been left in an unstable *status quo*.

The revocation of the company's license came as no surprise to the Greek market. Already since 2002 there were assumptions that there were issues with Aspis Pronia. Greek audit services have made discoveries over the company's financial assets such as properties in Cyprus in inexistent locations, or properties in Romania that were appearing to cost as much as four times over their real price, while officials pertained that the former CEO Pavlos Psomiadis and his family have had misappropriated funds that reached EUR 50 million during and over the last 10 years of the company's operation. The company was asked to find funds to cover the EUR 250 million deficit and as no solution was reached, the license of Aspis Pronia was

[105] Giomelakis et al. (2020).

revoked, leaving over one million people in limbo. The Greek government acted by binding 50% of the assets of the Aspis insurance fund to prevent a following liquidation of the remaining assets of Aspis Pronia that were estimated at around EUR 130 million, for the benefit of the employees and those that were insured with Aspis. But, up until a solution would be found for the insureds of Aspis—such as transferring the contracts to other insurance companies (in fact a large amount of the contracts were already transferred to other insurers and relatively rapidly, but because most of these insurance policies were concerning health-covering costs or pension funds programs that had to be covered soon enough, it would mean no profit for the companies and no insurance firm was willing to take them), the Public Auxiliary Fund was appointed to cover the losses of Aspis and cover them. Those insureds have had to be compensated by the Life Guarantee Fund with 70% of their demands.[106]

As in other financial sectors,[107] guarantee funds have been set up for the protection of insureds and third parties in the insurance sector.[108] The Auxiliary Fund was established in 1986 to cover damage caused by car accidents and to give to third parties access to financial cover for damage and personal injuries caused by motor vehicles for any reason, and in any case not due to intentional misconduct by the insured, or when the insured cannot be identified, thus allowing the exemplification of a socio-economic safety net and purpose that benefits the public and the market. All insurers have had to participate in the Auxiliary Fund, which aimed to restate the insurer to its obligations and covered the risks of third-party liability in the event of insolvency or revocation of the operation licence.

Following the revocation of the operating license of Aspis Pronia AEGA was revoked in 2009/2010 by *Greek Government Gazette* Vol 11292/21-09-2009 and *Greek Government Gazette* Vol 1468/26-02-2010 respectively, and the situation which evolved, i.e. the fact that thousands of Greek policyholders were left uncovered and uninsured in spite of having paid their premiums, a solution, albeit interim, was sought and it was under the ambit of the Greek Regulator (i.e. the Bank of Greece) that the Private Life Insurance Guarantee Fund was founded.[109] Hence, the Greek legislature attempted to regulate and supervise the operation of life insurers by introducing the Private Life Insurance Guarantee Fund and its Management Committee, which is composed of insurers (Articles 9, 11 and 12 of Law 3867/2010) also attempting to prevent any attempts to abuse the existence of funds and to protect policyholders. Further, the above special law on the Supervision of Private Insurance was introduced with the aim to achieve the rescue of the existing funds through the

[106] Xprimm (2012).

[107] Guarantee funds intended to protect customers of financial sector firms are established and operate in Greece in accordance with the respective EU directives (i.e. for credit institutions, the Deposit Guarantee and Investment Fund; for investment firms, the Co-guarantee Fund; and for credit risks relating to the settlement of the stock exchange transactions, the Auxiliary Fund); Issaias and Kalogerakou (2015).

[108] Issaias and Kalogerakou (2015).

[109] Ibid.

portfolio transfer of the above insurance companies in distress to a third party—successor of those insurance portfolios.[110] For the case whereby such portfolio transfer was not successful for any reason, this special law provided for a liquidation scenario and the termination of all relevant insurance policies.

In this respect, the Greek regulator (Bank of Greece) issued a decision on the special process of the portfolio transfer of the above insurance undertakings as well as the required qualifications of the potential successor of such portfolios.[111] The efforts of the portfolio supervisors to transfer the insurance portfolios of Aspis Pronoia remained unfruitful, among others, from failure to adequately estimate the exposure risk inherent in such transfer.[112] Finally, the deadline set by the Greek regulator for the completion of the transfer lapsed and a relevant decision was issued confirming the failure of the portfolio transfer process and also regulating the details of the inevitable liquidation scenario under the Legislative Decree 400/1970.[113]

In the case of Aspis Pronia, whose operating licence was revoked and which finally entered into liquidation, the Council of State has held[114] that the liability of the state and its organs (i.e. civil servants) exists only in case of major fault on the part of the regulator. The Supreme Administrative Court has also found[115] that the facts surrounding Aspis Pronia did not justify the triggering of such liability. Within the reasoning of this decision, the court held that the introduction of the law on the Private Life Insurance Guarantee Fund, which protected the insureds in that case, was a fundamental reason why the general basis of liability[116] for acts or omissions of state organs cannot apply directly in cases where the action is brought against the regulator for acts or omissions of its officers in the performance of their supervisory duties.[117]

On 1 February 2021, the insurance liquidator announced the allocation of € 20 million from the Private Life Insurance Guarantee Fund to meet claims from life insurance claims of Aspis Pronia AEGA which is under Insurance Liquidation. As per this announcement, the temporary distribution of each beneficiary, is to be made exclusively under the responsibility of the insurance liquidator after a proportional distribution, from his part, of the advance of € 20 million based on the amount of the claim of each beneficiary, which is amounting to circa 6.66%.[118]

---

[110] Article 2 par. 1 b) of Law 3867/2010; Sobolou (2016).

[111] Decision No. 37/5/20-4-2012 of the Credit and Insurance Committee of the Bank of Greece.

[112] See relevant decision of the Credit and Insurance Committee of the Bank of Greece (Decision No. 37/4/20-4-2012).

[113] Decision No. 41/1/1-6-2012 of the Credit and Insurance Committee of the Bank of Greece.

[114] Decision 3783/2014; Issaias and Kalogerakou (2015).

[115] Decision 3783/20141; Issaias and Kalogerakou (2015).

[116] Article 105 of the Greek Civil Code; Issaias and Kalogerakou (2015).

[117] Although this law was introduced only after the collapse of the insurer and the insureds and/or the failed insurer had paid no contributions to the Private Life Insurance Guarantee Fund, when the insurance policies were issued, they were covered by the fund; Issaias and Kalogerakou (2015).

[118] Asfalistiki Agora (2021).

5 Conclusions

The restructuring of insurance companies is at points needed, be it in company law through the mechanism of M&A, or under EU legislation via portfolio transfer, or be it as winding-up and/or portfolio transfer as per the Cross-Border Mergers directive, as well as under the Solvency II directive. The position under the EU legislation and the paradigm of the case study of the winding-up of Aspis Pronia in Greece in 2009 has shown that there exists fragmentation in the insurance portfolio transfers harmonisation in the EU. Our discussion has shown that asset sale has challenges within it as a process, but, when compared with other deal structures, is advantageous in that the liabilities can be left with the target company, and a major disadvantage is the existence of statutory measures asking the buyer to assume certain liabilities. Moreover, the large-scale formalities within asset sales presents its own significant costs, resulting in its limited application for most insurance companies. The contractual offer or the sale of shares is a method most common for companies seeking to take control of another company. There is also the route of adopting a scheme of arrangement, such as a share transfer scheme or a merger, which has the benefit of at the same time having the option to effect a merger and also implement a share sale for control. As our discussion has shown, schemes of arrangement for an insurance company in distress can be utilised to facilitate numerous restructuring methods, including restructuring of finance, mergers, and acquisitions.[119] The Directive on cross-border mergers sought to facilitate the cross-border merger of limited liability companies where at least two of the companies have their principal place of business governed by different Member States.[120] It is a Directive that provides clarity as to which domestic laws apply but often reverts back to domestic and local provisions. The application of the directive on cross-border mergers and how they apply in the UK context when a domestic company is merged with an EEA company if all required formalities and votes have been complied with, the court may approve the cross-border merger.[121] The consequences are similar to the domestic scheme of arrangement whereby the assets and liabilities are transferred, and the transferor companies are dissolved. Following Brexit, regulations governing the cross-border mergers have been revoked because of the UK's withdrawal,[122] and cross-border mergers have now ceased to be an option for insurance companies wishing to complete a merger with a company outside of the UK. As discussed, Solvency II created, for the first time, a fully harmonised regime for the

[119] Hostile takeovers have not been considered and are beyond the scope, for a detailed analysis of this as a method of control, see Kershaw (2016).

[120] Directive (EU) 2017/1132 of the European Parliament and of the Council of 14 June 2017 relating to certain aspects of company law, Art 118.

[121] Ibid, s 16.

[122] The Companies, Limited Liability Partnerships and Partnerships (Amendment etc.) (EU Exit) Regulations 2019, s 5.

prudential regulation of insurance and reinsurance businesses in Europe.[123] Insurance companies have the option to effect a winding-up process which even if it does not fall into the strict remit of reorganisation is worth consideration for insurance companies in distress, as its effect is that a liquidator taking control of the company[124] to facilitate the winding-up of the company and the distribution of assets, hence assisting in the dissolution of the company where restructuring may not be of economic benefit. In Greece, when the operating license of Aspis Pronoia AEGA was revoked in 2009/2010 and a large number of policyholders were left uncovered and uninsured in spite of having paid their premiums, the Greek state intervened and used the Private Life Insurance Guarantee Fund as a guardian interim mechanism to seek to protect the interests of policyholders. No solution has been found to date as there has been no interest in buying the bad portfolio of the defaulted insurance company. The above analysis and discussion, demonstrates the attempts to harmonise the legal landscape, and the struggles to achieve homogeneity, even more in a post Brexit era. On reorganisation and winding-up proceedings, Solvency II may fulfil the goal of ensuring coordination and cooperation between the supervisory authorities of the Member States in respect to the mutual and universal recognition of reorganisation measures and winding-up proceedings throughout the EU, but actually does little to achieve this homogeneity and finally the harmonisation of the national laws as it refers back to the procedure in the domestic company's jurisdiction to achieve the result of the reorganisation or the winding-up proceedings. The preceding analysis and discussion has identified how this can be problematic and that the application in multiple jurisdictions further exacerbates the challenges in identifying and applying the most beneficial procedure. The UK's withdrawal from the EU further limits the options available to UK insurance companies, which is likely to result in further winding-up, as opposed to rescue in times of distress. Further harmonisation efforts should seek to lift procedural burdens and simplify procedures including countries legally treated as EEA ones. Increasing harmonisation and the inclusion of simplified procedures has the potential to rescue more multi-jurisdictional companies in distress and thus adequately protect policyholders, as well as maintain financial stability in the EU.

References

Arden M (2010) Regulating the conduct of directors. JCLS 10:1

Asfalistiki Agora (2021) Developments in relation to Aspis Pronia and commercial value [in Greek], <https://www.aagora.gr/exelixeis-se-aspis-pronoia-kai-commercial-value/>. Accessed 17 Apr 2021

Astle T (2015) Pack-up your troubles: addressing the negative image of pre-packs. Insolv Int 28:72

[123] Maddock and Matthews (2020), p. 1.

[124] The Companies, Limited Liability Partnerships and Partnerships (Amendment etc.) (EU Exit) Regulations 2019, ss 135–140.

Baird D (2010) The elements of bankruptcy law

Bugden P (2005) Insurance business transfer schemes: creating an effective route to finality. L.L.I. D., Jul 15, p 5

Central Bank of Ireland (2020) Regulations for pre-emptive recovery planning for (re)insurers. Consultation Paper 131

Davis G (2004) Administration of insurance companies likely to be insolvent. Insolv Int 17 (8):124–126

Dentons LLP (2021) Brexit and the future of cross-border (re-)insurance and pensions business from the UK and Gibraltar in Germany – BaFin Issues New Post-Brexit Access Ruling, <https://www.dentons.com/en/insights/alerts/2021/january/29/brexit-the-future-of-cross-border-re-insurance-pensions-business-from-uk-and-gibraltar-in-germany>. Accessed 12 Apr 2021

EIOPA, Opinion on the 2020 Review of Solvency II (Chapter 12). EIOPA-BoS 20/749, 17 December 2020

European Commission, Winding-up of insurance undertakings: rules on reorganising and winding-up insurance companies. <https://ec.europa.eu/info/business-economy-euro/banking-and-finance/insurance-and-pensions/winding-insurance-undertakings_en>. Accessed 5 Apr 2021

Fama E, Jensen M (1983) Separation of ownership and control. J Law Econ 26:301

Finch V (2006) Pre-packaged administrations: bar-gains in the shadow of insolvency or shadowy bargains? JBL 568

Giomelakis D, Mathiopoulos N, Papagrigoraki M (2020) The insurance and reinsurance law review: Greece. <https://thelawreviews.co.uk/title/the-insurance-and-reinsurance-law-review/greece>. Accessed 5 Apr 2021

Gustafsson M (2017) Beating a dead horse? An assessment of wrongful trading. Co Law 38:239

Habersack M (2018) Non-frustration rule and mandatory bid rule–cornerstones of European takeover law? Eur Company Financ Law Rev 15:1

Issaias K, Kalogerakou P (2015) Policyholder protection funds. <https://www.internationallawoffice.com/OnDemand/Insurance/Policyholder-protection-funds/Greece/KG-Law-Firm>. Accessed 5 Apr 2021

Keay A (2011) Good faith and directors' duty to promote the success of their company. Co Law 32:138

Keay AR (2002) The duty of directors to take into account creditors' interests; has it any role to play?. J Bus Law:379–410

Kershaw D (2007) The illusion of importance: reconsidering the UK's takeover defence prohibition. Int Comp Law Q 56(2):267

Kershaw D (2016) Principles of take over regulation. Oxford University Press

Khomenko O (2017) Jurisdictional issues of cross border insurance portfolio transfers: a comparative analysis. Eur Ins Law Rev 1:36–50, <http://www.erevija.org/pdf/articles/eng/Khomenko%20engl.pdf>. Accessed 5 Apr 2021

Lim E (2013) Salomon reigns. Law Q Rev 129:480

Maddock D, Matthews A (2020) Solvency II: a new decade, a new regime? Or much the same as before? C.O.B. 174(Mar), 1–41

McCormack G (2020) The European Restructuring Directive - a general analysis. Insolv Int 33 (1):11–22

Milman D (2014) Further judicial enlightenment on UK restructuring law and practice. Co. L.N. 358, 1–5

Morse G, Worthington S (2010) Palmer's company law. Sweet & Maxwell

Mukwiri J (2019) Cross-border mergers directive and its impact in the UK. In: Papadopoulos T (ed) Cross-border mergers. Studies in European economic law and regulation, vol 17. Springer, Cham. https://doi.org/10.1007/978-3-030-22753-1_23

Omar PJ (ed) (2018) Directors' duties and liabilities. Routledge

Perakis E (2004) Some thoughts on International Bankruptcy Law after Regulation 1346/2000 and the model UNCITRAL law. In: Perakis E (ed) Issues of theory and practice in commercial law, pp 753–774 [in Greek]

Sobolou A (2016) The portfolio transfer of insurance undertakings under the new law 4364/2016 for Solvency II. In: Tzouganatos D, Kotsovilis V, Kontovazenitis T, Voglis E (eds) 'Studies in honor of Leonidas Georgakopoulos' Band I, Central bank of Greece, pp 827–850 [in Greek]

Tsagas G (2019) Use and abuse of power in changes of corporate control: transfer schemes and shareholders' voting practices in unchartered waters. J.B.L. 4:282–303

Umfreville C (2018) Review of the pre-pack industry measures: reconsidering the connected party sale before the sun sets. Insolv Intell 31(2):58–63

Van Zwieten K (2018) Goode on principles of corporate insolvency law. Sweet and Maxwell

Xprimm: Greece: Aspis Pronoia - The Black Sheep of the Greek Insurance Market, 2012 <http://www.xprimm.com/GREECE-ASPIS-PRONOIA-the-black-sheep-of-the-Greek-insurance-market-articol-2,143,140-2006.htm>. Accessed 5 Apr 2021

Insurance in M&A Transactions

Angelo Borselli

Abstract Mergers and acquisitions (M&A) involve transactional risks, no matter how extensive and accurate the due diligence process is. This raises the question as to how transacting parties can be protected. Representations and warranties and indemnification provisions as well as escrow requirements, typically included in the acquisition agreement, may often prove to be inefficient and inadequate to this end. When negotiating these terms, transacting parties clearly have contrasting interests, and there could also be cases, especially in public company transactions or distressed sales, where the buyer may have no effective remedies against the seller after the closing.

To overcome problems associated with seller's indemnities, transacting parties increasingly avail themselves of some innovative insurance products, generally known under the catch-all name of "transactional insurance," that provide coverage for risks arising out of extraordinary corporate transactions, including risks related to breaches of representations and warranties, tax liabilities, pending or potential litigation and other contingent liabilities.

This chapter explores the role that insurance can play in managing transactional risk, discussing whether it may represent an efficient alternative to more traditional, contractual solutions like indemnity and escrow requirements. The discussion suggests that transactional insurance can serve as an effective risk-transfer tool in M&A, which may act as a supplement or also a substitute for seller indemnity obligations. By spreading transactional risk, insurance can facilitate M&A transactions and enhance the overall social benefit, providing economic security at a fraction of the cost that it would take for transacting parties to protect themselves. No problems of

The author wishes to thank the Association Internationale de Droit des Assurances (AIDA) Europe for awarding the AIDA Europe Academic Prize to this work.

A. Borselli (✉)
Department of Law, Bocconi University, Milan, Italy

Scholar in Residence, Insurance Law Center, University of Connecticut School of Law, Hartford, CT, USA
e-mail: angelo.borselli@unibocconi.it

P. Marano, K. Noussia (eds.), *The Governance of Insurance Undertakings*, AIDA Europe Research Series on Insurance Law and Regulation 6,
https://doi.org/10.1007/978-3-030-85817-9_9

adverse selection or moral hazard peculiar to the M&A context seem to arise and a steadily increasing use of insurance in M&A can be expected.

1 Introduction

Mergers and acquisitions (M&A) involve transactional risks, no matter how extensive and accurate the due diligence process is. Information asymmetries are inherent in most M&A deals, and it is no surprise that post-M&A disputes arising from inaccuracies and misrepresentations in seller's disclosures are common, and severity of claims is on the increase.[1] This raises the question as to how transactional risk can be effectively managed and allocated.

Representations and warranties included in acquisition agreements typically address this issue, as they facilitate the transfer of information to the buyer, reducing information asymmetry.[2] In private transactions they are generally accompanied by indemnification provisions by which the seller or the selling shareholders undertake to indemnify the buyer if representations and warranties turn out to be inaccurate after the closing. Escrow arrangements may also be in place, providing that a portion of the sales price is placed in escrow and can be paid to the seller subject to certain conditions.

When negotiating representations and warranties and indemnification and escrow requirements transacting parties clearly have contrasting interests, as while the buyer wishes to obtain the maximum degree of protection, the seller seeks to minimize its liability. There could also be cases, especially in public company transactions or distressed sales, where the buyer may have no effective remedies against the seller after the closing.

To remedy issues related with seller's indemnities, insurance companies created some innovative products, generally known under the catch-all name of "transactional insurance," and providing coverage for risks arising out of extraordinary corporate transactions, including risks related to breaches of representations and warranties, tax liabilities, pending or potential litigation and other contingent liabilities.

This chapter explores the role that insurance can play in managing transactional risk, considering whether it can serve as an efficient alternative to more traditional, contractual solutions like indemnity and escrow requirements.

The chapter rests on both practical and theoretical grounds. From a practical point of view to consider the role of insurance in M&A is undoubtedly relevant, as global

[1] AIG, *M&A: A rising tide of large claims*, 2020, available at: https://www.aig.com/content/dam/aig/america-canada/us/documents/business/management-liability/aig-manda-2020-w-and-i.pdf; Norton Rose Fulbright, *After the deal: recent cases and trends in M&A disputes*, 2018, available at: https://www.nortonrosefulbright.com/en/knowledge/publications/09047a9c/after-the-deal-recent-cases-and-trends-in-ma-disputes.

[2] Gilson (1984), p. 267 ff.

demand for transactional insurance has grown substantially over the last decade and insurance is regarded ever more as a common risk management tool in M&A.[3] From a theoretical and systematic perspective, the question arises as to whether, by allowing parties to transfer transactional risks in exchange for a premium, insurance has the potential to enhance the overall social benefit facilitating the conclusion of beneficial M&A transactions or, on the contrary, may bring about distortion to M&A contracting, as it transfers liability from the parties that have superior access to information to the insurer, potentially triggering moral hazard and adverse selection problems.

In this context, the chapter proceeds as follows. After this Introduction, Sect. 2 focuses on traditional contractual solutions to manage transactional risk and mitigate potential liabilities, highlighting their main drawbacks. Section 3 turns to transactional insurance, examining representation and warranty insurance, tax liability insurance, litigation buyout and contingent liability insurance. Section 4 considers whether insurance can qualify as an efficient risk-transfer tool in M&A, also considering potential issues of moral hazard and adverse selection. Section 5 concludes.

2 Contractual Solutions

Representations and warranties are typically included in acquisition agreements to remedy information asymmetry and manage transactional risk. They are made by the buyer and the seller to each other to provide full disclosure of all information relevant to the transaction. Whereas the buyer's representations and warranties are mainly intended to prove its ability to legally execute the deal, the representations and warranties made by the seller are aimed at providing an accurate and complete description of different aspects of the company being sold.[4]

Representations and warranties generally concern a company's organization and good standing, capitalization, subsidiaries, organizational authority to enter into the agreement, financial statements, absence of undisclosed liabilities, property titles, contracts, litigation, compliance with law and agreements, taxes, employee benefit plans, labor disputes, environmental matters, and insurance policies.[5]

Transacting parties warrant in the acquisition agreement that their representations are complete and accurate. In particular, if the seller's representations and warranties turn out to be inaccurate before the closing, the buyer may reject or renegotiate the contract (bring-down clause), while if a breach is discovered after the closing, in

[3] AON, *Representations and Warranties Insurance Claim Study*, 2020, available at: https://www.aon.com/risk-services/amats/2019rwclaims.

[4] Gole and Morris (2007), p. 155; DePamphilis (2010a), p. 93.

[5] See Carney (2011), p. 1123 ss.; W. Gole, J. Morris, J. Ibidem, 154 ss.

private transactions, the buyer is normally entitled to get indemnification from the seller.[6]

Representations and warranties are among the most heavily negotiated provisions in the sale and purchase agreement. Unlike buyers, who want absolute representations and warranties, sellers insist on limiting their potential liabilities by using knowledge and materiality qualifiers. A knowledge qualifier limits the seller's statements to the best of its "knowledge," with the buyer insisting on interpreting the term as knowledge after a reasonable investigation, while the seller as knowledge of a fact without any duty to investigate.[7] Materiality clauses, on the other hand, limit the accuracy of representations and warranties by providing that the representations must be true and correct in all material respects. A fact is regarded to be material if a reasonable investor would consider it important in making a decision on an acquisition transaction. Besides, materiality may also refer to the effect of a breach of representations and warranties, excluding liability for inaccuracies that do not have a material adverse effect.[8]

If a breach of the seller's representations and warranties is discovered after the closing, as noted above, indemnification provisions would require the seller to pay damages. Indemnification provisions also permit to allocate specific risks pending on the acquired company, that have been disclosed in the representations and warranties and the consequences of which cannot be calculated before closing, such as pending litigation, unpaid tax obligations or violations of environmental or labor laws.[9] Indemnification provision are common in private transactions, while in transactions where a public company is being acquired, representations and warranties generally do not survive the closing and no indemnity may be available to the buyer for breaches discovered after the closing as, especially in listed corporations with dispersed shareholders, it would not be feasible to get indemnification from selling shareholders. In addition, a lower degree of information asymmetry is generally found in public deals than in private transactions, given the disclosure requirements imposed on public companies and the consequent amount of information that is publicly available.[10]

Normally the seller wants the indemnification periods to be short. The term may vary from one to three years after the closing except for some claims such as tax, environmental or property and title that may survive beyond.[11]

As for the indemnifiable damages, the buyer is likely to want unlimited coverage for the reasonable cost of satisfying the incurred liabilities in addition to the amount

[6]See DePamphilis (2010a), p. 93.

[7]See W. Carney, Ibidem, 238.

[8]W. Carney, Ibidem, 238 ff.

[9]See D.M. DePamphilis, *Mergers and Acquisitions Basics*, Ibidem, 94; W. Gole, J. Morris, Ibidem, 157.

[10]Hill et al. (2016), p. 409; Griffith (2020), p. 1851.

[11]W. Carney, Ibidem, 237; D.M. DePamphilis, *Mergers and Acquisitions Basics*, Ibidem, 94 f.; W. Gole, J. Morris, Ibidem, 157.

necessary to put the buyer in the position it would have been in without the breach of the representations and warranties. This may result in a request for damages in excess of the purchase price. Sellers, on the contrary, want to set a ceiling on the indemnity obligations and, at the most, agree to indemnify up to the purchase price.[12] Generally, indemnification limits are well under the purchase price.[13]

Moreover, the seller may insist on including a deductible or a "basket" to restrain claims for minimum damages. In the first case, when a loss suffered by the buyer exceeds the stipulated deductible amount, the seller is liable only for the amount of the loss above the deductible. If a "basket" is used, the buyer agrees not to assert indemnification claims until the aggregate amount of losses exceeds a specified basket amount. When the buyer's losses exceed the basket amount, the seller is liable for the total amount of the losses.[14]

It should be noted, however, that there may be virtually no remedy for a breach of representations and warranties where no identifiable seller remains after the closing. This, for example, may be typical of asset purchases from companies that go into liquidation after the transaction, and more generally in distressed sales. Where the seller is privately held, the buyer may demand that (large) selling shareholders participate in the representations and warranties and that indemnification rights are conferred against them.[15] If the shareholders consent, they will usually want the guarantee to survive for as short a time period as possible. This solution instead is impracticable where the seller is a publicly held corporation with dispersed shareholders.

To protect himself from potential liabilities associated with the transaction, the buyer may also seek to defer the payment of part of the purchase price and put the unpaid portion in a holdback or escrow account. Transacting parties, nevertheless, need to agree on the amount to place in escrow, the length of time the proceeds are escrowed, the conditions of the escrow. Further, the seller is not likely to accept escrow arrangements without an increase in the purchase price.[16]

---

[12] W. Carney, Ibidem, 242 ff.; W. Gole, J. Morris, Ibidem, 157 f.

[13] American Bar Association, M&A Market Trends Subcommittee of the Mergers & Acquisitions Committee, (2009) "2009 Private Target Mergers & Acquisitions Deal Point Study," 100, (showing that just 9% of the deals considered have indemnification limits between 50 and 100% of the purchase price); American Bar Association, M&A Market Trends Subcommittee of the Mergers and Acquisitions Committee (2008) "2008 Continental Europe Private Target Mergers & Acquisitions Deal Points Study," 37, (highlighting that deals with indemnification limits set between 50 and 100% of the purchase price account for the 22% of the sample); W. Carney, Ibidem, 245 f. (making reference also to other surveys).

[14] D.M. DePamphilis, *Mergers and Acquisitions Basics*, Ibidem, 95; W. Gole, J. Morris, Ibidem, 157. See also W. Carney, Ibidem, 245 f. (distinguishing between a basket and a threshold. With a basket, the seller bears the losses in excess of the basket, while in the case of a threshold, when a loss exceeds the threshold amount, the seller is liable for both the threshold amount and any excess).

[15] See W. Carney, Ibidem, 236 ff.

[16] Paar (2002), p. 2. See also D.M. DePamphilis, *Mergers, Acquisitions, and Other Restructuring Activities*, Ibidem, 88 f., 424 ff. (where also reference to other mechanisms for managing risk, such as post-closing price adjustments).

3 Transactional Insurance

When negotiating representations and warranties and indemnification provisions transacting parties have contrasting interests and need to reach agreement on several key points, including the scope of representations and warranties, the survival period, the definition of indemnifiable damage, indemnification limits, the portion of price to put in escrow. The possibility of deal breaker issues is strong. When disagreement does not result in the failure of the transaction, the compromise agreed to by the parties might be substantially different from their initial expectations. Should a breach of the seller's representations and warranties be discovered after the closing, the risk that the buyer is left with no effective remedies exists.[17]

In this context, to overcome the drawbacks associated with representations and warranties and indemnification provisions, and facilitate the conclusion of the deal, parties increasingly avail themselves of transactional insurance.

Introduced in the United Kingdom and the United States in the 1990s, transactional insurance was not widely used at first mainly due to its novelty and lack of confidence by parties, high premiums and limited availability of coverage. With time, however, the market for transactional insurance has evolved: available coverage is now broader, terms are more favorable, and rates are lower as there is more competition among insurers,[18] while risk aversion of transacting parties has risen.[19] Coverage has also become more widely known: global demand for transactional insurance nowadays is ever more on the rise, especially in the U.S. and U. K. markets,[20] but also in continental Europe where the use of this type of insurance is on the increase.[21]

[17] On the risk that representations and warranties and indemnification provisions might not adequately protect the buyer, see D.M. DePamphilis, *Mergers, Acquisitions, and Other Restructuring Activities*, Ibidem, 182; T.E. Lenson (2006), *Lies, Damn Lies, and Fraud Claims in M&A Transactions*, available at https://www.deallawyers.com/nonmember/podcast/lenson_item2.pdf.

[18] AON, *Representations and Warranties Insurance Claim Study*, 2020, 3, available at: https://www.aon.com/risk-services/amats/2019rwclaims.

[19] M.P. Lusk (2012) "Transactional Insurance: A deal Tool Whose Time Has Come," 1 f., available at: https://www.mondaq.com/unitedstates/Insurance/198526/Transactional-Insurance-A-Deal-Tool-Whose-Time-Has-Come; C. Sternberg (2012) "Transactional Risk Insurance: Deal-Enabling Risk Transfer Solutions," 1 f., available at: http://www.lockton.com/Resource_/PageResource/MKT/Transactional%20Risk_for%20web%20posting.pdf.

[20] AON, *Representations and Warranties Insurance Claim Study*, Ibidem, 3.

[21] See Monti (2010), p. 361; De Lousanoff O. (2003) "Warranty and Indemnity Insurance in M&A Transactions," International Law Office, available at: https://www.internationallawoffice.com/Newsletters/Corporate-FinanceMA/Germany/Hengeler-Mueller-/Warranty-and-Indemnity-Insurance-in-MA-Transactions, (noting that insurance for M&A is offered by a growing number of insurance companies and brokers in Germany).

In particular, insurance products for M&A transactions include: representation and warranty insurance,[22] tax liability insurance, litigation buyout and contingent liability insurance.

3.1 Representations and Warranties Insurance

Representations and warranties insurance is the most widely used type of transactional insurance.[23] It became available towards the end of the 1980s in the United Kingdom and about a decade later in the United States. This type of insurance provides coverage against financial losses resulting from breaches of representations and warranties. It can serve as either a surety or indemnity of the seller's indemnity obligations.[24] In the first case, the sale and purchase agreement includes indemnification provisions and the insurance policy serves the purpose of replacing completely or in part an escrow. In the latter case, insurance either can be entirely substituted for the seller's indemnity obligation or may be used as an additional layer of coverage over a lower amount of indemnification liability assumed by the seller.

Insurance is tailor-made to the needs of the individual transactions. Underwriting can be quite complex, and it is advisable that insurance companies and brokers are involved from the initial stage of the deal structuring process. Insurance companies and brokers, however, have gained adequate experience over time and are able to provide coverage within a limited period, meeting the deal timetable.[25] The applicant is expected to cooperate closely with the insurer and provide relevant information. The acquisition agreement is submitted to the insurer along with other relevant documents to promote underwriting review.[26] Once the insurer has reviewed all the materials, it issues a non-binding indication letter, presenting the general terms of the proposed coverage. If the applicant decides to execute the non-binding indication letter, then the insurer conducts a thorough review of the transaction with the possible assistance of outside counsel, basically re-examining the due diligence

[22] Representations and warranties insurance is commonly referred to in the Europe as warranties and indemnity insurance (W&I).

[23] Gerber et al. (2012), § 32.01, Matthew Bender & Company, Inc., available at: http://www.lexisnexis.com, [hereinafter New Appleman, Mergers and Acquisitions Insurance], § 32.02 [1][a].

[24] See New Appleman, Mergers and Acquisitions Insurance, § 32.02 [2][a].

[25] See C.C Zgutowicz, M.P. Lusk, Ibidem, 4 (noting that binding terms may be delivered within 1 to 2 weeks).

[26] The insured may not amend, supplement, or rescind the acquisition agreement, nor waive any rights thereunder, without the prior consent of the insurer if the modification or waiver would reasonably have an adverse effect on the insurer. See New Appleman, Mergers and Acquisitions Insurance, § 32.02 [5][c]. Among the other documents generally requested for underwriting review are: financial statements of the target company, a copy of the executed letter of intent, data room index or other due diligence document index, buyer's due diligence request list, buyer's due diligence memoranda, third party reports and opinions, working group list and other relevant materials.

process performed by the parties and makes a final decision as to whether to insure the risk and at what conditions.[27]

The insured under a representations and warranties insurance policy can be the buyer (buyer-side policy) or the seller (seller-side policy). A party to the transaction may also purchase coverage for the other party and vice versa.[28]

A buyer-side policy provides indemnity to the buyer for losses resulting from a breach of the seller's representations and warranties. It allows the buyer to recover losses directly from the insurer without having to pursue remedies against the seller.

A variety of reasons may lead buyers to purchase representations and warranties insurance. A buyer-side policy can be useful, for example, when the acquirer cannot successfully negotiate the desired level of indemnification from the seller or when it is concerned with its ability to recover damages because the seller may have financial difficulties or because recourse against the seller would be otherwise ineffective and expensive. Insurance can also be used strategically by a buyer to gain a competitive advantage over other bidders and avoid entering into endless negotiation with the seller over indemnification requirements. This way a buyer can accept a lower indemnification ceiling and may not need to insist on a holdback or escrow account, thus increasing the competitiveness of its offer.[29] A buyer may also consider that insurance coverage is less expensive than the growth of the purchase price demanded by the seller to afford the same level of indemnification. In addition, in public company transactions, where no indemnity is available to the buyer for breaches discovered after the closing, insurance can be a substitute for seller's indemnity.

A seller-side policy indemnifies the seller for, or pays on behalf of the seller, any loss resulting from claims made by the buyer for inaccuracies in the seller's representations and warranties. Seller-side policies may be used when sellers, especially private equity firms, want to reduce their potential liability post-closing to the smallest amount possible, exiting the business and distributing sale proceeds to their investors or immediately reinvesting the proceeds. A seller-side policy also permits the seller to provide potentially interested buyers with higher indemnification limits, thereby making the deal more attractive and reducing the need for a holdback or escrow.

No substantial differences typically exist in the structure and wording of representation and warranty insurance policies between the U.S. and the U.K. (and more generally European) market. The scope of coverage is determined in connection with the representations and warranties made by the seller in the sale and purchase agreement. The insurer normally selects the representations and warranties to insure

[27] New Appleman, Mergers and Acquisitions Insurance, § 32.02 [4].

[28] New Appleman, Mergers and Acquisitions Insurance, § 32.02 [2][a]. See also Marsh (2012) "Contribution of Insurance in Facilitating Mergers and Acquisitions," 10, available at: https://www.airmic.com/sites/default/files/legacy_files/Contribution%20of%20Insurance%20in%20Facilitating%20Mergers%20and.pdf (noting that sellers are increasingly suggesting buyer-side policies to bidders in an auction process).

[29] See New Appleman, Mergers and Acquisitions Insurance, § 32.02 [2][c]. See also Marsh "Contribution of Insurance in Facilitating Mergers and Acquisitions," Ibidem, 16.

and may also intervene on the wording of the representations and warranties, restricting or clarifying their scope for coverage purposes only. A policy may also be issued on a "blanket" basis, thereby covering all the seller's representations and warranties except for those excluded.[30]

Indemnification requests unrelated to representations and warranties are generally not covered. Some insurers, however, have also started offering a more innovative type of coverage—so-called synthetic representations and warranties insurance—that allows the buyer to agree to a set of representations and warranties directly with the insurer, removing the need for the seller to give representations and warranties in the sale and purchase agreement. This type of coverage can be advantageous for both transacting parties, as the seller would exit the transaction without the risk of facing liability for breaches of representations and warranties, while the buyer, in an auction scenario with multiple bidders, can make its acquisition offer more competitive.

Representation and warranty insurance policies typically contain a prior knowledge exclusion that excludes coverage where the insured had knowledge of circumstances leading to the breach at the time the policy incepted. The policy defines the persons who may have actual knowledge of a breach as those who supervised or conducted any due diligence in connection with the acquisition agreement, and/or those who supervised, prepared, or negotiated the acquisition agreement ("deal team members"). The names of the deal team members are generally listed in an appendix attached to the policy.[31]

Further, seller-side policies generally exclude coverage for breaches resulting from the seller's fraud. This exclusion may be subject to a final adjudication of fraud before becoming applicable, otherwise a mere allegation of fraud can be an argument for the insurer to deny coverage. A severability clause may be inserted, ensuring coverage for innocent co-insureds. Buyer-side policies, instead, do not contain a fraud exclusion and, therefore, are considered to provide broader coverage,[32] and they represent almost the totality of the policies issued.[33] Other exclusions specific to representation and warranty insurance may concern unfulfilled projections and

[30]New Appleman, Mergers and Acquisitions Insurance, § 32.02 [3][a].

[31]Representation and warranty insurance provides coverage for breaches of representations and warranties made by a definite set of persons (i.e., the deal team members) that may include not only directors and officers but also shareholders and various outside advisors. It follows that the scope of this type of insurance is different than that of Directors and Officers (D&O) insurance which, on the contrary, provides liability coverage for the company's directors and officers against claims that may arise from the decisions taken within the scope of their managerial duties. In addition, it should be noted that D&O insurance policies may include contractual liability exclusions, while coverage for claims against the company itself is typically limited to securities claims. On the differences between D&O insurance and Representations and Warranties Insurance, see New Appleman, Mergers and Acquisitions Insurance, § 32.02 [1][c].

[32]New Appleman, Mergers and Acquisitions Insurance, § 32.02 [5][b] (emphasizing that buyer-side policies may entail higher premium as a result).

[33]Marsh, *Transactional Risk Insurance Report*, 2019, available at https://www.marsh.com/us/insights/research/transactional-risk-insurance-outpaced-global-deal-activity.html.

forward-looking statements and losses due to price adjustments based on the seller's net worth determined after a post-closing audit.[34]

Insurance coverage usually begins with the closing of the transaction and is provided for at least the survival period set in the acquisition agreement. It is quite frequent, however, that the policy period lasts beyond the survival period indicated in the acquisition agreement, to the advantage of the parties involved in the transaction. In general, policy periods may vary between 18 months and four years. A different expiry date may also be set with respect to some of the seller's representations and warranties.[35]

Depending on the need for coverage that parties to the transaction may have, policy limits can be set up to $50 million, although larger programs may be structured on a case-by-case basis. Broader coverage may be achieved through tiered insurance programs that combine primary insurance with excess insurance, thereby increasing coverage limits even up to $200 million per transaction.[36]

Both buyer-side and seller-side policies contain some form of risk retention. Typically, deductibles between 1% and 3% of the transaction value are included, depending, for example, on the type of business being acquired, the due diligence performed, the nature and scope of the representations and warranties. The insurance premium generally ranges between 2% and 8% of the amount of insurance purchased, depending on the nature of representations and warranties, the policy period and the retention applied.[37]

3.2 *Tax Liability Insurance*

Tax liability insurance is another solution aimed at facilitating M&A deals. Tax considerations are clearly important in M&A transactions and often parties are not able to obtain in time an advance tax ruling clarifying the treatment that will be applied to a proposed transaction. Uncertainty regarding tax results may even obstruct the completion of a proposed deal.

---

[34]Losses resulting from pollution, bodily injury and property damage, consequential, multiplied, punitive or exemplary damages and criminal fines or penalties are generally not covered either since they may be covered under other liability policies. New Appleman, Mergers and Acquisitions Insurance, § 32.02 [5][b].

[35]New Appleman, Mergers and Acquisitions Insurance, § 32.02 [3][b] (highlighting that where the acquisition agreement establishes different survival periods for some of the seller's representation and warranties, the insurance policy may have different periods of coverage as well).

[36]Representation and warranty policies are deemed best suited to transactions where the value is $25 million to $1 billion. See New Appleman, Mergers and Acquisitions Insurance, § 32.02 [3][c].

[37]New Appleman, Mergers and Acquisitions Insurance, § 32.02 [4]; M.E. Betzen, M.T. Goglia (2005) "Insuring for Accuracy," 1, available at: https://www.jonesday.com/files/Publication/bff201d2-36a4-4c94-ad92-3a6a979c7229/Presentation/PublicationAttachment/a1a30e34-58f8-406e-a822-2eae225c46d1/BetzenGoglia050905.pdf.

Tax liability insurance allows parties to reduce or eliminate potential tax exposures resulting from the tax treatment of a transaction. It covers unexpected tax liabilities resulting from an unfavorable tax authority's ruling. Most policies also cover the costs of contesting the tax authority's ruling, including the expenses of outside counsels and accountants, as well as interest, non-criminal fines, and penalties,[38] provided that fines and penalties are insurable under the applicable law.[39]

Policies are generally written on a manuscript basis to meet the specific needs of the individual transactions. To promote underwriting review, the prospective insured is generally required to provide the insurer with a tax opinion prepared by the taxpayer's counsel, along with supporting documents and possible correspondence with the tax authorities.[40] After evaluating the tax risk, the insurer usually sends a non-binding indication letter, stating the general terms and conditions of the proposed coverage. Once the applicant decides to execute the indication letter, the insurer conducts a thorough review of the transaction, with the assistance of outside counsels and advisors, and a final coverage decision is made.

The coverage period usually is aligned with the applicable statute of limitations. Generally, up to $20 million in coverage is available for any transactions, although larger limits can also be available. Retentions and premiums are determined on a case-by-case basis, also considering the nature of the transaction, the probability of adverse tax results, the probable cost of defense.[41]

Tax liability insurance typically excludes coverage for purely tax motivated transactions, lacking a legitimate independent business purpose. Transactions qualified as tax shelter are not likely to be covered either. Further, coverage is generally not available for losses resulting from changes in the law and for transactions that are

[38] R. Paar, Ibidem, p. 2; New Appleman, Mergers and Acquisitions Insurance, § 32.03 [2].

[39] Restrictions on the insurability of fines and penalties are generally in place in Europe. See, e.g., Article 12 of the Italian Private Insurance Code providing that losses arising from administrative fines and penalties cannot be insured, otherwise the insurance contract is void. For an overview of the law on the insurability of fines and penalties in some European and non-European countries, see Banks, Richard (2007) "International Comparative Review of Liability Insurance Law," *Insurance Day*, available at: https://www.bld.de/fileadmin/bld/txt_pdf/ID_Int_l_Legal_guide_120607.pdf. See also Denslow A., Baks B., Daidone M. (2018) "10 Things Every Insurer Should Know," available at: https://cms.law/en/int/publication/ten-things-every-insurer-should-know.

[40] In some cases, insurance may also be issued without a supporting tax opinion, depending on the type of tax issue, the taxpayer's particular factual representations and the legal analysis provided. See AIG "Tax Liability Insurance," available at: https://www.aig.com/business/insurance/mergers-and-acquisitions/tax-liability-insurance.

[41] The overall structure of the insurance coverage clearly matters in determining the premium, since consideration should be given, for example, to retention, coinsurance arrangements or possible partial refunds of a significant premium when no losses occur during the policy period. See also New Appleman, Mergers and Acquisitions Insurance, § 32.03 [10]. See also AIG "Tax Liability Insurance," 1, available at: http://www.aig.co.uk/chartis/internet/uk/eni/Tax%20Liability%20Insurance%20-%20Information%20Sheet%20AI160739%201212_tcm2538-372590.pdf (stating that premiums so far charged range between 3% and 12% of the limit of liability purchased).

already under audit or are being contested by the tax authorities. A fraud exclusion is also included.[42]

Tax liability insurance is ever more common in M&A transactions.[43] Private letter rulings from tax authorities, in fact, are normally time-consuming, while relying merely on the professional liability or error and omissions insurance coverage owned by tax advisors may turn out to be unsatisfactory.[44] Tax liability insurance may then allow parties to manage tax uncertainty in M&A transactions, also considering that there could be cases where indemnity obligations of the seller might be unfeasible or otherwise ineffective.

3.3 Litigation Buyout Insurance and Contingent Liability Insurance

Litigation buyout insurance enables transacting parties to manage risks resulting from any anticipated or ongoing litigation, arbitration or other claim involving liabilities either uninsured or underinsured.[45] Litigation buyout insurance can prove particularly useful, as pending or threatened litigation may hinder the closing of a transaction where, for example, financial sponsors withdraw or the settlement of the claim cannot be negotiated in time for the deal. Insurance allows parties to exactly quantify future exposures by transforming contingent third-party claims into a fixed insurance cost.

The policies are tailor-made to fulfill specific needs of individual transactions[46] and can provide coverage for a wide range of matters, such as securities litigation, contractual disputes, products liability, intellectual property disputes, successor liability and employment practices liability.[47] Risks may relate to the litigation outcome or the amount of damages awarded. Insurance may cover either a particular

---

[42] New Appleman, Mergers and Acquisitions Insurance, § 32.03 [5][a] (noting that the accuracy of taxpayers' factual representation and the proper filing and compilation of tax returns are not generally covered).

[43] See Kahn (2009), p. 7 (where also reference to other mechanisms for shifting tax risk).

[44] In the event of a payment by the insurer under a tax liability insurance policy, the insurer is typically subrogated to all of the insured's rights of recovery against tax advisors and other persons or entities relating to such a payment. See New Appleman, Mergers and Acquisitions Insurance, § 32.03 [12].

[45] New Appleman, Mergers and Acquisitions Insurance, § 32.04 [1].

[46] The underwriting process is similar to that employed in connection with representation and warranty insurance and tax liability insurance and it is based on an initial review leading to a non-binding indication letter. A final coverage decision is made after the insurer conducts a thorough examination of the transaction, with the assistance of outside counsels and advisors. A non-refundable underwriting fee is normally charged. See New Appleman, Mergers and Acquisitions Insurance, § 32.04 [8].

[47] New Appleman, Mergers and Acquisitions Insurance, § 32.04 [9]. Issues may arise as to the need for confidentiality that the applicant has in connection with the underwriting review. To protect the

known lawsuit or a portfolio of lawsuits or claims. Considering the uniqueness of the insured risk, premiums, policy limits, and the amount of retentions are set on a case-by-case basis, considering the severity of the underlying risk and the policy structure.[48]

Litigation buyout insurance can be issued in three different versions: buyout, cap, and appeal hedge. The buyout provides coverage for all losses resulting from a specific dispute, including defense costs, while under the cap version the insurer assumes liability in excess of a certain amount that is retained by the insured and possibly covered through existing primary insurance. Appeal hedges, instead, permit the insured to secure the benefits from a favorable judgment against possible reversal on appeal.[49]

The degree of defense control exercised by the insurer differs among the three types of insurance. In particular, in a buyout, the insurer normally assumes the entire risk in exchange for the complete control of the litigation. The insured, nevertheless, is required to cooperate and participate in the litigation. In a cap or hedge, on the contrary, the insured may maintain control of the defense, considering that it shares the same interest with the insurer.[50]

In addition to fraud, insurance policies typically exclude coverage against claims for personal profit, including claims based on insider trading or for usurpation of corporate opportunities. Further, losses due to claims filed by governmental and quasi-governmental entities are not indemnified either.[51]

Finally, it is worth noting that contingent liability insurance is also available, providing tailor-made insurance coverage for risks specific to single transactions, ranging from potential successor liability and losses deriving from defects or failure of property titles, to government and regulatory approvals, contractual disputes, environmental liability, employment matters and intellectual property infringements. Premiums and other policy conditions are determined on a case-by-case basis according to the nature of the specific liability to be insured and the overall structure of the insurance policy.

privileged information transmitted by the applicant, the insurer is required to sign a confidentiality agreement.

[48] Insurance policies may include return premium or additional premium provisions. See New Appleman, Mergers and Acquisitions Insurance, § 32.04 [3] (explaining that return premium provisions provide for the return of part of the premium to the insured if the policy is canceled or certain claims do not occur, while additional premium provisions require the insured to pay some extra amount in premium because of losses paid or incurred under the policy).

[49] New Appleman, Mergers and Acquisitions Insurance, § 32.04 [3].

[50] In a cap or hedge policy, however, the insurer and the insured may also agree that control is given to one of them, subject to the consent of the other on major issues. See New Appleman, Mergers and Acquisitions Insurance, § 32.04 [7].

[51] New Appleman, Mergers and Acquisitions Insurance, § 32.04 [5][c].

4 Transactional Insurance in M&A Contracting

As discussed above, transactional insurance allows parties to overcome problems associated with seller's indemnities and reduce exposure to transactional risk. In principle, insurance can prove to be particularly useful in no indemnity deals involving public company targets or distressed sellers, where it can act as a substitute for seller's indemnity obligations, but it can also be used as a supplement to seller's indemnity, when the buyer cannot negotiate the desired level of indemnification or when it is concerned about its ability to recover from the seller after the closing. In an auction with multiple bidders, insurance may also give buyers a strategical advantage over other competitors. Moreover, it permits to reduce or eliminate the need for escrow arrangements, and this seems especially important after the COVID-19 pandemic outbreak, as companies have been experiencing a deepening liquidity crisis and avoiding escrow requirements can provide enhanced liquidity to sellers.

It has been argued, however, that insurance may introduce potential distortions to the M&A contracting process, since the transfer of risk from the seller (i.e., the party that has superior access to information) to the insurer can create a credible commitment problem, as the seller may exercise a lower degree of care in providing relevant information to the buyer and this can undermine efficiency in M&A contracting. The fact that transactional insurance may bring about adverse selection and moral hazard issues in M&A contracting has also been emphasized.[52]

The credible commitment problem is clearly more relevant to private transactions than public company transactions, since, as discussed above, when the target is a public company due diligence is mainly based on information that is publicly available and the buyer normally cannot rely on indemnity provisions to protect itself against inaccuracies in the representations and warranties, so that the concern for possible lower care exercised by the seller loses relevance in public company transactions. Even in private transactions, the transfer of transactional risk to the insurer seems not to exacerbate the credible commitment problem, which is ultimately counterbalanced by the buyer's interest to conduct a thorough due diligence to gather information about the target and decide whether to enter into the transaction, negotiate certain terms or adjust the consideration to offer.

Also, adverse selection and moral hazard, which are typical issues in insurance, seem not to pose peculiar problems in M&A. Adverse selection implies that a risk pool will progressively consist of high-risk individuals, that value insurance more than low-risk individuals and have an information advantage over the insurer, thereby preventing the formation of an insurance pool. It should be noted, however, that adverse selection normally does not create significant problems to properly designated insurance arrangements.[53] Due diligence and representations and

[52] S.J. Griffith, *Deal Insurance: Representation & Warranty Insurance in M&A Contracting*, Ibidem, 1839 ff.

[53] T. Baker, *Insurance against misinformation in the securities market*, 2006, 16, available at: https://papers.ssrn.com/sol3/papers.cfm?abstract_id=1010106.

warranties restrain information asymmetries in M&A and allow insurers to set rates that discriminate based on risk. Moreover, it is fair to assume that adverse selection in transactional insurance would operate not profoundly different than in other sectors, such as D&O insurance, where information asymmetries exist but do not prevent the formation of an insurance pool.[54]

As regards moral hazard, which basically implies that insurance reduces the insured's incentives to avoid a loss, it should be noted that transactional insurance policies seem well designed to address moral hazard concerns. Policy limits, deductibles and exclusions as well as, in buyer's policies, subrogation rights of the insurer in case of fraud by the seller align the insurer's and insured's interests, reducing parties' incentives to exercise a lower degree of care.

Transactional insurance thus appears as an effective risk-transfer tool that can facilitate the conclusion of M&A deals. It allows parties to transform potential future liabilities into a quantified insurance premium that can be allocated as part of the purchase price, providing certainty and strategic advantages. A steadily increasing use of insurance in M&A deals can be expected.

5 Conclusion

No matter how extensive the due diligence, losses related to transactional risks in mergers and acquisitions occur. Traditional mechanisms used to allocate risk between transacting parties may turn out to be inefficient and inadequate. Representations and warranties and indemnification provisions are among the most heavily negotiated provisions in the sale and purchase agreement. The parties have contrasting interests during the negotiation of these terms and the possibility of deal breaker issues is strong. When disagreement does not result in the failure of the transaction, the compromise agreed by the parties may be inefficient and unsatisfactory for either or both of them. In some cases, depending also on the form of acquisition, there is a fair chance that the buyer will have insufficient remedies against the seller after the closing.

Transactional insurance provides effective solutions to manage transactional risk, whether related to indemnity obligations, tax uncertainty, pending or threatened litigation or other contingent liabilities. Insurance is tailor-made to meet the needs of transacting parties and may be used as a supplement or also a substitute for seller indemnity obligations. By spreading transactional risk, insurance can promote beneficial transactions that might not otherwise occur and enhance the overall social benefit, providing economic security at a fraction of the cost that it would take for transacting parties to protect themselves.

[54] See generally T. Baker, Ibidem, 17.

References

AIG (2020) M&A: a rising tide of large claims, available at: https://www.aig.com/content/dam/aig/america-canada/us/documents/business/management-liability/aig-manda-2020-w-and-i.pdf

AIG "Tax Liability Insurance," available at: https://www.aig.com/business/insurance/mergers-and-acquisitions/tax-liability-insurance

American Bar Association (2008) M&A Market Trends Subcommittee of the Mergers and Acquisitions Committee, "2008 Continental Europe Private Target Mergers & Acquisitions Deal Points Study."

American Bar Association (2009) M&A Market Trends Subcommittee of the Mergers & Acquisitions Committee, "2009 Private Target Mergers & Acquisitions Deal Point Study."

AON (2020) Representations and Warranties Insurance Claim Study, available at: https://www.aon.com/risk-services/amats/2019rwclaims

Baker T (2006) Insurance against misinformation in the securities market, available at: https://papers.ssrn.com/sol3/papers.cfm?abstract_id=1010106

Banks R (2007) International Comparative Review of Liability Insurance Law. Insurance Day, Available at: https://www.bld.de/fileadmin/bld/txt_pdf/ID_Int_l_Legal_guide_120607.pdf

Betzen ME, Goglia MT (2005) "Insuring for Accuracy," 1. Available at: https://www.jonesday.com/files/Publication/bff201d2-36a4-4c94-ad92-3a6a979c7229/Presentation/PublicationAttachment/a1a30e34-58f8-406e-a822-2eae225c46d1/BetzenGoglia050905.pdf.

Carney W (2011) Mergers and acquisitions. Foundation Press, New York

De Lousanoff O (2003) Warranty and Indemnity Insurance in M&A Transactions. International Law Office, Available at: https://www.internationallawoffice.com/Newsletters/Corporate-FinanceMA/Germany/Hengeler-Mueller-/Warranty-and-Indemnity-Insurance-in-MA-Transactions

Denslow A, Baks B, Daidone M (2018) 10 Things Every Insurer Should Know. Available at: https://cms.law/en/int/publication/ten-things-every-insurer-should-know

DePamphilis DM (2010a) Mergers and acquisitions basics. Academic Press

DePamphilis DM (2010b) Mergers, acquisitions, and other restructuring activities. Academic Press

Gerber DW, Delaney SJ, McCormick PD (2012) Mergers and acquisitions insurance. In: Dunham WB Jr (ed) New Appleman on insurance law, vol. 4, Chapter 32. Matthew Bender & Company, Inc.

Gilson RJ (1984) Value creation by business lawyers: legal skills and asset pricing. Yale Law J 239

Gole W, Morris J (2007) Mergers and acquisitions, New Jersey

Griffith SJ (2020) Deal insurance: representation & warranty insurance in M&A contracting. Minnesota Law Rev, p 1839

Hill C, Quinn BJM, Davidoff Solomon S (2016) Mergers and acquisitions. West

Kahn JH (2009) Hedging the IRS – a policy justification for excluding liability and tax insurance proceeds. Yale J Regul 26:1

Lenson TE (2006) Lies, Damn Lies, and Fraud Claims in M&A Transactions. Available at https://www.deallawyers.com/nonmember/podcast/lenson_item2.pdf

Lusk MP (2012) Transactional insurance: a deal tool whose time has come. 1 f., Available at: https://www.mondaq.com/unitedstates/Insurance/198526/Transactional-Insurance-A-Deal-Tool-Whose-Time-Has-Come

Marsh (2012) Contribution of Insurance in Facilitating Mergers and Acquisitions. Available at: https://www.airmic.com/sites/default/files/legacy_files/Contribution%20of%20Insurance%20in%20Facilitating%20Mergers%20and.pdf

Marsh (2019) Transactional Risk Insurance Report. Available at https://www.marsh.com/us/insights/research/transactional-risk-insurance-outpaced-global-deal-activity.html

Monti A (2010) Editorial-Introduction. Geneva Papers 35:361
Norton Rose Fulbright (2018) After the deal: recent cases and trends in M&A disputes. Available at: https://www.nortonrosefulbright.com/en/knowledge/publications/09047a9c/after-the-deal-recent-cases-and-trends-in-ma-disputes
Paar R (2002) Protect your deals with M&A insurance. Corporate Board XXIII(136):2
Sternberg C (2012) Transactional risk insurance: deal-enabling risk transfer solutions. 1 f., Available at: http://www.lockton.com/Resource_/PageResource/MKT/Transactional%20Risk_for%20web%20posting.pdf

The Algorithmic Future of Insurance Supervision in the EU: A Reality Check

Andromachi Georgosouli and Jeremmy Okonjo

Abstract Recent developments in FinTech and RegTech marked the EU's pivot towards a digitally driven Capital Markets Union and a concomitant algorithmic turn in EU financial supervision under the leadership of the three European Supervisory Authorities (ESMA, EBA, EIOPA). Starting from the premise that the EIOPA's relevant initiatives are driven from the Authority's normative and institutional environment as well as the perceived technological affordances of RegTech, this chapter provides a 'reality check' of the algorithmic future of EU financial supervision in the field of insurance as an aspect of EU financial markets' governance. On the one hand, it finds that an important blind-spot in the EIOPA's agenda is the absence of a concrete plan for a system of digital reporting. On the other hand, it examines what it takes to set up a system of digital reporting. To that end, it focuses on three interrelated issues: The technology that will be required to provide the infrastructure of digital reporting and its limitations, difficulties with the conversion of regulatory content into code, and issues of reporting architecture and governance. The ultimate objective of this chapter is to inform the agenda of the digital transformation of EU financial market oversight in anticipation of future challenges while relevant policy and legal debates are still on-going.

We wish to thank the International Insurance Law Association (AIDA) Europe for awarding the paper the AIDA Europe Young Authors Award 2020. We would also like to thank the book's anonymous reviewers and the book editors for their comments on earlier versions of this chapter. Any errors remain our own.

A. Georgosouli (✉)
Centre for Commercial Law Studies (CCLS), School of Law, Queen Mary University of London, London, UK
e-mail: a.georgosouli@qmul.ac.uk

J. Okonjo
Kent Law School, University of Kent, Canterbury, UK
e-mail: j.okonjo@kent.ac.uk

P. Marano, K. Noussia (eds.), *The Governance of Insurance Undertakings*, AIDA Europe Research Series on Insurance Law and Regulation 6,
https://doi.org/10.1007/978-3-030-85817-9_10

1 Introduction

This article seeks to contribute to the relevant policy and legal discourse about the digital transformation of financial market governance in the EU focusing on issues of transnational insurance supervision. It explores the minimum steps required to integrate data sharing, data analytics and automated monitoring in EIOPA's supervision, and the opportunities and challenges that EIOPA is likely to encounter. At a more theoretical level, this article illustrates the explanatory power of current theoretical scholarship on algorithmic regulation in the field of EU insurance regulation. Developments in this specific field of EU law deserve special attention. Quite apart from the significance of a robust insurance market for EU economic growth and prosperity, as this chapter is going to show, the digitalisation of transnational insurance oversight in the EU exhibits a range of challenges that are not present when similar initiatives are confined within the jurisdictional boundaries of a specific sovereign State.

The main thesis of this chapter is that a system of digital reporting is an essential precondition for the implementation of insurance supervisory technology (SupTech) in the EU, but setting it up may prove to be an incredibly challenging project in reality. To substantiate this thesis, Sect. 2 provides a brief overview of EIOPA, its operating environment and how principles of EU administrative law shape its SupTech mission and mandate. Section 3 portrays the Authority's role in the digital transformation of insurance supervision in the EU and the evolution of its strategy to point to an important blind-spot: the absence of a comprehensive plan of action for the development of a digital system of regulatory reporting in the field of EU insurance supervision. Section 4 proceeds to discuss a series of themes in relation to the setting up and running of a system of digital reporting in anticipation of future challenges, and to briefly outline potential responses to those problems. These relate to the limitations of the technology that will be required for digital reporting given its current and foreseeable degree of sophistication, a series of difficulties with the conversion of regulatory content into code and, lastly, issues of reporting architecture and governance. The chapter concludes with a summary of its main findings.

Our methodology is partly theoretical, partly comparative, and partly diagnostic. On the one hand, it borrows insights from a burgeoning body of interdisciplinary literature in the field of algorithmic regulation to articulate the main tenets of EU supervisory technology in the field of insurance. On the other hand, it compares EU developments with experience in the UK and other jurisdictions to contextualise the discussion and explore potential solutions. For this article, the term algorithmic financial supervision will be understood in its broader possible sense as a decision-making system that undertakes regulatory activities by continuously generating knowledge through computation of real-time data collected from the regulated environment, in order to optimise regulatory processes.[1] EU public discourse on digital transformation of the governance of the EU Single Market draws a distinction

[1] Yeung and Lodge (2019), p. 5.

between Fintech and RegTech, and perceives SupTech as an aspect of RegTech. For this chapter, we adopt the same conceptual distinctions.[2]

2 EIOPA, Its Operating Environment and How EU Principles of Administrative Law Shape Its SupTech Mission

EIOPA executes its digital supervision strategy within the legal and institutional framework of the European System of Financial Supervision (ESFS), whose objective is to promote market integration through legal convergence, and also consumer protection and financial stability.[3] The ESFS shapes and constrains the feasibility of an EU-wide system of digital reporting significantly because it is structured along EU principles of administrative law which act as constitutional and administrative boundaries to the respective mandates of the European Supervisory Authorities (ESAs) including of course that of EIOPA.[4] For present purposes the following four are of particular relevance: the conferred powers principle, the subsidiarity principle, the proportionality principle, and the *Meroni* doctrine.

2.1 The Conferred Powers Principle

The principle of conferred powers provides that the EU's competencies are limited to those conferred on it under EU treaties.[5] The principle has three dimensions: (i) the EU's competence to establish an agency; (ii) whether the agency's powers form part of the EU's competencies; and (iii) whether the agency has been granted those powers under its founding EU legislation.[6] For present purposes, the discussion is limited to the last question: whether, under its founding legislation, EIOPA has the competencies to establish EU-level digital reporting. This necessitates an analysis of its objectives, tasks and powers.

EIOPA is an operationally independent Union agency with responsibility over the supervision of the insurance and occupational pensions sector in Europe. In pursuit of its mission, EIOPA undertakes a series of initiatives to promote supervisory convergence, strengthen consumer protection and preserve financial stability.

[2] For a different conception, see Buckley et al. (2020). See also EIOPA's SupTech definition in EIOPA (2020a): 'the use of technology by supervisors, to deliver innovative and efficient supervisory solutions that will support a more effective, flexible, and responsive supervisory system'.

[3] European Commission (2014), p. 2.

[4] See Chiti and Vesperini (2018), pp. 230–235.

[5] Article 5 of the Treaty of the European Union (TEU).

[6] See Chamon (2016), p. 136.

Specifically, the objectives of EIOPA include preventing regulatory arbitrage and promoting competition, regulatory harmonisation and supervisory convergence among national regulators.[7] It also includes strengthening international supervisory coordination, regulating and supervising risk-taking by regulated entities, enhancing customer and consumer protection, and enhancing supervisory convergence across the internal market.[8] These objectives ultimately feed into the objective of ensuring the integrity, transparency, efficiency and orderly functioning of the internal market.[9]

EIOPA's supervisory tasks include the development of draft regulatory and implementing technical standards, guidelines, recommendations, opinions, and other related measures.[10] In addition, EIOPA is tasked with contributing to the consistent application of legally binding Union acts; organising and conducting peer reviews of National Competent Authorities (NCAs); and undertaking market analysis to inform discharge of the authority's functions.[11] Other tasks include protection of insurance sector consumers, beneficiaries, customers, investors; and contributing to consistent and coherent functioning of college of supervisors.[12] The 2019 amendments have also included a related task in contributing to common regulatory and supervisory standards and practices: developing and maintaining a Union supervisory handbook, which sets out the best practices and high-quality methodologies and processes.[13] Notably, this mandates EIOPA's consideration of changing business practices and models, which certainly include digitalisation of the financial sector, and the emergence of Fintech, RegTech and SupTech.

The 2019 amendments have strengthened EIOPA's legal jurisdiction in relation to SupTech. EIOPA is required to monitor and assess market developments, including in innovative financial services.[14] In addition, it is tasked with contributing to the establishment of a common Union financial data strategy.[15] As discussed further below, data strategy is an essential precondition for digital regulatory reporting. More importantly, when carrying out all its tasks under the Regulation, EIOPA is also required to consider technological innovation, innovative sustainable business models, and the integration of ESG factors.[16] It is worth noting that before the 2019 amendments, the treaty and legislative provisions empowering EIOPA, ESMA and the EBA were broadly interpreted to include the consideration of developments in

[7] Articles 1(6) and 8(1) of Regulation (EU) No. 1094/2010 establishing EIOPA.

[8] Ibid.

[9] Ibid.

[10] See Articles 8(1) and (2) of Regulation (EU) No. 1094/2010 establishing EIOPA.

[11] See Articles 8(1) and (2) of Regulation (EU) No. 1094/2010 establishing EIOPA.

[12] Ibid.

[13] Article 8 (1)(aa) of Regulation (EU) No. 1094/2010. See also Regulation (EU) 2019/2175 of 18 December 2019, which amends the three ESA founding Regulations.

[14] Article 8 (1)(f) of Regulation (EU) No. 1094/2010.

[15] Article 8(1)(ia) of Regulation (EU) No. 1094/2010.

[16] Article 8(1a)(c) of Regulation (EU) No. 1094/2010.

technological innovation.[17] Nevertheless, the EU law makers considered it essential to be explicit in the legislative text, demonstrating the necessity of a SupTech strategy for ESAs in the evolving digital insurance ecosystem.[18]

EIOPA's powers under Article 8(2) largely mirror its roles enumerated under Articles 8 (1) and (1a), and include the powers to: develop draft regulatory and implementing technical standards; issue guidelines and recommendations; issue warnings relating to financial stability, take individual decisions addressed to NCAs; take individual decisions addressed to financial institutions in specific cases concerning directly applicable union law; issue opinions to the European Parliament, the Council and the EC. Other powers include: collecting from the NCAs (rather than regulated entities) the necessary information concerning financial institutions;[19] developing common methodologies for assessing the effect of product characteristics and distribution processes on the financial position of institutions and on consumer protection; and providing a centrally accessible database of registered financial institutions.[20]

2.2 *The Subsidiarity Principle*

The subsidiarity principle restricts EU action only to what is strictly necessary for EU governance needs.[21] It is evident in the composition of the ESFS, which consists of the three European Supervisory Authorities (EIOPA, ESMA and the EBA) a joint committee of the ESAs, the European Systemic Risk Board (ESRB), and NCAs.[22] Despite their designation as 'supervisory authorities', ESAs act largely as conveners of a technocratic transnational network of regulatory governance consisting of the so-called NCAs, which retain direct supervisory powers over market actors in their respective national jurisdictions.[23] Prima facie, ESAs enjoy indirect regulatory

[17] See European Commission (2014), p. 4. The EC notes that 'the scope of the mandate of the ESAs is sufficiently broad…'. See also European Commission (2019b), p. 64. The expert Group on Regulatory Obstacles to Financial Innovation (hereafter ROFIEG) recommended a collaboration between ESAs, NCAs and financial institutions in making EU financial regulations machine-readable and machine-computable.

[18] The reforms were also motivated by the need to avoid tensions in the interpretation of the *Meroni* Doctrine. The discussion of the Meroni doctrine appears on Sect. 2.4. See also Chiti (2015), p. 12 for a discussion of the concerns with the broad interpretation of ESA competencies.

[19] See Articles 8(1) and (2), and Article 35(1) of Regulation (EU) No. 1094/2010 establishing EIOPA.

[20] Ibid.

[21] Article 5(3) of the Treaty on the Functioning of the European Union (TFEU).

[22] See European Commission (2014), p. 2.

[23] See Simoncini (2015), p. 324. The author explores the tensions between the subsidiarity principles and the need to centralise supervisory tasks at the EU level, to ensure more financial market stability.

powers over regulated entities, in the form of supervision of national regulators. However, ESAs also enjoy last-resort powers to adopt individual decisions addressed to financial institutions, in three instances: in the event of a breach of EU law, in an emergency and, last but not least, to settle a dispute between two or more NCAs in a cross-border situation.[24] The main function of ESAs is therefore the convergence of NCAs' supervisory practices, in accordance with the subsidiarity principle.[25] However, the supervisory autonomy of NCAs has been critiqued as an impediment to the achievement of legal convergence and a capital markets union.[26] It can be argued that it may similarly stand as a potential obstacle to the digitalisation of regulatory reporting at the EU level, as EIOPA lacks the direct supervisory powers to access insurance market data directly from regulated entities.[27]

Nevertheless, in recent years there seems to be a steady albeit nuanced departure from the delegation of indirect supervisory powers to ESAs. The evolution of ESMA testifies to this trend.[28] Thanks to legal reform, ESMA enjoys direct supervisory powers over credit rating agencies (CRAs), and trade repositories.[29] In 2019, the European Commission (EC) successfully pushed for the amendment of the ESAs' supervisory powers, further expanding the ambit of ESMA's direct supervision to include third country central counter-parties (CCPs).[30] The 2019 legislative process signalled the EC's ill-fated but notable ambition to convert ESMA into a single, centralised, capital markets supervisor.[31]

This development is of special relevance in the case under examination. If the asymmetry between the supervisory powers of ESAs continues to grow, the SupTech strategies of the Authorities will also reflect this asymmetry. For example, on the one hand, ESMA makes clear that its leadership and strategy on EU-wide access to reporting data is driven by its expanding direct supervisory competencies, and the importance of the availability of high-quality data on a pan-European basis for supervision.[32] EIOPA's strategy, on the other hand, is shaped by its indirect supervisory mandate, and the allocation of direct supervisory powers to the national regulators. Consequently, it collects data (primarily from Solvency II templates)

[24] See Articles 17(6), 18(4) and 19(4) of Regulation (EU) No. 1094/2010 establishing EIOPA.

[25] Ibid, para 66 of the preamble.

[26] Schoenmaker (2011), p. 57.

[27] See European Court of Auditors (2018), pp. 8–9. The report notes that EIOPA's lack of access to information from insurance firms has impeded even its current oversight functions.

[28] See Howell (2017), p. 1027. The author argues that ESMA's credible performance as a direct supervisory could result in the allocation of direct supervisory powers to EIOPA and the EBA. See also Moloney (2016), p. 380. The author suggests that ESMA could have a significant influence on the evolution of the institutional governance of the CMU.

[29] See Articles 9 and 81 of the Regulation (EU) No. 648/2012 (European Markets Infrastructure Regulation).

[30] See Regulation (EU) 2019/2175 of 18 December 2019, which amends the three ESA founding Regulations.

[31] Gortsos and Lagaria (2020), p. 14.

[32] ESMA (2020), p. 20.

from national regulators rather than directly from regulated entities. In the past, national regulators have not easily given access to their data.[33] This ultimately creates SupTech implementation challenges in relation to the design of the technological architecture of the digitalised ESFS, the feasibility of a centralised data service provider, and the governance of the reporting framework.

2.3 The Proportionality Principle

The proportionality principle means that 'the content and form of Union action shall not exceed what is necessary to achieve the objectives of the Treaties'.[34] In *Ex parte Fedesa*, the European Court of Justice (ECJ) formulated a three-part proportionality test for an EU measure: whether it is suitable to achieve a legitimate aim, necessary to achieve that aim, and does not have an excessive impact on an applicant's interests.[35] In addition, the 2019 amendments to the EIOPA Regulation emphasise EIOPA's duty, in accordance with the principle of proportionality, to consider specific differences within the insurance sector, relating to the nature, scale and complexity of risks, to business models and practice as well as to the size of financial institutions and of markets to the extent that such factors are relevant to the rules considered.[36]

An implication of this principle is that both the digitalisation of the Capital Markets Union and the adoption of a system of EU algorithmic oversight are subject to the proportionality test, and relevant measures must be suitable, necessary and not excessive or disproportionate to the objectives sought. To the extent that uniform reporting requirements are essential for unlocking the full potential of digital reporting and EU algorithmic oversight,[37] the proportionality principle requires consideration of the costs implications of digitalisation to both small and large size insurance firms.[38] The principle is also relevant in determining the allocation of powers between EIOPA and NCAs as further progress with the integration of the latest technology into the EU system of financial supervision will most certainly require a rethink of their existing roles, powers and terms of interaction. Consequently, the proportionality principle will require a very nuanced exercise of the powers of EIOPA as regards initiatives for the development of a harmonised system of digital reporting.

[33] European Court of Auditors (2018), p. 8.

[34] Article 5(4) of the TFEU.

[35] Case C-331/88 *R v Minister of Agriculture, Fisheries and Food, ex parte Fedesa* [1990] ECR I-4023. See also Chalmers et al. (2010), p. 367.

[36] Article 1(6) and (7) as amended by Regulation (EU) No. 2019/2175 amending ESA regulations.

[37] See European Commission (2019b), p. 63.

[38] Joosen and Lehmann (2019), p. 71. See also Article 8(3) of Regulation (EU) No. 1094/2010 establishing EIOPA.

2.4 The Meroni Doctrine

The *Meroni* doctrine also restricts the ESAs' rule making duties and powers to technical rather than policy issues with a wide margin of appreciation.[39] Under the Lamfalussy legislative process, the ESAs have the mandate to promote legal convergence and market integration in two ways.[40] First, they draft Level 2 delegated Acts and Implementing procedures, which are then considered and adopted by the EC.[41] The Delegated Acts (which elaborate on the substantive content of Level 1 legislation) and implementing procedures of Level 1 legislation, ensure harmonisation of the implementation and application across Member States.[42] Second, ESAs formulate Level 3 non-binding (but 'comply or explain') guidelines and recommendations to establish consistent, efficient and effective supervisory practices in the Member States to achieve a uniform interpretation of the legislation.[43] The European Commission approves draft technical standards.[44]

The convoluted institutional design of the ESFS and the Lamfalussy procedure make it difficult to identify which institution should have the authority over the process of translating financial services legislation into machine readable and executable code. While it may be tempting to vest this authority on the Commission, this type of task (and relevant decision making) seems to have a strong technocratic component. In view of the intertwined co-existence of technical and public policymaking domains, especially in complex areas such as financial regulation, one possibility is to delegate this task to EIOPA under the approval of the European Commission.[45]

---

[39] Case 9/56 *Meroni & Co., Industrie Metallurgiche, SpA v High Authority of the European Coal and Steel Community* (1958). For a discussion on the different conception of the Meroni doctrine arising from Case **C-270/12,** *United Kingdom v. Parliament and Council (Short Selling Ban)* (Jan. 22, 2014), see Georgosouli (2016), p. 368.

[40] The Lamfalussy process, introduced in 2002 and later modified by the 2009 Lisbon Treaty, is a fast-track procedure for the EU-level legislation in the financial sector. It consists of four levels: framework Acts under Level 1, delegated and implementing Acts under Level 2, guidelines and recommendations under Level 3, and supervision of NCAs under Level 4. See Moloney (2014), p. 862.

[41] See, for example, Articles 8(2), 10, and 15 of Regulation (EU) No. 1094/2010 establishing EIOPA.

[42] See Simoncini (2015).

[43] See Schemmel (2016). See also Tridimas (2012), p. 70: the author argues that these instruments represent 'the heavy hand of soft law'.

[44] See Articles 10 and 15 of Regulation (EU) No. 1094/2010 establishing EIOPA. See also Georgosouli (2016), p. 350, noting the 'unprecedented range of powers and level of discretion that [ESAs] have been endowed with when compared with older generations of EU agencies'.

[45] See Tridimas (2012), p. 69.

3 The EIOPA's Recent Initiatives for the Digital Transformation of Insurance Supervision: An Incomplete Agenda?

3.1 Introduction

The purpose of this section is to offer a critical overview of the EIOPA's strategic plan for the digital transformation of EU insurance supervision. Specifically, it considers the origins, subject matter and objectives of EIOPA's plan of action, its compatibility with parallel initiatives from the other two ESAs and it assesses its completeness.

3.2 Origins of EIOPA's SupTech Strategy

EIOPA's SupTech strategy emanates from an over-arching policy framework of the EU. First is the EC's 2015 Action Plan on Building a Capital Markets Union (CMU), which aims to further integrate the capital markets, to ensure the free flow of capital within the Union.[46] Recognising the role of technology in an increasingly digitalised EU financial market, the EC in 2018 launched the Fintech Action Plan, as part of a wider strategy to create and strengthen a digital single market and the Capital Markets Union.[47] These two action plans strengthened the imperative for SupTech adoption by ESAs as a key factor in legal convergence within the CMU. The EC consequently launched a 2018 Fitness Check of EU Supervisory Reporting Requirements project, aimed at not only cutting the costs of regulatory compliance, but also securing data standardisation, a key pillar for the integration of SupTech into the model of EU financial markets governance.[48] The EC also recognised that establishing the CMU depended on ESAs' promotion of supervisory convergence among national regulators, with specific attention to innovation and technologies.[49] Consequently, in 2018, the EC launched a legislative proposal to further integrate supervision of EU financial markets, by granting more roles and powers to the ESAs.[50] The European Parliament and Council enacted the Regulation amending the ESA Regulations in December 2019, which clarified and strengthened the existing powers of the ESAs, and granted additional powers to ESMA and the

[46] See European Commission (2015).

[47] See European Commission (2018).

[48] See European Commission (2019a).

[49] See European Commission (2017).

[50] Ibid.

EBA.[51] ESMA received additional direct supervisory powers over critical benchmarks and third country benchmarks, while the EBA was granted a coordinating role over money laundering and terrorism financing issues.[52]

As outlined in Sect. 2 above, the roles of the ESAs (including EIOPA) were amended to include the monitoring and assessment of innovative financial services and also contributing to the establishment of a common Union financial data strategy.[53] In addition, the ESAs were mandated to consider technological innovation, as well as innovative and sustainable business models, when carrying out their tasks under the respective founding legislations.[54] These amendments placed the ESAs in strong legal footing to make SupTech policy without straying into policymaking roles.

In 2018, the EC also established the Expert Group on Regulatory Obstacles to Financial Innovation (ROFIEG), whose 2019 report recommended the development and implementation of 'a comprehensive and ambitious agenda to support the adoption of advanced RegTech and SupTech by the financial sector' by the EC, ESAs and international standard setters.[55] This prompted the EC's 2020 launch of the Consultation on a New Digital Finance Strategy for Europe, in which the EC endorsed an EU SupTech framework driven by machine-learning technology, and machine-readable and machine-executable technology.[56]

In addition to the EU's policy framework, other notable programmatic activities by EIOPA also foregrounded its SupTech Strategy. One is the industry-led Open Insurance initiative (OPIN). This refers to the accessing and sharing of consumers' insurance services-related data between insurers, intermediaries or third parties via Application Programming Interfaces (APIs), to enable faster and easier development of InsurTech.[57] EIOPA has identified this initiative as a catalyst for the uptake of SupTech, as Open Insurance may require real-time access to insurance services data by supervisors, to allow for automated monitoring and reporting, for regulatory compliance purposes.[58]

Second, EIOPA has rolled out specific EU-level regulatory initiatives in response to the challenges of InsurTech. These include the 2018 InsurTech Task Force, which brings together national supervisors for multidisciplinary backgrounds; the InsurTech Roundables, which facilitate dialogue with insurance stakeholders; and the European Forum for Innovation Facilitators.[59] EIOPA has also established the

[51] See Regulation (EU) 2019/2175 of 18 December 2019, which amends the three ESA founding Regulations.

[52] Ibid. See also Gortsos and Lagaria (2020), p. 14.

[53] See Articles 8(1) (aa), (f), and (ia) of Regulation (EU) 1094/2010.

[54] See Article (1a)(c) of Regulation (EU) 1094/2010.

[55] See European Commission (2019b).

[56] See European Commission (2020).

[57] See Husseini (2018), p. 2.

[58] See EIOPA (2020c).

[59] ibid 26.

Expert Group on Digital Ethics in Insurance (DGE), a total of 40 stakeholders from the insurance industry, consumer representatives and academics that are working to develop a set of principles of digital responsibility in insurance.[60]

Against this backdrop of developments, EIOPA adopted two milestone plans of action in early 2020. The first one is the Supervisory Convergence Plan for 2020, while the second one is its 2020 Supervisory Technology Strategy.

The Supervisory Convergence Plan for 2020 seeks to achieve a high, effective and consistent level of supervision across Europe. Its goal is to further improve the functioning of the internal market, by preventing supervisory arbitrage and guaranteeing a level playing field.[61] Supervisory convergence, according to the Plan, 'should be built on a common interpretation of law and regulations, and without prejudice to the application of supervisory judgment or the proportionality principle'.[62] The Plan identifies SupTech as one pillar of supervisory convergence, with the aim of 'joint development by EIOPA and NCAs of innovative and efficient supervisory solutions that will support a more flexible and responsive supervisory system'.[63] Examined in the context of the ESFS, the Plan is key to EIOPA's overall SupTech strategy in at least two ways. First, the Plan sets as an outcome the development of supervisory convergence tools, including EIOPA Guidelines, Supervisory Handbook, Supervisory Statements.[64] These supervisory tools will create the administrative and operational structures that will be subject to digitalisation by SupTech. Second, it entrenches the EU administrative law principles of subsidiarity and proportionality, which are key to the legality of the SupTech adopted by EIOPA.[65] Notably, the Convergence Plan neither engages with SupTech in detail, nor pre-empts the emerging issues of digitalised regulatory supervision. These include the technologies required, the limits of encoding EU regulations, and the architecture of regulatory reporting and related governance issues, discussed in Sect. 4.

In its turn, the Supervisory Technology Strategy seeks to establish 'a . . .coordinated plan for SupTech development which will deliver supervisory tools or processes, considering EIOPA's strategic objectives and the Supervisory Convergence Plan'.[66] This overarching goal is also reflected and further articulated in the four objectives of EIOPA's SupTech Strategy. These are the following: (a) Promotion of knowledge and experience; (b) improving cooperation and exchange of information; (c) improving data collection through the standardisation and efficiency of reporting framework; and (d) improving data analytics. The

[60] ibid 53.

[61] See EIOPA (2020a), pp. 1–2.

[62] Ibid, p. 1.

[63] Ibid, p. 3.

[64] Ibid p. 1.

[65] Ibid, p. 2.

[66] See EIOPA (2020b), p. 1.

technologies identified in the Strategy[67] include the Internet of Things (IoT),[68] Distributed Ledger Technology (DLT),[69] Artificial Intelligence (AI),[70] Machine Learning Technology (MLT),[71] and Natural Language Processing (NLP).[72] The supervisory functions EIOPA aims to digitalise include prudential and Conduct of Business (COBS). This entails digitising operational functions such as data sharing, data analytics (e.g. in common risk assessment frameworks), and market monitoring.[73]

As a result of the operating environment of the ESFS and the EU principles of conferred powers, subsidiarity, proportionality, and the *Meroni* doctrine, areas impacted by specific national administrative law (e.g. organisational changes and the enhancement of different processes) fall outside the scope of the SupTech Strategy of the Authority. Instead, EIOPA's SupTech Strategy focuses on areas where EIOPA and the NCAs can collaborate (e.g. improvement of supervisory processes and use of data). Further, it is noteworthy that (as the four strategic objectives bring beyond doubt) EIOPA intends to explore how technology could help improve regulatory reporting. This should not come as a surprise. Without a robust system of regulatory reporting that benefits from the latest predictive and communication technology, it is simply not possible for EIOPA (or ESMA and the EBA) to improve its business intelligence capability, enhance its analytical framework, risk reports and the publication of statistics.

While the EU's over-arching policy framework has indeed provided impetus for the adoption of the SupTech strategy, EIOPA has also (separately) outlined key rationales that necessitate its engagement. For example, in its response to the EC's 2020 Digital Finance Strategy Consultation, EIOPA identifies barriers to RegTech adoption within the Single Market, including lack of harmonisation of EU rules, and lack of harmonised approach to RegTech within the EU.[74] These rationales put into

---

[67] Ibid, p. 2.

[68] Internet of Things refers to the networked interconnection of everyday objects, which are often equipped with ubiquitous intelligence. IoT integrates every object for interaction via embedded systems, which leads to a highly distributed network of devices communicating with human beings as well as other devices. See Xia et al. (2012), p. 1101.

[69] Distributed Ledger Technology is 'an appended-only, distributed database that is collectively stored, maintained and updated across a network of computers with each computing "node" in the network storing an identical copy of the database.' See Yeung (2019), p. 210.

[70] Broadly speaking, Artificial Intelligence (AI) is the simulation of intelligent behaviour in computers. See Boden (2018), p. For a working definition of AI and Machine Learning and a brief description of their main difference, see Bank of England and Financial Conduct Authority (2019).

[71] See Bank of England and Financial Conduct Authority 2020. Machine learning is a type of Artificial Intelligence (AI) that enables computers not just do certain tasks but to learn without being explicitly programme.

[72] Ibid, p. 24. Natural language processing is a tree-based machine learning model that 'involves the application of algorithms—often neural networks—to identify and extract the natural language rules such that unstructured language data is converted into a form that computers can understand'.

[73] See EIOPA (2020b), p. 1.

[74] See EIOPA (2020c), p. 54.

perspective the role EIOPA has shaped for itself in the SupTech Strategy: to coordinate common work (at national level) by implementing a platform of on-going exchange of knowledge and experience, and organising and endorsing the analysis of potential developments of tools (e.g. by promoting proof of concepts).[75] These roles are fully compatible with EIOPA's current, supervisory role, including the development of draft Implementing Technical Standards on public disclosure and supervisory reporting of insurance and reinsurance undertakings, provision of XBRL taxonomies, as well assurance of data standardisation and data quality.[76]

3.3 Summary

EIOPA's strategic plan for the digital transformation of insurance supervision in the EU single market covers a lot of ground but takes a piecemeal, cautious and fragmented approach. Instead of implementing a general plan of action for regulatory technology, it focuses on the use of technology for supervisory purposes (SupTech) and in priority for the execution of reporting requirements. This cautious and rather tentative approach is in the right direction, but it leaves a lot to be desired. Digital reporting is clearly on the agenda and rightly so, but there is no systematic thinking about what course of action would be required for the development of such system in the future.[77] Although this could be partly explained by the fact that it is too early (for example, Member States are in different levels of digital transition; the harmonisation of EU law on all aspects of data privacy and other crucial governance aspects of technology is still incomplete etc), it is equally true that it is never too early to think about a roadmap of action in anticipation of future challenges and potential responses to those challenges. Some of those challenges are considered below.

---

[75] See EIOPA (2020a), p. 6.

[76] See EIOPA (2020c), p. 55. XBLR is an example of semantic technology. According to Wikipedia, XBLR is a framework for exchanging business information. It allows the expression of semantic meaning for business reporting using the so-called XML-based language and XML-based syntax and related XML technology. In its turn, XML is a software system through which data may be specified, stored, queried, transformed, exported and returned to a calling system according to a specific set of rules for encoding documents in a format that can be read by both humans and machines. Wikipedia at https://en.wikipedia.org/wiki/XBRL and at https://en.wikipedia.org/wiki/XML (last visited 12 February 2020).

[77] Similar data collection initiatives have been announced in other jurisdictions and largely remain at an earlier stage of development. These include the US Consumer Financial Protection Bureau (CFPB) and Commodity Futures Trading Commission (CFTC), the Monetary Authority of Singapore (MAS), the Hong Kong Monetary Authority (HKMA), the Japan Financial Services Agency (JFSA), and the Philippines Central Bank (BSP). Bank of England (2020), pp. 26–27.

4 A Reality Check: What Would It Take to Set Up a Digital System of Regulatory Reporting?

The recognition of the need for a system of digital reporting in EIOPA's agenda is a welcome development but the absence of any comprehensive plan of action is an important blind-spot in the Authority's strategy for the digital transformation of EU insurance supervision. In this section, we discuss a series of themes that emerge in relation to the development and implementation of a system of digital reporting in the field of EU insurance supervision in anticipation of problems and potential responses to those problems. Where appropriate we draw on recent experience from other jurisdictions.

4.1 Mapping the Extent of Sophistication of the Technology That Will Be Required for a System of Digital Reporting

At a minimum, a digital system of regulatory reporting requires a digital network providing the necessary infrastructure for the interconnection of the various users, and advanced predictive and communication technology for the generation, collection, storage and processing of high volumes of different types of data coming from different sources ideally in real time. Digital Ledger Technology (DLT), Machine Learning Technology (MLT) and Natural Language Processing (NLP) are essential components of this digital infrastructure.[78]

Originally, DLT came into being for Bitcoin[79] and its function was to enable peer-to-peer transfers of money without using banks. For Bitcoin transactions, DLT works as follows. Participating individuals are identified by a number (the 'public key') and are given a passcode (a 'private key') to access their own money. Each time they transact, a shared public record of the transaction is created and an identical copy of the entire record of the transaction (the 'distributed ledger') is kept on their personal computer and updated by the consensus of all the participants.[80] DLT is typically combined with a 'smart contract', a distinctive feature of which is its self-executing nature. Specifically, the terms of the smart contract are written into code, run on a distributed ledger and are executed automatically on the occurrence of a specified event.[81]

[78] See definitions in note 26, 28 and 29.

[79] Bitcoin is a form of money that is not backed up by the government of any State. See Narayanan et al. (2016), p. 59.

[80] See Micheler and Whaley (2020), p. 352.

[81] Ibid. An example of a specific event is the payment of a certain sum at regular intervals. There remains a debate on whether smart contracts are legal contracts, since smart contracts may not fulfil the legal requirements for the formation of a contract. See for example Brownsword (2019); De Filippi and Wright (2019), p. 87.

Since its first appearance, the application of DLT has expanded to IT compliance solutions amongst others. In the UK, Codra was the first DLT-enabled regulatory technology. It was initiated by the industry to match legal agreements between parties and operated according to a basic distributed consensus.[82] Being designed to complement the existing legal structures, Codra mandated its users to acknowledge explicitly the supremacy of the rules of the regulatory law for compliance purposes.[83] Furthermore, its running had a positive impact on the detection of money laundering, fraud or other illegal activity. DLT is very promising in providing the necessary digital network for the operation of a system of digital reporting. Pending further improvements, DLT could be used by the financial industry for the record-keeping and execution of a wide spectrum of financial transactions.[84] This is of particular relevance in the case under examination because, if this were to happen, it would be the first decisive step to connect financial authorities like EIOPA directly with all other users of this digital network and, hence, to open the way to an era of almost real-time financial reporting and oversight.[85]

MLT is a further component of a digital network of regulatory reporting. This is a type of artificial intelligence that can allow real time analysis of vast volumes of information for supervisory purposes.[86] Machines with learning capabilities excel humans in the identification of unusual patterns of activities and in spotting previously unnoticed correlations indicating the emergence of risks. Furthermore, when combined with NLP, it could be used for the processing, analysis and understanding of oral and written human communication. This would be particularly helpful for reporting purposes. Specifically, it could enable machines to read regulatory content and then process relevant data for the execution of reporting tasks as, for instance, the collection or submission of specific data. Currently, NLP supports the operations of Alexa, Siri and Google Translate.[87] Furthermore, it is increasingly becoming a useful tool for financial regulators like EIOPA. For instance, EIOPA itself is already exploring the benefits of this technology to extract information from packaged retail and insurance-based investment products' (PRIIPs) key information documents (KIDs) for supervisory purposes.[88]

For the enthusiastic advocates of digitalisation, the capabilities of these technologies are impressive, however, it is important to have a realistic sense of their current and projected potential. Recent experiments with digital reporting in the UK, for example, have established the feasibility of real time regulatory reporting in relation

[82] Yeung (2019), pp. 221–222.

[83] On the Codra project see Ibid (noting that in this manner it becomes clear that 'the understanding of the code of law prevails over code as law').

[84] Micheler and Whaley (2020), pp. 352–353.

[85] Yeung (2019), pp. 221–222.

[86] Micheler and Whaley (2020), pp. 353–354.

[87] Ibid p. 354.

[88] Ibid. This is further discussed on page 15.

to highly detailed technical requirements from the computer science point of view but, at the same time, have also brought onto the surface several challenges.[89]

Although it is possible for the industry to use DLT, the UK regulators have concluded that for the time being this technology is not sufficiently advanced to become fully integrated into a system of digital reporting. Similarly, the use of MLT is growing but it is not problem free. One of the thorniest issues is that the software that enables machines to engage in learning raises serious questions of ethics, fair use and privacy because of its conspicuous complexity, lack of transparency and inexplicability.[90] A further difficulty is that its use is not scaleable given its present and foreseeable development. Nevertheless, the future looks promising. The more access machines have to data, the smarter the machines become.[91] In this respect, the advent of quantum computing and the convergence of technologies like Advanced Software, Big Data and Big Compute is expected to enhance cloud storage and improve accessibility of data kept in large-scale storage, while Big Data will improve the machines' ability to analyse vast pools of data, detect patterns and generate insights.[92] Finally, NLP is at an early stage of development. According to the latest experiments with this technology, NPL is not sophisticated enough to cope with social context and the linguistic nuance of the content of regulatory law.[93] To be sure, it is desirable to integrate NLP and other semantic technologies into digital regulatory reporting but, by everyone's admission, the design and implementation of these technologies require further investigation.[94]

4.2 *The Limited Translatability of the EU Legal Content Into Instructions that Can Be Read and Executed by Machines*

EIOPA takes the view that machine readable and executable reporting requirements could prove beneficial for regulators and the insurance industry alike. It further projects that a future of regulatory compliance will be largely 'algorithm/code based' as the relevant technology promises to reduce compliance costs, eliminate the need for human interpretation and speed up the time that is otherwise required for

[89] See FCA (2017), p. 10, 14.

[90] See Jarrahi (2019), p. 5. He notes that '[t]hese AI systems often know more than they can explain in an intelligible way, and hence emerge as a black-box to human decision-makers'. See further Scantamburlo et al. (2019), p. 57.

[91] Lohr et al. (2019), p. 231.

[92] Big Data describes an extremely vast set of accessible data (e.g. the Internet of Things). Big Compute refers to a wide range of tools and approaches to run large-scale applications for business, science, and engineering performing complex modelling, simulations etc. Cloud computing is an example of Big Compute. NLP is an example of Advanced Software.

[93] See EIOPA response to the consultation -specifically, response to question 45. EIOPA (2020a), p. 57.

[94] Some firms currently use NLP technologies to extract key terms from legal documents.

regulators to identify emerging risks.[95] Transforming the legal requirements into code is technically challenging, however. Algorithms are the only language that machines can process. To ensure that the content of the EIOPA rulebook becomes machine readable and machine executable, it is necessary to convert it into its algorithmic version in order to enable machines to communicate with other machines in the same network for the automated execution of a series of regulatory tasks (e.g. data collection).

Machines of specialised intelligence do not process equally well all types of data.[96] To be at the peak of their performance, they need to be fed with highly structured data, namely data capturing a piece of information of a narrowly defined meaning. This is not to say that machines cannot cope at all with semi-structured or unstructured data namely data, the meaning of which is more open-ended and far less clearly pre-defined. They do, but the less structured the data, the more difficult it is for machines to engage in decision-making where meaning is to be inferred. The machines' need for highly structured data sets a crucial challenge to the conversion of regulatory content into algorithms.[97] Ultimately, this depends on how feasible it is to break down regulatory content into granular instructions, and then convert those instructions into micro-directives communicated in algorithmic language.

Many existing provisions of the EIOPA rulebook are not suitable for algorithmic conversion chiefly because it is difficult to interpret the content of those legal provisions into exhaustively precise terms without changing or losing part of their meaning. This task of translation is not as straightforward as it seems because it is impossible to fix the meaning of a word prior to its use. Take the example of the word 'sales'. To paraphrase Ludwig Wittgenstein, no meaning of the word 'sales' can include everything that is a sale and exclude everything that is not a sale.[98] The relationship between the various uses of the word 'sale' is like the relationship between various members of a family. A resemblance exists but it is not possible to give this resemblance any rigid definition ex-ante. Accordingly, the algorithmic conversion of legal rules of relative specificity is much more complex than, say, the identification and submission of the reference number of a specific product provider.

Consider for instance the Commission Delegated Regulation (EU) 2017/653 supplementing Regulation (EU) No 1286/2014 on key information documents (KIDs) for packaged retail and insurance-based investment products (PRIIPs).[99] This is a Level 2 regulation that lays down the regulatory technical standards for

[95] See EIOPA response to consultation, specifically response to question 43. EIOPA (2020a), p. 55.

[96] The UK financial regulators draw a distinction between three different types of data: 'structured', 'semi-structured', and 'unstructured-data'). A bank account balance offers an example of structured data. The pixels in an image offer an example of unstructured data, as they do not have a pre-defined meaning. See Bank of England and Financial Conduct Authority (2019), pp. 21–23.

[97] Ibid, p. 22 (noting that according to their survey responses 'structured data is used for more than 80% of ML use cases' but 'firms also use semi-structured or unstructured data in more than two thirds of cases, often in conjunction with structured data').

[98] See Anscombe and Rhees (1963), para 1–38. See also McGinn (2003), pp. 33–72.

[99] For a comprehensive discussion of PRIIP see Colaert (2016).

fulfilling the disclosure of KIDs. Annex 1 provides the template for the KID, which specifies in detail the data fields that must be completed. The substantive provisions of the Regulation outline in great detail how to populate the data template. For example, Art. 12 section 1(a) provides that in the section on risks and returns, PRIIP manufacturers shall specify 'the range of risk classes of all underlying investment options offered within the PRIIP by using a summary risk indicator having a numerical scale from 1 to 7, as set out in Annex III'. This provision can be relatively easily encoded into machine-readable language, as the numerical values are amenable to rephrasing into a set of more concrete instructions. On the other hand, section 1(c) requires PRIIP manufacturers to specify 'a brief description on how the performance of the PRIIP as a whole depends on the underlying investment options'. It is much more difficult to generate granular instructions for an open-ended data field like section 1(c). For example, it is not clear how brief the description will have to be and what should be the criterion for assessing the relevance of underlying investment options. The application of section 1(c) calls for a system of decision-making that displays normative reasoning and sensitivity to social context and the nuances of human language namely capabilities in which humans overperform machines of specialist intelligence.[100]

An additional limitation here is the following: although it is possible to convert the semantic content of legal rules into algorithmic language, it is not possible to capture the context within which these rules are meant to apply. Legal rules are also subject to change and so it does the regulatory content that is to be converted into algorithmic language. Consequently, the relevant computer programming that supports machine readability and machine executability will also need constant updates. Finally, an additional source of complication stems from the fact that quite often regulatory content comes from legal rules that have been made by different regulators with distinctive mandates and potentially conflicting agendas. As a result, the ex-ante standardisation of those rules and correspondent agreed definitions may simply not be feasible or it may be unsuitable.

At least in part, the challenges described above may be addressed by ensuring that data is subject to constant validation through human input and oversight, so that it is kept accurate and reliable; and by regulating those professionals that undertake to do this job. For instance, regulators like EIOPA can take the following measures amongst other things: (a) Draft and constantly update explanatory guidance for software developers and others professionals with the responsibility of overseeing machines and of validating machine outputs, (b) provide training or at least have some control over the training of software developers and other professionals; and

[100] See Colaert (2018), pp. 71–72 (highlighting the qualitative element underlying the method of calculation of the risk indicators in relation to the KID of Regulation (EU) No. 1286/2014 of the European Parliament of the Council of 26 November 2014 on key information documents for packaged retail and insurance-based investment products (PRIIPs) [2014] OJ L 352/1, namely the predecessor of the current Commission Delegated Regulation, and noting that, despite the recent legislative amendments, concerns remain over the potentially misleading nature of the risk indicators.

(c) supervise them to ensure compliance with best practice.[101] However, multiple checks, verifications and updates complicate the governance of algorithmic financial supervision, increase the cost of its administration and management and over-stretch the mandate of insurance regulators.[102]

To be sure, progress with the current on-going efforts to improve the consistency of definitions, formats and processes as well as the standardisation of data is expected to improve data quality in the context of digital reporting and, more generally, to make the governance of algorithmic financial supervision much more manageable.[103] However, this would not be enough. Law and code are not just two different normative domains of governance.[104] They are mutually exclusive forms of communication.[105] While natural language requires a degree of linguistic 'open-texture', algorithmic language leans towards granular precision. Conflict between the two is inevitable and it is paramount that it is resolved in a manner compatible with the rule of law.

A potential solution to the mutual exclusiveness of natural language and algorithmic language as forms of communication would be the following. First, to confine algorithmic conversion only to Level 3 legislation of the EIOPA rulebook since its extremely detailed content seems to better fit the picture of regulatory content eligible for coding albeit not without difficulties.[106] The next step would be to draft Level 3 legislation as two-tiered legal instrument so that its content is expressed in both forms of communication to accommodate both human decision making and algorithmic decision making. Finally, resolve potential conflict between the two by giving priority to human interpretation as a recognition of the fact that human language is the only form of communication that is capable of realising fundamental principles of the rule of law.[107] A future EIOPA rulebook of that sort would of course confine the use of digital reporting to a smaller fraction of insurance regulatory requirements, but it would make the digital transformation of EU insurance supervision compatible with the rule of law, safer and more manageable.

[101] See, for instance, FCA Data Reference Guides in FCA (2016).

[102] Phase 2 of the Pilot Programme looked into the economic viability of the DRR concluding that 'the business case for DRR is strongest when implemented for multiple domains and aligned to change initiatives already occurring at firms'. See Financial Conduct Authority et al. (2019), p. 5.

[103] The importance of data consistency and standardisation has been emphasised in various public policy communications. See notably, European Commission 2019. EIOPA has been supporting the development of standardised approaches to data and IT as for instance the development of an XBRL based taxonomy for both pensions and re-insurance reporting requirements and the LEI application in both sectors. See EIOPA (2020a), p. 56.

[104] Yeung (2019).

[105] Pasquale (2019), p. 3.

[106] The suggestion is likely to find a positive response from the EIOPA. See EIOPA's response to EC consultation in EIOPA (2020a), p. 55. Reporting frameworks / legislations which could benefit the most from being translated into machine-executable form are the ones already using machine-native international standards (such as ISO20022, XBRL, SDMX) for reporting and disclosure.

[107] Pasquale (2019), p. 5.

4.3 *The Architecture of Regulatory Reporting and Issues of Governance*

Broadly speaking, the debates on the architecture of regulatory reporting draw a conceptual distinction between two models of data collection: On the one hand the 'push model' of data reporting and, on the other hand, the 'pull model' of data reporting.[108] The push model is the traditional process of reporting in which regulated individuals have the obligation to submit certain information in compliance with the relevant regulatory law. The pull model stands at the opposite side of the spectrum in that the regulators are assumed to be able to pull data themselves instead of requiring members of the industry to submit data while keeping an eye on them to ensure that they will conform with the specific reporting instruction. Until recently, and as it is evident from the architecture of the existing legal design of reporting requirements, only the implementation of the push model was feasible. However, the advent of regulatory technology bears the potential of moving to a pull model of regulatory reporting.

EIOPA has already in place a common database for Solvency II reporting, but it is at an early stage of development.[109] Accordingly, it is worth asking whether the pull model or a variant of it would be an appealing proposition for EIOPA more generally. A notable advantage of a pull mechanism, at least on paper, is that it would make possible for EIOPA to collect the data it needs, in almost real time and at a minimum cost, as it will not have to store and handle large datasets. For the same reason, it would become easier for the Authority to ensure compliance with data security and personal data rules.

A potential candidate for EIOPA would be to opt for an architecture of digital regulatory reporting similar to the one that has been adopted by the National Bank of Rwanda (NBR).[110]

The NBR has in place a granular data extraction model (a pull mechanism like for example an API) connecting the NBR with reporting firms. This pull mechanism facilitates the submission of information on the request of the NBR. It operates based on pre-defined set of templates with guidelines, which are shared with all reporting institutions and make possible for the NBR to pull data from the firms' core systems.[111]

---

[108] Bank of England (2020), pp. 42–45.

[109] Solvency II data is to some extent standardised but further progress is required with standardisation because its present level does not guarantee data quality. Compared to Solvency II data, the standardisation of Conduct of Business data is at a very early stage of development.

[110] Kamali and Randall (2017); Dias and Straschen (2017), p. 27; Broeders and Prenio (2018), p. 6. See also Bank of England (2020), p. 27 (considering the recent experience with the digital reporting model of NBR in the context of current debates about the future shape of the Bank's digital data strategy).

[111] Bank of England (2020), p. 27. See also National Bank of Rwanda (2017), p. 73.

Despite its obvious benefits when compared to the traditional push model of regulatory reporting, the pull model would most probably not work equally well for all types of data collection. For example, its application would be problematic for the collection of fluctuating figures (e.g. data on aggregate financing). In that latter case, the traditional push model of data collection would be preferable. Projections about the net benefits of the pull model are also bound to be an imprecise science.[112] Ultimately, the efficiency of this model will depend on how its costs compare to the costs of generating and sending files manually, the number of data requests and other uncertain factors.

The implementation of a pull model would also require massive changes to data governance. Under the existing push model, reporting rules specify things like the time of data submission and content of the data submitted. However, if a pull model is to be implemented, then these rules would have to be replaced with a different set of rules as it would be necessary to specify when and how often firms must make data available, when and how often EIOPA could pull data, and under what circumstances data resubmissions might be allowed.

An alternative to the Rwandan model would exhibit a more centralised outlook. A distinctive feature of this model would be the presence of a central service provider ('central utility') which would carry out a variety of tasks and reporting processes as, for example, the collection of granular data, the interpretation of reporting instructions, and the transformation of firm source data into the data that is required for reports.[113] The reporting model of the Central Bank of Austria is an example of this more centralised variant of the pull model.[114] At the heart of this system of reporting lies the AuRep. The latter is a central utility co-owned by seven of the largest Austrian banking groups. AuRep serves as a reporting platform and works as follows: Reporting banks enter granular data into a standardised input layer. This data is then sent to AuRep, which processes it into regulatory data that meets different reporting requirements. Acting on behalf of the reporting banks, AutRep then reports directly to the Austrian Central Bank.[115] Currently, AuRep covers almost all statistical reporting of banks and financial stability reports, but the plan is to expand in the future.

One of the advantages of implementing an Austrian type of data collection for digital reporting is cost reduction though the avoidance of duplication. A further advantage is the increase of the quality of reported data, since several crucial functions—notably, the standardisation of the transformation of data, the interpretation of reporting instructions and their execution—will be carried out in one place. An additional advantage is that the collected standardised data could be used to feed

[112] Bank of England (2020), p. 31.

[113] Ibid, p. 43.

[114] Ibid, p. 26; Broeders and Prenio (2018), p. 6. The Austrian architecture follows the model of the European System of Central Banks' (ESCB) Integrated Reporting Framework (IReF). Here chose to refer to the Austrian model instead of the IReF one because the latter is under consultation.

[115] Bank of England (2020), p. 26.

valuable information back to regulated insurers taken individually, hence, providing value to the industry and policy analysts amongst others. Furthermore, the publication of a subset data in a central and easily accessible database could become instrumental to the improvement of public disclosures.[116]

The perceived benefits need to be weighed against the costs of running the centralised service provider. Again, this type of architecture may not be suitable for all types of data. Statistics reports consisting of aggregations of granular source data will probably be easiest to provide centrally. The opposite holds for data which requires firm-specific judgment. In that latter case, it would be desirable to ensure a degree of human involvement at firm level so that those legally responsible for any data omissions and inaccuracies have the opportunity to check the data that they are submitting.[117] The preservation of human input is crucial here because the purpose of centralisation of the various reporting functions is not to discharge firms from the responsibility to comply with the various reporting rules but to help them comply in a cost-efficient fashion. From the legal point of view, reporting firms need to continue to be legally responsible and accountable for the quantity and quality of the data that they submit. A further issue of concern is that any data errors are bound to affect the entire industry with potential systemic implications for as long as they remain undetected.

Not unlike the decentralised model, the implementation of an Austrian type of reporting architecture EU-wide in the context of insurance would also require crucial changes to the existing governance arrangements. For example, extra measures would have to be taken to respond to data security and other operational risks with clear lines of responsibility for decision-making and action. In addition, it would be necessary to change the reporting rules to respond to the emerging data architecture, while a separate set of rules might be needed to provide responses to errors or various other contingencies.

The Integrated Reporting Framework (IReF) of the European System of Central Banks (ESCB) which is currently under consultation, is very similar to the Austrian model and offers a hint of how the Austrian reporting architecture might look like at the EU level.[118] The aim of the IReF is to integrate a wide range of existing statistical reporting requirements of the various NCAs into a single reporting model. It is envisaged that the IReF would define a sufficiently granular set of requirements for reporting purposes and that its operations would benefit from the existing Bank's Integrated Reporting Dictionary (BIRD).[119] The BIRD provides a harmonised data

[116]The US Federal Financial Institutions Examination Council provides an interesting example of data transparency in terms of the depth, frequency and accessibility of the disclosures. See Ibid, p. 44.

[117]Human involvement would also be essential to ensure EIOPA is allowed to query part of the common input layer directly. Ibid, p. 42.

[118]Further information on the IRef is available at https://www.ecb.europa.eu/stats/ecb_statistics/co-operation_and_standards/reporting/html/index.en.html.

[119]Further information on BIRD is available at https://www.ecb.europa.eu/stats/ecb_statistics/co-operation_and_standards/reporting/html/index.en.html.

model which specifies the data which should be extracted from the internal IT systems of the reporting firms (the so-called 'input layer'). Furthermore, it contains a set of rules which govern the transformation of the extracted data into a specific final regulatory figure (the so-called 'transformation rules').

An interesting question to ask is whether EIOPA should undertake the role as central service provider or whether instead this role should be entrusted to a separate EU agency which will be designed specifically for that role. EIOPA is primarily an EU-supervisory agency with nuanced range of powers to perform regulatory functions specific to its insurance mandate. Prima facie, it is not a technology or data services provider. As discussed above, EIOPA perceives its role as focusing on the promotion of the development of a common SupTech framework and strategy in the field of insurance. In pursuit of this role, EIOPA has been particularly active in the coordination of common work with NCAs, the facilitation of experience sharing and the organisation and endorsement of analysis for the potential development of tools (e.g. by promoting proof of concepts). Historically, the management of large quantities of data is not its core specialism. If it were to be entrusted with the additional role of central service provider, this would also generate significant reputational risks to the EIOPA in relation to data quality assurance failures, data security and other operational risks. A further issue of concern is that, if EIOPA were to take up additional powers and responsibilities in pursuit to its new role, the desirability of calibrating the powers and responsibilities of the other two ESAs would have to be considered too, hence, potentially opening the floodgate of far-reaching and for that reason more time-consuming reforms of the current ESFS.

While the above considerations militate against the idea of expanding the existing mandate of EIOPA and turning it in effect into a central service provider for reporting purposes in the field of EU insurance, a host of other issues point to the opposite direction. Consider, for example, the use of MLT. A key feature of machine learning is that it is driven by a statistical model, whose design embeds a system of scoring and typically involves impenetrably complex calculations.[120] The statistical model serves a specific goal in relation to which machines learn to mine data from vast datasets, identify correlations and patterns, infer information, make predictions and produce outputs. This goal may address a legitimate concern as, for example, that of cost efficient reporting and compliance but from that it does not follow that it fully captures the policy objectives of financial regulators, or that it indeed yields correct legal results. To pre-empt this mismatch, EU rule-makers should continue to be the ones to write rules in natural as well as in algorithmic language. Moreover, EU rule-makers should assume responsibility over the regulation of data specifications and the validation of standards (with the cooperation of EU and other NCAs including the European Data Protection Supervisor (EDPS) as well as input from expert software developers, the industry and other stakeholders) so that they will be able to address issues of data quality assurance and other operational risks at source.

[120]This aspect of machine learning is known as algorithmic opacity, and it explains the inscrutability of algorithmic decision-making. On this point, see Cobbe (2019), pp. 638–639.

This will be easier said than done. The institutional design of the ESFS is complex and additional supervisory responsibilities over the governance of the relevant regulatory technology will most certainly overstretch EIOPA's current supervisory mandate and powers. To be sure, one does not have the crystal ball to make projections about whether the EU governance of regulatory technology in the field of insurance will provide the impetus for a radical reshuffling of the existing convoluted institutional architecture of the ESFS. This notwithstanding, ignoring the elephant in the room does not help for planning purposes. Given space constraints, it is not possible to explore all possible institutional options taking things forward. One possibility, however, might be to set up a joint central service provider for all three ESAs the task of which would be to coordinate and streamline the administration of digital regulatory reporting for all three sectors of the EU financial systems. This would be consistent with economies of scale and scope and would facilitate cross-sectoral knowledge generation and sharing.

5 Conclusion

In this chapter we sought to offer a reality check of the algorithmic future of insurance supervision in the EU. Specifically, we examined EIOPA, its operating environment, and how principles of EU administrative law shape its SupTech mission and mandate. We then portrayed the Authority's role in the digital transformation of insurance supervision in the EU and the evolution of its strategy to point to an important blind-spot: the absence of a comprehensive plan of action for the development of a digital system of regulatory reporting in the field of EU insurance supervision. Against this backdrop, we considered a series of themes in relation to the setting up and running a system of digital reporting in anticipation of future challenges and potential responses to those problems. These relate to the limitations of the technology that will be required for digital reporting given its current and foreseeable stage of development, a series of difficulties with the conversion of regulatory content into code and, lastly, issues of reporting architecture and governance.

The analysis makes plain that the EIOPA's approach to supervision is at a stage of transition and it is fast moving towards a digital model of EU insurance supervision in response to the relevant initiatives of the EU Commission to foster technological innovation and promote the implementation of a digital strategy in all three sectors of the EU financial system. Specifically, three findings emerge from our analysis.

The first finding is that digital reporting is not new to EIOPA. The Authority has in place a digital system for Solvency II reporting. However, its scope is narrow, and the system has faced challenges with data quality and standardisation. Building on the current experience with Solvency II reporting, EIOPA is increasingly assuming a leadership role in coordinating EU-level initiatives, including OPIN, the InsurTech Task Force, InsurTech Roundtables, EFIF and DGE. While these initiatives are welcome, establishing an EU-level system of digital reporting requires an ambitious and detailed strategy, which may over-stretch the Authority's mandate in the future.

The second finding is that EIOPA perceives its role as a coordinator rather than a centralised data service provider, within the emerging digital ecosystem of reporting. This can be explained by the impact of the EU administrative law principles of proportionality and subsidiarity, the *Meroni* doctrine, and the concomitant structure of the ESFS on the objectives, tasks and powers of EIOPA. Proportionality requires the adoption of digital reporting by EIOPA to be guided by the suitability, necessity and balancing of any adverse impact of EU action. The *Meroni* doctrine restricts EIOPA rulemaking to technical rather than policymaking domains. Subsidiarity vests NCAs with direct supervisory powers, which promote national supervisory autonomy but undermine the prospect of an EU-level centralised system of digital reporting. Indeed, it is difficult to strike a satisfactory trade-off between a common supervisory approach and maintaining national supervisory autonomy.

Finally, the third finding is that the setting up and running of an EU wide system of digital reporting in the field of insurance will prove to be particularly challenging due to a series of factors which yet have escaped thorough consideration. These are (a) the degree of current and projected sophistication of the relevant technology that will be required to provide the necessary digital infrastructure; (b) the limited translatability of rulebook content into algorithms to enable machine readability and machine executability, and (c) difficulties with data architecture and governance.

Our findings point to concrete themes that could provide the building blocks for a more comprehensive blueprint for an EU system of digital reporting as an integral aspect of insurance supervision with wider implications given their relevance to the other two European Supervisory Authorities. To be sure, this chapter did not address the full spectrum of themes that are intertwined with digital reporting and the advent of EU algorithmic financial regulation more generally. The impact of EU regulatory technology on the use of administrative discretion both at the EU level as well as at national levels, automation bias[121] and the concomitant problem of deskilling,[122] the compatibility of regulatory technology with the principles of EU administrative and constitutional law – to mention a few – are equally important and call for systematic investigation in their own right which, given space constraints, will have to be postponed for another occasion.

[121] Automation bias is the general belief that—compared to humans—computers are more rational and objective in their decision-making. The belief of the superior rationality of machines is in many respects unfunded but nonetheless strong. See Lohr et al. (2019), p. 231; Cobbe (2019), p. 641. The phenomenon has been observed in criminal prosecution with judges using the aid of AI to decide whether to bail an alleged offender or determine the length of sentence and finding it extremely hard to ignore machines making predictions on the chances of re-offence. See Fry (2020).

[122] Deskilling is intertwined with automation bias. Financial supervision involves a wide range of normative reasoning skills including the capacity to sense a degree of social connection, critical judgment, empathy and moral imagination all of which will atrophy because of growing reliance on automation. See Scantamburlo et al. (2019), pp. 75–76. On the degradation of cognitive skills, see further, Volz et al. (2016); Shiffrin (2010), p. 1222, 1244. For a more general discussion see Alexander and Sherwin (2001).

References

Alexander L, Sherwin E (2001) The rule of rules: morality, rules and the dilemmas of law. Duke University Press, Durham

Anscombe GEM, Rhees R (1963) Philosophical investigations. Blackwell, Oxford

Bank of England (2020) Transforming data collection from the UK financial sector. https://www.bankofengland.co.uk/-/media/boe/files/paper/2020/transforming-data-collection-from-the-uk-financial-sector.pdf?la=en&hash=6E6132B4F7AF681CCB425B0171B4CF43D82E7779. Accessed 08 September 2020

Bank of England and Financial Conduct Authority (2019) Machine Learning in the UK Financial Services. https://www.bankofengland.co.uk/-/media/boe/files/report/2019/machine-learning-in-uk-financial-services.pdf. Accessed 12 February 2020

Boden M (2018) Artificial intelligence: a very short introduction. OUP, Oxford

Broeders D and Prenio J (2018) Innovative Technology in Financial Supervision (SupTech): The Experience of Early Users. FSI Insights 9: 1. https://www.bis.org/fsi/publ/insights9.pdf. Accessed 17 December 2020

Brownsword R (2019) Coding the transactions, decoding the legal debates. In: Lianos I, Hacker P, Eich S, Dimitropoulos G (eds) Regulating Blockchain: techno-social and legal challenges. OUP, Oxford

Buckley RP, Arner DW, Zetzsche DA, Weber RA (2020) The road to RegTech: the (astonishing) example of the European Union. J Bank Regul 21(1):26–36

Chalmers D, Davies G, Monti G (2010) European Union law. CUP, Cambridge

Chamon M (2016) EU agencies: legal and political limits to the transformation of the EU administration. Oxford University Press, Oxford

Chiti E (2015) In the aftermath of the crisis: the EU administrative system between impediments and momentum. http://cadmus.eui.eu/bitstream/handle/1814/35498/LAW_2015_13.pdf. Accessed 14 December 2020

Chiti E, Vesperini G (2018) The administrative architecture of financial integration. In: Merloni F, Pioggia A (eds) European democratic institutions and administrations: cohesion and innovation in times of economic crisis. Springer, Cham

Cobbe J (2019) Administrative law and the machines of government: judicial review of automated public sector decision making. Legal Stud 39(4):636–655

Colaert V (2016) Regulating PRIIPs: great ambitions, insurmountable challenges? J Financ Regul 2 (2):203–224

Colaert V (2018) RegTech as a response to regulatory expansion in the financial sector. Int J Financ Serv 3:56–77

De Filippi P, Wright A (2019) Blockchain and the law: the rule of code. Harvard University Press, Cambridge

Dias D, Straschen S (2017) Data Collection by Supervisors of Digital Financial Services. https://www.cgap.org/sites/default/files/publications/Working-Paper-Data-Collection-by-Supervisors-of-DFS-Dec-2017_1.pdf. Accessed 18 December 2020

European Commission (2014) Report from the Commission to the European Parliament and the Council on the Operation of the European Supervisory Authorities and the European System of Financial Supervision. https://ec.europa.eu/info/sites/info/files/140808-esfs-review_en.pdf. Accessed 17 September 2020

European Commission (2015) Action Plan on Building a Capital Markets Union. https://eur-lex.europa.eu/legal-content/EN/TXT/PDF/?uri=CELEX:52015DC0468&from=EN accessed 8 September 2020

European Commission (2017) Reinforcing Integrated Supervision to Strengthen Capital Markets Union and Financial Integration in a Changing Environment. http://ec.europa.eu/finance/docs/law/170920-communication-esas_en.pdf. Accessed 8 September 2020

European Commission (2018) FinTech Action Plan: For a More Competitive and Innovative European Financial Sector. https://eur-lex.europa.eu/resource.html?uri=cellar:6793c578-22e6-11e8-ac73-01aa75ed71a1.0001.02/DOC_1&format=PDF. Accessed 8 September 2020

European Commission (2019a) Fitness Check of EU Supervisory Reporting Requirements. https://ec.europa.eu/info/sites/info/files/business_economy_euro/banking_and_finance/documents/191107-fitness-check-supervisory-reporting-staff-working-paper_en.pdf. Accessed 8 September 2020

European Commission (2019b) Expert Group on Regulatory Obstacles to Financial Innovation (ROFIEG): 30 Recommendations on Regulation, Innovation and Finance - Final Report to the European Commission. https://ec.europa.eu/info/files/191113-report-expert-group-regulatory-obstacles-financial-innovation_en. Accessed 8 September 2020

European Commission (2020) Consultation on a new digital finance strategy for Europe/FinTech action plan. https://ec.europa.eu/info/sites/info/files/business_economy_euro/banking_and_finance/documents/2020-digitalfinance-strategy-consultation-document_en.pdf. Accessed 5 October 2021

European Court of Auditors (2018) EIOPA Made an Important Contribution to Supervision and Stability in the Insurance Sector, But Significant Challenges Remain. https://op.europa.eu/en/publication-detail/-/publication/09d83bb1-2e78-11e9-8d04-01aa75ed71a1. Accessed 8 September 2018

European Insurance and Occupational Pensions Authority (2020a) Supervisory Technology Strategy. https://www.eiopa.europa.eu/sites/default/files/publications/supervisory-technology-strategy-february-2020.pdf. Accessed 8 September 2020

European Insurance and Occupational Pensions Authority (2020b) Supervisory Convergence Plan for 2020. https://www.eiopa.europa.eu/sites/default/files/publications/supervisory-convergence-plan-for-2020.pdf. Accessed 8 September 2020

European Insurance and Occupational Pensions Authority (2020c) European Commission's Digital Finance Strategy Consultation - EIOPA's Draft Response. https://www.eiopa.europa.eu/sites/default/files/publications/submissions/eiopa-response to-digital-finance-strategy-consultation.pdf. Accessed 7 September 2020

European Securities and Markets Authority (2020) ESMA's Strategic Orientation 2020-2022. https://www.esma.europa.eu/sites/default/files/library/esma22-106-1942_strategic_orientation_2020-22.pdf. Accessed 8 September 2020

Financial Conduct Authority (2016) Data Reference Guides. https://www.fca.org.uk/firms/gabriel/data-reference-guides. Accessed 12 February 2020

Financial Conduct Authority (2017) Digital Regulatory Reporting Pilot Phase 1 Report. https://www.fca.org.uk/publication/discussion/digital-regulatory-reporting-pilot-phase-1-report.pdf. Accessed 12 February 2020

Fry H. 'Seven secrets of the online world (aka a beginner's guide to algorithms). https://www.bbc.co.uk/programmes/articles/4ssWY6xdQKx23n97sWNvbck/seven-secrets-of-the-online-world-aka-a-beginner-s-guide-to-algorithms. Accessed 12 February 2020

Georgosouli A (2016) Regulatory incentive realignment and the EU legal framework of bank resolution. Brooklyn J Corp Financ Commer Law 10:343–382

Gortsos C, Lagaria K (2020) The European supervisory authorities (ESAs) as 'Direct' supervisors in the EU financial system. Eur Bank Inst 57:14

Howell E (2017) The evolution of ESMA and direct supervision: are there implications for EU supervisory governance? Common Mark Law Rev 54(4):1027–1057

Husseini F (2018) Open Insurance Initiative: Whitepaper. https://openinsurance.io/?smd_process_download=1&download_id=394. Accessed 14 August 2020

Jarrahi MH (2019) In the age of the smart artificial intelligence: AI's dual capacities for automating and informating work. Bus Inform Rev 36(4):178–187

Joosen B, Lehmann M (2019) Proportionality in the single rule book. In: Chiti M, Santoro V (eds) The Palgrave handbook of European Banking Union Law. Springer, Berlin

Kamali W and Randall D (2017) Leveraging 'SupTech' for Financial Inclusion in Rwanda. https://blogs.worldbank.org/psd/leveraging-SupTech-financial-inclusion-rwanda. Accessed 18 December 2020

Lohr JD, Maxwell WJ, Watts P (2019) Legal practitioners' approach to regulating AI risks. In: Lodge M, Yeung K (eds) Algorithmic regulation. Oxford University Press, Oxford, pp 224–247

McGinn M (2003) Routledge philosophy guidebook to Wittgenstein and the philosophical investigations. Routledge, London

Micheler E, Whaley A (2020) Regulatory technology: replacing law with computer code. Eur Bus Organ Law Rev 21(2):349–377

Moloney N (2014) EU securities and financial markets regulation. OUP, Oxford

Moloney N (2016) Institutional governance and capital markets Union: incrementalism or a "Big Bang"? Eur Comp Financ Law Rev 13(2):376–423

Narayanan A, Bonneau J, Felten E, Miller A, Goldfeder S (2016) Bitcoin and cryptocurrency technologies: a comprehensive introduction. Princeton University Press, Princeton

National Bank of Rwanda (2017) Annual Report. https://www.bnr.rw/news-publications/publications/annual-reports/. Accessed 30 September 2020

Pasquale F (2019) A rule of persons, not machines: the limits of legal automation. Geo Wash Law Rev 87(1):1–55

Scantamburlo T, Charlesworth A, Christianini N (2019) Machine decisions and human consequences. In: Yeung K, Lodge M (eds) Algorithmic regulation. OUP, Oxford, pp 49–81

Schemmel J (2016) The ESA guidelines: soft law and subjectivity in the European financial market – capturing the administrative influence. Indian J Glob Leg Stud 23(2):455–504

Schoenmaker D (2011) The financial Trilemma. Econ Lett 111:57–59

Shiffrin SV (2010) Inducing moral deliberation: on the occasional virtues of fog. HLR 123: 1214, 1222, 1244

Simoncini M (2015) Legal boundaries of European supervisory authorities in the financial markets: tensions in the development of true regulatory agencies. Yearb Eur Law 34(1):319

Tridimas T (2012) Financial supervision and agency power: reflections on ESMA. In: Shuibhne NN, Gormley LW (eds) From single market to Economic Union: essays in memory of John A Usher. Oxford University Press, Oxford

Volz K, Yang E, Dudley R, Lynch E, Dropps M, Dorneich MC (2016) An evaluation of cognitive skill degradation in information automation. SAGE, Thousand Oaks

Xia F, Yang LT, Wang L, Vinel A (2012) Internet of things. Int J Commun Syst 25(9):1074–5351

Yeung K (2019) Regulation by blockchain: the emerging battle for supremacy between the code of law and the code as law. Modern Law Rev 82(2):207

Yeung K, Lodge M (2019) Algorithmic regulation. OUP, Oxford

Financial Reporting in Insurance and International Financial Reporting Standards

Katica Tomic

Abstract Financial reporting obligations for financial institutions, including insurance companies, have increased in recent years and insurers needs to stay up-to-date on the latest revisions of International Financial Reporting Standards and data reporting requirements and to comply with it. Many of these reporting obligations on listed and large non-listed insurers will benefit the insurance industry in the long term but it is challenging and costly task for insurance companies. The complexity of organizing high-quality data, transparent and structured reporting processes for different purposes (e.g., financial and regulatory reporting, CSR reporting, and many other types of reporting at local level) with internal and external stakeholders within a specified time frame, have become a strategic initiative, value-based investment, and opportunity for growth of insurance companies. To meet the various reporting requirements while overcoming reporting challenges, insurance companies need to ensure effective data governance and oversight in their reporting processes, which require considerable staff resources, and expertise in a wide variety of area, including appropriate IT architecture setup. In this chapter, we will analyze financial reporting obligations for insurance companies and evolution of the international accounting standards for the insurance industry. Moreover, we will discuss some practical issues facing insurers to comply with different regulatory, financial, and business reporting requirements to fulfill their reporting obligations.

1 Introduction

The global financial crisis of 2007–2008 and subsequent world recession affected large numbers of financial institutions by slowing down their business activities and decreasing their earnings. Although banks were at the center of the financial crisis, for many individual insurers, direct exposure of the crisis has revealed inefficient and ineffective business processes, which were misaligned with a company's activities

K. Tomic (✉)
Rechtsanwälte BVM, Vienna, Austria

P. Marano, K. Noussia (eds.), *The Governance of Insurance Undertakings*, AIDA Europe Research Series on Insurance Law and Regulation 6,
https://doi.org/10.1007/978-3-030-85817-9_11

and strategic direction (e.g., risk management, rationality in making financial decisions, investment, pricing, reserving or business grow) and inadequate minimum level of capital.[1]

The crisis in financial markets was also indicative of market and government failures, unsatisfactory supervisory practice of the financial sector as a whole at both national and international level. In addition, the crisis has exposed shortcomings in financial regulation that left considerable discretion to the Member States by the primary directives that governed the area.[2] The economic downturn revealed that the solvency regime for the insurance sector is not sufficiently risk sensitive, i.e., it does not contain an incentive to improve risk management and it is necessary to establish more effective financial reporting framework.

Numerous changes in the regulatory frameworks, policy measures, standards tools and practice have been brought forward for both the insurance and banking sectors to build a more resilient financial system.[3] For insurance sector, this includes Directive 2009/138/EC (Solvency II)[4] which is analogous to Basel II's capital adequacy requirements for banks, Insurance distribution Directive[5] and International Financial Reporting Standard (IFRS) 17 Insurance Contracts.

The global financial crisis helped with re-assessing the value of corporate reporting and modernizing and optimizing reporting processes. Corporate reporting has become very sophisticated in the last years and in most insurance undertakings is carried out in a very professional manner.[6]

Despite substantial evidence of capital-market benefits from corporate disclosures, the multiplicity of different reporting and disclosure requirements poses great functional and technical challenge for an insurance companies who needs to adapt their businesses to new regulations and to maintain ongoing compliance.[7] Most of the directives and regulations dealing with financial services are supplemented by various regulatory technical standards, implementing standards and guidance from

---

[1]Schich (2010a), p. 15.

[2]Craig (2015), pp. 243–267; Reifner et al. (2011), p. 9.

[3]Marano (2017), pp. 5–29.

[4]Directive 2009/138/EC of 25 November 2009 on the taking-up and pursuit of the business of Insurance and Reinsurance, Official Journal of the European Union, L 335/1.

[5]Directive (EU) 2016/97 of 20 January 2016 on insurance distribution, Official Journal of the European Union.

[6]Reporting to supervisory authorities help regulators in terms of monitoring the regulatory capital, safety, and soundness of the legal entity. Public disclosure by insurance companies: leads to more competition and offers a unique opportunity for self-assessment of the situation on the ground, including through data collection and analysis for legislative and policy review. Corporate reporting is very flexible to adapt to changing environment and new risks (e.g., technological, demographic, climate and political changes, cyber risks).

[7]For a selective literature review about reporting obligation and disclosure by insurance companies, see representative bibliography as follows: Bloomer (2005), pp. 101-107; Pucci (2012), pp. 115–138; De Mey (2009), pp. 228–241; Höring and Gründl (2011), pp. 380–413, Jovković (2018), pp. 110–126; Chiaramonte, et al. (2020), p. 5530.

EU and national regulators and insurance companies are expected to be compliant with all the applicable laws and regulations.

Producing and submitting structured financial and regulatory reports and other type of reports by collecting and combining data from multiple sources, for internal or external stakeholders, is a challenging and time-consuming task. For many financial institutions, including insurance companies, reporting obligations and disclosure is a mandatory obligation and exists only as a subsidiary function within different departments. Many insurance companies struggled how to organize skilled professional team responsible for regulatory compliance with a line of sight over reporting strategy, execution and an understanding of the full regulatory environment.

Additional problem represent how to deliver accurate and timely reports to regulators and the market and to ensure data security, data privacy, and data compliance. Some reporting requirements imposed by different supervisors are additionally costly, inconsistent, and duplicative, and the similar information needs to be delivered to different regulators in different ways and through different technology platforms.[8]

There are significant unrecognized costs associated with errors, duplication of data and inefficient or incorrectly reporting processes that accrues for a variety of reasons (for example, data compiled for a specific purpose was reused for another report, with different underlying requirements and constraints). Some information demands are often excessive or unnecessary (sometimes, data are collected and not used) which leads to inefficiency. There are many open questions about relevance of the information contained in different mandatory reports and usefulness of reporting information for users.[9]

This chapter aims to analyze the evolution of the international financial reporting standards and accounting requirements for insurance contracts. The development of an international standard for the accounting of insurance contracts, which reflects the complexity of the underlying insurance and reinsurance business, was a long and challenging process. Significant diversity in insurance contracts accounting practices has raised several issues regarding a successful implementation of new international standard for insurance contracts by insurers and its contribution to financial stability.

2 The Evolution of the International Financial Reporting Standards

The globalization of financial market and rapid growth of the trade in goods and services that goes beyond national borders, have triggered the need for a free movement of capital, goods, services and access to information included in the

[8] Nagari et al. (2017).

[9] Cascino et al. (2021).

financial statements of companies that operate in several countries.[10] However, there were legal and accounting standard difficulties to achieve corporate disclosure, due to interest group resistance and the variety in national laws of the Member States.[11]

Companies engaged in foreign trade (multinational, international, transnational and global companies) needed to comply with the different accounting frameworks and standards applicable in countries in which they operate. Information from financial statements of these companies created confusion and had limited value to users in other countries if they were not familiar with the accounting standards underlying these statements.

Many national interest groups in various countries realized that the growth in global trade is possible to achieve with international accounting harmonization system and uniform EU company law, which involves harmonization of company financial reporting.[12] A number of international organizations engaged in process of development of accounting standard such as: United Nations, the OECD, the European Economic Community (EEC), Accounting Standards Committee (independent professional accounting body—IASC)[13] and the International Federation of Accountants. The aim was to develop understandable and enforceable accounting standard, which will serve equity investors, lenders, creditors, and others in globalized capital markets.

However, the harmonization of financial statements by developing standards that could serve as a model on which national standard setters could base their own standards was a long-term process. The first steps towards harmonizing accounting standards were to align accounting standards in Europe.[14]

The harmonization of accounting standard started with the adoption of the Fourth Council Directive 78/660/EEC of 25 July 1978 on the annual accounts of certain types of companies and Seventh Council Directive 83/349/EEC of 13 June 1983.[15] Those two directives had a significant impact on company reporting in the Member States and they have remained largely unchanged until 2013.

The Fourth Council Directive's first draft was published in 1971, amended drafts were issued in 1974 and adopted in 1978.[16] Member States were supposed to implement the Fourth Council Directive 78/660/EEC until 1980 but they have failed

[10] Held et al. (2000), pp. 14–28.

[11] Nobes (1998), pp. 162–187; Buxbaum (1991), p. 407.

[12] There were groups who were mainly interested in regulations that imposes stricter reporting, auditing, and accounting requirements for international companies with the goal to exercise greater control over their business activities.

[13] The IASC was replaced by the International Accounting Standards Board in 2001.

[14] Van Hulle (2002), pp. 357–365.

[15] The Fourth Company Law Directive (78/660/EEC) establishes the content of financial information that should be made available to the public by limited liability companies and the content of annual accounts (balance sheet, profit and loss account and the notes to the accounts), the publication and auditing requirements of the annual accounts depending on the size of the company; Diggle and Nobes (1994), pp. 319–333.

[16] Botez and Pravat (2009), pp. 791–795.

to do so. The Directive was transposed with considerable delay in some countries. For example, the Fourth Council Directive was transposed into German law in 1985,[17] Spain and Portugal in 1989, Austria in 1990,[18] Italy in 1991 and Sweden in 1995, etc.

To ensure agreement between Member States on a numerous issue, existing due to the different legal accounting rules and policy approaches, the Directive allowed Members States with a lot of flexibility on how to individually implement it. Moreover, certain flexibility were left to companies to prepare their financial statements to meet the needs of users. Thus, the Fourth Council Directive 78/660/EEC served more as recommendation, which provides guidance on how the provisions of the Directive should be used than an agreed standard.

Despite the fact that Fourth Council Directive 78/660/EEC was first stage of the harmonization process of accounting standards and it improved the comparability of annual financial statements of companies throughout Europe, there were some practical problems of its implementation.[19]

There are a number of very significant accounting issues on which the Fourth Council Directive 78/660/EEC is silent. For example, the Fourth Council Directive 78/660/EEC does not include provisions about translation of foreign currency transactions, accounting for the effects of changing prices on financial statements or problem of deferred-tax accounting.[20]

A few years later, The Council took additional steps towards a harmonized European accounting system with the adoption of two Directives dealing specifically with annual accounts and consolidated accounts specific to banks[21] and insurance undertakings.[22]

The International Accounting Standards Committee (IASC) has undertaken even bigger task to produce accounting standards that would be implemented worldwide.[23] During the period between 1973–1987, the IASC generated most of the International Accounting Standards (IAS).[24]

---

[17] German legislature transposed The Fourth Directive by the Accounting Directives Law (Bilanzrichtliniengesetz, BGBl (1985 I), p. 2355) and applied its rules to the capital companies and all traders, including subsidiaries of companies registered in other Member States.

[18] Alexander and Eberhartinger (2009), pp. 571–594.

[19] Walton (2015), pp. 135–151.

[20] The IASC was formed in 1973 through an agreement made by the leading accounting bodies of ten countries: Australia, Canada, France, Germany, Japan, Mexico, The Netherlands, the U.K., Ireland, and the U.S. The IASC decided to restructure in April 2001 and became the International Accounting Standards Board ((IASB) and International Financial Reporting Standards (IFRS) replaced the IAS; Camfferman and Zeff (2007), p. 21; Zeff (2011), pp. 807–837.

[21] Council Directive 86/635 of 8 December 1986 Annual Accounts and Consolidated Accounts of Banks and Other Financial Institutions, 1986 O.J. (L 372) 1, 1.

[22] Council Directive 91/674 of 19 December 1991 Annual Accounts and Consolidated Accounts of Insurance Undertakings, 1991 O.J. (L 374) 7, 7.

[23] Samuels and Piper (1985), p. 7; Camfferman and Zeff (2007), p. 93.

[24] Knežević et al. (2013), p. 64.

The IAS (which were all prefixed with "IAS"—e.g., IAS 10 Events After the Reporting Period, IAS 14 Segment Reporting, IAS 21The Effects of Changes in Foreign Exchange Rates, IAS 34 Interim Financial Reporting) represent an attempt to find "middle ground" between national accounting regulations, where the financial reporting standards are already highly developed, as opposed to an effort on international standardization in financial reporting. The level of harmony of financial reporting within and between countries depends on the degree of compliance with the IAS. IAS standards were increasingly used as a model by national accounting standards setters but they were not implemented by a significant number of large companies.[25]

Some commentators questioned the scope and authority of IAS Standards.[26] IASC was established in 1973 as a part-time, voluntary organization, run by the professional accounting bodies from nine countries. The IASC was not a government body and the IAS Standards could not be imposed as a set of accounting rules that could be part of a standard international listing agreement and applied by all national regulators.[27]

The Restructuring structure of the IASC started in 2001. IASC handed over its functions to the International Accounting Standards Board (IASB). The newly formed IASB took over the standards of the IASC and decided to name new accounting standards issued by the IASB as International Financial Reporting Standards (IFRS).

In June 2002, the European Union has endorsed the International Accounting Standards (IAS/IFRS) for all EU companies (including many of the largest insurance companies in Europe) that are listed on European exchanges through the adoption of the Regulation (EC) No 1606/2002.[28] From 2005 all companies were required to prepare and publish their consolidated financial statements in accordance with IFRS.[29] The Regulation (EC) No 1606/2002 authorizes EU Member States to extend the IFRS requirement to the consolidated financial statements of non-listed companies.[30]

[25] Walton (2003), pp. 59–65.

[26] Danjou and Walton (2012), pp. 1–15; Pelger and Spieß (2017), pp. 64–90; Richardson and Eberlein (2011), pp. 217–245.

[27] Flower and Ebbers (2002), p. 239.

[28] Regulation (EC) No 1606/2002 of the European Parliament and of the Council of 19 July 2002 on the application of international accounting standards, Official Journal L 243, 11/09/2002 p. 0001-0004.

[29] Some types of listed company did not need to comply with IFRS until 01.01. 2007. Individual Member States had option to decide about this delayed implementation. Temporary exceptions are made for companies with a listing outside the EU who were using internationally accepted standards.

[30] Article 5 of the Regulation (EC) No 1606/2002.

Since 2011, the European Commission has taken steps with the goal of imposing obligations on listed and large non-listed entities to disclose certain non-financial information about sustainable development and environmental policy in the annual reports.[31]

The result was a new law on accounting, the Directive 2013/34/EU of 26 June 2013[32] on the annual financial statements, consolidated financial statements and related reports of certain types of undertakings, which also applies on credit institutions and insurance companies.[33] Directive 2013/34/EU combines and updates the requirements of the 4th and 7th Council Directives and refers both to the individual financial statements and consolidated financial statements.[34]

The main focus of Directive 2013/34/EU is to harmonize accounting and simplify reporting and disclosure requirements which will lead to reducing administrative burdens and the lower costs of financial reporting for small- and medium-sized enterprises ((SMEs) and micro-enterprises. However, the reduction of the administrative burden for SMEs has not been fully achieved due to the different transposition of the Directive 2013/34/EU in some Member States, and the fact that there are no middle-sized entity categories in some countries.[35]

Directive 2014/95/EU amended Directive 2013/34/EU and represents first step in the field of mandatory sustainability reporting. This directive requires large companies (exceeding 500 employees) to include annual non-financial statements on sustainability and diversity, either as a part of their management report or as a separate document from 2017 onwards.[36]

[31] European Commission, Communication from the Commission to the European Parliament, the Council, the Economic and Social Committee and the Committee of the Regions, Single Market Act—Twelve levers to boost growth and strengthen confidence—"Working together to create new growth", Brussels, 13 April 2011, COM(2011) 206 final; European Commission, Communication from the Commission to the European Parliament, the council, the European economic and social committee and the committee of the regions. A renewed EU strategy 2011-14 for Corporate Social Responsibility, adopted on 25 October 2011.

[32] Directive 2013/34/EU of 26 June 2013 on the annual financial statements, consolidated financial statements and related reports of certain types of undertakings, amending Directive 2006/43/EC of the European Parliament and of the Council and repealing Council Directives 78/660/EEC and 83/349/EEC, Official Journal of the European Union, L 182/19.

[33] Pakšiová (2018), pp. 736–745; Marius (2014), pp. 197–205.

[34] Directive 2013/34/EU contains definition of Public Interest Entities (PIEs) and includes all insurance undertakings in the EU, regardless of whether they are listed or not and regardless of whether they are life, non-life, insurance or reinsurance undertakings; Hýblová and Kolčavová (2017), pp. 1349–1357; Strampelli (2018), pp. 541–579.

[35] Hýblová (2019), pp. 604–621.

[36] Directive 2014/95/EU of 22 October 2014 amending Directive 2013/34/EU as regards disclosure of non-financial and diversity information by certain large undertakings and groups, Official Journal of the European Union L 330/1.

3 Evolution of Accounting Rules and Financial Statements for Insurance Companies

The lack of quality and consistency in insurance reporting and accounting practices has resulted in weak usefulness of financial statement information for investors, creditors and analysts to evaluate a company's financial position and performance. Compared with the banking sector, the insurance sector in the EU was not known for its transparency in financial reporting that reflects economic reality towards supervisory authorities and stakeholders. Moreover, insurance sector has not followed financial reforms that was developed by the Basel Committee on Banking Supervision (BCBS) in banking (Basel reforms).[37]

An internationally accepted accounting standard for the measurement of insurance contracts did not exist until 2004.[38] The absence of international standards for insurance industry, both in accounting and in solvency, has resulted to the fragmentation of the existing insurance accounting practices, which are often inconsistent with accounting practices of other industries. Significant diversity in insurance contracts accounting practices was also the result of different accounting standards and different types of insurance products in each jurisdiction.[39]

The IASB (formerly IASC) has been working on a new international standard for insurance contracts based on fair value for many years to reduce the differences among the accounting principles used in insurance industry and improve comparability and understanding of the income statement of companies issuing insurance contract across entities, jurisdictions, and capital markets.[40]

The development of an international standard for the accounting of insurance contracts has raised several conceptual and practical issues regarding its application. Some issues are general and affect all financial institutions and some specific to the insurance sector.

Insurance is a unique financial service and preparation of financial statements of insurance business requires the application of actuarial science to determine results, and then to integrate those results with accounting rules.[41] The preparation and production of high quality financial statements of insurance business can be very complicated; whether the insurance business is long-term such as life insurance or

---

[37] O'Shea (2013), p. 2; Kozarevic et al. (2018), pp. 225–246; Gatzert and Wesker (2012), pp. 539-570; Chiaramonte (2018), pp. 167–188.

[38] Insurance contracts have been excluded from the scope of the accounting standard for financial instruments in the United States, FAS 133, as it was a common opinion that financial market is not ready to determine fair values for insurance contracts; Dickinson (2003a), p. 151; Nguyen and Molinari (2013), p. 384.

[39] Foroughi et al. (2012), p. 570.

[40] Dickinson (2003a), pp. 151–175.

[41] Insurance Europe (2019), p. 3.

health and long-term care insurance; or short insurance business duration with a long term such as workers' compensation insurance.[42]

Insurance is interdisciplinary topic and interacts with various fields of law, accounting, marketing, economics and finance.[43] It can be defined from legal aspect (contract of law,) risk management and risk transfer tool, social or commercial device providing financial compensation and for accounting , insurance is an intangible product of insurance business.[44] Definition of insurance contracts are relevant regarding insurance accounting standards for insurance contracts and determines whether a contract is within the scope of IFRS or another standard.

Another debate concerns the question of fair value accounting for insurance contracts in financial reporting. Insurance contracts are not tradable financial instruments (unless considering their tradeable stock or debt in the secondary market) and market values cannot be objectively presumed. Insurance accounting measurement models involves using judgment, estimation and clear and precise rules for fair value for insurance.[45]

The IASC/IASB and Financial Accounting Standards Board (FASB) have been dealing with the challenges in auditing fair value measurements on assets and liabilities arising from insurance contracts for a number of years.[46] IASC/IASB and FASB have promulgated a number of conceptual frameworks for Financial Reporting and fair value measurement Standards requiring fair value accounting for selected (largely financial) assets and liabilities.[47] There is still ongoing discussions among professionals with respect to the application of fair value accounting of Insurance Contracts but it is difficult to reach complete consensus about this topic.

There are many other challenges involved in adopting and implementing international standards for insurance contracts which involves, how to ensure effective accounting rules, how to increase reporting transparency and give users a better understanding of the sources and trends of earnings or excessive implementation costs. Another important challenge is how to ensure that the long-term nature of insurers' business is captured in annual reporting.

The development of the new international accounting standards for insurance contracts is part to a European Union's initiative to converge their financial reporting

[42] Albrecher et al. (2018), pp. 9-25; LaDou (2011), p. 103.

[43] Hollman et al. (1991), p. 714; Rohrbach (2018), p. 7.

[44] Stanić and Glavaš (2013), p. 654.

[45] Center for Excellence in Accounting & Security Analysis (2008), p. 44; Araceli (2019), pp. 1–19. Walton (2013), p. 423.

[46] Alexander et al. (2012), p. 84.

[47] The Financial Instruments Joint Working Group of standard setters (JWG) proposed in its "Draft Standard and Basis for Conclusions Financial Instruments and Similar Items" a hierarchy of methods for determining fair value of financial instruments. Since many insurance contracts are included within its definition of financial instruments, this hierarchy presumably would apply to insurance liabilities.

standard to International Financial Reporting Standards.[48] There was no accounting standard for insurance contracts before the establishment of the European Union (EU) in 1992, and IFRS for insurance contracts relied on local GAAP.[49]

In 1997, the IASB initiated a two-phase project called "Insurance Contracts" and set up a steering committee to carry out the initial work on new accounting requirements for insurance contracts.[50] This project was split in two-phase, mainly because of complexity to develop a full standard by the time of EU's 2005 year-end deadline for the mandatory adoption of IFRS. About the same time, the EU started work on Solvency II, a framework directive aimed at enhancing policyholder protection; improve (international) competitiveness of EU insurers and streamlining and strengthening solvency requirements across the EU in an effort to create a single market for insurance.[51]

In December 1999, the IASC Steering committee published an Issues Paper on Insurance and in June 2001 developed first Draft Statement of Principles—Insurance contract (DSOP) which was based on its work and the 138 comment letters to the issue paper.[52] The DSOP was never approved because of many issues raised by actuaries, insurance companies but it created a foundation for further work. In October 2001, the IASC Steering committee published last DSOP and in July 2003, the IASB Published Exposure Draft ED 5—Insurance Contracts.[53]

The IASB's insurance accounting project, phase 1, was completed in March 2004 when IFRS 4 was released an interim standard. IFRS 4 provides only limited improvements to accounting practices for insurance contracts until comprehensive accounting standard (IFRS 17) could be finalized. IFRS 4 permits an entity to continue of existing accounting practices (paragraph 25) and requires to disclose information that identifies and explains the amount, timing and cash flow assumptions from insurance contract (paragraph 15). Thus, many IFRS jurisdictions where IFRS is used for general purpose financial reporting do not also use IFRS 4 for regulatory purposes because of the absence of a consistent accounting framework for all insurance contracts in IFRS 4. They instead specify supervisory methods for the determination of insurance contract liabilities. For example, in the European context, solvency assessment is not based on IFRS but on balance sheets using the Solvency II framework.[54]

[48]The notion of harmonization was replaced by the concept convergence by the 1990s. The definition of convergence refers to the development of a unified set of high-quality, international accounting standards that would be used in capital markets; Pacter (2005), p. 2; Mohd et al. (2019), p. 506.

[49]Ortiz (2005), pp. 36–51; PWC (2017).

[50]Dickinson (2003b), pp. 151–176.

[51]Directive 2009/138/EC of 25 November 2009 on the taking-up and pursuit of the business of Insurance and Reinsurance (Solvency II), Official Journal of the European Union L 335/1; Marano (2017), pp. 5–29.

[52]Altenburger (2006), p. 323.

[53]Dickinson (2003a), pp. 151–175.

[54]Engeländer and Kölschbach (2006), p. 512.

On 18 May 2017, IASB published IFRS 17 "Insurance Contracts" which replaces interim standard, IFRS 4 Insurance Contracts. The IFRS 17 Standard will be effective for annual reporting periods beginning on or after 1 January 2023. Subsequently, after a period of consultation, the IASB issued amendments to IFRS 4[55] which allows an insurance entity to use the overlay approach[56] and temporary exemption from applying IFRS 9 Financial Instruments to annual reporting periods beginning on or after 1 January 2023. This means that insurers will still be able to apply IFRS 17 and IFRS 9 at the same time, thus reducing implementation costs and possibly accounting mismatches.

4 Financial Stability and the Insurance Sector

Financial reporting transformation and development of an international standard for the accounting of insurance contracts started much later than in banking sector.[57] There were several reasons for a late start: global insurance market is characterized by differences between developed and developing countries; thus, insurance business model is less globalized than other areas in finance (e.g., capital markets or investments).[58] There were also limited research of the insurer's business model and its interactions with financial and other financial intermediaries.[59]

As mentioned, the financial crisis of 2008 and the subsequent recession had negative effects on economy, including decreased of business activities of global and regional financial and insurance companies. Some insurers experienced substantial capital deterioration, some of them required government support (e.g., the

[55]The amendments in Applying IFRS 9 "Financial Instruments" with IFRS 4 "Insurance Contracts" on 12 September 2016 and Extension of the Temporary Exemption from Applying IFRS 9 on 25 June 2020.

[56]The overlay approach mitigates some of the effects from the volatility caused by misalignment of the implementation of IFRS 9 and IFRS 4. It allows an insurance entity to exclude from profit or loss certain effects of IFRS 9 and regrouped these amounts to other comprehensive income (OCI) for certain financial assets.

[57]The case is the same with the Basel Committee on Banking Regulations and Supervisory Practices (BCBS) which was founded in 1974. The first set of principles for sharing supervisory responsibility for banks' foreign branches, subsidiaries, and joint ventures between host and parent (or home) supervisory authorities ("Concordat") was issued in 1975. The BCBS developed over several years. The Basel Accords (Basel I in 1988, Basel II in 2004, Basel III in 2010) and BCBS report on Basel III implementation in October 2012. Similarly, insurance regulators developed the First Council Directive 79/267/EEC of 5 March 1979, Directive 2002/83/EC (Solvency I) was adopted in 2002 and Solvency II in 2009; Basel Committee on Banking Supervision 2012; Loguinova (2019), p. 19; Zweifel (2014), pp. 135–157.

[58]Olasehinde-Williams and Balcilar (2020).

[59]Trichet (2005), pp. 65–71.

case of American International Group—AIG) or some insurers needed to seek changes to accounting rules to provide capital relief.[60]

For insurers, financial crisis and economic recession simultaneously influenced the decrease in the value of assets and an increase in the value of liabilities because it had strong negative impact on all insurers' business activities (underwriting, investments and risk transfer).[61] The financial crisis has exposed multiple failures in the financial system and their implications for financial system stability. A number of tighter regulations of the financial sector have been issued to prevent future financial crise, including set of changes to accounting practice (US GAAP and IFRS).[62]

One of the key issues in the post-crisis environment was a restoring public confidence through the structural changes in the insurance industry. Some of legislator's objective were: to strengthen the oversight of insurance companies that are considered important for systemic financial stability in the global financial system; and to develop a credible and coherent accounting standards and prudential capital standard for internationally active insurance groups (IAIGs).

Traditionally, banks have been connected with concept financial stability (i.e., the absence of systemic risk) because of their maturity transformation and their leading role in the transmission of monetary policy, the payment system and the reallocation of savings to investments.[63] The contribution to systemic risk by insurers has been regarded less significant than in banks.

Insurance industry is going through a period of transformation driven by a number of factors, such as changes in the insurance sector environment, new disruptive technologies, regulatory activities. Insurers are expanding their activities beyond their core business which leads to a closer integration between insurance and banking undertakings.[64] This is especially the case in the OTC derivatives markets, bancassurance or unit-linked or index-linked products.[65] For this reason, the role of

[60] In the aftermath of financial crisis, American Insurance Group (AIG) faced liquidity problems. AIG achieved positive financial results in the underwriting business. Due to AIG excessive exposures to subprime mortgages that resulted from credit default swaps business of its financial products division and its negative investment results, the company declared a loss of $13 billion in August 2008. The government had to bail out the AIG by providing credit line of $85 billion in return for 79.9% share in AIG, factually nationalizing the company, and later by providing additional $37.8 billion. The other example is the case of Swiss Re. Swiss Re reinsurer losses came from a unit that was involved in writing credit default swaps, providing credit protection and capital market trading outweighed the profits from (well performing) core business to be had at the consolidated level of the group; Baluch et al. (2011), pp. 126–163; Hunt (2011), p. 1667; Schich (2010b), p. 45.

[61] Society of Actuaries (2017), p. 5.

[62] Bender (2005), p. 13.

[63] Rambure and Nacamuli (2008), p. 69; Pascal (2020), p. 2.

[64] Pavić Kramarić et al. (2019), pp. 163–178.

[65] Rockas and Siafarika (2019), p. 2; Tomic (2017), p. 199.

insurance companies in financial market and relevance of the insurance sector for the overall stability of the financial sector has gained importance over the years.[66]

Discussions about remedial measures to address financial stability risks and vulnerabilities in the insurance sector started after the financial crisis and failure of AIG's CDS (credit default swaps) business in 2008, decline in equity markets that began in 2000 and subsequent low interest rate environment.[67] Moreover, strong interconnections between the insurance industry and the rest of the financial system, non-traditional or non-insurance activities of insurance companies (including their activities in credit risk transfers) has become increasingly relevant for maintaining a stable financial system. It is necessery to understand interaction between insurance companies with financial markets, banks and other financial intermediaries and the fluctuations in the business cycle to determine potential risk transfer from one sector to another.

Banks and insurance companies are both financial institutions but very different in terms of business models, funding structure, financial products, different nature of underlying risks which is the result of many factors such as demographics, the structure of liabilities, the scale of operations, regulation, accounting practices and distribution channels.[68] There have been attemps to push towards convergence between banking and insurance setor, including integration insurance regulation with the regulation of banking and investment business at EU level.[69] However, this regulatory approach is not sufficiently taking account dfferences between banks and insurers.

Bearing in mind contrasting business models and balance sheet structures of banks and insurers, different roles of capital, leverage, and risk absorption, it is clear that the banking model of capital cannot be applied to insurance. The case is the same with the accounting regime.

The primary goal of IFRS 17 insurance contract is transparency, accountability and efficiency to financial markets which at same time promotes the long-term financial stability of the global economy. Insurers can be consider systematicly important because of the economic role of the insurance sector.[70]

It is hard to assess the extent to which insurers can be originators or transmitters of systemic risk in the financial system.[71] However, IFRS 17 will contribute to financial stability by providing more granular contractual data about insurers's current and future profitability.

[66]Central bank of the Republic of Austria defines financial stability as a financial system being "capable of ensuring the efficient allocation of financial resources and fulfilling its key macroeconomic functions even if financial imbalances and shocks occur." https://www.oenb.at/en/financial-market/financial-stability.html.

[67]McDonald and Paulson (2015), pp. 81–106.

[68]Beltratti and Corvino (2008), pp. 363-388.

[69]Noussia and Siri (2019), p. 28.

[70]Dickinson (1998), p. 519.

[71]Baranoff (2011), p. 21.

5 Conclusion

Financial institutions and insurance companies are facing with a regulatory environment that changes rapidly, complex and expensive reporting requirements and numerous regulatory disclosures obligations. Many of these reporting requirements are not only limited to the financial performance of a company, but also include a relevant non-financial information statement on company's impact on social and environmental matters. International Financial Reporting Standards and high quality of financial statement information have two main objectives. First, to bring high transparency, accountability and efficiency to financial markets through the international standards and second, transparency in financial reporting and accountability derived from accounting standard represent a significant factor for achieving financial stability and underpin the trust that investors creditors and other interest groups place. IFRS 17 insurance contract represents first harmonized accounting model for insurance contracts. This new accounting requirements for insurance contracts was created to provide more transparent information about the effect and revenue of insurance contracts on financial statements for stakeholders, investors, analysts, and consumers. IFRS 17 insurance contract is complex regulation, which will require insurers to take a different approach to measuring and reporting insurance and reinsurance assets and liabilities for insurance contracts. Complying with this regulation will raise many practical implementation issues, including significant operational costs for most companies. Another challenging task will be the organization of IFRS 17 compliance reporting structures, assigning roles and reporting responsibilities between different departments in a company. Smaller insurers, whose resources are limited, will need to consider outsourcing compliance processes to fulfill their reporting obligations.

References

Albrecher H, Bauer D, Embrechts P, Filipović D, Koch-Medina P, Korn R, Loisel S, Pelsser A, Schiller F, Schmeiser H, Wagner J (2018) Asset-liability management for long-term insurance business. Eur Actuarial J 8:9–25. https://doi.org/10.1007/s13385-018-0167-5

Alexander D, Eberhartinger E (2009) The true and fair view in the European Union. Eur Account Rev 18(3):571–594 Available at SSRN: https://ssrn.com/abstract=1331387

Alexander D, Bonaci C, Mustata R (2012) Fair value measurement in financial reporting. Proc Econ Financ 3:84–90. https://doi.org/10.1016/S2212-5671(12)00124-4

Altenburger OA (2006) IFRS 4 insurance contracts — verbesserte Versicherungsrechnungslegung?. ZVersWiss 95:323–332. https://doi.org/10.1007/BF03353452

Araceli M, McGeachin A, Barth M, Barker R, Wagenhoffer A, Joos P (2019) Fair value accounting: the eternal debate – AinE EAA Symposium, May 2018. Account Eur 16(3):1–19. https://doi.org/10.1080/17449480.2019.1664754

Baluch F, Mutenga S, Parsons C. (2011) Insurance, systemic risk and the financial crisis. Geneva Pap Risk Insur Iss Pract 36(1):126–163. https://doi.org/10.1057/gpp.2010.40

Baranoff EG, Haefeli D, Liedtke PM (2011) Insurers as systemically important financial institutions (SIFIs)? Activities-based methodology, systemic risk, Basel III, Financial Stability and Regulation 2011, Available at SSRN: https://ssrn.com/abstract=1772089 or https://doi.org/10.2139/ssrn.1772089

Basel Committee on Banking Supervision (2012) Progress report on Basel III implementation. http://www.g20ys.org/upload/auto/829497400add53d124cefbe8b3f3820290340e02.pdf

Beltratti A, Corvino G (2008) Why are insurance companies different? The limits of convergence among financial institutions. Geneva Pap Risk Insur Iss Pract 33(3):363–388. https://doi.org/10.1057/gpp.2008.13

Bender C (2005) Umsatzerfassung nach US-GAAP und IFRS Konzeption, Problembereiche, Lösungsansätze Gabler Edition Wissenschaft

Bloomer J (2005) Developments in international financial reporting standards and other financial reporting issues. Geneva Pap Risk Insur Iss Pract 30(1):101–107. https://doi.org/10.1057/palgrave.gpp.2510002

Botez D, Pravat I (2009) Study concerning the differences between the Fourth directive and accounting standards from Romania. Ann Faculty Econ 3(1):791–795

Buxbaum RM, Hirsch A, Klaus J, Hopt KJ, Hertig G (1991) European business law: legal and economic analyses on integration and harmonization. De Gruyter

Camfferman K, Zeff AS (2007) Financial Reporting and global capital markets: a history of the international accounting standards committee. Oxford University Press, pp 1973–2000

Cascino S, Clatworthy M, Osma GB, Gassen J, Shahed I (2021) The usefulness of financial accounting information: evidence from the field. Account Rev 96(1):117–146. https://doi.org/10.2308/TAR-2019-1030

Center for Excellence in Accounting & Security Analysis (2008) Principles for the application of fair value accounting. https://www0.gsb.columbia.edu/mygsb/faculty/research/pubfiles/3029/FairValue.pdf

Chiaramonte L (2018) The implications of Basel III liquidity regulatory reform. In: Bank liquidity and the global financial crisis. Palgrave Macmillan Studies in Banking and Financial Institutions. Palgrave Macmillan, Cham. https://doi.org/10.1007/978-3-319-94400-5_7

Chiaramonte L, Dreassi A, Paltrinieri A, Pisera S (2020) Sustainability practices and stability in the insurance industry. Sustainability 12(14):5530. https://doi.org/10.3390/su12145530

Craig P (2015) The financial crisis, the European Union institutional order, and constitutional responsibility, maastricht treaty, democracy deficit, lisbon treaty. Indiana J Glob Legal Stud 22 (2):243–267. Available at: https://www.repository.law.indiana.edu/ijgls/vol22/iss2/2

Danjou P, Walton P (2012) The legitimacy of the IASB. Account Eur 9(1):1–15. https://doi.org/10.1080/17449480.2012.664396

De Mey J (2009) Reporting on the financial performance of life insurers. Geneva Pap Risk Insur Iss Pract 34(2):228–241. https://doi.org/10.1057/gpp.2009.6

Dickinson G (1998) The economic role of the insurance sector in the risk transfer - capital market nexus. Geneva Pap Risk Insur Iss Pract 23(89):519–529. https://doi.org/10.1057/gpp.1998.45

Dickinson G (2003a) The search for an international accounting standard for insurance: report to the accountancy task force of the Geneva Association. Geneva Pap Risk Insur Iss Pract 28 (2):151–176. www.jstor.org/stable/41952682. Accessed 27 Apr 2021

Dickinson G (2003b) The search for an international accounting standard for insurance: report to the accountancy task force of the Geneva association. Geneva Pap Risk Insur Iss Pract 28 (2):151–175. https://doi.org/10.1111/1468-0440.00215

Diggle G, Nobes C (1994) European rule-making in accounting: the seventh directive as a case study. Account Bus Res 24(96):319–333. https://doi.org/10.1080/00014788.1994.9729490

Engeländer S, Kölschbach JA (2006) Reliable fair value for insurance contracts. Geneva Pap Risk Insur Issues and Practice 31(3):512–527. https://doi.org/10.1057/palgrave.gpp.2510093

Flower J, Ebbers G (2002) The IASB: its origins and structure. In: Global financial reporting. Palgrave, London. https://doi.org/10.1007/978-1-137-10538-7_11

Foroughi K, Barnard RC, Bennett RW, Clay DK, Conway EL, Corfield SR, Coughlan AJ, Harrison JS, Hibbett GJ, Kendix IV, Lanari-Boisclair MC, Brien DO, Straker JSK (2012) Insurance accounting: a new era? Br Actuarial J 17(3):562–649. Accessed 27 April 2021. http://www.jstor.org/stable/23356789

Gatzert N, Wesker HA (2012) Comparative assessment of Basel II/III and Solvency II. Geneva Pap Risk Insur Iss Pract 37(3):539–570. https://doi.org/10.1057/gpp.2012.3

Held D., McGrew A., Goldblatt D., Perraton J (2000) Global transformations: politics, economics and culture. In: Pierson C, Tormey S (eds) Politics at the edge. Political Studies Association Yearbook Series. Palgrave Macmillan, London. pp 14–28. https://doi.org/10.1057/9780333981689_2

Hollman KW et al (1991) The structure and disciplinary boundaries of insurance: a citational analysis of JRI Articles. J Risk Insur 58(4): 714–721. JSTOR, www.jstor.org/stable/253082. Accessed 24 Apr 2021

Höring D, Gründl H (2011) Investigating risk disclosure practices in the European insurance industry. Geneva Pap Risk Insur Issues Pract 36(3):380–413. https://doi.org/10.1057/gpp.2011.13

Hunt JP (2011) Credit ratings in insurance regulation: the missing piece of financial reform. Washington Lee Law Rev 68(4):1667–1697. https://scholarlycommons.law.wlu.edu/wlulr/vol68/iss4/3

Hýblová E (2019) The current problems of harmonization of accounting for small and medium-sized enterprises. Econ Res-Ekonomska Istraživanja 32(1):604–621. https://doi.org/10.1080/1331677X.2018.1561317

Hýblová E, Kolčavová A (2017) The consequences of "Options" in the Directive 2013/34/EU of the European Parliament and of the Council on the Financial Statements. Acta Universitatis Agriculturae et Silviculturae Mendelianae Brunensis. 65(4):1349–1357. https://doi.org/10.11118/actaun201765041349

Insurance Europe (2019) Why insurance is unique And offers unique benefits for consumers. https://insuranceeurope.eu/sites/default/files/attachments/Why%20insurance%20is%20unique_0.pdf

Jovković BČ (2018) Karakteristike finansijskih izveštaja osiguravajućih kompanija i njihova revizija. Bus Econ 12(1):110–126. https://doi.org/10.5937/poseko13-16143

Knežević G, Stanišić N, Mizdraković V (2013) Analiza finansijskih izvještaja. Univerzitet, Singidunum

Kozarevic S, Kozarevic E, Porretta P, Santoboni F (2018) Implementation of Basel and solvency risk assessment standards in banks and insurance companies of South-Eastern Europe Countries. Risk Assessment:225–246. https://doi.org/10.5772/intechopen.70605

LaDou J (2011) The European influence on workers' compensation reform in the United States. Environ Health 10:103. https://doi.org/10.1186/1476-069X-10-103

Loguinova K (2019) A critical legal study of the ideology behind Solvency II, Economic and financial law & policy – shifting insights & values. Springer. https://doi.org/10.1007/978-3-030-26357-7

Marano P (2017) Sources and tools of the insurance regulation in the European Union. In: Marano P, Siri M (eds) Insurance regulation in the European Union. Palgrave Macmillan, Cham, pp 5–29. https://doi.org/10.1007/978-3-319-61216-4_2

Marius D (2014) The New EU Accounting Directive – A Comparison of Reporting Requirements (1 May 2014). Annals of "Constantin Brâncuşi" University of Târgu-Jiu, 2014, Available at SSRN: https://ssrn.com/abstract=2775921

McDonald R, Paulson A (2015) AIG in Hindsight. J Econ Persp 29(2):81–106. https://doi.org/10.1257/jep.29.2.81

Mohd A, Mohd A, Mohd A (2019) Barriers in adoption of IFRS in developed and developing economies: TIFS framework. Int J Recent Technol Eng 8(4):506–512. https://doi.org/10.35940/ijrte.D7105.118419

Nagari F, Muriithi A, Marshall R (2017) Data management in the new world of insurance fiancial and actuarial, Deloitte. https://www2.deloitte.com/content/dam/Deloitte/cn/Documents/financial-services/deloitte-cn-fs-data-management-in-new-world-of-insurance-finance-and-actuarial-en-171207.pdf

Nguyen T, Molinari P (2013) Accounting for "insurance contracts" according to IASB exposure draft—is the information useful? Geneva Pap Risk Insur 28(2):376–398. https://doi.org/10.1057/gpp.2012.11

Nobes C (1998) Towards a general model of the reasons for international differences in financial reporting, Abacus 34(2):162–187. https://doi.org/10.1111/1467-6281.00028

Noussia K, Siri M (2019) The legal regime and the relevant standard, distribution of insurance-based investment products the EU regulation and the liabilities: the EU regulation and the liabilities. Springer, pp 27–58. https://doi.org/10.1007/978-3-030-11668-2

O'Shea M (2013) Comparison of the Regulatory Approach in Insurance and Banking in the Context of Solvency II, European actuarial consultative group. https://actuary.eu/documents/SII%20vs%20Basel%20II_Dec_12_final.pdf

Olasehinde-Williams G, Balcilar M (2020) Examining the effect of globalization on insurance activities in large emerging market economies. Res Int Bus Financ 53(C):101228. https://doi.org/10.1016/j.ribaf.2020.101228

Ortiz E (2005) GAAP choice by European companies. Eur Bus Rev 17(1):36–51. https://doi.org/10.1108/09555340510576258

Pacter P (2005) What exactly is convergence? Int J Account Audit Perform Eval 2(1–2):67–83. https://doi.org/10.1504/IJAAPE.2005.006893

Pakšiová R (2018) The comparison of requirements for a disclosure of non-financial information according to legal regulations in Slovakia and EU directives, Fourth international scientific conference ERAZ 2018 pp 736–745. https://doi.org/10.31410/eraz.2018.736

Pascal P (2020) Banks, Maturity Transformation, and Monetary Policy, Federal Reserve Bank of San Francisco Working Paper 2020-07. https://doi.org/10.24148/wp2020-07

Pavić Kramarić T, Miletić, M, Kožul Blaževski R (2019) Financial stability of insurance companies in selected CEE countries. Bus Syst Res J 10(2):163–178. https://doi.org/10.2478/bsrj-2019-025

Pelger C, Spieß N (2017) On the IASB's construction of legitimacy – the case of the agenda consultation project. Account Bus Res 47(1):64–90. https://doi.org/10.1080/00014788.2016.1198684

Pucci S (2012) Insurance financial statements, Bancassurance in Europe. Palgrave Macmillan, pp 115–138

PWC (2017) IFRS adoption by country https://www.pwc.ru/ru/ifrs/ifrs-17-hub-int/pwc-ifrs-by-country-2016.pdf

Rambure D, Nacamuli A (2008) The role of payment systems in the economy. In: Payment systems. Palgrave Macmillan Studies in Banking and Financial Institutions. Palgrave Macmillan, London, pp 69–73. https://doi.org/10.1057/9780230227217_5

Reifner U, Clerc-Renaud S, Knobloch RA M, Flach L (2011) Financial Supervision in the EU A consumer perspective Institut für Finanzdienstleistungen e.V Hamburg https://www.beuc.eu/publications/2011-00396-01-e.pdf

Richardson AJ, Eberlein B (2011) Legitimating transnational standard-setting: the case of the international accounting standards board. J Bus Ethics 98(2):217–245. www.jstor.org/stable/41475812. Accessed 27 Apr 2021

Rockas I, Siafarika A (2019) The notion of insurance-based investment products, distribution of insurance-based investment products the EU regulation and the liabilities: the EU regulation and the liabilities, pp 3–25. https://doi.org/10.1007/978-3-030-11668-2

Rohrbach W (2018) Značaj istorije osiguranja. Tokovi osiguranja 3:7–26. http://tokoviosiguranja.edu.rs/wp-content/uploads/2018/12/18-03_1.pdf

Samuels JM, Piper A (1985) International accounting: a survey croom helm series on international accounting and finance. St. Martin's Press

Schich S (2010a) The role of insurance in the recent financial crisis. Insur Mark Comp Anal Actuarial Comput 1(1):45–53. https://businessperspectives.org/images/pdf/applications/publishing/templates/article/assets/2819/IMC_2010_1_Schich.pdf

Schich S (2010b) Insurance companies and the financial crisis. OECD Journal: Financial Market Trends. https://www.oecd.org/pensions/insurance/44260382.pdf

Society of Actuaries (2017) Reviewing Systemic Risk within the Insurance Industry. https://www.soa.org/globalassets/assets/files/research/projects/reviewing-systemic-risk.pdf

Stanić L, Glavaš J (2013) Uloga i značenje menadžmenta u osiguranju, Ekonomski vjesnik: Review of Contemporary Entrepreneurship, Business, and Economic Issues 16(2):637–653

Strampelli G (2018) The EU issuers' accounting disclosure regime and investors' information needs: the essential role of narrative reporting. Eur Bus Organ Law Rev 19:541–579. https://doi.org/10.1007/s40804-018-0112-8

Tomic K (2017) Bankoosiguranje na tržištu osiguranja zemalja Europske Unije, XVIII Conference Proportionality and Legal Certainty in Insurance Law, Palic ISBN 978-86-920975-0-8. 199-215.

Trichet JC (2005) Financial stability and the insurance sector. Geneva Pap Risk Insur Iss Pract 30 (1):65–71. https://doi.org/10.1057/palgrave.gpp.2510021

Van Hulle VK (2002) International convergence of accounting standards: a comment on Jeffrey. Duke J Comp Int Law 12:357–196. Available at: https://scholarship.law.duke.edu/djcil/vol12/iss2/8

Walton P (2003) International Accounting Standards: The New Regime, International accounting and reporting issues 2001 review, United Nation Geneva https://unctad.org/system/files/official-document/iteteb14_en.pdf

Walton P (2013) Fair value and accounting, handbook of key global financial markets, institutions, and infrastructure. In: Caprio G, Arner DW, Beck T, Calomiris CW, Neal L, Veron N (eds) Academic Press, pp 423–433. https://doi.org/10.1016/B978-0-12-397873-8.00251-6

Walton P (2015) IFRS in Europe – an observer's perspective of the next 10 years. Account Eur 12 (2):135–151. https://doi.org/10.1080/17449480.2015.1095306

Zeff S (2011) The evolution of the IASC into the IASB, and the challenges it faces. Account Rev 87 (3):807–837. https://doi.org/10.2308/accr-10246

Zweifel P (2014) Solvency regulation of insurers: a regulatory failure? J Insur Iss 37(2):135–157. JSTOR, www.jstor.org/stable/43151297. Accessed 28 Apr 2021

Recent Directions in the Regulation of Insurance Claims Handling in the United Kingdom and Australia: A Model for Other Jurisdictions to Consider?

Robin Bowley

Abstract This chapter examines recent developments in the regulation of insurance claims handling in the United Kingdom and in Australia. It commences by reviewing the relevant Insurance Core Principles developed by the International Association of Insurance Supervisors which articulate the standards that national supervisors should implement to effectively regulate the handling of claims and the resolution of disputes with policyholders. From this basis, it then examines the various rules developed by the Financial Conduct Authority to regulate claims handling in the United Kingdom, and through the use of case studies discusses how compliance with these rules has been monitored and enforced. The chapter then examines the legal framework for regulating insurance claims handling in Australia, which has been significantly expanded following the implementation of the reforms recommended by the 2019 Royal Commission into Misconduct in the Banking, Superannuation and Financial Services Industry. The chapter concludes that the approaches adopted in these two jurisdictions could provide a model for similar jurisdictions considering similar regulatory challenges.

1 Introduction

The handling of insurance claims can be a long and complex process, involving factual investigations, consideration of the application of policy conditions, the engagement of external service providers and negotiated forms of settlements. Unsurprisingly, the claims handling process can frequently give rise to disputes between policyholders expecting the timely settlement of their claim, and insurers being mindful of managing their liabilities within the scope of their contractual obligations. This chapter discusses how insurance supervisory authorities in the United Kingdom and in Australia have used a variety of approaches over the recent

R. Bowley (✉)
Faculty of Law, University of Technology Sydney, Sydney, NSW, Australia
e-mail: robin.bowley@uts.edu.au

P. Marano, K. Noussia (eds.), *The Governance of Insurance Undertakings*, AIDA Europe Research Series on Insurance Law and Regulation 6,
https://doi.org/10.1007/978-3-030-85817-9_12

years to regulate the handling of insurance claims to ensure fairness for policyholders.

Section 2 reviews the relevant international standards for regulating the handling of insurance claims, with a particular focus on the Insurance Core Principles developed by the International Association of Insurance Supervisors which articulate the standards that national supervisors should implement to ensure a fair balance between the expectations of insurers and policyholders. From this basis, Sect. 3 examines the legal framework for regulating insurance claims handling in the United Kingdom under the various rules developed by the Financial Conduct Authority (FCA). It discusses how the FCA has worked to ensure fair outcomes for consumers through both thematic reviews to encourage insurers to improve their practices, and formal enforcement action involving the imposition of financial penalties against a major insurer in 2018.

The remainder of the chapter discusses the regulation of insurance claims handling in Australia. Section 4 provides an overview of the Australian legislation relating to claims handling and the key cases in which insurers' claims handling practices have been challenged. It then discusses the functions of the Australian Securities and Investments Commission (ASIC) in regulating the insurance industry, with a particular focus on the key findings from ASIC's reviews of insurers' claims handling practices. Section 5 examines the significant reforms to the regulation of insurance claims handling resulting from the recommendations of the 2019 Royal Commission into Misconduct in the Banking, Superannuation and Financial Services Industry (FSRC). These include bringing insurance claims handling within the ambit of being a 'financial service'; making industry codes of practice legally enforceable and extending the existing unfair contract terms regime to insurance contracts. As well as considering how these new measures might apply in practice, Sect. 5 also reviews two recent cases where ASIC has taken action against insurers in the courts for unsatisfactory claims handling practices. Section 6 draws together the key observations in the preceding parts and concludes that the approaches to regulating insurance claims handling in Australia and the United Kingdom could provide a model for similar jurisdictions to consider.

2 International Standards for Regulating the Handling of Insurance Claims

At an international level, a good starting point when examining national arrangements for the regulation of insurance claims handling are the Insurance Core Principles (ICPs) which have been progressively developed by the International Association of Insurance Supervisors (IAIS) since its establishment in 1994.[1] The

[1] International Association of Insurance Supervisors, *Insurance Core Principles and ComFrame* https://www.iaisweb.org/page/supervisory-material/insurance-core-principles. For an overview of

IAIS ICPs provide benchmarks on the key elements that should be addressed in the national supervisory regimes to ensure both financially sound insurance industries and adequate levels of consumer protection for policyholders. Each of the 26 ICPs include further guidance on the recommended measures to implement the relevant principles.

ICP 19 'Conduct of Business' envisages that 'The supervisor requires that insurers and intermediaries, in their conduct of insurance business, treat customers fairly, both before a contract is entered into and through to the point at which all obligations under a contract have been satisfied.'. ICP 19.0.2 elaborates on this general statement by explaining that 'fair treatment of customers' encompasses achieving outcomes such as: (inter alia) 'dealing with customer claims, complaints and disputes in a fair and timely manner'.

ICP 19.10 addresses claims handling and envisages that supervisors in each jurisdiction will require insurers to handle claims in a timely, fair and transparent manner, and to have dispute resolution policies and procedures in place. To achieve these benchmarks, the guidance to ICP 19.10 on effective claims handling recommends that insurers should maintain written documentation on their claims handling procedures; clearly inform claimants about procedures, formalities and common timeframes for claims settlement; ensure that claimants are given information about the status of their claim in a timely and fair manner; and clearly explain in comprehensible language claim-determinative factors (such as depreciations, discounting or negligence) that could result in claims being denied in whole or in part.[2]

The guidance to ICP 19.10 on claims handling goes on to explain that a fair claims assessment process requires the avoidance of conflicts of interest as well as appropriate competence and ongoing training of the staff involved, with the competence requirements for claims handlers likely to differ depending on the types of insurance policies involved.[3]

In relation to claims disputes, the guidance on ICP 19.10 emphasises that dispute resolution procedures should be fair, impartial and transparent with procedural complexities minimised as far as possible; and that staff handling claims disputes being appropriately qualified and experienced in claims handling.[4] Similar recommendations are included in the European Insurance and Occupational Pensions Authority's Guidelines on Complaints Handling by Insurance Undertakings.[5]

The guidance on ICP 19.10 also recommends that if claims handling processes are outsourced (either in part or in full), supervisors should require insurers to

---

the evolution and function of the IAIS generally, see Lowry et al. (2011); Walker and Purves (2014), pp. 18–19; Steinberg (2011), pp. 302–304.

[2] International Association of Insurance Supervisors, *Insurance Core Principles* 19.10.2–19.10.5.

[3] International Association of Insurance Supervisors, *Insurance Core Principles* 19.10.7–19.10.8.

[4] International Association of Insurance Supervisors, *Insurance Core Principles* 19.10.9–19.10.11.

[5] European Insurance and Occupational Pensions Authority (2012) *Guidelines on Complaints Handling by Insurance Undertakings*, EIOPA-BoS-12/070.

maintain close oversight and ultimate responsibility for fair and transparent claims handling and claims dispute resolution.[6] Similar recommendations on appropriate oversight are contained in ICP 19.11 which addresses situations where intermediaries are involved in claims handling processes.

Section 3 below shows how the legal framework for regulating the handling of insurance claims in the United Kingdom reflects the standards envisaged in ICP 19.10, and Sect. 4 explains how because of recent reforms Australian legislation governing the handling of insurance claims now also adheres to the principles set out in ICP 19.10.

3 The Regulation of Insurance Claims Handling in the United Kingdom

In the United Kingdom, since 1 December 2001,[7] the *Financial Services and Markets Act* 2000 (the FSMA) has governed the conduct of insurance businesses. Between 2001 and April 2013, the FSMA was administered by the Financial Services Authority. In the aftermath of the Global Financial Crisis, the regulatory functions of the Financial Services Authority were divided between two new agencies. The Prudential Conduct Authority assumed responsibility for the prudential regulation of the UK's financial sector (including the insurance industry) and the Financial Conduct Authority (FCA), assumed responsibility for regulating the conduct of financial services firms.[8]

The FSMA provides the FCA[9] with wide powers to make rules, issue codes, to give guidance and to develop rules, policy and guidance to regulate financial markets and services in the UK. The FSMA prevents a person from carrying on a 'regulated activity' unless the person is authorised by the FCA or an 'exempt person'.[10]

The FCA Handbook provides the primary re-statement of relevant rules, codes and general guidance in force at a given time, and consists of several 'blocks'. These 'blocks' in turn contain a number of 'source books' on specific regulatory requirements, which contain both legally enforceable rules (denoted by an 'R' after the relevant rule) and regulatory guidance (denoted by an 'R' after the relevant principle).[11]

[6] International Association of Insurance Supervisors, *Insurance Core Principles* 19.10.12.

[7] Walker and Purves (2014), p. 743.

[8] Walker and Purves (2014), pp. 3–6.

[9] Although the *FSMA* (which is jointly administered by the FCA and the PRA) refers to 'the Authority', this chapter focuses only on the role of the FCA.

[10] *Financial Services and Markets Act* 2000 (UK) s 19 (containing the general prohibition—unless the person is authorised or exempt).

[11] Walker and Purves (2014), p. 5.39.

The Insurance Conduct of Business Sourcebook (ICOBS) sets out the obligations of firms that carry on a business of insurance in the United Kingdom. ICOBS 8 sets out the obligations of insurers in relation to claims handling. ICOBS 8.1.1R requires insurers to (1) handle claims promptly and fairly; (2) provide reasonable guidance to help a policyholder make a claim and appropriate information on its progress; (3) not unreasonably reject a claim (including by terminating or avoiding a policy); and (4) settle claims promptly once settlement terms are agreed.

For contracts agreed before the commencement of the *Insurance Act* 2015 (UK) on 1 August 2017, ICOBS 8.1.2R explains that the rejection of a consumer policyholder's claim may be unreasonable unless there was evidence of fraud; non-disclosure or misrepresentation of a fact that was material to the risk to be transferred; or breach of a warranty or condition under the contract.

For contracts agreed after 1 August 2017, ICOBS 8.1.2AR explains that the rejection of a consumer policyholder's claim may be unreasonable unless the consumer made a qualifying misrepresentation within the meaning of the *Consumer Insurance (Disclosure and Representations) Act* 2012 (UK); or for claims subject to the *Insurance Act* 2015 (UK), where the consumer breached a warranty or engaged in fraudulent conduct.

The FCA's Dispute Resolution: Complaints sourcebook sets out the requirements for firms to have arrangements in place for the handling of complaints by consumers. DISP 1.3.1R requires firms to establish, implement and maintain effective and transparent procedures for the handling of complaints. DISP 1.4.1R elaborates on these obligations, by requiring firms to investigate and assess complaints fairly, consistently and promptly; to offer redress or remedial action where appropriate; and to clearly and fairly explain its assessment of the complaint to consumers in a manner that is not misleading. The DISP sourcebook includes further guidance for firms to meet these mandatory requirements.

At a broader level, the FCA's Senior Management Arrangements, Systems and Controls (SYSC) sourcebook places responsibility on the directors and senior managers of firms to take reasonable care to ensure compliance with applicable requirements and to implement appropriate risk management arrangements.

Over the recent years, the FCA has undertaken several reviews of British insurers' claims handling practices. In May 2014, the FCA published the report of its thematic review of insurers' management of claims in the household and retail travel sector. This review was based on both consumer research and the FCA's engagement with the claims handling staff of insurers. Whilst consumer research for this revealed that consumers levels of satisfaction with their claims experiences were overall reasonably high, the review highlighted some issues for future improvement by insurers. These included working to ensure that policy documentation was clear and understandable to consumers (particularly around policy exclusions), and keeping consumers informed during the claims process (particularly where third party providers such as builders and loss adjusters were involved).[12] This thematic review also involved a survey of members of the Chartered Insurance Institute about the members' perceptions of insurers' practices for handling household and travel insurance claims. Whilst responding members indicated that insurers were adequately informing customers about how to make claims and providing relatively straightforward claims notification processes, the survey highlighted several areas for insurers to improve their claims handling practices. These included keeping claimants informed throughout the claims process; clearly informing claimants about the coverage of their policies; proactive management of third-party suppliers (such as tradespersons); and clearly informing claimants about the evidence needed to support their claims.[13]

A year later in May 2015, the FCA published the findings of its thematic review of the handling of claims lodged by policyholders in the Small and Medium-sized Enterprise (SME) sector. Whilst noting that claims by SMEs were more complex than those examined it its earlier review of household and travel claims, the FCA identified several areas for insurers to improve their claims handling practices. These included many SME claimants reporting a lack of clarity about who was responsible for managing their claims (particularly where external providers such as loss adjusters were involved), and poor communication about the progress of their claims.[14]

The FCA has a wide range of enforcement powers to respond to breaches of its rules, which are set out in its Enforcement Guide. One of the FCA's enforcement options is its power under s 206(1) of the FSMA to impose financial penalties where it determines that an authorised person has contravened a requirement under the FMSA. The FCA's approach to exercising its powers to impose financial penalties is set out in Chapter 7 of its Enforcement Guide, and its policy on the determining the appropriate quantum of financial penalties is set out in Chapter 6 of its Decision Procedure and Penalties Manual (DEPP).

The application of these sanctions was illustrated on 29 October 2018 when the FCA imposed a financial penalty of £5,280,800 on Liberty Mutual Insurance Europe SE (Liberty) following its investigation into Liberty's failure to exercise appropriate oversight of claims on mobile phone insurance policies which it had underwritten between 2010 and 2015.

By way of background, in 2010 Liberty entered into an arrangement to underwrite mobile phone insurance, with a third party[15] providing this insurance to retail customers in the UK. Under this arrangement, the third party managed the

---

[12] Financial Conduct Authority (May 2014) 'Thematic Review TR 14/8: Insurers' management of claims - household and retail travel.

[13] Financial Conduct Authority (May 2014) 'Perceptions of insurers management of claims: Findings from a survey of members of the Chartered Insurance Institute' See https://www.fca.org.uk/publication/research/tr14-08-cii-survey.pdf.

[14] Financial Conduct Authority (May 2015) 'Thematic Review TR 14/19: Handling of insurance claims for Small and Medium-sized Enterprises (SMEs)'.

[15] The third party was not identified in the FCA's media release.

administrative functions associated with the mobile phone insurance on Liberty's behalf, including the handling of claims and complaints. However, as the authorised insurer, Liberty retained primary responsibility for ensuring that these outsourced claims and complaints handling arrangements complied with regulatory requirements.

Following numerous complaints by customers to the UK's Financial Ombudsman Service, an investigation by the FCA determined that Liberty had failed to exercise appropriate oversight of the third party's handling of claims on the mobile phone insurance policies. The FCA's investigation found that around 6000 customers had been unfairly denied cover for claims for loss or theft if they had failed to comply with a requirement to download and install a Mobile Rescue App; that in many of the 3171 claims declined on suspicion of fraud there had been insufficient evidence to support such suspicions due to an overreliance on voice analytics software; and that approximately 1707 customers had been unfairly denied cover through the inappropriate use of a policy exclusion for unattended loss. Based on these findings, the FCA investigation determined that Liberty had failed to comply with its obligations under ICOBS 8.1.1R to handle claims promptly and fairly, and to not unreasonably reject claims.

The FCA also found that Liberty had failed to ensure that the third party had adequate complaint handling processes in place, noting with concern that the great majority of the 1627 customers who complained about denials of cover for late notification of their claim or for failure to install the Mobile Rescue App had the original decision overturned. These failings meant that Liberty had failed to adhere to its obligations DISP 1.3.1R and 1.4.1R discussed above, as well as its obligations under SYSC 3.1.1R, which requires firms to establish and maintain appropriate systems and controls.[16]

More recently, on 19 March 2020, the FCA outlined set out its expectation of firms when handling insurance claims in the context of the COVID-19 pandemic. Emphasising the importance of treating customers fairly, the FCA made clear that it expected firms to clearly communicate policy exclusions, and to take a more flexible approach to motor and home property claims given the increased number of consumers working from home.[17]

In summary, this part has shown how in the FCA is empowered to regulate the handling of insurance claims in the United Kingdom in accordance with the standards envisaged in ICP 19.10. The following part of the chapter and discusses how significant reforms in Australia now provide for the effective regulation of all parties involved in the handling of insurance claims in accordance with the ICP 19.10 standards.

---

[16]Financial Conduct Authority (29 October 2018) Press Release 'The FCA has fined Liberty Mutual Insurance Europe SE £5.2 million for failures in its oversight of mobile phone insurance claims and complaints handling'. See also Financial Conduct Authority (29 October 2018) Final Notice - Liberty Mutual Insurance Europe SE.

[17]Financial Conduct Authority, Press Release 'Insurance and coronavirus (Covid-19): our expectations of firms' 19 March 2020.

4 The Evolution of the Australian Legal Framework Relating to Insurance Claims Handling

4.1 Australian Insurance Contract Law Relating to Claims Handling

Since 1 January 1986, most classes of insurance contracts in Australia have been governed by the *Insurance Contracts Act* 1984 (Cth) (the ICA).[18] The ICA regulates the relationship between insurers and insureds[19] throughout the life cycle of a contract of insurance. It includes provisions governing pre-contractual disclosure, the ability of insurers to refuse (or limit their liability) when determining claims, and the circumstances under which insurers may cancel contracts.

Section 13 of the ICA imposes duties of utmost good faith on both parties to insurance contracts. Whilst the meaning of the generalised duty of utmost good faith is challenging to conclusively define—and will depend on the circumstances of each case—it has been noted to encompass notions of fairness, reasonableness and community standards of decency and fair dealing, and require both parties to an insurance contract to have due regard to the interests of the other party.[20]

A leading Australian insurance lawyer has helpfully described the duty of utmost good faith under the ICA as consisting of four quadrants.[21] The first of these quadrants concerns the insured's pre-contractual obligations, which under Part IV of the ICA require the insured to disclose[22] (and not misrepresent[23]) information that is relevant to the risk to be transferred. The ICA includes specific Part IV of the ICA also provides remedies for insurers in cases where the insured has failed to comply with the duty of disclosure.[24] The second quadrant is the insurer's pre-contractual obligations, with Part IV of the ICA requiring the insurer to clearly inform the

[18] The exceptions to the application of the ICA include contracts of marine insurance, insurance that is required under state or territory legislation (including workers compensation and compulsory third-party insurance for motor vehicles), private health insurance and reinsurance.

[19] The terms 'policyholder', 'consumer' and 'insured' are used interchangeably in this chapter.

[20] Enright and Merkin (2015), pp. 471–476.

[21] These 'four quadrants' of utmost good faith were first conceptualised by Mann (2016), pp. 176–184.

[22] *Insurance Contracts Act* 1984 (Cth) s 21.

[23] *Insurance Contracts Act* 1984 (Cth) s 26. Under amendments to the *Insurance Contracts Act* 1984 (Cth) which took effect on 1 January 2021, when entering into a 'consumer insurance contracts' (defined in s 11AB as 'a contract of insurance obtained wholly or predominantly for the personal, domestic or household purposes of the insured') the insured's pre-contractual obligations under s 20B are to take reasonable care not to make a misrepresentation to the insurer before the relevant contract of insurance is entered into.

[24] These remedies are set out in *Insurance Contracts Act* 1984 (Cth) s 28 (for contracts of general insurance) and in s 29 (for contracts of life insurance).

insured in writing of the duty of disclosure before the insured enters into an insurance contract.[25]

The third quadrant of utmost good faith focuses on the insured's post-contractual obligations after an insurance policy comes into effect. Section 54 of the ICA provides remedies to insurers that have been prejudiced by the insured's failure to comply with terms of an insurance contracts—which may involve the insurer reducing its liability in respect of the insured's claim or avoiding the claim in its entirety. Section 56 of the ICA also provides remedies to the insurer in the event of fraudulent claims. The fourth quadrant of utmost good faith relates to the insurer's post-contractual conduct—which in most cases concerns the insurer's conduct in handling claims (the focus of the present chapter).

Section 14 of the ICA prevents parties to a contract of insurance from relying on a provision of the contract except in the utmost good faith, and to date s 15 of the ICA has provided that relief under other legislation does not apply to contracts of insurance governed by the ICA. Whilst to date this has meant that the unfair contract terms regime under the *Australian Securities and Investments Commission Act* 2001 (Cth) (the ASIC Act)—which renders void unfair contractual terms that cause a significant imbalance in the contracting parties' rights and obligations—has thus far not applied to insurance contracts, as Sect. 5.2 below discusses the recommendations by the 2019 FSRC for extending the unfair contract terms regime to apply to insurance contracts subject to the ICA.

Over the recent years, there have been an increasing number of cases in which aggrieved policyholders have challenged the decision-making processes of insurers in refusing their claims. In several cases aggrieved policyholders have questioned the insurers' adherence to the duty of utmost good faith under s 13 of the ICA—particularly in cases where the insurers were not open and frank in their dealings with the insureds. The decisions of Australian courts on such challenges have progressively clarified the standards expected of insurers when determining claims.

The leading Australian decision on s 13 of the ICA is *CGU Insurance Ltd v AMP Financial Planning Pty Ltd* [2007] HCA 36. During 1999 two representatives of the financial services company AMP had acted outside the terms of their respective authorities, resulting in losses for their clients. AMP then faced pressure from the corporate regulator ASIC[26] to devise a protocol for settling claims by the affected clients in a timely manner. However, AMP's professional indemnity policy with CGU prevented it from admitting liability or settling claims without obtaining the CGU's written consent, and also required AMP's liabilities to clients (and hence its right to indemnity under the policy) to be conclusively established by advice from a senior counsel. Whilst CGU indicated through its lawyers that it 'agreed in principle' to the protocol for compensating the affected clients, it also advised that it reserved its decision on its liability to indemnify AMP and advised AMP to act as a 'prudent uninsured'. After almost two years of delays and changes of lawyers, CGU refused

[25] *Insurance Contracts Act* 1984 (Cth) s 22.

[26] ASIC's role in regulating the Australian financial services industry is discussed below at Sect. 4.2.

AMP's claim. Following a succession of legal proceedings, the majority of the High Court of Australia upheld CGU's refusal of AMP's claim due to its failure to comply with the policy's requirement to obtain CGU's consent before settling the clients' claims. However, in his dissenting judgement Kirby J was highly critical of CGU's failure 'to act with clarity, candour and decisiveness',[27] as well as what he characterised as the 'dilatory, prevaricating, confused, uncertain, inattentive and misleading way in which, over two years, CGU, with its four successive firms of solicitors, delayed and postponed its decision to deny indemnity'.[28] Whilst the High Court found by a 4:1 majority that CGU had not breached its duty of utmost good faith in its refusal of AMP's claim, in other cases Australian insurers have been found to have breached this duty in their determination of claims.

In the field of Total and Permanent Disability (TPD) insurance there have been several cases where insurers have been found to be in breach of their duty of utmost good faith in determining claims. In Australia TPD insurance policies are commonly arranged on a 'group insurance' basis by trustees of superannuation funds to provide benefits for incapacitated members of the fund. Whilst such claimants are not parties to the insurance contract arranged between the superannuation fund trustee and the insurer, Australian courts have recognised that insurers' duties of utmost good faith also extend to third party claimants.[29] This position was confirmed through amendments to the ICA in 2013,[30] which extended insurers' duties of utmost good faith to third party beneficiaries.[31]

Whilst TPD definitions vary between insurers, one typical example of the criteria that must be satisfied for TPD benefits to be payable is that 'the Insured Person is unable to follow their usual occupation by reason of an accident or illness for six consecutive months and in our opinion, after consideration of medical evidence satisfactory to us, is unlikely ever to be able to engage in any Regular Remuneration Work for which the Insured Person is reasonably fitted by Education, Training or Experience'.[32]

Determining claims for TPD benefits can be a complex process for insurers, requiring the evaluation of sometimes conflicting evidence from medical specialists, allied health professionals, investigative surveillance and labour market analyses to decide whether a claimant has satisfied the applicable TPD definition. If an insurer's

---

[27] *CGU Insurance Ltd v AMP Financial Planning Pty Ltd* (2007) 235 CLR 1; 14 ANZ Ins Cas 61-739; [2007] HCA 36 at [72].

[28] *CGU Insurance Ltd v AMP Financial Planning Pty Ltd* (2007) 235 CLR 1; 14 ANZ Ins Cas 61-739; [2007] HCA 36 at [139].

[29] For an overview of these cases see Bowley (2016), pp. 194–213.

[30] For an overview of the 2013 reforms to the ICA, see Box and Webster (2013), pp. 114–119; Tarr (2015), pp. 68–74.

[31] *Insurance Contracts Act* 1984 (Cth) s 13(4). Since 2013 s 11 of the ICA has defined a 'third party beneficiary' as a person who is not a party to the contract but is specified or referred to in the contract, whether by name or otherwise, as a person to whom the benefit of the insurance cover provided by the contract extends.

[32] *Hannover Life Re of Australasia Ltd v Dargan* [2013] NSWCA 57 at [16].

decision-making process is found to be unreasonable, the court may determine the TPD claim on the available evidence.[33] Examples of claims handling processes that have been found to breach of the duty of utmost good faith have included failing to inform an assessing doctor of the criteria that a claimant would need to satisfy to qualify for TPD benefits, and refusing a request by the claimant (an accountant who had suffered a stroke) for access to the documentation relied upon to declining his claim;[34] failing to inform a manual worker claiming TPD benefits for a back injury of adverse reports from an assessing doctor and private surveillance agents that were relied upon to refuse his claim;[35] failing to inform a manual worker with limited English about the information that would be required to substantiate his claim, and failing to give appropriate consideration to a specialist medical report that was favourable to the claimant;[36] and providing a claimant (a police officer claiming for psychological injuries) with only 14 days to respond to a 'procedural fairness' letter enclosing the full volume of information relating to her claim that had been collected in the three years since she had lodged her claim, after having failed to respond to three requests by her solicitors and the trustee of her superannuation fund to release medical reports relating to her claim.[37]

Whilst these decisions finding insurers to be in breach of the duty of utmost good faith through their deficient claims handling practices have resulted from civil challenges by policyholders to the refusal of claims by insurers, the following sections outline how in in more recent years the regulators of the Australian insurance industry have become increasingly active in their monitoring of insurers' claims handling practices.

4.2 The Powers of the Australian Insurance Industry Regulators

There are two key regulators of the Australian insurance industry, which have existed in their present form since 1998.[38] The first of these is the Australian

[33] *Lazarevic v United Super Pty Ltd* [2014] NSWSC 96 at [147].

[34] *Wyllie v National Mutual Life Association of Aust Ltd* (1997) 217 ALR 324 at 342; [1997] NSWSC 146.

[35] *Sayseng v Kellogg Superannuation Pty Ltd and Anor* [2003] NSWSC 945 at [93]–[97]; upheld on appeal: *Hannover Life Re of Australasia Ltd v Sayseng* (2005) 13 ANZ Ins Cas 90-123; [2005] NSWCA 214.

[36] *Dumitrov v SC Johnson and Son Superannuation Pty Ltd and Anor* [2006] NSWSC 1372. In a subsequent decision Gzell J awarded the claimant interest under s 57 of the ICA to compensate for the insurer's unreasonable withholding of insurance monies: *Dumitrov v SC Johnson and Son Superannuation Pty Ltd (No 2)* (2007) 14 ANZ Ins Cas 61-722; [2007] NSWSC 42.

[37] *Wheeler v FSS Trustee Corp Atf First State Superannuation Scheme* [2016] NSWSC 534.

[38] Australia's current regulatory system was an outcome of the Wallis Financial System Inquiry which was held between 1996 and 1997. The Wallis Inquiry recommended the replacement of

Securities and Investments Commission (ASIC), which has responsibility for the general administration of the ICA.[39] ASIC's wide range of responsibilities include the regulation of Australian companies, financial markets and financial services.[40] The focus of ASIC's regulation of the Australian financial services industry (which as explained below, encompasses most forms of insurance) is on consumer protection, ensuring accurate disclosure for consumers and investors, and licensing providers of financial services. As also explained below, ASIC has a wide range of powers to investigate and take enforcement action in response to suspected non-compliance with the various laws that it administers, and it also publishes extensive regulatory guidance for the sectors that it oversees.[41]

The other regulator of the Australian insurance industry is the Australian Prudential Regulation Authority (APRA). In comparison to ASIC's focus on consumer protection, APRA focuses on the prudential regulation of Australian financial institutions (including general and life insurers) to ensure they remain financially viable and able to satisfy their obligation to policyholders. As part of this prudential regulatory role, the *Financial Sector (Collection of Data) Act* 2001 (Cth) enables APRA to collect and analyse data from the financial institutions it supervises on an ongoing basis. As explained below in Sect. 4.3 in recent years ASIC has worked collaboratively with APRA by drawing on its data collection and analysis capabilities in its reviews of the Australian insurance industry.

Chapter 7 of the *Corporations Act* 2001 (Cth) (the Corporations Act) sets out an over-arching consumer protection regime for the Australian financial services industry. Many of the key provisions of Chapter 7 are expressed broadly, with numerous 'carve-outs' as exceptions in both the Corporations Act and the *Corporations Regulations* 2001 (Cth).[42] A foundational term in Chapter 7 is the concept of a 'financial product', defined in s 763A as 'a facility through which, or through the acquisition of which a person makes a financial investment; manages a financial risk, or makes a non-cash payment'. Section 763C includes 'taking out insurance' as an example of 'managing a financial risk', and s 764C includes 'contracts of insurance' as 'financial products'. Section 765A provides exceptions to these general

Australia's previous over-lapping and sector-specific regulatory system with the 'twin peaks' model of financial sector regulation: Wallis (1997). For an excellent overview of the evolution of the current regulatory arrangements for the Australian insurance industry, see Tarr (2010), pp. 332–350.

[39] *Insurance Contracts Act* 1984 (Cth) s 11A.

[40] ASIC also regulates consumer credit and business names, which are outside the scope of the present chapter.

[41] ASIC publishes Regulatory Guides to set out its interpretation of, and for outlining its recommended best practice for complying with, the various laws that it administers; and Information Sheets which provide concise guidance on a specific process or compliance issue or an overview of detailed guidance: ASIC, Regulatory Resources: https://asic.gov.au/regulatory-resources/.

[42] For an interesting critique of the broadly expressed nature of Chapter 7 of the *Corporations Act*, see Lewis (2004), pp. 103–134.

definitions by specifying the forms of insurance that are not classified as 'financial products' under Chapter 7.[43]

Proceeding from these definitions of 'financial product', s 766A explains that a person 'provides a financial service' if they (inter alia) provide financial product advice,[44] or deal in a financial product. As this definition captures the busines activities of most forms of insurance in Australia, under s 911A general and life insurers must hold an Australian Financial Services (AFS) Licence issued by ASIC.[45]

Section 911A imposes wide-ranging obligations on AFS licensees, which include ensuring that financial services are provided efficiently, honestly and fairly; complying with financial services laws; and ensuring that representatives are adequately trained and are competent to provide the relevant financial services.[46]

When financial services are provided to consumers (who are classified as 'retail clients' under the Corporations Act[47]), s 912A(1)(g) requires AFS licensees to have in place systems for resolving disputes. These must include internal dispute resolution (IDR) arrangements that comply with the standards made by ASIC,[48] and in cases where a firm's IDR processes do not result in the resolution of the consumer's dispute, external dispute resolution (EDR) arrangements. The Australian Financial Complaints Authority (AFCA) scheme is the sole EDR body for resolving consumer disputes in the financial services industry. The AFCA commenced operations on 1 July 2018 after a review of Australia's financial services dispute resolution framework had recommended the replacement of the three previous EDR bodies[49] (which were overlapping and inconsistent) with a single unified body for resolving

[43] These include contracts of reinsurance; insurance provided by commonwealth, state and territory governments; private health insurance; and insurance entered into by the Export Finance and Insurance Corporation.

[44] *Corporations Act 2001* (Cth) s 766B(1) defines 'financial product advice' as a recommendation or statement of opinion that is intended to influence a person in making a decision in relation to a financial product or class of financial products, or an interest in a particular financial product or class of financial products; or could reasonably be regarded as being intended to have such an influence.

[45] *Corporations Act* 2001 (Cth) ss 913A–913B; See also ASIC Regulatory Guide 36 'Licensing: Financial product advice and dealing (updated July 2016).

[46] *Corporations Act* 2001 (Cth) s 912A.

[47] *Corporations Act* 2001 (Cth) s 761G—which provides that a retail client is a client that does not qualify as a wholesale client. See also *Corporations Act* 2001 (Cth) s 761G(5)(b)(vii) and *Corporations Regulations* 2001 (Cth) Reg 7.1.17, which explains that a general insurance product will be provided to a person as a 'retail client' if the product is a motor vehicle, home building, home and contents, sickness and accident, consumer credit, travel or a personal and domestic insurance product.

[48] ASIC's expectations in relation to internal dispute resolution arrangements for AFS Licensees is set out in Regulatory Guide 271 'Internal dispute resolution' (30 July 2020).

[49] Prior to the formation of AFCA, Australia's three previous EDR bodies had included the Financial Ombudsman Service, the Credit Ombudsman Service and the Superannuation Complaints Tribunal.

consumer disputes.[50] The AFCA dispute resolution process (which is funded by the compulsory levies on AFS licensees[51]) is free to consumers[52] and seeks to resolve disputes firstly through informal methods such as negotiation, or through a conciliation conference.[53] If these methods fail to resolve the complaint, AFCA may then proceed to make a final determination in relation to the complaint, which is binding on the AFCA member.[54] Under Part 7.10A of the Corporations Act, AFCA is subject to oversight by ASIC and must report matters including serious contraventions of the law and systemic issues.[55]

A significant focus of ASIC's consumer protection efforts is on ensuring complete and accurate disclosure about financial products when these are sold retail clients. In most cases, a Product Disclosure Statement which clearly sets out the key terms and conditions of the insurance contract, including the policy wording.[56] must be provided to the retail client either by the insurer,[57] or by their insurance broker or financial adviser.[58] ASIC utilises a risk-based approach to monitor the adequacy of Product Disclosure Statements in informing consumers about the terms and conditions of financial products.[59]

Chapter 7 of the Corporations Act includes provisions that prohibit dishonest conduct[60] and misleading or deceptive conduct[61] in relation to financial products or financial services. These provisions are paralleled in the ASIC Act, which also includes prohibitions on misleading or deceptive conduct[62] and false or misleading representations[63] in relation to financial services.

---

[50] Ramsay et al. (2017).

[51] Under *Corporations Act* s 912A(2) all AFS licensees that provide financial services to retail clients must be members of the AFCA scheme.

[52] Australian Financial Complaints Authority, Funding - https://www.afca.org.au/about-afca/corporate-information/funding.

[53] Australian Financial Complaints Authority, *Complaint Resolution Scheme Rules* (25 April 2020), Rule A.8.1.

[54] Australian Financial Complaints Authority, *Complaint Resolution Scheme Rules* (25 April 2020), Rule A.15.

[55] See ASIC (July 2018) Regulatory Guide 267 'Oversight of the Australian Financial Complaints Authority'.

[56] *Corporations Act* 2001 (Cth) s 1012D; *Corporations Regulations* 2001 (Cth) Reg 7.9.15 D-F.

[57] In cases where the contract of insurance is issued directly by the insurer: *Corporations Act* 2001 (Cth) s 1012B.

[58] In cases where the retail client has been provided with personal advice (which considers a client's person's objectives, financial situation and needs) before entering into the relevant contract of insurance *Corporations Act* 2001 (Cth) s 1012A.

[59] For an overview of ASIC's approach to monitoring disclosure about financial products, see ASIC (October 2011) Regulatory Guide 168 Disclosure: Product Disclosure Statements and other disclosure obligations.

[60] *Corporations Act* 2001 (Cth) s 1041G.

[61] *Corporations Act* 2001 (Cth) s 1041H.

[62] *Australian Securities and Investments Commission Act* 2001 (Cth) s 12DA.

[63] *Australian Securities and Investments Commission Act* 2001 (Cth) s 12DB.

ASIC utilises a range of measures to regulate the financial services industry, including engagement with the industry and other stakeholders, consumer education, the development of regulatory guidance, targeted surveillance to assess compliance, and formal enforcement action. ASIC has extensive powers to monitor and enforce compliance with the legislation it administers. These include the powers to conduct examinations of individuals;[64] obtain records relating to financial products[65] and financial services;[66] and apply for warrants to enter premises to obtain records.[67] ASIC may also direct AFS licensees to provide written statements about the financial services they provide.[68]

Depending on its assessment of the seriousness of breaches that come to its attention, there are a range of regulatory enforcement tools that ASIC may utilise.[69] ASIC's enforcement strategies encapsulate the principles of 'responsive regulation', which combines both compliance and deterrence through an 'enforcement pyramid' of progressively more punitive measures in response to breaches of the law.[70] Whilst to date the bulk of ASIC's enforcement actions have tended to be at the lower levels of the enforcement pyramid, as Sect. 5.2 explains the recommendations from the 2019 FSRC have urged ASIC to firstly ask the question 'why not litigate?' when taking enforcement strategies in response to future instances of misconduct in the financial services industry.

At the lowest level of the enforcement pyramid, ASIC may issue informal warnings or recommendations for changing business practices.[71] In situations where ASIC is satisfied that a regulated entity is willing and capable of implementing appropriate measures to ensure compliance with the law and/or to compensate adversely impacted persons, ASIC may consider entering into an enforceable undertaking as an alternative to formal administrative or civil action.[72]

The next level up on the 'enforcement pyramid' are administrative actions against regulated entities and individuals.[73] Examples of administrative actions include the powers to suspend or cancel AFS Licences;[74] the power to ban individuals from

---

[64] *Australian Securities and Investments Commission Act* 2001 (Cth) s 19.

[65] *Australian Securities and Investments Commission Act* 2001 (Cth) s 31.

[66] *Australian Securities and Investments Commission Act* 2001 (Cth) s 32A.

[67] *Australian Securities and Investments Commission Act* 2001 (Cth) ss 35–36A.

[68] *Corporations Act* 2001 (Cth) s 912C.

[69] See ASIC (September 2013) Information Sheet 151 ASIC's approach to enforcement.

[70] Legg and Speirs (2019), pp. 244–246.

[71] For an overview of the factors that ASIC would ordinarily consider in determining whether to enter into an enforceable undertaking, see ASIC Information Sheet 151 (September 2013) 'ASIC's approach to enforcement' and ASIC (February 2015) Regulatory Guide 100 Enforceable Undertakings.

[72] *Australian Securities and Investments Commission Act* 2001 (Cth) s 93AA; see also ASIC (February 2015) Regulatory Guide 100, Enforceable Undertakings.

[73] ASIC (30 July 2013) Regulatory Guide 98 Licensing: Administrative action against financial services providers.

[74] *Corporations Act* 2001 (Cth) s 915C.

providing financial services;[75] and issuing infringement notices under the ASIC Act 2001.[76] In contrast to civil litigation and criminal prosecutions, decisions to impose administrative sanctions are made within ASIC by authorised delegates, after providing the regulated entity or individual with the opportunity for a hearing.[77]

The higher levels of the enforcement pyramid involve ASIC pursuing action through the courts, which can include civil litigation such as seeking injunctions[78] and/or the pursuit of recovery actions.[79] For more serious breaches of the law which adversely impact on consumers and/or investors, ASIC may pursue proceedings for the imposition of civil penalties. Section 1317E designates a number of provisions of the Corporations Act as 'civil penalty provisions', and when a court declares a contravention of a civil penalty provision it may impose a range of penalties. These include pecuniary penalty orders,[80] compensation orders[81] and/or orders disqualifying a person from specified roles such as managing a company or providing financial services for the period that it considers appropriate.[82] Civil penalties were introduced into Australian corporate legislation in the 1990s to expand the enforcement powers of regulatory authorities such as ASIC and its predecessors by providing an alternative to pursing criminal prosecutions (which involve the very high standard of proof beyond reasonable doubt. By contrast the civil standard of proof of the balance of probabilities applies to civil penalty proceedings. Civil penalties are intended to have both a deterrent effect both specifically (through punishing the offending individual or entity through the imposition of fines and/or disqualification orders) and generally (through providing high profile examples of punishment for wrongful conduct to the relevant regulated sectors).[83]

Reforms to the ICA which took effect from 12 March 2019 have enabled ASIC to pursue civil penalty proceedings for contraventions of designated provisions of the ICA, including the duty of utmost good faith under s 13. As discussed in Sect. 5, recent reforms resulting from the recommendations of the 2019 FSRC report which took effect from 1 January 2021 have introduced civil penalties for a range of other legislative provisions relating to insurance claims handling.

---

[75] *Corporations Act* 2001 (Cth) s 920A

[76] *Australian Securities and Investments Commission Act* 2001 (Cth) s 12GX; See also ASIC's infringement notices register http://asic.gov.au/about-asic/asic-investigations-and-enforcement/infringement-notices/.

[77] ASIC's practice in relation to administrative hearings is set out in ASIC (March 2002) Regulatory Guide 8 'Hearings practice manual'.

[78] *Corporations Act* 2001 (Cth) s 1324.

[79] See for example *Australian Securities and Investments Commission Act* 2001 (Cth) s 50.

[80] *Corporations Act* 2001 (Cth) s 1317G.

[81] *Corporations Act* 2001 (Cth) s 1317H (in relation to corporation / scheme civil penalty provisions) and s 1317HA (in relation to financial services civil penalty provisions).

[82] *Corporations Act* 2001 (Cth) s 206C.

[83] For an overview of the evolution of the Australian civil penalties regime, see Comino (2015), pp. 141–171.

In the most serious cases, ASIC may refer matters to the Commonwealth Director of Public Prosecutions, which may prosecute under both commonwealth and state and territory legislation.[84]

The following Sect. 4.3 explains how ASIC has become increasingly active in its monitoring of the practices of the Australian insurance industry over the recent years. Although since 2013 s 14A of the ICA has empowered ASIC to suspend, cancel or impose conditions on AFS licenses in cases where an insurer has failed to comply with the duty of utmost good faith in the handling or settlement of claims, to date it has been limited in its ability to seek the imposition of civil penalties in cases where an insurer has engaged in unfair conduct in the determination of a claim. In comparison to the selling of insurance (which has been designated as a financial service[85] since the inception of the Corporations Act in 2001), s 766A(2) of the Corporations Act has to date exempted 'handling insurance claims' from the ambit of 'financial services'. Until 1 January 2021, Regulation 7.1.33 of the Corporations Regulations 2001 (Cth) explained this exemption as encompassing the handling and/or settling of actual and potential claims, and provided non-exhaustive list of examples of such services as negotiations of settlement amounts; interpretation of relevant policy provisions; estimates of loss or damage; estimates of value or appropriate repair; recommendations on mitigation of loss; recommendations on changing cover limits; and claims strategy such as the making of claims under alternate policies.[86] However, as Sect. 5.2 explains, the FSRC has made recommendations to remove this exception.

In addition to the legal requirements set out in the ICA and the Corporations Act, codes of practice have progressively developed as an important source of self-regulation for the Australian insurance industry. Since 1994 there have been various iterations of the General Insurance Code of Practice, with the most recent iteration coming into effect on 1 January 2020.[87] The General Insurance Code of Practice is subscribed to by the majority of Australia's general insurers and sets out standards of business practice for insurers to adhere to when selling insurance; when issuing policies (and explaining the basis for rejecting applications for policies); determining claims (including timeframes and special arrangements in response to catastrophes); and when dealing with complaints and disputes. Codes of practice for the Australian life insurance industry have been developed over more recent years, covering similar issues to the General Insurance Code of Practice. These include the Life Insurance Code of Practice developed by the Financial Services Council which came into

---

[84] See Memorandum of Understanding: Australian Securities and Investments Commission and Commonwealth Director of Public Prosecutions – 1 March 2006, which is accessible at https://download.asic.gov.au/media/3343247/asic-cdpp-mou-march-2006.pdf.

[85] *Corporations Act* 2001 (Cth) ss 766A and 766B.

[86] *Corporations Regulations* 2001 (Cth) Reg 7.1.33.

[87] Insurance Council of Australia, *General Insurance Code of Practice*, 1 January 2020. See http://codeofpractice.com.au/2020/10/ICA001_COP_Literature_Code_OnScreen_RGB_DPS_10.2_LR2.pdf.

operation on 1 July 2017,[88] and the Association of Superannuation Funds of Australia's Insurance in Superannuation Voluntary Code of Practice, which commenced on 1 July 2018.[89] Whilst to date breaches of the provisions of these industry codes of practice have only been enforceable by the respective code governance committees (which are empowered to impose such sanctions as they see fit), as Sect. 5.2 explains reforms that took effect from 1 January 2021 to implement the recommendations of the 2019 FSRC now enable ASIC to pursue a variety of enforcement measures in the event of breaches of the provisions of financial services industry codes of practice.

4.3 *Reviews of Insurance Claims Handling Practices by Australian Regulators*

Over the recent years, ASIC and APRA have increased their scrutiny of the claims handling practices of Australian insurers. In response to media reports about the practices of life insurer CommInsure (including reliance on outdated medical definitions to deny claims; assessing doctors being pressured to change their reports; and the delaying of claims[90]) in 2016 ASIC reviewed the claims handling practices of Australian life insurers. Whilst ASIC's Report 498 on this review did not identify evidence of industry-wide misconduct, it noted with concern that declined claims were higher for policies that were sold directly to consumers in comparison to those that were sold through adviser channels. Report 498 also identified the need for more detailed, consistent and transparent data about life insurance claims to better enable consumers to compare performance indicators between insurers. As an example of good practice Report 498 pointed to the Association of British Insurers' practice of publishing claims payout rates each year, which ASIC noted as having prompted standardisation of policy definitions and improved transparency for consumers.[91] Over the next two years, ASIC and APRA worked collaboratively to improve the consistency in the data about life insurance claims,[92] and in March 2019 the

[88] Financial Services Council, *Life Insurance Code of Practice*, 2017. See https://www.fsc.org.au/policy/life-insurance/code-of-practice/.

[89] Association of Superannuation Funds of Australia, Insurance in Superannuation Voluntary Code of Practice, 1 July 2018 https://www.superannuation.asn.au/policy/insurance-in-superannuation-voluntary-code-of-practice; see also ASIC (13 December 2019) Report 646 'Insurance in Superannuation 2019-20: Industry implementation of the Voluntary Code of Practice'.

[90] See for example Sarah Ferguson 'Money for Nothing' *ABC News* 7 March 2016 http://www.abc.net.au/4corners/money-for-nothing-promo/7217116.

[91] ASIC (12 October 2016) Report 498 'Life insurance claims: An industry review', 6–7.

[92] ASIC 'APRA and ASIC publish key industry data on life insurance claims' (Media Release 17-43MR, 9 November 2017).

regulators published their first joint report on life insurance claims and dispute statistics.[93]

In October 2019, ASIC published Report 633 which set out the findings from its review of over 35,000 TPD claims lodged in 2016 and 2017 with seven of Australia's largest life insurers.[94] ASIC noted with concern the widespread use of restrictive definitions in policies which only provided benefits to claimants that were unable to undertake the activities of daily living, which was a factor in nearly a third of declined TPD claims.[95] ASIC and APRA published a further report on life insurance claims data in June 2019 which summarised the percentage of claims accepted, the length of time taken to pay claims, the number of disputes and policy cancellation rates for life insurance claims lodged in 2018. Similarly to its findings in Report 498 this review found declined claims were higher in policies that were sold directly to consumers than in the case of policies arranged by financial advisors.[96]

In July 2019, ASIC published the findings of its review of industry practices for investigating motor vehicle claims lodged between September 2016 and September 2017.[97] For this review, ASIC examined the records of five insurers accounting for 62% of written premiums in the general insurance market, and also interviewed policyholders whose claims had been investigated. The concerning practices identified by ASIC including delays in the resolution of claims; the failure to inform claimants about the investigation process and their rights to make complaints; the practice of requesting onerous amounts of information from claimants[98] and several examples of unfair practices by claims investigators.[99] ASIC's report concluded with several recommendations to improve claims handling practices, including a four-month timeframe for finalising claims. ASIC also warned that in future cases where it identified poor claims handling practices it would consider using its various

[93] ASIC 'APRA and ASIC publish world leading life insurance data' (Media release 19-070MR, 29 March 2019).

[94] ASIC (17 October 2019) Report 633 'Holes in the safety net: A review of TPD insurance claims'.

[95] ASIC (17 October 2019) Report 633 'Holes in the safety net: A review of TPD insurance claims' (17 October 2019), 31–47; 86–96.

[96] ASIC 'APRA and ASIC publish latest data on life insurance claims and disputes' (Media Release 19-160MR, 27 June 2019).

[97] ASIC (4 July 2019) Report 621 Roadblocks and roundabouts: A review of car insurance claim investigations.

[98] Examples of information requested from some claimants included criminal record checks, social media histories, birth certificates, telephone and text message records, financial statements for each of their bank and loan accounts and information about family members and friends. ASIC's review noted that one insurer required some consumers to provide telephone records with an annotated explanation for each call: ASIC Report 621 'Roadblocks and roundabouts: A review of car insurance claim investigations' (4 July 2019), 9.

[99] Examples of the harmful investigative practices included the use of lengthy interviews, contacting claimants at irregular hours and interviewing some claimants in their homes: ASIC (4 July 2019) Report 621 'Roadblocks and roundabouts: A review of car insurance claim investigations', 7.

enforcement powers, including the power to pursue civil penalty proceedings for breaches of the s 13 duty of utmost good faith.[100]

In addition to the reviews of claims handling practices discussed above, ASIC has conducted a number of reviews of industry practices in the selling of insurance.[101] ASIC also conducted a more broadly-focused review of corporate governance practices of seven of Australia's largest financial institutions in 2018, which included four banks, one general insurer and two large diversified financial institutions (one of which issued life insurance), and released its findings from this review in Report 631 in October 2019.[102] ASIC's review focused on the oversight by directors and officers of non-financial risk—which ASIC's review defined as encompassing operational risk,[103] compliance risk[104] and conduct risk.[105] In its report ASIC emphasised the importance of directors formulating clear 'risk appetite statements' with both leading and lagging indicators, and holding management to account against the metrics in such risk appetite statements.[106] Report 631 also highlighted the important role of board risk committees in ensuring the timely flow of material information to boards about non-financial risk matters.[107]

It is also relevant to note that under s 180 of the Corporations Act, directors and officers of Australian corporations[108] have generalised obligations to discharge their duties with the degree of care and diligence that a reasonable person would exercise if they had the same responsibilities in a corporation in similar circumstances. Contraventions of s 180 may be attract civil liability (for example, claims for

---

[100] *Insurance Contracts Act* 1984 (Cth) Part IXA - Enforcement.

[101] See for example ASIC (October 2014) Report 415 'Review of the sale of home insurance'; ASIC (February 2016) Report 470 'Buying add-on insurance in car yards: Why it can be hard to say no'; ASIC (September 2016) Report 492 'A market that is failing consumers: The sale of add-on insurance through car dealers'; and ASIC (11 July 2019) Report 622 'CCI Poor value products and harmful sales practices'.

[102] ASIC (October 2019) Report 631, Corporate Governance Taskforce: Director and officer oversight of non-financial risk report.

[103] ASIC defined 'operational risk' as encompassing the risk of loss resulting from inadequate or failed internal processes, people and systems or from external events, and explained that it included legal risk but excluded strategic and reputational risk.

[104] ASIC defined 'compliance risk' as encompassing the risk of legal or regulatory sanctions, material financial loss or loss to reputation an organisation may suffer as a result of its failure to comply with laws, regulations, rules, related self-regulatory organisation standards and codes of conduct applicable to its activities.

[105] ASIC defined 'conduct risk' as encompassing the risk of unethical or unlawful behaviour on the part of an organisation's management or employees.

[106] ASIC (October 2019) Report 631, Corporate Governance Taskforce: Director and officer oversight of non-financial risk report, 11–24.

[107] ASIC (October 2019) Report 631, Corporate Governance Taskforce: Director and officer oversight of non-financial risk report, 26–50.

[108] Under the *Insurance Act* 1973 (Cth), which regulates the authorisation by APRA of general insurers, and the *Life Insurance Act* 1995 (Cth), which regulates the authorisation by APRA of life insurers, insurers must be registered Australian corporations to carry on an insurance business in Australia.

damages by members, creditors and/or other affected persons) and also be subject to civil penalty proceedings by ASIC.[109] All decisions thus far by Australian courts on alleged breaches of s 180 have related to financial liabilities incurred by the relevant companies—particularly the failure by listed companies to disclose market-sensitive information to financial markets such as the Australian Securities Exchange in a timely manner. However, in light of both the enhanced focus by ASIC on the oversight of non-financial risk by directors and officers of financial institutions, and as Sect. 5.2 discusses, ASIC's 'why not litigate?' mantra following the recommendations of the 2019 FSRC, it is quite possible that the coming years may see decisions by Australian courts on the duties of directors and officers in relation to the oversight of non-financial risk.

5 The 2019 FSRC: Key Findings and Reform Recommendations

On 1 December 2017, in response to widespread reports of misconduct within the Australian financial services industry, the federal government announced the appointment of former High Court of Australia judge the Honourable Kenneth Hayne AC QC to chair a Royal Commission into Misconduct in the Banking, Superannuation and Financial Services Industry. Following seven rounds of hearings throughout 2018 involving the examination of over 130 witnesses and the review of over 10,000 public submissions, Commissioner Hayne presented his final report to the Federal Treasurer on 1 February 2019, which was made public on 4 February 2019. Whilst the final report of the FSRC identified numerous instances of misconduct within Australian banks and superannuation funds (including the charging of fees on the accounts of deceased customers, delays in reporting breaches to regulators and pressure selling), the discussion below focuses on the findings of misconduct within Australian insurers.

5.1 FSRC Findings in Relation to Insurance Claims Handling and ASIC's Enforcement Practices

In its sixth round of hearings, the FSRC examined the practices of Australian general and life insurers across all stages of the insurance process from design and sale of insurance products to the handling of insurance claims. In relation to the design of insurance products, the FSRC identified several examples of policies with outdated definitions and/or overly restrictive exclusions, which lessened the circumstances under which consumers might be entitled to successfully claim on such policies. The

[109] Under s 1317E of the *Corporations Act* 2001, s 180 is a designated civil penalty provision.

FSRC also identified several instances of problematic selling of insurance products, including misrepresentations or omissions about policy premiums and/or payment arrangements, and pressure selling whereby sales agents did not provide consumers with sufficient opportunities to review policy documents before committing to purchase insurance products.

The final report of the FSRC included three case studies of unsatisfactory claims handling practices. The first of these case studies concerned the practices of TAL Life Ltd in handling claims under income protection policies. These included the excessive use of private surveillance; bullying tactics and offensive communications with claimants; and misuse of daily activities diaries by claimants. The FSRC also found that TAL had failed to provide several claimants with an adequate opportunity to respond to the proposed declinature of their claims; that its IDR processes lacked independence from its claims management functions; and that it had failed to engage with the former Financial Ombudsman Service[110] in an open and cooperative manner.[111]

The FSRC's final report included two case studies of misconduct in the handling of general insurance claims. The first of these case studies concerned the insurer Youi Pty Ltd which had failed to exercise appropriate oversight of a builder that it had engaged to repair a policyholder's house in the NSW mining town of Broken Hill following a hailstorm. The delays in repairing the hail-damaged property (which totalled almost two years) had left the pregnant homeowner exposed to lead dust. In another claim following a tropical cyclone, Youi had failed to ensure the completion of repairs to the damaged house of a policyholder's house, and had also failed to arrange emergency accommodation for the policyholders in a timely manner. These omissions lead Commissioner Hayne to conclude that Youi had breached several provisions of the General Insurance Code of Practice in force at the time.[112]

The second of the FSRC's general insurance claims handling case studies examined the practices of insurer AAI Ltd (AAI) in handling of a claim for storm damage. The FSRC found that AAI had breached several provisions of the General Insurance Code of Practice that required it to handle claims in an honest, fair, transparent and timely manner; and other Code provisions requiring it to keep the policyholders updated about the progress of their claim. Commissioner Hayne also condemned AAI for its failures to properly inform the policyholders about its internal dispute resolution processes—noting that whilst AAI had initially offered to settle the policyholders' claim for $30,000, the former Financial Ombudsman Service later awarded the policyholders $744,000 for the cost of repairing their house.[113]

The final report of the FSRC was also highly critical of ASIC's tendency to respond to instances of misconduct in the Australian financial services industry by

[110] As explained in Sect. 4.2, the functions of the former Financial Ombudsman Service were assumed by the Australian Financial Complaints Authority on 1 July 2018.

[111] Hayne (2019). Volume 2: Case Studies, pp. 331–352.

[112] Hayne (2019). Volume 2: Case Studies, pp. 415–431.

[113] Hayne (2019). Volume 2: Case Studies, pp. 445–455.

resorting to enforcement measures at lower levels of the enforcement pyramid such as enforceable undertakings and infringement notices. As Commissioner Hayne put it:

> It is wholly consistent with the analyses that are expressed by the metaphor of the regulatory pyramid, that serious breaches of law by large entities call for the highest level of regulatory response. And that is what has been missing . . . Too often serious breaches of law by large entities have yielded nothing more than a few infringement notices, an enforceable undertaking not to offend again (with or without an immaterial "public benefit payment") or some agreed form of media release.[114]

Commissioner Hayne therefore recommended that when determining the enforcement action(s) to take in response to future instances of misconduct in the financial services industry, ASIC's first question should be: 'Why not litigate?'.[115] ASIC accepted Commissioner Hayne's recommendations by revising its enforcement strategy to involve greater use of court-based sanctions.[116]

Commissioner Hayne referred a total of 17 instances of misconduct to ASIC for further investigation, which included the misconduct by Youi in its handling of general insurance claims, and by TAL in its handling of life insurance claims discussed above. ASIC subsequently commenced proceedings against both insurers in the Federal Court of Australia (the Federal Court).

On 27 November 2020, Chief Justice Allsop declared that Youi had breached its duty of utmost good faith under s 13 of the ICA through its failure to exercise appropriate oversight of the contracted builder in its handling of the Broken Hill hail damage claim that had been reviewed by the FSRC. As Youi's misconduct had occurred before 13 March 2019 (when as noted in Sect. 4.1 reforms were made to the ICA enabling ASIC to seek pecuniary penalties for breaches of the duty of utmost good faith came into effect) ASIC was only able to seek declarations that Youi had breached the s 13 duty.[117]

ASIC also commenced proceedings in the Federal Court against TAL in respect of its handling of life insurance claims. ASIC alleged that through its misconduct TAL had breached its duty of utmost good faith under s 13 of the ICA, and that it had engaged in false or misleading conduct in breach of ss 12DA and 12DB of the ASIC Act, and s 1041H of the Corporations Act. In his judgement on 9 March 2021, Allsop CJ found that whilst ASIC's claims of false or misleading conduct had not been made out. Nevertheless, his Honour found that through its failure to inform the policyholder that it was examining her medical history; its failure to provide her with the opportunity to address the material that TAL was relying upon to decline her

[114] Hayne (2019). Volume 1, p. 433.

[115] Hayne (2019). Volume 1, p. 427.

[116] ASIC 'ASIC update on implementation of Royal Commission recommendations' (Media Release 19-035MR, 19 February 2019).

[117] *Australian Securities and Investments Commission v Youi Pty Ltd* [2020] FCA 1701.

claim; and its failure to make inquiries of her treating medical professionals, TAL had breached its duty of utmost good faith under s 13 of the ICA.[118]

5.2 *FSRC Reform Recommendations*

In his final report, Commissioner Hayne made a total of 76 recommendations for law and/or policy reform, with the Australian government accepting all these reform recommendations.[119] Following a consultation process during which exposure drafts of the new legislative provisions were released for feedback from stakeholders, these reforms were enacted to take effect at various times during 2021. The discussion below focuses on the reforms that relate most closely to insurance claims handling.

5.2.1 Making Insurance Claims Handling a Financial Service

A significant recommendation of the 2019 FSRC was the removal of the exemption of insurance claims handling from the definition of 'financial services' under the Corporations Act.[120] Commissioner Hayne accepted ASIC's submission that 'for consumers, the intrinsic value of an insurance product lies in the ability to make a successful claim when an insured event occurs',[121] and from this basis reasoned that:

> There can be no basis in principle or in practice to say that obliging an insurer to handle claims efficiently, honestly and fairly is to impose on the individual insurer, or the industry more generally, a burden it should not bear. If it were to be said that it would place an extra burden of cost on one or more insurers or on the industry generally, the argument would itself be the most powerful demonstration of the need to impose the obligation.[122]

Reforms to implement Commissioner Hayne's recommendation for removing the exemption of claims handling from the ambit of 'financial services' under the Corporations Act were introduced through the *Financial Sector Reform (Hayne Royal Commission Response) Act* 2020 (Cth), with the new measures taking effect from 1 January 2021.[123] The explanatory memorandum to the *Financial Sector Reform (Hayne Royal Commission Response) Bill* 2020 (Cth) to implement these reforms explained that a person will provide a 'claims handling service' if the person

---

[118] *Australian Securities and Investments Commission v TAL Life Limited (No 2)* [2021] FCA 193.

[119] Department of Treasury (4 February 2019), Restoring trust in Australia's financial system: Government response to the Final Report of the Royal Commission into Misconduct in the Banking, Superannuation and Financial Services Industry - https://treasury.gov.au/publication/p2019-fsrc-response.

[120] Hayne (2019), pp. 308–310.

[121] Hayne (2019), p. 309.

[122] Hayne (2019), p. 309.

[123] *Financial Sector Reform (Hayne Royal Commission Response) Act* 2020 (Cth), s 2.

makes a recommendation or states an opinion that could influence a decision whether to make an insurance claim; assists another person to make an insurance claim; assesses whether an insurer is liable under an insurance product; makes a decision to accept or reject all or part of an insurance claim; quantifies an insurer's liability under an insurance product; offers to settle all or part of an insurance claim; or satisfies a liability of an insurer under an insurance claim.[124]

The explanatory memorandum went on to explain that the persons required to either hold an AFS Licence covering claims handling (or become an authorised representative of such an AFS Licensee), will include an insurer; a loss assessor or loss adjustor acting on behalf of an insurer; an 'insurance fulfilment provider' (a new category of persons including smash repairers, builders and any other tradespeople contracted by an insurer) with authority to reject all or part of a claim; an insurance claims manager; an insurance broker who handles an insurance claim on behalf of the insurer; or a financial adviser who provides claims handling services on behalf of the insurer.[125]

The new measures will require such authorised persons to handle and settle insurance claims in a timely way, without undue delay, balancing the negative effects of delay on consumers with the insurer's reasonable requirements for handling an insurance claim; in the least onerous and intrusive way possible, including requesting information, medical examinations, surveillance and undertaking other assessment methods if it is strictly relevant to the claim; fairly and transparently, with information about the handling process, the reason for information requests, and reasons for decisions provided to consumers; and in a manner that ensures adequate support is provided for consumer, particularly for vulnerable consumers (for example those experiencing financial hardship).[126]

The explanatory memorandum provided indicative examples of conduct that could be inconsistent with the new requirements for ensuring that claims are handled efficiently, honestly and fairly and therefore possibly result in ASIC enforcement action.[127]

In cases where an insurer is offering to settle a claim through a cash settlement instead of repairing or replacing the insured property or product, the insurer will be required to provide a Cash Settlement Fact Sheet, which will be required to set out the basis for the proposed settlement amount and statements that the client should

[124] Explanatory memorandum, *Financial Sector Reform (Hayne Royal Commission Response) Bill* 2020, para 7.13.

[125] Explanatory memorandum, *Financial Sector Reform (Hayne Royal Commission Response) Bill* 2020, para 7.16.

[126] Explanatory memorandum, *Financial Sector Reform (Hayne Royal Commission Response) Bill* 2020, para 7.28.

[127] Explanatory memorandum, Financial Sector Reform (Hayne Royal Commission *Response) Bill* 2020, paras 7.27–7.40.

consider obtaining independent financial advice in respect of the proposed settlement.[128]

The explanatory memorandum also explained that an insurer's failure to provide a Cash Settlement Fact Sheet, or the provision of a defective Cash Settlement Fact Sheet, could trigger the general offence, civil penalty and civil liability provisions in Division 7 of Part 7.7 of the Corporations Act.[129]

On 27 November 2020, ASIC released a draft information sheet setting out its approach to regulating insurance claims handling as a financial service, which sets out further details of ASIC's expectations on the contents of 'Cash Settlement Fact Sheets' for general insurance claims.[130] It is likely that ASIC will release further regulatory guidance on these matters in the near future.

5.2.2 Making Industry Codes Legally Enforceable

Whilst the industry codes of practice overviewed in Sect. 4.2 have to date only been enforceable by the relevant code governance committees,[131] as Sect. 5.2.1 explained the 2019 FSRC Report identified several instances where the sales and claims handling practices of Australian insurers had breached the provisions of the General Insurance Code of Practice. Commissioner Hayne therefore recommended that the provisions of Australia's financial services industry codes should be legally enforceable.[132]

Reforms to implement this recommendation were introduced into the Corporations Act through the *Financial Sector Reform (Hayne Royal Commission Response) Act* 2020, with these new measures taking effect from 1 January 2021. Under these new measures, ASIC now has the role of approving financial services industry codes of conduct, and may designate certain provisions of such codes as enforceable code provisions.[133] If a person (such as an insurer) holds out that they comply with an approved code of conduct, the Corporations Act now provides for the imposition of civil penalties in the event of a breach of an enforceable code provision.[134]

---

[128] Explanatory memorandum, *Financial Sector Reform (Hayne Royal Commission Response) Bill* 2020, para 7.41–7.48.

[129] Explanatory memorandum, *Financial Sector Reform (Hayne Royal Commission Response) Bill* 2020, para 7.49–7.59.

[130] ASIC 'ASIC releases draft information sheet for insurance claims handling' (Media Release 20-300MR, 27 November 2020).

[131] However, as Enright and Merkin explained in 2015, adherence to the provisions of codes of practice may be one of the factors for ASIC and/or the courts to consider in determining whether an insurer had engaged in unconscionable conduct, or a breach of the duty of utmost good faith under s 13 of the ICA: Enright and Merkin (2015), p. 340.

[132] Hayne (2019), p. 24 - Recommendation 1.15 (Enforceable code provisions).

[133] *Corporations Act* 2001 (Cth) s 1101A.

[134] *Corporations Act* 2001 (Cth) s 1101AC.

5.2.3 Extension of the Unfair Contract Terms Regime to Insurance Contracts

As Sect. 4.1 explained, the unfair contract terms regime under the ASIC Act has until now not applied insurance contracts. Whilst the extension of the ASIC Act unfair contract terms regime to insurance contracts was previously considered at the time of the consultations leading to the 2013 amendments to the ICA,[135] prompting mixed reactions from industry commentators,[136] these proposed reforms were not implemented at that time. However, following the recommendations of a 2017 Senate Economics Committee inquiry into the Australian general insurance industry,[137] the Australian government announced that it would extent the unfair contract terms regime to insurance contracts.[138] In light of the misconduct identified during the 2019 FSRC, Commissioner Hayne also recommended that the ASIC Act unfair contract terms regime be extended to contracts of insurance governed by the ICA.[139]

These recommendations were implemented through the *Financial Sector Reform (Hayne Royal Commission Response - Protecting Consumers (2019 Measures)) Act* 2020, which makes several amendments to both the ASIC Act and s 15 of the ICA to extend the ASIC Act unfair contracts regime to insurance contracts governed by the ICA with effect from 5 April 2021.

Under Division 2 of the ASIC Act, a term in a consumer financial services contract may be considered unfair if it meets the three criteria in s 12BG of the ASIC Act—which are that the term would cause a significant imbalance in the parties' rights and obligations arising under the contract; that the term is not reasonably necessary to protect the legitimate interests of the party that would be advantaged by the term; and that the term would cause detriment to a party if it were to be applied or relied on.[140] If a term of a consumer contract is found to be unfair, the term may be declared void.[141]

The explanatory memorandum to the *Financial Sector Reform (Hayne Royal Commission Response – Protecting Consumers (2019 Measures)) Bill* 2019 which implemented these reforms provided several indicative examples of terms in

---

[135]The *Insurance Contracts Amendment (Unfair Terms) Bill* 2013 (Cth) proposed to incorporate a mirror provision to s 12BG of the *ASIC Act* into a new s 15B of the ICA; however, this proposal was not adopted. See e.g. Mann and Drummond (2016), p. 10.

[136]See for example Merkin (2012), pp. 272–298 (arguing against the proposed extension) and Nattrass (2012), pp. 299–311 (arguing in favour of the proposed extension).

[137]Parliament of Australia (August 2017) Senate Economics References Committee, Australia's general insurance industry: Sapping consumers of the will to compare, 65.

[138]Australian Government (December 2017) Response to the Senate Economics References Committee Report - Senate Economics References Committee, Australia's general insurance industry: Sapping consumers of the will to compare.

[139]Hayne (2019), p. 32 – Recommendation 4.7 (Application of unfair contract term provisions to insurance contracts).

[140]*Australian Securities and Investments Commission Act* 2001 (Cth) s 12BG.

[141]*Australian Securities and Investments Commission Act* 2001 (Cth) s 12BG.

insurance contracts that could be unfair. These include a term that allows the insurer to, instead of making a repair, elect to settle the claim with a cash payment calculated according to the cost of repair to the insurer, rather than how much it would cost the insured to make the repair; a term that is an unnecessary barrier to the insured lodging a legitimate claim (for example, requiring the payment of a large excess before the insurer considers a claim or requiring the insured to lodge the claim within an unreasonably short timeframe); a term in a disability insurance contract that uses an outdated, and therefore inaccurate and restrictive, medical definition to determine whether the consumer meets the criteria to be eligible to have a claim paid; or a term in a contract that significantly reduces the cover offered where compliance with the preconditions for being covered is unfeasible (for example, a term in a travel insurance policy that only covers loss of luggage when it has been personally attended by the insured at all times).[142]

In preparation for the commencement of these reforms, on 20 October 2020 ASIC released updated regulatory guidance on the extended protections under the new unfair contract terms laws, and advised that it would engage with the industry in preparation for the commencement of these new measures.[143]

In summary, the new measures introduced through the reforms enacted in response to the FRSC's recommendations now enable ASIC to respond more effectively to instances of deficient claims handling practices such as those highlighted by the FSRC in the Youi and AAI case studies. These newly enacted reforms bring Australia's regulatory framework in line with the standards envisioned by ICP 19.10.

6 Conclusion and Key Lessons for Other Jurisdictions Considering Similar Regulatory Reforms

In conclusion, whilst the handling of insurance claims can often be a lengthy and complex process involving factual investigations, consideration of the application of policy conditions, the engagement of external service providers and negotiated forms of settlements, it is imperative to bear in mind that for policyholders their perceptions of the value of their insurance arrangements will usually be determined by their claims experiences. These perceptions will in turn influence consumer confidence in specific insurance markets. This chapter has provided two examples of how the legal frameworks in the United Kingdom and in Australia now enable the respective supervisory agencies to effectively regulate the claims handling process in a manner that reflects the standards envisioned under the IAIS Insurance Core

[142] Explanatory Memorandum, *Financial Sector Reform (Hayne Royal Commission Response – Protecting Consumers (2019 Measures)) Bill* 2019, para 1.23.

[143] 'ASIC updates information sheets on new protections under the unfair contract terms laws' ASIC Media Release 20-248MR (20 October 2020).

Principles. As it is probable that the FCA in the United Kingdom and ASIC in Australia will be increasingly active in utilising their enforcement powers in response to future instances of poor claims handling practices, it is suggested that the application of the laws relating to claims handling in these two jurisdictions will be of interest to governments, regulators, insurers and policyholders in other jurisdictions in the years to come.

References

Legislation

Australian Securities and Investments Commission Act 2001 (Cth)
Corporations Act 2001 (Cth)
Corporations Regulations 2001 (Cth)
Financial Sector Reform (Hayne Royal Commission Response) Act 2020 (Cth)
Financial Services and Markets Act 2000 (UK)
Insurance Act 1973 (Cth)
Insurance Contracts Act 1984 (Cth)
Life Insurance Act 1995 (Cth)

Bills and Explanatory Memoranda

Explanatory Memorandum, *Financial Sector Reform (Hayne Royal Commission Response – Protecting Consumers (2019 Measures)) Bill* 2019
Explanatory memorandum, *Financial Sector Reform (Hayne Royal Commission Response) Bill* 2020
Insurance Contracts Amendment (Unfair Terms) Bill 2013 (Cth)

Cases

Australian Securities and Investments Commission v TAL Life Limited (No 2) [2021] FCA 193
Australian Securities and Investments Commission v Youi Pty Ltd [2020] FCA 1701
CGU Insurance Ltd v AMP Financial Planning Pty Ltd [2007] HCA 36
Dumitrov v SC Johnson and Son Superannuation Pty Ltd and Anor [2006] NSWSC 1372
Dumitrov v SC Johnson and Son Superannuation Pty Ltd (No 2) [2007] NSWSC 42
Hannover Life Re of Australasia Ltd v Dargan [2013] NSWCA 57
Hannover Life Re of Australasia Ltd v Sayseng [2005] NSWCA 214
Lazarevic v United Super Pty Ltd [2014] NSWSC 96
Sayseng v Kellogg Superannuation Pty Ltd and Anor [2003] NSWSC 945
Wheeler v FSS Trustee Corp Atf First State Superannuation Scheme [2016] NSWSC 534
Wyllie v National Mutual Life Association of Aust Ltd [1997] NSWSC 146

Policy Statements and Regulatory Guidelines

ASIC (March 2002) Regulatory Guide 8 'Hearings practice manual'
ASIC (July 2016) Regulatory Guide 36 Licensing: Financial product advice and dealing
ASIC (July 2013) Regulatory Guide 98 Licensing: Administrative action against financial services providers
ASIC (February 2015) Regulatory Guide 100 Enforceable Undertakings
ASIC (October 2011) Regulatory Guide 168 'Disclosure: Product Disclosure Statements and other disclosure obligations'
ASIC (July 2018) Regulatory Guide 267 'Oversight of the Australian Financial Complaints Authority'
ASIC (July 2020) Regulatory Guide 271 'Internal dispute resolution'
ASIC (September 2013) Information Sheet 151 'ASIC's approach to enforcement'

Other Rules

Australian Financial Complaints Authority, *Complaint Resolution Scheme Rules* (25 April 2020)

Memoranda of Understanding

Memorandum of Understanding: Australian Securities and Investments Commission and Commonwealth Director of Public Prosecutions (1 March 2006). https://download.asic.gov.au/media/3343247/asic-cdpp-mou-march-2006.pdf

Official Reports

Wallis S (1997) Financial System Inquiry, Final Report of the Financial System Inquiry. Canberra: Australian Government Publishing Service
Parliament of Australia (August 2017) *Senate Economics References Committee, Australia's general insurance industry: Sapping consumers of the will to compare*
Hayne K (4 February 2019) Royal Commission into Misconduct in the Banking, Superannuation and Financial Services Industry Final Report. Canberra, Australian Government Publishing Service. https://financialservices.royalcommission.gov.au/Pages/reports.aspx
Ramsay I, Abramson J, Kirkland A (2017) Final Report: Review of the Financial System External Dispute Resolution and Complaints Framework Canberra Department of the Treasury. https://treasury.gov.au/sites/default/files/2019-03/R2016-002_EDR-Review-Final-report.pdf

Regulatory Reports

Financial Conduct Authority (May 2014) Thematic Review TR 14/8: Insurers' management of claims - Household and retail travel

Financial Conduct Authority (May 2014) Perceptions of insurers management of claims: Findings from a survey of members of the Chartered Insurance Institute. https://www.fca.org.uk/publication/research/tr14-08-cii-survey.pdf
ASIC (October 2014) Report 415 Review of the sale of home insurance
Financial Conduct Authority (May 2015) 'Thematic Review TR 14/19: Handling of insurance claims for Small and Medium-sized Enterprises (SMEs)
ASIC (February 2016) Report 470 'Buying add-on insurance in car yards: Why it can be hard to say no'
ASIC (September 2016) Report 492 'A market that is failing consumers: The sale of add-on insurance through car dealers'
ASIC (12 October 2016) Report 498 'Life insurance claims: An industry review'
ASIC (4 July 2019) Report 621 'Roadblocks and roundabouts: A review of car insurance claim investigations'
ASIC (11 July 2019) Report 622 'CCI Poor value products and harmful sales practices'
ASIC (October 2019) Report 631 'Corporate Governance Taskforce: Director and officer oversight of non-financial risk report'
ASIC (17 October 2019) Report 633 'Holes in the safety net: A review of TPD insurance claims'
ASIC (13 December 2019) Report 646 'Insurance in Superannuation 2019-20: Industry implementation of the Voluntary Code of Practice'

Industry Codes of Practice

Association of Superannuation Funds of Australia, Insurance in Superannuation Voluntary Code of Practice, 1 July 2018. https://www.superannuation.asn.au/policy/insurance-in-superannuation-voluntary-code-of practice
Financial Services Council, *Life Insurance Code of Practice*, 2017. https://www.fsc.org.au/policy/life-insurance/code-of-practice/
Insurance Council of Australia, *General Insurance Code of Practice*, 1 January 2020. http://codeofpractice.com.au/2020/10/ICA001_COP_Literature_Code_OnScreen_RGB_DPS_10.2_LR2.pdf

International Principles

International Association of Insurance Supervisors, *Insurance Core Principles and ComFrame*. https://www.iaisweb.org/page/supervisory-material/insurance-core-principles
European Insurance and Occupational Pensions Authority (2012) *Guidelines on Complaints Handling by Insurance Undertakings* EIOPA-BoS-12/070

Media Releases

ASIC 'APRA and ASIC publish key industry data on life insurance claims' (Media Release 17-43MR, 9 November 2017)
ASIC 'ASIC update on implementation of Royal Commission recommendations' (Media Release 19-035MR, 19 February 2019)

ASIC 'APRA and ASIC publish world-leading life insurance data' (Media release 19-070MR, 29 March 2019)

ASIC 'APRA and ASIC publish latest data on life insurance claims and disputes' (Media Release 19-160MR, 27 June 2019)

'ASIC updates information sheets on new protections under the unfair contract terms laws' ASIC Media Release 20-248MR (20 October 2020)

Australian Government, *Response to the Senate Economics References Committee Report - Senate Economics References Committee, Australia's general insurance industry: Sapping consumers of the will to compare*, December 2017

ASIC 'ASIC releases draft information sheet for insurance claims handling' (Media Release 20-300MR, 27 November 2020)

Department of Treasury, *Restoring trust in Australia's financial system: Government response to the Final Report of the Royal Commission into Misconduct in the Banking, Superannuation and Financial Services Industry*, 4 February 2019 - https://treasury.gov.au/publication/p2019-fsrc-response

Financial Conduct Authority, Press Release 'The FCA has fined Liberty Mutual Insurance Europe SE £5.2 million for failures in its oversight of mobile phone insurance claims and complaints handling' 29 October 2018

Financial Conduct Authority, Final Notice - Liberty Mutual Insurance Europe SE, 29 October 2018

Financial Conduct Authority, Press Release 'Insurance and coronavirus (Covid-19): our expectations of firms' 19 March 2020

Media Reports

Sarah Ferguson 'Money for Nothing' *ABC News* 7 March 2016. http://www.abc.net.au/4corners/money-for-nothing-promo/7217116

Website Links

Australian Financial Complaints Authority, Funding - https://www.afca.org.au/about-afca/corporate-information/funding

ASIC, Regulatory Resources: https://asic.gov.au/regulatory-resources/

ASIC, Infringement Notices Register http://asic.gov.au/about-asic/asic-investigations-and-enforcement/infringement-notices/

Books

Comino V (2015) Australia's 'Company Law Watchdog': ASIC and Corporate Regulation. Thomson Reuters Law Book Co, Sydney

Enright I, Merkin R (2015) Sutton on insurance law, 3rd edn. Thomson Reuters, Sydney

Lowry J, Rawlings P, Merkin R (2011) Insurance law: doctrines and principles, 3rd edn. Hart Publishing

Walker G, Purves R (eds) (2014) Financial services law, 3rd edn. Oxford University Press

Chapters

Steinberg L (2011) International organisations: their role and interconnectivity in insurance regulation. In: Burling P, Lazarus K (eds) Research handbook on international insurance law and regulation. Edward Elgar Publishing

Journal Articles

Bowley R (2016) The progressive evolution of Australian insurers' duty of utmost good faith to third party claimants. Insur Law J 27:194–213

Box R, Webster T (2013) Evolution not revolution - Insurance Contracts Amendment Act finally passed. Aust Insur Law Bull 28(8):114–119

Legg M, Speirs S (2019) 'Why Not Litigate?' The Royal Commission, ASIC and the Future of the Enforcement Pyramid. Aust Bus Law Rev 47:244–259

Lewis K (2004) When is a financial product not a 'financial product'? Companies Secur Law J 22:103–134

Mann P (2016) The elusive second quadrant of utmost good faith: what is the scope of an insurer's pre-contractual duty of utmost of good faith? Insur Law J 27:176–184

Mann P, Drummond S (2016) Utmost good faith, unconscionable conduct and other notions of fairness - where are we now? Insur Law J 29:1–55

Merkin R (2012) Unfair terms in insurance contracts: a solution in search of a problem (2012). Insur Law J 23:272–298

Nattrass R (2012) Extending the unfair contract terms laws to insurance contracts: is the duty of utmost good faith fair enough? Insur Law J 23:299–311

Tarr J-A (2010) The regulation of insurance intermediaries in the Australian financial services market. Aust Bus Law Rev 28:332–350

Tarr J-A (2015) Accountability 30 years on: Insurance Contracts Act Reform. Aust Bus Law Rev 43:68–74

Business Registration Data as the Best Vehicle to Achieve KYC and AML for Business

Erick Rincón Cárdenas and Valeria Martinez Molano

Abstract To achieve the corporate purpose of a company, it is necessary to follow the regulations that exist in its respective sector, which include not only the adoption of policies and protocols, but also the prevention of fraudulent activities, which can be done through a sufficient knowledge of the customer. It is of greater relevance in the case of insurance companies, which must sufficiently know their client, taking into account their transactions and activities, since the internal decisions that the company takes in relation to the risks it assumes are based on its own corporate governance policies.

For this purpose, this chapter proposes the alternative of implementing RegTech tools through the adoption of a Single Business Registry. This registry contains all the required information from a company, including financial statements for the respective periods, which can be supplemented with records already existing in a country, as this would facilitate regulatory compliance.

1 Introduction

RegTech is a FinTech segment that, through technology, creates solutions to help companies comply with regulatory requirements.[1] Its main objectives are to improve the parameters of regulatory compliance of companies, optimize processes, promote business efficiency, and improve customer service. They are the technological tools that help different entities, mainly financial ones, to comply with the applicable legislation, especially with the normative and regulatory burdens that could be verified through the use of data.

[1] Cermeño (2016).

E. R. Cárdenas (✉) · V. M. Molano (✉)
Universidad del Rosario, Bogotá, D.C., Colombia
e-mail: erick.rincon@urosario.edu.co; valeria.martinez@urosario.edu.co

P. Marano, K. Noussia (eds.), *The Governance of Insurance Undertakings*, AIDA Europe Research Series on Insurance Law and Regulation 6,
https://doi.org/10.1007/978-3-030-85817-9_13

A major category within RegTech is primarily dedicated to compliance, providing the tools for Know Your Customer (KYC) and Anti-Money Laundering (AML) as part of a Customer Due Diligence (CDD) process.

On the other hand, corporate governance is made up of the set of rules, principles, and procedures that regulate the structure and operation of the governing bodies of a company.

The strategic decisions made by the corporate governments of an insurance company must have an accurate data analysis to acquire adequate information about the client and the possible business that may be undertaken with the latter. Thus, having accurate and complete corporate data enables in-depth analysis of agents and customers, which generates appropriate product offering strategies and direct marketing programs.

Properly analyzing the data and knowing the customer causes a significant demand for time and cost, as compliance with the standard implies an essential information requirement. However, it is also necessary to avoid crimes such as money laundering, corruption, and crimes related to drugs and terrorism that may occur in any country through adequate knowledge of the client and the origin of its assets by virtue of the coherence between income and different bank movements.

The certification and business registration entities are essential component within the statistics and operation of the business sector. However, to make its activity more efficient, it is necessary to improve public records at the time of data capture. Under this scenario, this article aims to solve the question: How can insurance companies adopt corporate governance that uses business records to develop KYC or AML to improve their own compliance?

To improve public records and possess the tools for an adequate KYC and AML in insurance companies, it is necessary to consider financial information, including the definition of income, expenses, and profits for the respective period. This is considered the best vehicle to achieve a complete KYC and AML that may benefit the entire industry, especially the insurance industry.

In this context, the information provided during registration could be verified against external sources of information, as well as the set of other delegated registries existing in a country which facilitate business registration to avoid money laundering and other practices. In this way, business records are shown as the central axis of KYC in our society, with the aim of preventing the risk of identity theft both for the ones who hold the status of merchant, as well as for companies, generating greater precision in the analyzation of data when insurance company conducts business.

Obtaining company information from public commercial registers provides the insurance industry protection in its relationships with clients, suppliers, and counterparties, through watch list filtering solutions, KYC, and transaction filtering and monitoring.

Finally, these projects are relevant as most of the registries in a country share data, and the commercial public registries have accurate and updated information on their operations and provide accurate corporate data for an efficient aggregation of risk, obtaining even a more precise actuarial price or profitability relationship and improving compliance with regulations such as KYC and AML, among others, thus providing the insurance market with legal and operational security.

2 An Overview on RegTech

Broadly, it might be thought that regulatory developments and technological advances are not closely related to each other. However, these advances have changed in recent times the nature and way in which financial services are provided. Thus, they have evolved to be in tune with the context that exists at a given time, going from being reactive to the crisis, to considering the digital transformation in developed countries and the growth in digital financial services in developing countries, and finally, to considering the increase in the roles of FinTech and RegTech companies.[2]

In protecting financial consumers, especially insurance consumers, a complete regulation has been generated that implies an increase in costs in the financial system involving insurance companies. For this matter, companies seek mechanisms that tend to facilitate compliance with all regulations, which increased considerably, thus avoiding the imposition of fines.[3]

RegTech was born in this context, as were the technological tools applied to regulatory compliance. This makes it possible to solve the legal problem of a lack of incentive, thus improving competitiveness. RegTech performs online monitoring, which identifies problems or irregularities that may arise; thus, in the event of an atypical value, it is transmitted to the financial institution in charge of determining whether a fraudulent activity was carried out, looking for and identifying possible threats to financial security from the beginning, minimizing risks and costs related to loss of funds and data breaches.[4]

Other authors, like Jake Frankenfield, defined it as "Regtech, or RegTech, consist of a group of companies that use cloud computing technology through software-as-a-service (SaaS) to help businesses comply with regulations efficiently and less expensively. RegTech is also known as regulatory technology."[5]

Under this scenario, RegTech makes it possible to comply with the regulatory burden that currently exists in the different countries on the financial system, which includes insurers, avoiding not only simple breaches, but also the imposition of sanctions for failure to adequately comply with the regulatory burden with respect to multiple aspects. Consumer protection has a special relevance, for which its adequate knowledge is required to guarantee the protection of data, as well as the

[2] Arner et al. (2017), p. 377.
[3] Rincon (2020).
[4] Rincon (2020).
[5] Frankenfield (2019).

possibility of avoiding fraudulent activities that can be committed in the development of these activities.

Likewise, and for the specific case, RegTech represents an important advantage and has an essential purpose in the regulatory compliance of insurance companies. Using technology to manage data and information facilitates compliance with KYC and AML regulations, as well as internal regulations of each state. The foregoing is based on the sense of organization of the information and compliance as having adequate information systems facilitates a permanent audit that guarantees quality and success in insurance companies.

Deloitte[6] establishes that RegTech provides permanent monitoring that improves efficiency in the provision of financial services, freeing up the time generated by the investigation not only of the different regulations and capital invested in it, but also of those related to the sanctions for a certain breach. In this sense, RegTech acts as a tool that enables companies to act proactively and not only reactively, which in turn generates significant economic impacts.

To fulfill the purpose of these technologies that promote compliance, different mechanisms such as artificial intelligence or big data can be used, organizing the multiple data into information that may be useful in regulatory compliance and generating algorithms that identify suspicious activities being carried out, and the existing probabilities that a certain activity can be considered fraudulent within a company.

In addition, RegTech companies collaborate with financial institutions and regulatory bodies, using mechanisms such as cloud computing and big data, which allow information to be shared, since cloud computing is evidently a low-cost technology where data can be shared quickly and securely. In this sense, these companies combine the large volumes of financial information with the data they have from previous regulatory failures to determine, through predictions, areas of potential risk in which special emphasis should be placed.

It is important to note that it is not possible to simplify the entire RegTech panorama as a simple FinTech tool since FinTech has the "know-how" of innovation, but RegTech provides expert knowledge of the industry with special emphasis in the risks that need to be mitigated, offering security to users of financial services.[7]

In this way, although FinTech has an approach that is inherent in the financial system, RegTech has the potential to be applied in a wide range of contexts, based on principles such as Know Your Customer, which is transformed into Know Your Data, consolidating as a regulatory paradigm that must consider multiple aspects and new axes more broadly than the financial sphere.[8]

[6] Deloitte (2016), 07.

[7] Deloitte (2016), 07.

[8] Arner et al. (2017), p. 383.

3 KYC and AML Within Corporate Governance

RegTech favors the incorporation of technological solutions regarding improved regulatory processes and their compliance through new technological developments such as artificial intelligence, machine learning, among others, seeking regulatory reforms using technology in important issues such as anti-money laundering and KYC compliance.[9]

RegTech application can generate important impacts on the financial system, especially in insurance companies taking advantage of the potential that they have to automate and centralize Know Your Consumer (KYC) processes through blockchain technology. This kind of technology is more resistant to modifications and records activities in a transparent manner, which supports the integrity of costs, reducing them when incorporating new clients.[10]

The ease of centralizing KYC processes represents important benefits in companies such as insurance since it streamlines security and management processes in compliance with the regulations of the countries. In this sense, by automating this kind of process, companies can spend less time and resources in the in-depth and manual study of each client with respect to the state guidelines and focus on central tasks of special interest within their business.

The expression "Know Your Customer" or KYC first emerged in the United States in the late 1960s, with the purpose of referring to the specific obligation of loyalty that the broker had, where he must sufficiently know his client to make the appropriate investment recommendations, which are adjusted to one's conditions and needs. However, it was at the beginning of the 1990s that the obligation to know the customer permeated other banking and financial activities, gaining greater relevance since it acquired functions in preventing money laundering; thus, it was consolidated as the obligation to identify and to control clients, thereby seeking to fight money laundering.[11]

In tune with KYC is due diligence in anti-money laundering and fraud detection controls, where together the digitization of the client and partner incorporation processes, information exchange and analysis of data, clients, and transactions is sought.[12]

Considering that the information requirements on clients have increased to prevent terrorist activities and SARLAFT fraudulent businesses, RegTech provides reporting regulation systems, which in turn facilitates regulatory compliance by the actors involved.

On anti-money laundering, RegTech companies have had great relevance since they tend to improve the fight of different financial institutions against financial crimes. As an example, by 2017, based on a Global FinTech study, of 341 RegTech

---

[9] Arner et al. (2017), p. 377.

[10] Rincon (2020).

[11] Bonzom (2011).

[12] Rincon (2020).

companies, more than 53% were mainly dedicated to AML and KYC-related issues.[13]

The need for financial companies, such as insurance companies, to adapt RegTech- related alternatives for KYC and AML is given because of the use of sophisticated methods implemented by crime that aims to make money obtained by illegal means as well as from legitimate funds. Therefore, greater regulation and controls on money laundering are necessary by institutions dedicated to this purpose, which also manage resources from their different clients.[14]

Under this context of the rise of crime by different means, it is necessary to place special emphasis on KYC and AML. Thus, each client or potential client of a financial institution or an insurance company should be properly studied under the requirements that these two precepts bring with them. This process requires special attention and having sufficient documentation regarding identity, income, and provenance of similar funds.[15] Basic and superficial information are not enough, it is requiring depth for the technological tools to acquire the data sufficient to foresee situations that may compromise entities or insurance companies.

The need arises because currently, at the time of making transactions with different companies, whether involved in banking services or providing insurance, insurance entities no longer have enough confidence in traditional risks management systems. These have shown significant shortcomings that raise questions not only to the companies themselves, but also to the insurers, engaging in activities that may be criminal from not having sufficient regulatory support.

Therefore, insurance companies sought technology and apply it to comply with the regulation and different standards, with an emphasis on adequate knowledge of their clients and potential clients by processing the large amount of information and data that they can count on, thereby avoiding the carrying out by the insured of fraudulent activities such as money laundering.

It should be noted that the AML and KYC requirements regarding RegTech were established by the FATF and the Basel Committee, which seek to promote the implementation in different countries of RegTech solutions that not only simplify processes and guarantee regulatory compliance, but also identify transactions that may be suspicious.[16]

In this sense, the importance of RegTech in insurance companies is clear, where it is necessary to have adequate customer information before providing the respective insurance, thus guaranteeing an adequate origin of funds and the legality of all movements made by the insured company, which makes it possible to control not only the activity of the insured but also compliance with the regulation.

The implementation of RegTech tools is not a measure that can be used within an insurance company suddenly and indiscriminately. It is necessary to start making a

[13] Kurum (2020).

[14] Kurum (2020).

[15] Arner et al. (2017), p. 391.

[16] Arner et al. (2017), p. 395.

series of decisions within the company that come from its different organs and are in tune with all its policies and objectives. It is also necessary to consider how these emerging changes that have been brought about by technological advances may have repercussions on insurance companies, making it necessary for the existence of an interaction between corporate law and insurance regulation.

Within any company, especially insurance companies, taking into account the activities they are engaged in, there are circumstances that may make them more or less prone to risk. Therefore, it is not possible to completely eliminate the risks that arise in a company, the most relevant being the conscious acceptance of risk levels, communicating decisions to shareholders to take actions for their mitigation and control, using the tools and standards available.[17]

Based on the above and considering that companies will always have some kind of risk, even the more they try to moderate them, the author Javier Ísmodes Cascón[18] points out that an adequate corporate governance should seek to ensure that risks are understood, managed, and communicated appropriately. Thus, although at the time of conducting legal business controls and audits are carried out, there is no adequate qualification of *ex-ante* risks or those indicators that alert potential risks before they occur. Therefore, to prevent this class of risks in insurance companies, it is required to have an adequate KYC, which tends to identify future clients by investigating the origin of funds and their history of transactions and exchanges.

With respect to insurance companies, in Colombia specifically, the "Federación de Aseguradores Colombianos"—Fasecolda—is constituted, a non-profit entity that groups and represents the insurance sector mainly against surveillance and control entities. In 2007, this body approved the guidelines for establishing a corporate governance code for the Colombian insurance sector, which had as its main objective to offer a framework of behaviors and actions for insurance companies that would provide security, projection of interests, and in general, a responsible management of the entire company.[19]

The code of corporate governance above seeks to mitigate risks, provide transparency, and facilitate decision-making, generating greater confidence and better management of resources to reduce risks.[20]

The relationship between adequate corporate governance, which seeks to make correct decisions and regulatory compliance, is found in Legal Compliance. The action that aims to comply with the standard is the activity of obedience to the standard that is agreed or imposed. In this way, it is aimed at ensuring compliance with the company obligations, providing mechanisms that require adherence, and the study of compliance with current regulations, whether they are mandatory rules or different obligations voluntarily assumed by the company.[21]

---

[17] Cascón (2019), p. 197.

[18] Cascón (2019).

[19] Montañez et al. (2017), p. 27.

[20] Fasecolda (s.f.).

[21] Tejeira (2015).

Under this scenario, the corporate governance of insurance companies is in charge of implementing an adequate legal compliance within their organization, including current regulations. For this, it is important to use the tools that the world provides us, which not only ensure greater compliance, but also create cost effectiveness and efficiency. Thus, it is important that the different corporate governments duly study the possibility of applying RegTech tools within their organization.

4 The New Solution: Business Records

As mentioned, certification and business registration entities currently occupy a crucial role for the proper functioning of companies. They cause the registration of the main information of each society, generating with it a general database with basic information.

Most of the information available to these entities is obtained, in the Colombian case, from the records voluntarily made by the people of their companies, such as notification addresses, subscribed, paid, and authorized capital, corporate purpose, legal representative, among other information, which, although it is highly relevant, is inadequate to fully understand a company and all the activities it carries out, as well as different asset movements.

This lack of information creates the possibility that insurers may provide their services to companies whose assets may be made up of illicit money. This occurs from having inadequate knowledge of the client and lack of a large public database that guarantees transparency in the actions of the different market participants.

In this context, it is proposed as an alternative the obligatory nature of financial and accounting information, including income, expenses, and profits that must be registered in a single business registry, thereby seeking a KYC and AML. Thus, the corporate governance of insurance companies can be based on such records to have the well-founded and sufficient knowledge in insuring a respective client, preventing fraudulent activities and identity theft, and improving the internal compliance of each company.

A single business registry with sufficient information results in in-depth knowledge of the different clients of the insurance companies, taking into account their accounting history and income origin. This translates into an adequate KYC that facilitates better data treatment for AML policies based on RegTech, which are consolidated and capable of carrying out specific actions aimed at preventing fraudulent activities.

It should be noted that, in addition to the implementation of the Single Business Registry with sufficient information, the decisions to adapt it must be implemented within each company, also taking into account the adoption of RegTech tools.

For the implementation of the proposed Single Business Registry, it is important to know some aspects that the legislator must consider for the consolidation of a project of such magnitude. In this sense, a regulation that enables interoperability between the different registration systems present in a country is necessary so that an exchange of information is carried out, reducing costs for entrepreneurs while increasing the quality and updating of the data for the knowledge of the interested parties.

In the case of a country like Colombia, different registration systems have specific functions. There are records for merchants and records for natural or legal persons who intend to carry out contracting processes with the state. In this case, it would be necessary to have a regulation that would enable interoperability between these information systems, enabling the transmission of information. Additionally, the legislature must analyze the possibility of a consolidated system where interested parties can consult the information in the registers without having to go to each one individually.

Additionally, special emphasis must be placed on the legislator at the time of its regulation concerning the information that can be considered sensitive. Although greater publicity and transparency are sought to guarantee the KYC and AML, the monitoring of the personal data protection policies of each state must be considered to have an appropriate regulation that only represents benefits for the market participants.

Based on the above, RegTech promotes good corporate practices in compliance management and improves the results of regulatory compliance. In this sense, it enables the ordinary fulfillment of tasks, reducing operating costs related to the performance of daily tasks in a company.[22]

Given the importance of RegTech's application, Christopher Woorlard, Director of Strategy and Competition at the Financial Conduct Authority—the regulatory body for financial services in the United Kingdom—identified several uses of RegTech that can be highlighted in this case, which, when in tune, may result to the proper functioning of RegTech tools in compliance with the objectives set:

1. Facilitates compliance of companies with legal requirements, such as reports, documentation, among others.
2. By promoting efficiency in compliance, it is aimed at closing the gap between the intention of the regulatory requirements, their subsequent interpretation, and the effective implementation within a company.
3. The implementation of RegTech tools simplifies and helps companies to manage and exploit existing data, facilitating the best decision-making and finding in real time those who are not following the regulations.
4. Finally, the author points out that technologies and innovations give rise to more efficient regulation and compliance processes.[23]

For RegTech to function properly in areas such as KYC and AML, which are the most structured applications to date in financial companies, proper data management must be had, implementing structured data under provisions and rules, using mechanisms such as predictive analytics and machine learning, which help identify inside

---

[22] Geslevich (2018), p. 198.

[23] Woolard (2016).

information, threats and information that may be suspicious and related to fraud and financial crimes, as well as the use of privileged information and misconduct, all of which are collected through data exchanges in the network, such as telephone calls, exchanges in emails, commercial transactions, among others.[24]

As the authors Tom Blutler and Leona O'Brien[25] point out, for the proper management of KYC and AML, a traditional approach of technologies has been used that seek to transform and map the regulation of legal provisions through rules in software codes. However, this can create a solution called "black box" since violations of the regulation may be presented by the client that are not encoded in all its variables. That is, the commission of a certain conduct may be codified, however, there is not only one way to commit it. Hence, when coding it, it generates multiple existing combinations which cannot be entered in the code for the same act, thus some fraudulent behaviors could not be properly avoided.

In this sense, Nizan Geslevich Packin[26] says about the problem, "it requires a carefully tailored design of the technology, a joint effort of the regulators and the private sector, and some shifts in corporate thinking." Therefore, the application of technological tools should not be carried out in isolation, but in tune with the entities and the needs of the private sector and insurance companies.

Under this scenario, there must be an agreement and joint effort between the companies interested in the application of RegTech tools to improve their compliance in relation to KYC and AML and both public and private entities, such as, in the Colombian case, the Chambers of Commerce and DIAN, where they were able to unify the information to a single database, which by implementing tools such as predictive analytics, AI, among others, facilitate the prevention of the commission of crimes and provides sufficient knowledge for companies before carrying out the respective hiring or underwriting.

In addition, the legislator must also consider whether there are limitations for each entity to transfer its information. In this sense, it is necessary to analyze the total legislative panorama of each country to determine the extent of the integration of registers. It is not a question of the elimination of a particular record, since each one seeks the satisfaction of specific objectives, but of a consolidation of information that is complete, updated, and truthful, based on the existing data.

One of the main problems for a correct implementation of the proposal is the proper handling of the data, as it does not only refer to a few of them but to big data, that is, "data that contains a greater variety and that is presented in increasing volumes and at a higher speed."[27]

Among the main challenges that regulators faced and that the Single Business Registry that arises could have is the management and processing of the big data. However, it is at this point where the different regulators must work in tune with

[24] Butler and O'Brien (2019), p. 97.

[25] Butler and O'Brien (2019), p. 40.

[26] Geslevich (2018), p. 194.

[27] Oracle (s.f).

FinTech and Insurtech tools, determining not only the information that is considered relevant for its adequate treatment in line with the proposed objectives, but also the ideal means to collect it, such as through the expansion of the necessary information in the Single Tax Registry, or that which is registered at the time of the renewal of the Commercial Registry or other existing registry systems in the country. For this, regulation is necessary that not only guarantees the implementation of the appropriate tools, without limiting them, but also flexible to the changes necessary for proper operation.

In this sense, an adequate management of information resources and the data themselves is a potential agent of change and transformation for KYC and AML, which paved the way to the introduction of the concept of Know Your Data (KYD), since it is not only a matter of the insurance companies having an incalculable variety of information in their bases, but of the proper use given to it. Therefore, if this information is in the hands of the industry at a general level, efforts in the fight against laundering can be strengthened while reducing certain compliance costs and guaranteeing regulatory compliance of companies.

In this way, by implementing the Single Business Registry for insurance companies, with the goals that have been previously noted, compliance is achieved, which means acting in accordance with internal rules, regulations, laws, and procedures. Thus, when it is indicated that a company is compliant, this means that it complies with the regulations that the regulatory bodies impose, depending on the activities undertaken by it.[28]

For its fulfillment, it now depends to the respective body of each entity responsible for making decisions to implement the information in the Single Business Registry after it has been created, to prevent money laundering and obtain sufficient internal controls for normative compliance and its specific purposes.

The importance of the proposal is given because having an adequate RegTech through a Single Business Registry facilitates the KYC, which provides security on the legality of the clients. However, this has an important precedent in the Financial Action Task Force (FATF), which in 2007 published an important document that addresses market risks, how these should be managed efficiently, as well as the mechanisms to establish minimum due diligence parameters with the client.[29]

Aside from sufficient documentation as support and presence in the registry where insurance companies have access to, it is important to bear in mind that adequate KYC policies must contain the following:

1. Customer acceptance policy
2. Customer identification

[28] Falotico (2017).

[29] Falotico (2017), p. 24.

2.1. General identification requirements
2.2. Specific identification issues such as: trust accounts, corporate vehicles, business presented, client accounts, political persons, clients not present, and correspondent banking

3. Continuous account and transaction tracking
4. Risk management[30]

In this sense, both banks and insurance entities implementing RegTech policies must seek to sufficiently know the identity of their clients, control the activities they carry out, and take into account their account information to determine the transactions that are not within their normal business or those that are expected for the type of client or account. In this sense, the KYC is a necessary element in risk management and control, and it is essential that it is supported by compliance evaluations and internal audits.[31]

Finally, as an additional aspect for a possible RegTech implementation in the insurance area, in 2018 the IV International Congress of Insurance Law was held in Colombia, where the Financial Superintendence of Colombia, the body in charge of regulating the country's the financial market, announced that it will launch three tools that aim to promote and seek to facilitate innovation in the financial system, namely:[32]

- The hub, which acts as a meeting point for entities so that those interested in the FinTech sector can exchange information.
- "La Arenera," which through a control environment and in real time, facilitates the development of products, technologies, or business models.
- Finally, and with special relevance for this work, the aim is to implement RegTech, aiming through its use, by the Superintendency, to streamline and optimize internal processes in regulatory matters, thanks to the use of technological developments.

By implementing RegTech tools, the Financial Superintendency, in tune with the chambers of commerce, could exchange their information and generate a complete source of information that can be consulted by those interested. Thus, not only would it provide companies with an adequate KYC, the same superintendence could also more efficiently exercise its supervisory function, seeking compliance with the regulations by all insurance companies.

---

[30] Bank of Spain (2002).

[31] Bank of Spain (2002).

[32] Bermúdez (2018), p. 62.

5 The Sources of Information in the Business Registry

To have a single business registry that contains all the necessary information for RegTech to have an adequate management of KYC and AML, it is necessary that such information is complete and is obtained by contrasting the different external and internal sources of information on which a company can count. Hence, the importance of information is evident, as indicated by Arias and Portela,[33]

Las organizaciones empresariales son concebidas como entidades procesadoras de información, independientemente de su actividad, ya que todas las empresas tienen necesidad de obtener y analizar información actualizada sobre mercados, costos, ventas y procesos de producción. Esta información procede tanto de fuentes internas como fuentes externas a la organización, y, una vez procesada y utilizada, genera, a su vez, nueva información que será difundida dentro y fuera de la empresa (p. 11).

Translated to English as follows:

Business organizations are conceived as information processing entities, regardless of their activity, since all companies need to obtain and analyze updated information on markets, costs, sales, and production processes. This information comes from both internal and external sources to the organization, and once processed and used, generates, in turn, new information that will be disseminated inside and outside the company (p. 11).

It is the information which provides enough tools for adequate compliance that promotes knowledge of the client and avoids fraudulent activities. Although the company may possess internal information provided by the client, it is necessary that this information be contrasted with external sources for verification, granting a greater degree of certainty and transparency in the actions.

The Single Business Registry must have information systems that take raw data and transform them into knowledge that can be used by companies such as insurance. Thus, the information system can be defined as *"un conjunto de procedimientos ordenados, que proporcionan información efectiva para apoyar la Toma de Decisiones y, con ello, asegurar el control de la organización"*; translated to English as "a set of ordered procedures, which provide effective information to support Decision Making and, with it, ensure control of the organization."[34]

In this measure, it is not enough to indiscriminately obtain the information reported by companies and potential clients, it is necessary to organize and adapt it in a way that represents a true utility. In the case of insurance companies, they must contain clearly and easily accessible information on potential policyholders, with access to assets, liabilities, and current income, in addition to the requirements that insurance companies consider aspects of study at the time of making an assurance.

Having the information that facilitates the adequate execution of the company's corporate purpose and proper management is a key element for the development or

[33] Arias and Portela (1997), p. 11.

[34] Arias and Portela (1997), p. 12.

maintenance of advantages within a company; in this way, the required information and the possible sources of collection for such information must be clearly identified to define a structure for its processing, communication, and implementation with respect to clients and in decision-making.[35]

The information that business records should have should be obtained mainly from external sources of information. The internal sources are those internal documents and records of operations of a company, generated through reports of departments, procedures, and products. This kind of information makes it possible to know the conditions of insurance companies to insure other companies, analyzing the level of risk that it can assume, among others—factors necessary for making decisions from within.

In this regard, as indicated by UMB Virtual, external sources provide information generated outside the company, such as publications by public entities, development or international organizations, associations, directories, databases, or the press. It is generally the information to which a company refers because it is outside its scope and normal course of business and operation. In this sense, a Single Business Registry must go to these external sources to obtain its information, based on existing registries and on the obligation to register certain information by companies.

In this sense, insurance companies could have a wide range of information not only internal for them to know their business scope, but also about potential clients by consulting a single information system complete enough to avoid isolated consultation of different information bases. In the same Registry, everything that is necessary for an adequate management of all its objectives is found.

It is necessary to note that although there are already records that contain different information from companies, the majority have basic information such as: (i) general data (including ID number, address, corporate purpose, among others), (ii) establishment and branches, (iii) administrators, (iv) legal publications, (v) press publications, and (vi) commercial references and suppliers. These show the lack of information regarding the commercial activities of the companies and the relationships between assets, liabilities, and profits.

The foregoing is relevant because it is known that in a country like Colombia a company can have broad social objects, where "any legal activity" is indicated, which can open multiple possibilities that a company can carry out, making it difficult to really monitor and control by the interested parties, such as insurance companies. Additionally, although what is related to the publicity of a company's accounting information is questionable, certain information is necessary for entities such as banks, as its record makes it easier to detect the possible performance of suspicious activities.

Companies such as "Einforma" in Colombia prepare reports on different companies, which include not only basic information, but also evaluations of commercial risk, financial situation, of establishments, commercial references, commercial policies, shareholders, and occupational risk, among others. This platform uses sources

[35] Virtual UMB (s.f).

of primary business information, taken from public sources and the media, and sources of secondary business information, which comes directly from the company.

While it has a complete record of essential information that could be useful for insurance companies, this information is not public, so payment must be made to access it. This is understood at present since a private company collects the data and consolidates it as useful information. However, if there were already a public access tool where it is mandatory for companies to register certain information, the costs to access it could decrease, the tool being public makes access simpler and updated.

In conclusion, it can be established that the different companies, especially insurance entities, rely on external sources of information to implement RegTech tools for an appropriate KYC and AML, facilitating the fulfillment of the information needs, providing updated, relevant, reliable, and valid information—information that is necessary to solve questions and make hiring and assurance decisions[36].

6 Some Difficulties in Its Application

Finally, following the concept of the author Nizan Geslevich Packin[37], it is worth highlighting some difficulties in the RegTech application that cause it to be infrequently used with respect to the challenges of corporate governance, among which the following can be highlighted:

1) The motivation of market participants to assist in the formation of a common solution is unclear. In this sense, the cost/benefit analysis for compliance with regulatory obligations is partial, since it only covers the individual operational response of a specific entity, rather than the entire industry, which limits the ability to devise a common solution.

This difficulty would not be visible in the proposed registry, since a Registry with the aforementioned information and characteristics would provide important solutions for a large percentage of companies not only in the insurance industry but also in different sectors of the economy. In this sense, as indicated above, a Registry with general and accounting information, and with the main transactions, would provide assurances to companies at the time of hiring, having security of the identification and knowledge of their client, which in turn facilitates regulatory compliance and prevents fraudulent activities.

2) There is a lack of a general mandate or even an established standard on RegTech solutions. As indicated by the author, technology providers, finance companies, and legislators are reluctant to establish dialogue on common solutions, making their implementation more difficult for companies.

[36] ComuExter13 (2017).

[37] Geslevich (2018), p. 211.

This approach is shared with the author since RegTech and the possible solutions that its implementation can provide are currently seen as a scenario in the development process, which is why the information about it is scarce, even more so its possibilities of implementation.

Colombia is still in a process of identifying, recognizing, and starting the implementation of technology in different fields, which is why the lack of general knowledge and guidelines on RegTech results in its lack of use and homogeneity in policies that would have benefited all participants in an industry such as insurance.

Thus, a solution to this difficulty is the dialogue between the different parties that provide managing solutions for regulatory compliance, implementing technological tools, thereby providing greater visibility to RegTech solutions in achieving objectives and reducing operating costs.

3) The complexity in the connection and interaction of regulatory initiatives makes it difficult to adopt common solutions. In addition, difficulties in relation to data protection can constitute an obstacle to the efficient exchange of information.

As stated, the difficulty related to the security of the information and the privacy of the same within a company is recognized. Although the obligation for certain information is proposed to facilitate its access and consultation, the problems that this could bring with it on data protection is undeniable. Thus, it is necessary for RegTech tools and the proposed single business registry to use technology not only to guarantee the transparency of the information and provide access to it for multiple actors, but also to give security in the proper handling of such information by the companies.

7 Conclusions

Aiming for an adequate regulatory compliance within a company, as well as the need for business efficiency in relation to decision-making for contracting with different clients, thereby preventing and controlling the performance of illegal activities by the insured, the implementation of RegTech was shown as an alternative that facilitates the fulfillment of such objectives, allowing in its application not only the adequate compliance with the legislation and regulatory loads through utilization of data but also providing security and reducing costs.

As authors such as Douglas W. Arner, Jànos Barberis & Ross P. Buckley[38] point out, the implementation of RegTech is not only justifiable in making a financial regulation more effective and affordable for the different stakeholders, but it can also be implemented as a mechanism to reconceptualize and redesign financial regulation, taking into account the transformations that the market has undergone in this regard.

[38] Arner et al. (2017), p. 402.

Considering the relevance of the certification and business registration entities, the implementation of a single business registry with sufficient data for each company taken from different entities within a country, such as the Chamber of Commerce and DIAN, in the Colombian case, was shown as an important element of RegTech application for the consultation of customer information, thus generating an adequate KYC and AML.

Insurance entities can adopt a single registry to develop customer awareness or anti-laundering tools and improve their own compliance from the decisions made by corporate government, thus, a corporate government that is solely responsible for making decisions is not enough. Decisions which are usually based on internal information sources must necessarily use external sources such as the single registry to have sufficient knowledge and provide the insurance company with tools for an adequate risk analysis.

To this extent, for the insurance companies to achieve optimal KYC and AML, the single registry must have the general accounting and financial information of each period as mandatory information. This registry and its subsequent implementation by the corporate government of each company is the best vehicle to achieve a complete business KYC and AML that favors not only the insurance industry, but generally the important sectors of the industry in decision-making.

The idea that business records are the central axis of the KYC of our society is defended, having important functions in preventing the risk of identity theft, such as knowledge of the activities and transactions made, alerting risky actions.

Based on the above, it can be pointed out that the way companies use information is an aspect that allows them to generate competitive advantages between organizations. Thus, as Patricia González and Tatiana Bermúdez[39] point out, the strategic use of information is useful in decision-making, providing changes that have representation and create knowledge.

In the field of insurance companies, having sufficient information through a complete business registry that has the adequate resources and data for greater facilities when providing their services is extremely important, since taking into account the insurance activity which is based mainly on the acceptance and management of risks from third parties, the use of such information reduces the risks inherent to the activity, generating significant advantages for companies not only in their processes but also in economic terms.

Based on the above, to the extent that insurance companies have access to a varied information system associated with clients and therefore to risks, they will have more adequate tools for making business decisions. Having a greater knowledge of the insured object, that is, of the risk and its client, which, as the author Andrea Londoño[40] points out, empowers the insurance companies to implement:

---

[39] González and Bermúdez (2010), p. 86.

[40] Londoño (2018).

(i) *Mejores políticas de suscripción y mitigación de riesgos (contragarantías o garantías en los Contratos de Seguros), mejores esquemas de tarifación* (Pricing)
(ii) *Mejores y más adecuados productos a ser ofrecidos a los consumidores, a la luz de sus necesidades reales y hábitos de consumo y*
(iii) *Mejor y más eficiente diseño y manejo de reclamaciones y políticas antifraude*

Translated to English as follows:

(i) Better underwriting and risk mitigation policies (counter-guarantees or guarantees in Insurance Contracts), better pricing schemes (Pricing)
(ii) Better and more suitable products to be offered to consumers, considering their real needs and consumption habits
(iii) Better and more efficient design and handling of claims and anti-fraud policies

In conclusion, it is important that corporate governments, especially the ones at the insurance market, seek the implementation of RegTech tools that facilitate regulatory compliance. A crucial strategy is the single business registry that has a complete and detailed information on each of the companies to guarantee an efficient KYC and AML appropriate to their needs.

Finally, it can be seen how the application of RegTech still present some difficulties that must be solved so it can be implemented optimally. However, with existing tools, it is possible to use RegTech in a country like Colombia to facilitate information-based decision-making for insurance companies, which minimizes their risks and facilitates regulatory compliance.

References

Arias A, Portela I (1997) Sistema de información y sistema de calidad: relación y dependencia en las organizaciones empresariales. Documentación de las ciencias de la información 20:11

Arner D, Barberis J, Buckley R (2017) Fintech, Regtech, and reconceptualization of financial regulation. Northwest J Int Law Bus 37:371. https://scholarlycommons.law.northwestern.edu/cgi/viewcontent.cgi?article=1017&context=njilb

Bank of Spain (2002) Debida diligencia con la clientela bancaria. Notas de estabilidad financiera/Banco de España, 2

Bermúdez D (2018) Principales conclusiones del IV Congreso Internacional de Derecho de Seguros. Revista Fasecolda 170:62–65. https://revista.fasecolda.com/index.php/revfasecolda/article/view/440

Bonzom A (2011) La règle "know your customer" en droit bancaire et financier (Doctoral dissertation, Paris 1) https://www.theses.fr/2011PA010320

Butler T, O'Brien L (2019) Understanding RegTech for digital regulatory compliance. In Disrupting Finance. Palgrave Pivot, Cham, pp 85–102. https://library.oapen.org/bitstream/handle/20.500.12657/23126/1007030.pdf?sequence=1#page=106

Cascón JI (2019) GRC: Gobierno Corporativo, Riesgo y Cumplimiento Regulatorio. Primera edición. https://www.researchgate.net/profile/Javier_Ismodes2/publication/335273095_GRC_Gobierno_Corporativo_Riesgo_y_Cumplimiento_Regulatorio/links/

5d5c076b92851c37636c1543/GRC-Gobierno-Corporativo-Riesumpdfldf-Corporativo-Regulatordf
Cermeño JS (2016) Diez claves para entender qué es el "Regtech". BBVA. https://www.bbva.com/es/10-claves-para-entender-que-es-el-regtech/
ComuExter13 (2017) Las fuentes de información externa de la empresa. https://comuexter13.wordpress.com/2013/04/17/las-fuentes-de-informacion-externa-de-la-empresa/
Deloitte (2016) Regtech, el lado B de la innovación ¿Regulación e innovación son términos opuestos?: https://www2.deloitte.com/content/dam/Deloitte/ar/Documents/financial-services/Reg_Tech_El-Lado_B_de_la_innovaci%C3%B3n.pdf
Falotico M (2017) Know Your Customer, contribuição de prevenção à lavagem de dinheiro em instituições financeiras. INSPER: Instituto de Ensino e Pesquisa. http://dspace.insper.edu.br/xmlui/bitstream/handle/11224/1673/MARIANA%20FALOTICO%20COELHO%20COSTA_Trabalho.pdf?sequence=1
Fasecolda. Gobierno Corporativo. https://fasecolda.com/fasecolda/sostenibilidad/gobierno-corporativo/
Frankenfield J (2019) What you should know about Regtech. https://www.investopedia.com/terms/r/regtech.asp
Geslevich N (2018) RegTech, compliance and technology judgment rule. Chic-Kent Law Rev 93:193. https://scholarship.kentlaw.iit.edu/cgi/viewcontent.cgi?article=4198&context=cklawreview
González P, Bermúdez T (2010) Fuentes de información, indicadores y herramientas más usadas por gerentes de Mipyme en Cali, Colombia. Contaduría y administración 232:83–108. http://www.scielo.org.mx/scielo.php?script=sci_arttext&pid=S0186-10422010000300005&lng=es&tlng=es
Kurum E (2020) RegTech solutions and AML compliance: what future for financial crime? J Financ Crime. https://www.emerald.com/insight/content/doi/10.1108/JFC-04-2020-0051/full/html
Londoño A (2018) Preocupaciones de Big Data en materia de seguros: de la segmentación de riesgos o de eventuales situaciones de exclusión o problemas de acceso al mercado asegurador. Revista Ibero-Latinoamericana de seguros 27(49)
Montañez ME, Suárez AJ, Álvarez MF, Torres L (2017) Valor agregado del gobierno corporativo en el sector de seguros generales en Colombia. Pontificia Universidad Católica del Perú. http://tesis.pucp.edu.pe/repositorio/bitstream/handle/20.500.12404/8997/MONTA%c3%91EZ_SUAREZ_VALOR_SEGUROS_COLOMBIA.pdf?sequence=3&isAllowed=y
Oracle. What is big data? https://www.oracle.com/co/big-data/what-is-big-data.html
Rincon E (2020) El desarrollo jurídico de Fintech. Las bases regulatorias de la tecnología financiera. Editorial Tirant lo Blanch. In printing process
Tejeira M (2015) Legal Compliance: Conceptualización en el marco de la regulación corporativa. Estudios sobre el futuro Código Mercantil: libro homenaje al profesor Rafael Illescas Ortiz. Madrid, Universidad Carlos, 3, 935–948
Virtual UMB. Identificación y registro de proveedores. Módulo 1: Identificación de proveedores. http://virtualnet2.umb.edu.co/virtualnet/archivos/open.php/125/2eabe_2037/TGPC002037/mod1/profundizacion_tema3_m1.html
Woolard C (2016) Innovation in Regtech. London Fintech Week 2016. Financial Conduct Authority. https://www.fca.org.uk/news/speeches/london-fintech-week-2016-innovation-regtech

The Influence of Public and Corporate Insurance Law on the Application of Private International Law: Selected Issues

Mariusz Fras

Abstract The regime of obligations arising under insurance relationships, as expressed in Art. 7 of the Rome I Regulation is, however, relatively complex. The criticism seems legitimate of academic authors who quite clearly express their negative attitude to the wording of that provision, calling it a "labyrinth" or even "pandemonium of international law." As a result of the not particularly transparent nature of that regime, it can be doubted if in all situations the "weaker party" was afforded due protection. Negative answer to that question prompts a search for other solutions which allow to achieve the effect of conflict of laws designation of a law giving effect to the postulate of protecting the weaker party to the insurance relationship. The purpose of the study is to indicate, in the first place, the existing criteria of the division into public law and private law in the context of private international law. The second purpose is to analyze the phenomenon of mutual interpenetration of private and public law in the private international law of insurance contracts. The purpose of considerations was to indicate the mutual interpenetration between EU provisions of public and corporate law, as well as the impact of national provisions of the same type on private international law.

1 Introduction

The specificity of insurance contracts was noticed already in the applicability period of the Rome Convention.[1] Already at that time, it was proposed to introduce a special conflict of laws rule for direct insurance contracts.[2] These intentions,

This research was funded in whole by National Science Centre, Poland, Grant Number 2020/39/B/HS5/02631.

[1] Convention on the Law Applicable to Contractual Obligations, open for signature in Rome on 19 June 1980 (Dz.U. 2008, No. 10, item 57).

[2] Seatzu (2003), pp. 128–129.

M. Fras (✉)
Department of Civil Law and Private International Law, Silesian University, Katowice, Poland

P. Marano, K. Noussia (eds.), *The Governance of Insurance Undertakings*, AIDA Europe Research Series on Insurance Law and Regulation 6,
https://doi.org/10.1007/978-3-030-85817-9_14

however, were not put into practice. This did not follow from any revision of the assumptions made by the authors of the Convention at an early stage of legislative works. The absence of rules offering protection to the non-professional party of an insurance contract in the Convention itself was a consequence of exclusion of insurance relationships from its material scope. The relevant conflict of laws provisions were included in subsequent insurance directives.[3] On the entry into force of the Regulation (EC) No 593/2008 of the European Parliament and of the Council of 17 June 2008 on the law applicable to contractual obligations (Rome I)[4] this state of affairs was underwent a major change. The endeavor to afford special protection to the "weaker party" found manifestation already in Recital 23 of the Regulation, in which it was stipulated that "[a]s regards contracts concluded with parties regarded as being weaker, those parties should be protected by conflict-of-law rules that are more favorable to their interests than the general rules." This thought was developed in Recital 32 sentence 1 of the Regulation, where it is emphasized that "[o]wing to the particular nature of contracts of carriage and insurance contracts, specific provisions should ensure an adequate level of protection of passengers and policy holders." It should be noted that the EU legislator avoids using the term consumer in relation to parties of insurance transactions.[5] However, private international law offers a special treatment both to insurance agreements and already mentioned consumer contracts. Bearing the above in mind, the legislator decided to apply different protection mechanisms. While in the case of consumer contracts (Art. 6) protection is afforded by means of alternative corrective connectors, in the event of insurance agreements the legislator adopted a less complex solution based on a limited choice of law (Art. 7).

When making a holistic analysis of the Rome I Regulation, one may differentiate between four insurance categories, which are covered by the scope of application of different conflict of laws rules.[6] The mutual differences among them are significant enough that one may speak of several separate conflict of laws mechanisms.[7] It is even indicated that in Art. 7 of the Rome I Regulation there are various "subsystems" of conflict of laws rules,[8] which some refer to as "sets of conflict of laws rules,"[9] while others call them "situation groups."[10]

The first category in this classification system are insurance contracts relating to large risks, the second one—insurance contracts involving other risks, referred to as mass ones, which are situated in the territory of the Member States of the European Union, the third one—compulsory insurance contracts. The last of the categories for

[3] Fras (2008), pp. 59–61.

[4] OJ EU L 177 of 4 July 2008.

[5] Wojewoda (2007a, b), pp. 91–92.

[6] Kramer (2008), p. 37; Lando and Nielsen (2009), p. 1711.

[7] See Basedow (1991), p. 785.

[8] See Pilich (2012), pp. 332–334.

[9] Bělohlávek (2010), p. 1192.

[10] Kropka (2015), p. 301.

which the EU legislator provided special conflict of laws rules are insurances relating to mass risks situated in the territory of third countries and reinsurance contracts.

Pinpointing the appropriate conflict of laws rules for a given insurance agreement requires, in the first place, to determine the character of the insured risk. Such procedure allows to ascertain if the agreement is a large risk contract or a mass risk contract. As far as agreements belonging to the latter category are concerned, it also becomes necessary to identify the legal area in which the risk is situated. As a part of the qualification procedures, one must not overlook the special character of compulsory insurances. In a situation where the obligation to enter into the insurance contract is imposed by a Member State of the European Union, a distinct "subsystem" of conflict of laws rules applies.[11]

The regime of obligations arising under insurance relationships, as expressed in Art. 7 of the Rome I Regulation is, however, relatively complex. The criticism seems legitimate of academic authors[12] who quite clearly express their negative attitude to the wording of that provision, calling it a "labyrinth"[13] or even "pandemonium of international law."[14] As a result of the not particularly transparent nature of that regime, it can be doubted if in all situations the "weaker party" was afforded due protection. Negative answer to that question prompts a search for other solutions which allow to achieve the effect of conflict of laws designation of a law giving effect to the postulate of protecting the weaker party to the insurance relationship. The purpose of the study is to indicate, in the first place, the existing criteria of the division into public law and private law in the context of private international law. The second purpose is to analyze the phenomenon of mutual interpenetration of private and public law in the private international law of insurance contracts.

2 The Legal Qualification of the Concept of Insurance Contract and the Concept of Insurer in Private International Law

Analysis of the concept of insurance contract in the understanding of Art. 7 should start with identification of such contract's characteristic features.[15]

Protection of the insurance interest is realized by a transfer (assumption) of the insurance risk. For that reason, the concepts of insurance risk and insurance interest account for the essence of insurance as a method of transferring risk.[16] The transfer of risk, approached through the prism of collectively understood insurance, is

[11] More on that in Fras and Pacuła (2014), p. 141 et seq.

[12] Heiss (2008), p. 261; Gruber (2009), p. 110.

[13] Kramer (2008), p. 41.

[14] Heiss (2008), p. 261.

[15] Fras (2019a), pp. 131–148; Fras (2020), pp. 1–49.

[16] Kowalewski (1997), p. 73.

uniformly regarded as distribution of risk between parties participating in an insurance fund.[17] On the other hand, the analysis of the risk transfer through the prism of contents of the insurance obligational relationship allows to conclude that such transfer may generally take place in two ways, according to the dichotomous division of insurance into its economic types. Under the commercial type, the insurer takes over the risk from each insured party separately.[18] Under the mutual type—within the relation between the mutual insurance institution and its members (*Mitgliederversicherung*)[19]—the insurer does not take over the insurance risk, which is distributed among insured parties.[20]

Contracts under which the insurance risk is assumed by the insurer (commercial insurance type), are generally referred to as insurance contracts. The insurance nature of the assumed risk allows to distinguish that contract from other ones under which risk is transferred.[21] On the other hand, the source of the insurance relationship between a mutual insurance institution and its member may be a contract named otherwise than insurance contract. Examples are provided by German and French law. Under the second sentence of § 2 of the German VAG,[22] member of a mutual insurance society (*Versicherungsverein auf Gegenseitigkeit*) "may only be a person establishing an insurance relationship with the society." Therefore, it is assumed that, on such occasions, the source of the insurance relationship is an agreement for the accession or admission to the mutual society (*Beitritts- oder Aufnahmevertrag zum Gegenseitigkeitsverein*).[23] Such contract is also the source of the membership relationship.[24] By contrast, *institutions de prévoyance* (prudence institutions) incorporated under the French law[25] establish insurance relationships by collective acts with compulsory adhesion (*opérations collectives ŕ adhésion*

[17] See Präve (2005), pp. 38, 40.

[18] Dickstein (1995), pp. 118, 152, 155 (comments on the insurance relationship concept *sensu stricto*).

[19] Dickstein (1995), pp. 116–117.

[20] Dickstein (1995), p. 117.

[21] See in: Dickstein (1995), pp. 47–52 i 67–115. This author, using the examples of contracts which show similarity with specific insurance types (guarantee agreement—*Garantievertrag*, proper factoring—*echte Factoring*, financial leasing—*Finanzierungsleasing*), concluded that mere assumption of risk does not amount to the characteristic feature of the insurance contract (p. 51) and that such feature is the insurance interest. This is the case since—in that author's opinion—transfer of risk is only a means to achieve the purpose of the contract, that is, protection of the insurance interest (pp. 84–85).

[22] Versicherungsaufsichtsgesetz (accessed: 15.09.2020). https://www.gesetze-im-internet.de/vag_2016/VAG.pdf.

[23] Dickstein (1995), p. 123 and the literature cited therein.

[24] Roth (1999), p. 2290.

[25] *Institutions de prévoyance* are one of legal organizational forms prescribed in French law for insurance undertakings. Article L. 931-1 (Code de la sécurité sociale, accessed 15.09.2020). http://www.ilo.org/dyn/travail/docs/2315/Code%20de%20la%20Securite%20Sociale%201.pdf.

obligatoire),[26] collective acts with optional adhesion (*opérations collectives ŕ adhésion facultative*)[27] or individual acts (*opérations individuelles*).[28] The source of an insurance relationship may not be only a contract but also declarations of adhesion to the terms and conditions applied by *institution de prévoyance.*[29]

The contract establishing an insurance relationship between the mutual insurance institution and such institution's member may be qualified from the conflict of laws perspective as an insurance contract in the understanding of Art. 7.[30]

National legal systems require that insurance activity, which consists in the conclusion and performance of insurance contracts, be pursued by entities authorized under licenses granted by public authorities. This requirement is one of the aspects of legal regulation of the insurance activity. However, the requirement does not have to come in pair with recognition of an insurance contract as subjectively qualified agreement. In German law, the status of insurance contract is also

[26] In case of *opérations collectives ŕ adhésion obligatoire,* the undertaking (*entreprise*), understood as employer, joins the prudence institution (*adhésion*) by signing a declaration of adhesion to its terms and conditions (*adhésion par signature d'un bulletin au rčglement*) or by concluding with the institution an agreement for its employees (*contrat au profit de ses salariés*), who compulsorily become member participants (*membres participants*—art. L. 932-2 Code de la sécurité sociale). The terms and conditions, the declaration or the agreement specify the rights and obligations of the entity joining the institution and member participants.

[27] In case of *opérations collectives ŕ adhésion facultative,* employees have the right to decide to associate with the prudence institution (*affiliation*). Upon such decision, the employee becomes a member participant (Art. L. 932-14 k. Code de la sécurıté sociale).

[28] In case of *opérations individuelles,* employees themselves join the prudence institution by signing the declaration of adhesion to the terms and conditions or by concluding the agreement with that institution (Art. L. 932-14 Code de la sécurité sociale).

[29] Under Aer. L-932-23 Code de la sécurité sociale, the concepts of bulletin of adhesion to the terms and conditions (*bulletin d'adhésion ŕ un rčglement*), collective acts with compulsory adhesion and participant (*participant*) correspond, respectively, to the terms: insurance contract (*contrat d'assurance*), group insurance contract (*contrat d'assurance de groupe*) and insured party (*assuré*). This terminology is reflected in conflict of laws provisions on the law applicable to acts with the participation of *institutions de prévoyance* and reciprocity institutions (*mutuelles*), implementing the conflict of laws provisions of insurance directives (in respect to *institutions de prévoyance* regulated in Arts. L. 932-25–L. 932-34 Code de la sécurité sociale, wherein those provisions apply also to *institutions de prévoyance* regulated in *Code rural*, under Art. L. 727-2(2) of that Code; as regards *mutuelles*, the basis are Arts. L. 225-1–L. 225-10 Code de la mutualité (http://codes.droit.org/CodV3/mutualite.pdf). Those provisions were *leges speciales* in relation to the same conflict of laws provisions of the French Insurance Code (http://codes.droit.org/CodV3/assurances.pdf) on the law applicable to insurance contracts concluded by insurance companies (*entreprises d'assurance*). In those provisions—on *institutions de prévoyance*—the term "contract," present in conflict of laws rules of the Community insurance directives, refers also to the expression "declaration of adhesion to the terms and conditions" (see, e.g., Art. L.932-26(1) Code de la sécurité sociale, according to which, when the risk is located in France and the person making the declaration of adhesion to the terms and conditions of an *institution de prévoyance* or concluding an insurance contract with the *institution de prévoyance* has their habitual residence or seat of the management board in France, the applicable law shall be French law, to the exclusion of any other country's law), and the term "policyholder"—refers to the expressions "acceding party" and "participant."

[30] Dörner (1997), pp. 39–40.

recognized in relation to contracts whose party is an insurer not undergoing insurance supervision.[31] Moreover, an agreement having objective features of an insurance contract, concluded by an insurer which does not hold the required license for the pursuance of insurance activities, may be qualified from the substantive law perspective as insurance contract.[32] In the conflict of laws context, insurance contract should, in principle, be denied the status of subjectively qualified agreement.

The reasons of public law also justify the non-inclusion, within the scope of application of the EU insurance directives, of insurance undertakings seated in a third country which do not pursue insurance activities in the Member States in the form of agency or branch. This follows from a *ratione materiae* restriction of the scope of application of EU law. Also, this restriction should be ignored in the conflict of laws context.[33] There are apparent influences of commercial and public law on the interpretation of the concept of insurer.

Policyholder's counterparty in the insurance contract, in the understanding of the Rome I Regulation, may be any person. Art. 7(2), second indent, mentions "insurers" (German *Versicherer*, French *assureur*, Italian *assicuratore*, Spanish *asegurador*). The concept of "insurer" may be treated as superordinate to the terms "insurance undertaking" and "organisation other than undertaking." The approved qualification result allows to include as insurance contracts, within the meaning of the Rome I Regulation, contracts having the characteristics of insurance contracts concluded by entities claiming to be an insurance undertaking, pursuing insurance activities but, in fact, unauthorized to undertake such activities or acting in violation of the basic principles of pursuing such activities.[34] In the conflict of laws context, insurance contract should be denied the status of subjectively qualified contract. There are exceptions to this principle. One example can be provided by the insurance guarantee agreement. To delimitate the insurance guarantee agreement from the bank guarantee agreement, it is necessary to use the subjective criterion relating to the status of the insurer as policyholder's counterparty.[35] The question of the insurer's qualified status boils down to whether and to what extent a given entity is authorized to pursue insurance activities. This question forms a part of the law applicable to the insurance contract. Provisions of such law will be given effect, including in space, within the limits of their applicability. The will of being applied may be attributed to the rules specifying the policyholder's status from outside the law applicable to contractual obligations, either of the forum or a third country. Examples of substantive law qualification of insurance acts, which are interesting

[31] Prölls and Martin (2010), p. 72 ("die Unterstellung eines Unternehmens unter die Aufsicht impliziert also nicht die Anwendung des VVG und umgekehrt").

[32] Example is provided by Polish law where such contracts qualify as invalid insurance contracts, see Malinowska (2003), pp. 138–139.

[33] Gruber (1999), pp. 18–19.

[34] Dickstein (1995), pp. 43–45 (*Scheinversicherer*).

[35] Kropka (2010), pp. 39–42.

from the point of view of the discussed subject matter, are provided by the case law of the German Federal Administrative Court (Bundesverwaltungsgericht).[36]

3 Reinsurance and Co-Insurance Contracts

The reinsurance contract plays the same social and economic function and has the same characteristic features as the insurance contract.[37] However, this conclusion must give way to the effect of the qualification based on the provisions of the Rome I Regulation explaining the term insurance contract. It follows from Art. 7(1), second sentence, in conjunction with Recital 32, that reinsurance contracts do not amount to insurance contracts. By reinsurance contract, one should also understand the retrocession contract and further reinsurance contracts. Such position is in line with the definition of reinsurance as included in Art. 13(7) letter (a) of the Directive 2009/138/EC (Slovency II)[38] ("the activity consisting in accepting risks ceded by an insurance undertaking or third-country insurance undertaking, or by another reinsurance undertaking or third-country reinsurance undertaking"). Reinsurance is also the subject of an agreement under which the risks assumed by the insurer or reinsurer are further taken over by a so-called insurance special purpose vehicle (*Versicherungs- Zweckgesellschaft*, *véhicule de titrisation*). German law permits the establishment of special purpose vehicles.[39] Operation of a special purpose vehicle involves the transfer of insurance risks to the capital market.

An insurance type interesting for the subject matter of these considerations is insurance of additional contributions (*Nachschussversicherung*). Its parties are the reinsurer and the mutual insurance institution acting on behalf of its members. Such insurance makes an alternative to obligating the mutual insurance institution's

[36] The following were recognized as insurance operations in the understanding of § 1 of the German VAG: guarantee of maintaining (*Wartungsgarantie*) technical equipment if it is exhausted by the obligation to assume the relevant maintenance costs and unrelated in any way to other operations (Präve 2005, p. 45); permanent guarantee (*Dauergarantie*) granted for technical equipment involving non-gratuitous coverage of costs of any repairs necessary as a result of wear and tear if the guarantor restricts himself only to such promise of performance and does not sell any equipment covered by the guarantee (Präve 2005, p. 45).

[37] Eichler (1966), pp. 324–325.

[38] Directive 2009/138/EC of the European Parliament and of the Council of 25 November 2009 on the taking-up and pursuit of the business of Insurance and Reinsurance (Solvency II) (Text with EEA relevance) (Official Journal of the European Union, L 335/1, 17 December 2011).

[39] Paragraph 121g(1), first sentence, VAG defines *Versicherungs-Zweckgesellschaft* as company or partnership with a seat or central management in Germany which, being neither insurance undertaking nor reinsurer, assumes risks from insurance undertakings or reinsurers, wherein the risks of materialization of damage are secured by such partnership or company in full by issuing debt instruments or by another financing mechanism, and whereby recourse monetary claims under loans or other financial mechanisms give way to the entity's liabilities under reinsurance.

members to make additional contributions.[40] It comes in two forms. Under the former, the mutual insurance institution acts in its own name as the insurer, dedicating the funds received from the reinsurer to cover its losses;[41] under the latter, the mutual insurance institution acts in the name of its members as policyholders, collecting for that purpose additional premiums and transferring them to the reinsurer who, in exchange, makes the required additional contributions.[42] In German literature, the latter of the discussed *Nachschussversicherung* forms is compared to civil liability insurance.[43]

The above effect of qualification of the concept of insurance contract should extend to co-insurance contracts. The co-insurance contract—bearing in mind its social and economic function and characteristic features—is an insurance contract. This conclusion is in line with the provisions of the Rome I Regulation and the provisions of EU insurance directives. They do not contain any qualification guidelines to the contrary.[44] An opinion expressed in the doctrine is illegitimate that the law applicable to co-insurance contracts is regulated by the Council and European Parliament Directive 2009/138. That Directive does not include any conflict of laws provisions. One should also evaluate critically the opinion that it is ungrounded to apply, to co-insurance contracts, the conflict of laws norms implementing the conflict of laws provisions of the insurance directives since protection of the policyholder is unnecessary in case of such contracts.[45]

4 "Insurance Contracts" Covered by the Exclusion Under Art. 1(2) Letter (j) of the Rome I Regulation

4.1 Initial Comments on Art. 1(2) Letter (j)

Article 1(2) letter (j) reads that the following shall be excluded from the scope of the Regulation: "insurance contracts arising out of operations carried out by organisations other than undertakings referred to in Article 2 of Directive 2009/138 of the European Parliament and of the Council of 25 November 2009 concerning life assurance the object of which is to provide benefits for employed or self-employed persons belonging to an undertaking or group of undertakings, or to a trade or group of trades, in the event of death or survival or of discontinuance or curtailment of activity, or of sickness related to work or accidents at work." This provision contains a description of specific risks relating to employed and self-employed persons. That

[40] Dickstein (1995), p. 31.

[41] Ibid.

[42] Ibid., pp. 31–32.

[43] Ibid., p. 32 and the literature cited therein.

[44] Schnyder (2004), p. 1025.

[45] Fuchs (1999), p. 20.

is why "insurance the object of which is to provide benefits for employed [...] persons," concluded by an "undertaking" or "group of undertakings" is a contract for account of a third party. The same apparently refers to situations when an "insurance contract the object of which is to provide benefits for [...] self-employed persons" is concluded, in his or her own name, by a representative of their "trade" of "group of trades." Presently, this issue is regulated by Art. 9(2) of Directive 2009/138/EC (Solvency II).[46]

A characteristic feature of insurance contracts for account of a third party is that only the third party may take advantage of such insurance.[47] The way in which the third party takes such advantage depends on whether the insurance for account of the third party is direct or indirect.[48] In the former case, the subjective law claim against the insurer for the payment of benefit is vested in the third party, whereas in the latter in the policyholder, who is legally bound to deliver the benefit received from the insurer to the third party. This distinction is of secondary importance from the point of view of the conflict of laws qualification.[49]

Textual interpretation of Art. 1(2) letter (j) in conjunction with Art. 2 of the Directive 2009/138/EC of 25 November 2009 concerning life insurance, leads to the conclusion that Art. 1(2) letter (j) does not refer to insurance undertakings pursuing in the EU business of direct insurance in the life assurance branch. Such undertakings are both insurance undertakings seated in a Member State of the EU and insurance undertakings seated outside the EU.

Reasoning *a contrario* from Art. 1(2) letter (j) in conjunction with Art. 2 of Directive 2002/83/EC (currently Article 2 of the Directive 2009/138/EC) allows to include among "organisations other than undertakings referred to in Article 2 of Directive 2002/83/EC" (currently Article 2 of the Directive 2009/138/EC): (1) insurance undertakings engaging in re-insurance activities, (2) insurance undertakings engaging in insurance activities of direct insurance other than life assurance, (3) insurance undertakings pursuing outside the EU insurance activities of direct insurance in the life assurance branch, (4) organisations other than insurance undertakings. However, such reasoning—in my opinion—is illegitimate. The prototype of Art. 1(2) letter (j) is Art. 9 item 2 of the Directive 2009/138/EC. Nevertheless, when drafting Art. 1(2) letter (j), the legislator overlooked that the Directive 2009/138/EC, according to its general provisions, does not refer to any of the four abovementioned groups of entities. One should interpret the expression: "organisations other than undertakings referred to in Art. 2 of the Directive 2002/83/EC" (currently Art. 2 of

[46] "In regard to life insurance, this Directive shall not apply to the following operations and activities operations carried out by organisations, other than undertakings referred to in Article 2, whose object is to provide benefits for employed or self-employed persons belonging to an undertaking or group of undertakings, or a trade or group of trades, in the event of death or survival or of discontinuance or curtailment of activity, whether or not the commitments arising from such operations are fully covered at all times by mathematical provisions."

[47] Hełczyński (1927), p. 95; Maixner and Steinbeck (2008), p. 48.

[48] Hełczyński (1927), p. 82.

[49] Cf. Basedow and Fock (2002), p. 104.

the Directive 2009/138/EC), in the understanding of Art. 3(3) of the Directive 2002/83/EC (currently Art. 9(2) of the Directive 2009/138/EC), in the context of those general provisions. The same expression used in Art. 1(2) letter (j) is affected by a legislative error. In consequence, establishment of the scope of the subjective exclusion under Art. 1(2) letter (j) requires further investigations.

The expression: "organisations other than undertakings referred to in Article 2 of Directive 2002/83/EC" (currently Art. 2 of the Directive 2009/138/EC) in the understanding of Art. 1(2) letter (j) refers to one of the parties to the insurance contracts specified in that provision. As a result, this expression should be distinguished from the concept of "undertaking," used here in its subjective meaning to denote employer.

The formulation: "the object of which is to provide benefits for employed or self-employed persons belonging to an undertaking or group of undertakings, or to a trade or group of trades, in the event of death or survival or of discontinuance or curtailment of activity, or of sickness related to work or accidents at work" must be referred to the expression "insurance." As far as Art. 1(2) letter (j) mentions benefits in the event of sickness related to work or accidents at work, this provision relates both to the insurance of risk of invalidity caused by accident or sickness as a type of additional insurance in the understanding of Art. 2(3) letter (a) point (iii) of the Directive 2009/138/EC (I insurance group in the life assurance branch) and insurance against accidents at work and occupational diseases (I insurance group from the branch of insurance other than life assurance). Consequently, it must be concluded that "insurance undertakings" in the expression "organisations other than insurance undertakings" are all insurance undertakings pursuing in the European Union (including in Denmark) activities in the area of direct insurance. This means, at the same time, that the expression "organisations other than insurance undertakings referred to in Art. 2 of the Directive 2002/83/EC" (currently Art. 2 of the Directive 2009/138/EC) covers organizations other than insurance undertakings operating in the EU.

The wording of Art. 1(2) letter (j) suggests that the provision relates only to intra-Union situations, i.e., insurance contracts referred to in that norm concluded by organizations other than insurance undertakings as a part of their activities in the European Union. Nevertheless, this question must be finally resolved by purposive interpretation based on the final conclusions as to what "insurance contracts" the discussed provision refers to.

4.2 The European Law of Occupational Pension Schemes

Article 1(2) letter (j) makes a conflict of laws section of the EU regime of occupational pension schemes. This is indicated by the connection of that norm with Art. 9 item 2 of the Directive 2009/138/EC. The Directive's provision was adopted with a view to the works harmonizing the laws of the EU Member States in the occupational pension schemes.[50] The effect of those works was the Directive 2016/2341/EU.[51] It contains a comprehensive substantive law regime of occupational pension schemes. Its provisions are helpful in the interpretation of Art. 1(2) letter (j). This refers, in particular, to the definition of institution for occupational retirement provision (Art. 6(1) of the Directive 2016/2341/EU) and definition of retirement benefits (Art. 6(4)) of the Directive 2016/2341/EU), showing similarity to that provision. For that reason, it is legitimate to determine—in interpreting Art. 1 (2) letter (j)—the circle of institutions for occupational retirement provision to which the provisions of the Directive 2016/2341/EU apply. For that purpose, one should, in the first place, consider the catalogue of subjective exclusions under Art. 2 (2) of the Directive 2016/2341/EU.

The principle of separateness of institutions for occupational retirement provision, as expressed in their definition (Art. 6(1) of the Directive 2016/2341/EU), from financial institutions (as defined in Art. 6(3) of the Directive 2016/2341/EU) relates to the exclusion of companies using book-reserve schemes with a view to paying out retirement benefits to their employees (Art. 2(2) letter (e) of the Directive 2016/2341/EU). This exclusion refers to employers performing the obligations incurred vis-a-vis their employees under occupational pension schemes by establishing reserves with a view to paying out future benefits. The source of such obligations may, for instance, be direct promise (*Direktzusage*) under German law, direct promise of benefit (*direkte Leistungszusage*) under Austrian law[52] or—by all appearances—self-administered pension scheme under the law of the United Kingdom[53] or individual pension obligations (*engagements individuels de pension/individuele pensioentoezeggingen*) under Belgian law.[54] In connection with Art. 2(2) letter

---

[50] Dickstein (1995), p. 28.

[51] Directive (EU) 2016/2341 of the European Parliament and of the Council of 14 December 2016 on the activities and supervision of institutions for occupational retirement provision (IORPs) (Text with EEA relevance) (Official Journal of the European Union L 354/37, 23.12.2016).

[52] The essence of both the direct promise (*Direktzusage*, *unmittelbare Leistungszusage*) under German law and direct promise of performance (*direkte Leistungszusage*) under Austrian law is employer's obligation vis-a-vis employee to pay benefits within the framework of occupational pension provision (German Law—Blomeyer and Otto 2006, p. 113; Kemper 2003, p. 49) following from the given promise (*Zusage*) as the source of legal relationship of occupational pension provision (Blomeyer and Otto 2006, pp. 80–81). The employer may choose the form of fulfilling that promise. It may be fulfilled by the employer itself, in the form of *Direktzusage* or *direkte Leistungszusage*, or through an authorized institution. Regardless of the chosen form, the employer remains obliged against the employee under the *Zusage* to satisfy claims under that *Zusage* (*Einstandspflicht*—Kemper 2003, p. 51).

[53] It is a pension plan organized and managed by the employer whose agents (*directors*) play at the same time the role of the plan's *trustees* (Harpen 1991).

[54] See Art. 75 of the Belgian Act on the control of occupational retirement institutions (Loi relative au contrôle des institutions de retraite professionnelle/Wet betreffende het toezicht op de instellingen voor bedrijfspensioenvoorzieningen, of 27 October 2006, Moniteur Belge/Belgisch Staatsblad, 10 November 2006, p. 60162), http://www.ejustice.just.fgov.be/cgi_loi/change_lg_2.pl?language=fr&nm=2006023149&la=F (Last accessed: 22.12.2020).

(e) of the Directive 2016/2341/EU, attention should also be drawn to the Italian law construction known as *trattamento di fine rapporto.*[55]

Just as insurance undertakings ensure benefits in accordance with insurance contracts, institutions for occupational retirement provision, in the understanding of the Directive 2016/2341/EU, ensure pension benefits in accordance with the pension scheme, defined as "contract, an agreement, a trust deed or rules stipulating which retirement benefits are granted and under which conditions" (Art. 6(2) of that Directive). On the other hand, the concept of pension scheme does not refer to contracts relating to the occupational pension scheme regime but having as their subject obligations other than the obligation to provide pension benefits. This relates, among others, to contracts the object of which is investment of the entrusted funds on capital markets. Such contracts form a part of the activities of entities covered by the exclusion under Art. 2(2) letter (b) of the Directive 2016/2341/EU. This refers to investment firms as well as undertakings for collective investment in transferable securities (UCITS) and companies managing UCITSs.

The customers of "investment firms" may be, according to section I point 1 letter (f) of Annex II to the Directive 2014/65/EU,[56] "pension funds and management companies of such funds." Furthermore, under Art. 6(3) letter (a) of the Directive 2009/65/EC,[57] management companies may, by operation of national law of a given Member State, be entitled to manage investment portfolios belonging to pension funds.

An institution for occupational retirement provision covered by the norms of the Directive 2016/2341/EU may only be such entity against which the financing institution's employees have a claim for the provision of benefit (argument *a contrario* from Art. 2(2) letter (d) of the Directive 2016/2341/EU). Such entity is not the institution for occupational retirement provision known to German and Austrian laws under the name *Unterstützungskasse* (provident society). In German law, *Unterstützungskasse* provides benefits within the framework of occupational retirement provision under the contract concluded with the employer or under the institution's statute.[58] Under that relationship, *Unterstützungskasse* acquires against

[55] *Trattamento di fine rapporto* is, under Art. 2120 of the Italian Civil Code (CC) a special monetary provision owed to the employee (*il prestatore di lavoro*) from the employer because of termination of the employment relationship (*il rapporto di lavoro subordinato*). In practice, *Trattamento di fine rapporto* plays the function of an obligatory form of occupational pension provision (Wesselmann 2007, p. 49). https://noipa.mef.gov.it/web/mypa/tfr-e-tfs-dei-dipendenti-previdenziale (Last accessed: 27.01.2021).

[56] Directive 2014/65/EU of the European Parliament and of the Council of 15 May 2014 on markets in financial instruments and amending Directive 2002/92/EC and Directive 2011/61/EU Text with EEA relevance (*Dz.U. L 173 z 12.6.2014*).

[57] Directive 2009/65/EC of the European Parliament and of the Council of 13 July 2009 on the coordination of laws, regulations and administrative provisions relating to undertakings for collective investment in transferable securities (UCITS) (Text with EEA relevance) (Dz.U. L 302 z 17.11.2009).

[58] Blomeyer and Otto (2004), p. 521.

the employer a claim for the return of the funds expended on benefits.[59] As a result, the contract is not accompanied by the transfer of risk.[60] As a rule, employees do not acquire any claims against *Unterstützungskasse* for the payment of pension benefits.

Unterstützungskasse must be distinguished from *Contractual Trust Arrangement*, i.e., special purpose vehicle established by the employer in performance of obligations under *Direktzusage* with a view to managing the funds provided in trust within the framework of occupational retirement provision.[61] *Contractual Trust Arrangement* undertakes to manage those funds under a contract with the employer by the same name. This model is encountered, among others, in German practice.[62]

Pension benefits may be ensured by institutions managing social security schemes. Such institutions ("institutions managing social-security schemes which are covered by Regulation (EEC) No 1408/71(5) and Regulation (EC) No 987/2009 (6)") are covered by the subjective exclusion under Art. 2(2) letter (a) of the Directive 2016/2341.[63] The concept of social security schemes is explained in Art. 4(2) of the Regulation 1408/71.

The ensuring of pension benefits within the framework of social security schemes subject to the provisions of the Regulation 1408/71 may be grounded not only in the provisions of law. This is indicated by Art. 1 letter (j), second indent, of the Regulation 1408/71. A notification mentioned in that provision was made by France.[64] Under that notification, the Regulation 1408/71 applies to the operation of pension funds (*caisses de retraite*[65]—II pillar of the pension system, *régime complémentaire*) forming a supplementary pension scheme for hired labourers

---

[59] Ibid, p. 520.

[60] For this reason, no analogy can be drawn between that contract and so-called external self-insurance (*Externe Selbstversicherung*), consisting in the transfer by an entrepreneur of its own risks to an insurance undertaking specially created by the entrepreneur (or with its participation), known as *captive insurance company* (Präve 2005, p. 44).

[61] Weigel (2005), p. 1144.

[62] Ibid, pp. 1864–1865.

[63] This exclusion refers to national institutions of individual Member States of the EU, as defined in Art. 1 letter (n) of the Regulation 1408/71. Such institutions are listed in Annex II to the Regulation 574/72.

[64] Notification of the Government of the French Republic to the Commission of 29 March 1999, OJ EC C 215, 28 July 1999, p. 1.

[65] *Caisses de retraite* are covered by Arts. L-922-1–L-922-3 and Art. L-922-6–L-922-14 Code de la sécurité sociale. Under the first sentence of Art. L-922-1, first indent, of that Code, the institutions paying out supplementary pensions (*complémentaires*) are non-profit private law entities fulfilling the social mission, administered on parity basis by their members and participants (defined in Art. L. 922-2 Code de la sécurité sociale) or by their agents.

(ARRCO[66]) and supplementary pension scheme for management staff (AGIRC[67]). The source of each such scheme is a collective agreement.[68] In addition, *Caisses de retraite* pay benefits in respect of accidents at work or occupational diseases. Collective agreements are also a source of supplementary pension benefits under Danish law.[69]

The exclusion of institutions managing social security schemes tallies, in principle, with the exclusion relating to institutions which operate on a pay-as-you-go basis (Art. 2(2) letter (c) of the Directive 2016/2341/EU). The essence of pay-as-you-go financing (*Umlageverfahren, répartition*) is the financing of pension benefits from contributions paid on an ongoing basis by persons currently professionally active.[70] This principle, in specific situations, may be subject to modifications. The abovementioned *caisses de retraite* operate on pay-as-you-go basis. However, that modus is accompanied by a system of points (*systéme de points*) based on such criteria as the duration of the contributory period and the amount of contributions.

4.3 Article 1(2) Letter (j) of the Rome I Regulation as a Fragment of the Conflict of Laws Issue of Occupational Pension Schemes

The above considerations allow to consider the exclusion under Art. 1(2) letter (j) in the context of conflict of laws problems of protection against pension risk.

Nowadays, the legal instruments of protection against pension risk have ceased to be a domain of social security.[71] This issue is subject to legal provisions of different type.[72] As a result, it is necessary to demarcate—both in the substantive law and conflict of laws dimension—diverse relationships, including in the area of social security, employment law, financial markets law, private insurance law[73] or law of

[66] ARRCO is a federation of 33 institutions supplementing the pension system of the total of employees in the private sector of industry, commerce, services, and agriculture, including managerial staff. ARRCO's tasks comprise provision of information to, coordination and control of the institutions grouped within ARRCO, as well as collecting statistical and financial data (see www.agirc-arrco.fr).

[67] The AGIRC federation supplements the pension system of the managerial staff in the private sector of industry, commerce, services, and agriculture. It unites 21 pension funds (see www.agirc-arrco.fr, accessed: 15.09.2020).

[68] ARRCO—collective agreement of 8 December 1961 on supplementary pensions, concluded by national representative organizations of employers and employees.

[69] Bittner (2000), p. 7.

[70] Szubert (1987), pp. 228–229.

[71] Jędrasik-Jankowska (2004), p. 69.

[72] Muszalski (2007), pp. 13–15.

[73] Pacud (2006), pp. 46–47.

obligations.[74] On the level of private international law, the total of norms delimiting—in the relations within the framework of legal protection against pension risk—the impact spheres of different national legal systems by designating which of them should apply may be referred to as conflict of laws law of pension security. Such norms comprise both conflict of laws rules of private international law and conflict of laws rules of social security law or, in a wider perspective, of social law.[75]

The subject of demarcation by means of so understood conflict of laws law of social security are miscellaneous sets of public law and private law norms. Their delimitation is a difficult task. It has been noticed in literature that "public law and private law border one another in a distinguishable but inseparable manner."[76]

The justification of the exclusion under Art. 1(2) letter (j) is the fact that the contractual obligations in question make a source of pension benefits supplementary to the basic pension under the statutory system of pension security (I pillar of the pension system). Non-inclusion in that exclusion of contractual obligations under *Direktzusage,* as prescribed in German law, or similar legal constructions is an effect of a strict connection of such obligations with the basic relationship. This connection is reflected in the conflict of laws qualification of the obligations. However, one may wonder why Art. 1(2) letter (j) does not refer to insurance contracts concluded with insurance undertakings within the framework of occupational pension insurance. Such contracts are also intended to supplement the basic pension from the statutory pension security system. The ensuing insurance relationship (cover relationship) is, in large measure, determined by the cash relationship, as in the case of the cover relationship involving occupational pension funds. Insurance contracts concluded with insurance undertakings within the framework of occupational pension insurance were, however, treated in the Rome I Regulation in the same way as other insurance contracts.

---

[74] See the judgment of the French Cassation Court (Cour de cassation) of 24 February 2004 in the case République fédérative du Brésil c. Mme L. de Azevedo Werneck—Revue Critique de Droit International Prive 2005, pp. 62–64. The Court acknowledged compensatory liability of the Brazilian state as employer for the losses incurred by an employee delegated to work in France because of failure to register the employee for statutory social insurance. See also the glossator's comments on the interpenetration in the area of social insurance between relationships of public (vertical dimension) and private law (horizontal dimension)—d'Avout (2005), pp. 65–67. https://journals.openedition.org/nuevomundo/66375 (Last accessed: 27.01.2021).

[75] Eichenhofer (1994), p. 2. This means that the conflict of laws law of pension insurance belongs neither exclusively to private international law nor exclusively to international social law.

[76] Eichenhofer (1987), p. 22.

4.4 Article 1(2) Letter (j) as Fragment of the Conflict of Laws Regime of Protection Against Accidents at Work and Occupational Diseases

Article 1(2) letter (j), to the extent it refers to benefits in respect of occupational disease or accident at work, reaches beyond the conflict of laws issue of occupational pension schemes.

Accident at work or occupational disease may cause interruption or limitation of gainful activity, resulting not only in the acquisition of the right to benefits from occupational pension schemes but also of the right to benefits on other grounds. It is the case since accident at work or occupational disease may lead to an increase of financial needs which is unrelated to pension risk.

As in case of pension risks, risks of accidents at work or occupational diseases are governed by legal norms of various type. In consequence, it becomes necessary to demarcate diverse relationships, including relationships in the area of private insurance law,[77] social security,[78] employment law and law of obligations. In the conflict of laws context, the total of norms delimitating—in relationships within the framework of legal protection against the risks of accidents at work and occupational diseases—the impact spheres of different national legal systems, by designating which system should apply, may be referred to as conflict of laws law of protection against accidents at work and occupational diseases.

4.5 The National Conflict of Laws Rule on the Law Applicable to the Contractual Obligations Covered by the Exclusion Under Art. 1(2) Letter (j)

In the conflict of laws law of the insurance contract, the insured party's claim against the insurer is, as a rule, subject to the law applicable to the insurance contract. The same guideline should be followed in relation to employee claims against institutions for occupational retirement provision under the "insurance contract" in the understanding of Art. 1(2) letter (j). According to the position expressed in German doctrine, the relation between the entitled employee and *Pensionsfonds* is subject, as "subordinate legal relationship" (*dienendes Rechtsverhältnis*), to the law applicable to the "principal legal relationship" (*hauptsächliches Rechtsverhältnis*), i.e.,

[77] Risks of accidents at work or occupational diseases may be covered a voluntary or compulsory insurance contract concluded with an insurance undertaking (Gasińska 2003, pp. 212–213, 218–219).

[78] Risks of accidents at work or occupational diseases may also be covered by the objective scope of the social security system.

relationship forming the basis of occupational pension (*Recht der Betriebsrentenbeziehung*).[79]

Legitimacy of that position raises doubts. It must be admitted that the contract concluded by the employer with *Pensionsfonds* remains in connection with the principal contract between the employer and the employee. In German and Austrian laws this connection is stronger because the choice by the employer of the implementation of an occupational pension scheme in the form of *Pensionsfonds* does not relieve the employee from its obligations vis-a-vis employees under the employer's own promise of benefit (*Einstandspflicht*). The employer's promise to employees forms a constituent element of every form of occupational pension scheme.[80]

The terms "employed person" and "undertaking" ("employer"—in the subjective sense) used in Art. 1(2) letter (j) constitute primary (entry) questions.[81] The law relevant to their evaluation is the law designated by the national conflict of laws norm on the law applicable to life situations covered by Art. 1(2) letter (j). Provisions that may be given effect in such manner are norms clarifying the term "employed person," deviating from its meaning in employment law and in social security law.

Example is provided by German law. Under § 17(1) BetrAVG, first sentence,[82] employees (*Arbeitnehmer*) are blue collar workers (*Arbeiter*) and white-collar workers (*Angestellte*), including persons hired for professional training (*die zu ihrer Berufsausbildung Beschäftigten*).[83] Under the second sentence of that provision, BetrAVG norms apply respectively to persons other than employees if they have been promised benefits in consideration of their activities for the undertaking. The group of such persons includes, among others, *Geschäftsführer* in a limited liability company (GmbH).[84]

5 General Rules of the Definition of the Country in Which the Risk Is Situated (Art. 13(8) Letter d(i) and Art. 13(14) of the Directive 2009/138 in Connection with Art. 7(6) Rome I

The concept of legal person in the understanding of Art. 13(8) letter d(i) and Art. 13 (14) of the Directive 2009/138 with the expression: "companies and other bodies, corporate or unincorporated" in the understanding of Art. 19(1) Rome I, first indent.

[79] Bohne (2004), p. 158.

[80] Blomeyer and Otto (2006), p. 80.

[81] On primary (entry questions)—Pazdan (2008), p. 63.

[82] Gesetz zur Verbesserung der betrieblichen Altersversorgung (https://www.gesetze-im-internet.de/betravg access:15 September 2020; hereinafter also BetrAVG).

[83] Kemper (2003), p. 43.

[84] Bohne (2004), p. 96.

In autonomous qualification of that concept, one should use the experience of judicial practice against the background of Art. 4(2) of the Rome Convention.[85]

One should address critically the proposal of clarifying the concept of "establishment, to which the contract relates" in the understanding of Art. 13(8) letter d(i) of the Directive 2009/138 by the definition of "establishment" in Art. 13(12) of the Directive 2009/138.[86] Such interpretation is illegitimate since that definition refers *expressis verbis* to the insurer's establishment. This was confirmed by the CJEU in the judgment in the case Kvaerner.[87] "Establishment to which the contract relates" should be understood as organizational unit of the policyholder to whose activities the risk covered by the insurance contract relates.[88] The seat of the establishment to which the insurance contract relates is the place where such unit has its centre of activities.[89] At the same time, it is not required that such unit have its own agents or the capacity to conclude contracts.[90]

For conflict of laws rules under Art. 7, the term "establishment" should also cover a daughter company, i.e., legal entity separate from the mother company in a situation when the mother company insures the risks relating to operations of the daughter company. This conclusion is grounded in the justification of the CJEU judgment in the Kvaerner case. The CJEU included in the concept of establishment, in the understanding of the last indent of Art. 2 letter (d) of the Directive 88/357 (Present: Art. 13(13) letter d of the Directive 2009/138), all companies belonging to a given capital group if one of those companies concludes an insurance contract for the others.[91] The CJEU inferred that the purpose of the Directive's provision is, in particular, to establish a general rule specifying the place in which a given economic risk is situated when the risk does not relate to a building, vehicle or travel (specific rules of the definition). In the same way, the provision, in CJEU's opinion, refers to the place where the activities are pursued to which the risk covered by the contract relates. Therefore, in the Court's opinion, the provision uses the criterion of

---

[85] Spickhoff (2003), p. 2464 ("gemeint ist jede Personenvereinigung oder Vermögensmasse, die sich vertraglich verpflichten kann").

[86] Gruber (1999), p. 49.

[87] Case C-191/99. According to paragraph 35 of the justification of that judgment, "the definition of 'establishment' in Article 2(c) of the Directive therefore relates only to the establishment of an insurance company."

[88] In German: *risikoträchtige Teilorganisation*—Kramer (1995), p. 161.

[89] Broad understanding of the term "undertaking" (within the meaning associated above with the term "establishment") of the policyholder in the definition of the country where the risk is situated, was adopted by the law of the United Kingdom. Regulations 2001 (The Financial Services and Markets Act 2000: https://www.legislation.gov.uk/ukpga/2000/8/contents), by defining A's *establishment* as: (a) seat of A's management; (b) each of A's agencies; (c) each of A's branches; (d) any permanent presence of A in a member state of the EEA, which does not have to take the form of agency or branch and which may consist in having an office managed by A's personnel or by a person independent of A who, however, has been permanently authorized to act on A's behalf as though he was A's agent (Dicey et al. 2006, p. 1718).

[90] Cf. Martiny (2004), p. 133.

[91] Kropka (2010), p. 112.

policyholder's habitual residence and the criterion of domicile of the policyholder's establishment to which the contract relates (paragraph 46). Moreover, The CJEU pointed out (paragraph 54) that the presented interpretation of the term "establishment" in the understanding of the last indent of Art. 2 letter (d) of the Directive 88/357 (Present: Art. 13(13) letter d od the Directive 2009/138) is confirmed by the statement of the Insurance Committee on the interpretation of that rule. The statement reads that "if a single insurance contract covers risks relating to the policyholder's daughter companies or establishments, the location of different risks covered by the contract must be established individually for each risk, according to the provisions of Art. 2 letter (d) of the Directive 88/357 (Present: Art. 13(13) letter d of the Directive 2009/138), especially the last indent of that provision, and norms of Art. 2 letter (e) of the Directive 90/619 (Present: Art. 13 (14) of the Directive 2009/138)."

Article 19 may also be of help in the evaluation of situations where the insurance contract relates to a legal person as a whole or where it is impossible to unambiguously associate the contract with the legal person's specific establishments.[92] In such cases, the criterion of the place of policyholder's central administration should apply.[93]

6 Law Applicable in the Absence of Choice of Law (Art. 7(2), Second Indent Rome I)

The impact of corporate law is apparent in the establishment of the law applicable to the insurance contract in the absence of choice of law. Much importance for the delimitation of scopes of the abovementioned conflict of laws rules attaches to the determination if, as a part of qualification of the expression "in the course of the operations of a branch, agency or any other establishment of the insurer," one should consider Art. 145 of the Directive 2009/138 clarifying the concept of establishment of an insurance undertaking. Under that provision, "any permanent presence of an undertaking in the territory of a Member State shall be treated in the same way as a branch, even where that presence does not take the form of a branch, but consists merely of an office managed by the own staff of the undertaking or by a person who is independent but has permanent authority to act for the undertaking as an agency would."[94]

Consideration of Art. 145 of the Directive 2009/138 requires to assume that in the absence of choice of law an insurance contract concluded by an insurer present in the territory of a given Member State not in the form of agency or branch but in "an

[92] As an example, one can take a D&O (Directors & Officers) insurance contract concluded by a company for a member of its management board.

[93] Bull (2019), pp. 23–27.

[94] See Bigot (1989), pp. 25–27, 34; de Meireles (2020), pp. 141–152.

office managed by the undertaking's own staff or by a person who is independent but has permanent authority to act for the undertaking as an agency would" shall be subject to the law of that Member State. This means that the law applicable to the contract will generally be the law of the country to which the policyholder's vital interests are connected. By contract, a contrary conclusion leads to the submission of the contract to the law of the country where the insurer's central administration is domiciled, or the insurer's establishment to whose activities the contract relates. Such qualification result will generally favor, in the discussed situations, the conflict of laws interests of the insurer. The argument for considering Art. 145 of the Directive 2009/138 as a part of qualification of the expression "in the course of the operations of a branch, agency or any other establishment of the insurer" is the CJEU judgment in the case Kvaerner (C-191/99). The Court, by invoking its previous findings in paragraph 21 of the judgment in the case Commission v. Germany (205/84), concluded that Art. 3 of the Directive 88/357 (Present: Art. 145 of the Directive 2009/138) expands the scope of the concept "agency and branch" in the understanding of Art. 2 letter (c) of that Directive (paragraph 39) (Present: Art. 13 (12) of the Directive 2009/138). It must be noted that transposition of that finding to the qualification of the expression "branch, agency or any other establishment of the insurer" opens a breach in the uniform understanding of the term "establishment" in the provisions of the Rome I Regulation.[95]

The status of the insurer's establishment should not be referred to daughter companies. The same position was assumed by the CJEU in the judgment in the case Kvaerner in respect of interpretation of the term establishment in the understanding of Art. 2(c) of the Directive 88/357 (paragraph 41) (Present: Art. 13(12) of the Directive 2009/138).

The above opinion is confirmed by a judgement of CJEU in the case A Ltd,[96] the first subparagraph of Article 157 (1) of Directive 2009/138/EC of the European Parliament and of the Council of 25 November 2009 on the taking-up and pursuit of the business of Insurance and Reinsurance (Solvency II), as amended by Directive 2013/58/EU of the European Parliament and of the Council of 11 December 2013, read in conjunction with Article 13 (13) of Directive 2009/138, must be interpreted as meaning that, when an insurance company established in a Member State offers insurance covering the contractual risks associated with the value of the shares and the fairness of the purchase price paid by the buyer in the acquisition of an undertaking, an insurance contract concluded in that context is subject exclusively to the indirect taxes and parafiscal charges on insurance premiums in the Member State where the policyholder is established.

[95] Bull (2019), pp. 23–27.

[96] Judgment of the Court (Sixth Chamber) 17 January 2019, C-74/18.

7 The Model Regime of Applicable Law

Lege non distinguende, the connector of domicile of a branch, agency or other establishment of the insurer will apply when no law has been chosen, regardless of whether the activities of the establishment are separated from the operation of the headquarters or if they fit into the latter's operation. However, in each of those two situations, the connector of seat of the insurer's establishment leads to different consequences. Description of such consequences calls for a discussion of the doctrine of the law applicable to the place of pursuing insurance activities (*Betriebsstatut*).

The doctrine of law applicable to the place of pursuing insurance activities was created and developed within Savigny's classical school, centring the objectives of private international law around designation of a legal relationship's "seat." In academic literature, it was explained why in case of insurance contracts the place to be considered the "obligation's seat" (*Sitz der Obligation*) should be the place of pursuing insurance activities (*Ort des Betriebs der Versicherung*).[97] This conception gained the dominant status.[98] It requires treating the total of identical insurance contracts concluded by the same insurer as an economic whole.[99] A necessary condition is to legally frame, in a uniform manner, all insurance contracts covering a specific type of risk. Otherwise, the insurer will not have a uniform operating plan as the basis for the insurer's insurance activities.[100] As a result, the "seat" of the legal relationship is the country of pursuing insurance activities, as the place in which many individual legal relationships are integrated into one insurance portfolio (*Versicherungsbestand*[101]), into a single community of risks (*Gefahrengemeinschaft*[102]). Uniform legal assessment of the total of contracts concluded by a given insurer allows the insurer to pursue activities, which is not without impact on the protection of insurance interests.

The place where insurance activities are pursued is, generally, the insurer's seat (*Sitz des Versicherers*).[103] However, if the insurer has opened an establishment abroad (*Niederlassung*), the "seat" of legal relationship for contracts concluded as a part of operation of that establishment is its seat. The law applicable to the establishment's seat (*Statut der Niederlassung*) supersedes, on such occasions, the law applicable to the place of pursuing insurance activities (*Betriebsstatut*).[104] It was argued in literature that, in such context, establishment is understood as an

[97] Bruck (1924), p. 11.

[98] Reichert-Facilides (1976), p. 1028.

[99] Richter (1980), p. 70.

[100] Bruck (1924), p. 10.

[101] Keller (1962), pp. 16–17.

[102] See Sieg (1971), pp. 45–46.

[103] Richter (1980), p. 79.

[104] Bruck (1924), p. 12.

organizational unit appointed to handle a national insurance portfolio.[105] Authors indicate that the designation of law relevant to the seat of an insurer's establishment is not substantiated by the nature of insurance activities as such.[106] If an establishment may undertake activities under (as a part of) the operating plan of the headquarters, it is not necessary to deviate from the principle of applying the law of the country of the insurer's domicile.[107] These are the requirements of insurance supervision legislation that may necessitate deviations from the rule designating the law of domicile of the insurer's headquarters in favour of the law applicable in the country of the insurer's establishment.[108] *De lege lata,* operations of an establishment created in one Member State of the European Union by an insurer whose central administration is seated in another Member State are subject to supervision of the Member State of origin. The operating plan of such establishment may, but does not have to, make that establishment an enterprise separated in technical and organizational means from the headquarters.

In the light of the above, relevance of the law of the country of the insurer's establishment (Art. 7(2), second indent, in conjunction with Art. 19(2)) is not in conformity with the doctrine of the law applicable to the place of pursuing insurance activities inasmuch as the law of the country of the insurer's establishment will apply in situations when the establishment has not been separated in technical and organizational terms from the headquarters. Correction of the result of designation of applicable law is possible only within the limits of the second sentence of Art. 7(2), second indent.[109]

The abovementioned inconformity affects the insurer's cross-border activities pursued in the form of establishment which has not been separated from the headquarters in technical and organizational terms.[110] From the point of view of such insurer, significance attaches to the unlimited choice of law. Taking advantage of such possibility, the insurer may submit insurance contracts concluded by an establishment to the law of the same country which governs identical contracts concluded as a part of the headquarters. Without offering such possibility, private international law would lead to an actual separation of the establishment from its headquarters.

[105] Richter (1980), p. 80.

[106] Roth (1985), p. 343.

[107] Cf. Richter (1980), p. 72.

[108] Prölls and Martin (2010), p. 204.

[109] Roth (2004).

[110] Sodolska (2005), pp. 1282–1283.

8 The Influence of Corporate Law and Public Law on the *Ratio Legis* of the Regime Under Art. 7(3), First and Third Indents, of the Rome I Regulation

It must be noted that the contemporary private international law of the insurance contract, to the exclusion of insurance contracts covering a large risk, is intended to offer twofold protection: of the policyholder by applying the law of the country in which the centre of the policyholder's activities is situated (*Umweltrecht*),[111] and of insurers' equal chances in their efforts to attract customers. The need for conflict of laws protection of such interests is a consequence of current market conditions in the European Union. Such conditions are determined, first, by the missing harmonization of law on the insurance contract and, second, by the harmonized terms of pursuing insurance activities in the Community. Under the model approach, the need for such protection is directly proportional to the level of policyholders' (and insured parties') protection, as provided in the given national legislation and, in consequence, to the level of costs of pursuing insurance activities in that national market. This statement supports a compromise in the conflict of laws context, which would consider, on one hand, the need to protect policyholders and the need to protect insurers from undue distortions of competition and, on the other one, the need to realize the Community freedoms, especially the freedom to provide services. The uniform market lies, in particular, in the interest of insurers domiciled in those Member States whose law offers a relatively low level of policyholder protection. Such insurers would aspire—in the conditions of uniform market—to submit the total of their insurance contracts concluded by their foreign establishments to the law of one country, i.e., the country of their domicile.[112]

9 Overriding Mandatory Provisions as Instrument Protecting the "Weaker Party" to an Insurance Contract

It is argued in the doctrine that insurance law is "indeed a textbook example of a legal discipline in which legislators use mandatory provisions." It should be no surprise that legislators are accustomed to treating the norms they enact as mandatory rules also with regard to relationships involving a foreign element. Their expectation was partly met by the Community lawmaker at the stage of drawing up the Rome I Regulation. The discussed piece of legislation envisaged the possibility to give effect to legal provisions from outside the contract statute, which may derive from the law of the *forum* (Art. 9(2)) or from the country of performance of the contract (Art. 9(3)), as long, however, as such provisions make an important

[111] Roth (1985), p. 357.

[112] See Roth (1985), p. 365.

element of public interests protection.[113] The two most important (so far) European court decisions relating to the discussed subject matter are the cases: C-369 and 376/96 Arblade[114] and C-381/98 Ingmar.[115] The difference in terms of *rationes decidendi* of those judgments of the Court of Justice illustrates the difference between approaching mandatory rules merely as norms serving the protection of public interests of the state, such as political social or economic organization (Arblade), and a wider conception covering also norms intended to protect private interests (Ingmar). At this point, it is worth noting that the difference between specific norms whose application was considered in both factual situations was not huge. In the Ingmar case, the rule at stake was the provision granting an agent the right to receive commission on a contract concluded after the termination of the agency agreement where the proposal of concluding the contract was received by the principal or the agent prior to the termination of the agency agreement. On the other hand, the Arblade case related to non-application of the provisions of Belgian employment law in respect of: retaining employment records, payment of minimum wage, monitoring of labor conditions, including occupational health and safety. Protection of employee and agent has a common axiological source in the concept of so-called weaker party to contractual relationships. Undoubtedly, the Ingmar case referred to norms giving rise to a private law claim and the Arblade case to public (employment) law norms, both sanctioned and sanctioning ones. However, I consider it disputable if the norms are important enough, from the point of view of the Belgian state, to fulfil the demanding normative pattern under Art. 9(1) of the Rome I Regulation. It seems that in examining if a given provision of the Member State is intended to protect public interests in the understanding of Art. 9(1) of the Rome I Regulation, it will be possible to apply by analogy the methods of interpretation developed in German science in the context of § 823(2) Bürgerliches Gesetzbuch,[116] allowing to establish if a given norm is protective and, secondarily, what type of interests (public or only private) it protects.[117] Overriding mandatory provisions not only have to realize the abovementioned public interests but also apply to factual situations covered by their scope regardless of what law is applicable to a given legal relationship. The question if overriding mandatory provisions are to be applied irrespective of the proper law is generally decided by *lex fori* (it is different in case of so-called foreign rules). The fact if they are indeed overriding follows either from the express wording of the provision (textual interpretation) or from other interpretation methods. That said, the former type of situations will be rare.[118] Since this is a matter of other interpretation methods, a question arises—according to what criteria

[113]More on overriding mandatory provisions Pilich (2012), pp. 374–380.

[114]Case C-376/96 Arblade and Leloup. ECR 1999 Page I-08453.

[115]Case C-381/98 Ingmar versus Eaton. ECR 2000, p. I-9305.

[116]See http://www.gesetze-im-internet.de/bgb/ [Accessed: 2.10.2019].

[117]C.f. broadly on the subject: Mataczyński (2011), pp. 97–104 and the ample German literature cited therein against the background of § 823(2) BGB.

[118]C.f. Mataczyński (2005), p. 50.

interpretation should proceed. At this point, a significant scope of discretion is open for interpreters.

The starting point for the considerations on the scope of application of the law of a given country is the principle of territorial application of the country's law.[119] In purely general terms, it boils down to the recognition of the legislative competence of the state within the area of its sovereignty, understood as actual dominion. Private international law is an exception to that principle, justified at the *ratio legis* level by the aspiration to ensure protection to rights acquired under foreign legal systems, to ensure fair resolutions or to maintain good international cooperation (comity),[120] or even by an international law obligation of the state.[121] This exception—which is indisputable—is thetically justified by the binding force of proper regimes of national conflict of laws statutes, unifying legislation, in particular, bi- and multilateral international treaties or secondary legislation of regional integration organizations, especially ones which are crucial from our perspective of EU regulations. According to the opinion dominant in European doctrine, the mechanism of applying mandatory norms was explained by the conception of so-called latent conflict of laws rule.[122] In the light of that opinion, the basis for operation of overarching mandatory rules is an unwritten, hidden in the contents of substantive law provisions, unilateral conflict of laws norm which makes *lex specialis* in relation to the complete conflict of laws norm relevant to a given type of situation.[123] This conception is based on the universalist assumption of application of private international law (i.e., every act of applying law relies on a conflict of laws rule, however, in purely internal matters this procedure is unconscious). I have been of the opinion[124] that the problem of international mandatory rules may be approached as if from the other side, without the need to always rely on the latent conflict of laws rule, by regarding the application of substantive law norms of a given state as "return" to the basic territorial principle.[125]

By definition, overriding mandatory provisions stand in opposition to the proper law. This is the case since they are provisions which are effective beside the statute relevant for the evaluation of a given obligation.[126] Any decision concerning recognition of a given norm as an overriding mandatory provision necessitates a case-to case evaluation of the particular state of affairs, and the analysis of legal provisions should, as such, have a "functional" character.[127]

[119]Brownlie (1998), p. 301. So, Mann (1984), p. 20.

[120]Dicey et al. (2015), pp. 4–11.

[121]Wolff (1933), p. 7.

[122]Mataczyński (2005), pp. 113–116.

[123]Zachariasiewicz (2014), pp. 433–469.

[124]Mataczyński (2005), p. 116.

[125]Baker and Logue (2015), pp. 1–31.

[126]Fuchs (2003), p. 70 et seq.

[127]Zachariasiewicz (2010), p. 12; Zachariasiewicz (2014), pp. 443–444, 468; Baker and Logue (2015), pp. 1–31.

It is settled case law of the Court that it is, in that context, for the national court, in the course of its assessment of whether the national law which it proposes to substitute for that expressly chosen by the parties to the contract is a "mandatory rule," to consider not only of the exact terms of that law, but also of its general structure and of all the circumstances in which that law was adopted to determine whether it is mandatory in nature in so far as it appears that the legislature adopted in it order to protect an interest judged to be essential by the Member State concerned.[128] This opinion corresponds with the position taken by the CJEU according to which article 16 of Regulation (EC) No 864/2007 of the European Parliament and of the Council of 11 July 2007 on the law applicable to non-contractual obligations (Rome II) must be interpreted as meaning that a national provision, such as that at issue in the main proceedings, which provides that the limitation period for actions seeking compensation for damage resulting from an accident is three years, cannot be considered to be an overriding mandatory provision, within the meaning of that article, unless the court hearing the case finds, based on a detailed analysis of the wording, general scheme, objectives and the context in which that provisions was adopted, that it is of such importance in the national legal order that it justifies a departure from the law applicable, designed pursuant to Article 4 of that regulation. Article 27 of Regulation No 864/2007 must be interpreted as meaning that Article 28 of Directive 2009/103/EC of the European Parliament and of the Council of 16 September 2009 relating to insurance against civil liability in respect of the use of motor vehicles, and the enforcement of the obligation to insure against such liability, as transposed into national law, does not constitute a provision of EU law which lays down a conflict-of-law rule relating to non-contractual obligations, within the meaning of Article 27 of that regulation.[129]

At this point, it should be noted that the doctrine of private international law makes a consequent distinction between *lois de police "de direction"* and *lois de police "de protection"* (*lois de police protectrice*),[130] the equivalents of which in the German-language literature are *Eingriffsnormens* i *Parteischutzvorschriften.* The former protect public interests of the state. These may include provisions regulating supervision over insurance activities or imposing the requirement of compulsory insurance of a business. The latter restore the equilibrium between the parties to the contract and protect the weaker party (policyholder, insured party, injured person).[131] It is legitimate to treat both groups of situations separately, i.e., apply widely the construction of overriding mandatory rules in relation to consumer insurance; on the other hand, in case of entrepreneurs possible refusal to apply foreign norms compromising the protective principles of German insurance law should be based on the public policy clause. The proposed division into norms protecting public

[128] Judgment of 17 October 2013, Unamar, C-184/12, EU:C:2013:663, paragraph 50.

[129] CJEU Judgement 31 January 2019, C-149/18, Agostinho da Silva Martins v. Dekra Claims Services Portugal SA.

[130] Piroddi (2008), p. 606.

[131] Zachariasiewicz (2010), p. 22; Zachariasiewicz (2013), pp. 266–267.

interests (being the content of "overriding mandatory rules") and norms protecting merely individual interests (which should be eliminated *a priori* from the scope of the discussed concept) seems very attractive from the point of view of European law. It is supported especially by the quite rigorous wording of Art. 9(1) of the Rome Regulation, referring to state interests. It is not excluded that the status of "overriding mandatory provisions" can be assigned to national law norms intended to protect collective policyholder interests under Art. 9 of the Rome I Regulation.[132]

In French judicial practice, a liberal approach is outlined on overriding mandatory provisions in cross-border relationships. It is assumed that both provisions enacted in the interest of the state (*lois de police de diréction*) and provisions which protect individual interests (*lois de police protectrice*) may potentially amount to overriding mandatory provisions. By way of example, norms governing the language of an insurance contract are perceived as such overriding mandatory rules. It is indicated that provisions which implement the principle prohibiting the insured party's enrichment (rules on the consequences of over-insurance or "multiple" insurance) may also count as overriding provisions.[133] The status of overriding mandatory provisions may also be granted to rules which prohibit insurance of certain specific types of risk. The function of such provisions may be performed by norms containing general clauses to be applied by national insurance supervision authorities while permitting introduction of new insurance types on the domestic insurance market.[134] As a result, if a given norm protects both public and private interests, it may be recognized in a particular case—as long as the other prerequisites are met—as an overriding mandatory provision in the understanding of Art. 9 of the Rome I Regulation. Moreover, in the case law of the Court of Justice, one may speak of liberal interpretation of overriding mandatory provisions. It is pointed out that provisions protecting the weaker party from abusive contractual clauses are enacted in the public interest.[135]

A good illustration of the application of the discussed type of provisions is the decision by the French Court of Cassation of 2 October 2009,[136] based on a state of affairs in which a company incorporated under the laws of France entrusted the execution of maintenance works to an entity using materials supplied by their Belgian manufacturer. As a result of detachment of one of the structural elements, the orderer was injured. The ordering party brought the case before a French court

---

[132] Baker and Logue (2015); or Pilich (2012).

[133] Auclair (2003), pp. 64–67.

[134] Kropka (2007), p. 147. The author discusses the general clause of protection of insured persons' interests (*Belange der Versicherten*) in German law.

[135] In the judgment of 26 October 2006 in the case C-168/05 *Elisa María Mostaza Claro v. Centro Móvil Milenium SL*, ECR 2006, p. I-10421, the Court admitted that provisions of the Council Directive 93/13/EEC of 5 April 1993 on unfair terms in consumer contracts (OJ EU L 95 of 21.04.1993, p. 29) concerning unfair contract clauses form a component of the public order.

[136] Cass., Chambre civile 2, 8 octobre 2009, N° de pourvoi: 08-13149. Available in the Internet: http://www.legifrance.gouv.fr/affichJuriJudi.do?idTexte=JURITEXT00002114 1550 [last accessed: 10 October 2017].

for compensation against the contractor. The defendant requested that the manufacturer and the latter's insurer be called on to join the proceedings as entities against which the defendant had a guarantee claim.[137] In the course of the process, the insurer invoked a clause limiting its liability which had been stipulated in the civil liability insurance concluded between the insurer and the manufacturer. That solution was in conformity with Belgian law, which governed the insurance contract. The essence of the dispute brought before the Court of Cassation boiled down to the decision if in the depicted state of affairs Art. 113-1 of the French Insurance Code[138] could be given effect as an overriding mandatory provision. According to the interpretation line adopted in case law with regard to the relatively unfortunately formulated first sentence of Art. 113-1 of the Insurance Code,[139] the insurer is liable for damages caused by mishap or reasons attributable to the insured person unless the insurance agreement expressly provides for exemptions of the insurer's liability which are rendered precisely enough to permit their understanding without any special interpretative endeavors[140] and which are of "exceptional" character in the sense that they may not result in excessively far-reaching limitation of the scope of insurance protection or affording protection which is merely illusory.[141] The Court of Cassation reached the conclusion that in the examined case Art. 113-1 of the Insurance Code should have been applied as an overriding mandatory provision, and on that basis the insurer should have been refused the right to invoke the contractual clause limiting the its liability. Such recourse to French legislation was considered justified although the insurance contract was concluded in the territory of Belgium by a company incorporated under Belgian law with an insurer of the same domicile and the liability of the contracting parties was derivative from the liability of the contractor. It is symptomatic that the Court of Cassation did not accept the argument raised by the insurer that an obstacle to the application of Art. 113-1 of the Insurance Code was the fact that the provision was intended only to protect individual interests and did not strive to protect the public interest in any way. In the justification of the discussed judgment, it was highlighted that the exclusion of liability stipulated in the insurance agreement amounted to an excessively far-reaching restriction of insurance protection as compared to the principal function which was to be fulfilled by the insurance contract.[142]

In a judgment, dated 5 March 2013, the Periguex Court of First Instance held that the provisions of Article L121-10 of the French Insurance Code relating to the

[137] This institution of French procedural law is discussed in more detail in Herzog (1967), pp. 292–293.

[138] Code des assurances. "Journal Officiel de la République française" 1978, p. 1088, modifié.

[139] The provision of Art. 113-1 first sentence of the Insurance Code reads: "Save formal (formelle) and limited (limitée) exclusions contained in the policy, the insurer shall bear the losses and damage caused by unforeseen accident or caused by the insured's fault."

[140] Cass., civ. 2e, 8 octobre 2009, n° 08-19646. Available on the Internet: http://www.legifrance.gouv.fr/affichJuriJudi.do?idTexte=JURITEXT000021140120 [last accessed: 23 October 2017].

[141] Cass., civ. 3e, 8 juin 2010, n° 09-12968. Available on the Internet: http://www.legifrance.gouv.fr/affichJuriJudi.do?idTexte=JURITEXT000022342519 [last accessed: 23 October 2017].

[142] Pacuła (2014), p. 44.

automatic transfer of property insurance in case of sale of the covered good amounted to an overriding provision of French insurance law. The court therefore disregarded English law, which was provided for in the insurance policy underwritten between an English national and an English insurer to cover a building in France, which provides that the policy is automatically terminated in case of sale of the covered good.[143]

An analysis of the written justification of the ruling gives rise to the conclusion that the application of the conception of overriding mandatory provisions was to produce the desired substantive law outcome. Following the conclusions of such analysis, it seems that that provisions with the features of *lois de police protectrices* which could be potentially recognized as overriding mandatory provisions include insurance law rules intended to protect the policyholder and the insured party and to prevent negative consequences of the inequivalent position of the parties to an insurance contract. However, a reservation should be made that the foregoing refers to provisions which serve the purpose of preserving the essence of the insurance contract or its principal functions, including predominantly the function of insurance protection. Overriding mandatory provisions, by defending specific legislative objectives, are to ensure the substantive law outcome desired from the point of view of *lex fori*, and not to level the differences between particular systems of national law. Consequently, an intervention is probable by provisions which express the fundamental principles of insurance law, including the good faith principle based on mutual loyalty between the parties to an insurance agreement[144] and the principle of compensation[145] in a situation where these are not cherished by *lex causae*. Parties to an insurance contract should consider the possibility of effect being given to legal provisions imposing the requirement of the insured person's consent to the commencement of insurance protection granted under a life insurance. In case of artificial intelligence, we may have to do with provisions which should apply regardless of the law applicable to a given relationship. One example are traffic accidents caused by autonomous vehicles. Such provisions are given effect beside the law relevant to the relationship. Those are overriding mandatory provisions.[146] For example, some French scholars declare that only the following provisions should be considered as overriding mandatory provisions: (a) Article L310-2 of the French Insurance Code, which provides that insurance contracts with insurers not licensed in France are null and void; (b) Article L113-1 of the French Insurance Code, which condemns willful misconduct; (c) the general rule, which prohibits criminal liability insurance; (d) Article L113-6 of the French Insurance Code, which prohibits the unilateral termination of policy in the event of bankruptcy od liquidation of the insured; (e) the principle that benefits of the policy cannot exceed the insured's loss.[147] Part of the

143 Study on the law applicable to insurance contracts, Final Report, https://op.europa.eu/s/olTo.

144 More on that in Auclair (2003), pp. 64–67.

145 Dubuisson (2004), pp. 742–743.

146 Świerczyński (2019).

147 Study on the law applicable to insurance contracts, Final Report, https://op.europa.eu/s/olTu.

Italian legal literature pointed out examples. At first example might be rules states have adopted to assure the preservation of the "indemnity character" of insurance contracts. The need to avoid that insurance contracts can change from a private system of indemnity from risks to a mean for profit seems to fall with the definition of those rules that define the social and economics shapes of a country. If insurance contracts were—for the policyholder or the beneficiary—to become means for profits, it could be believed policyholders and beneficiaries would be induced to somehow favour the occurrence of the event they seek relief from, with negative and detrimental consequences, for example, in the field of life insurance. A second example, already discussed in the legal literature, might concern those substantive insurance law rules limiting the insurer's dominating position in the insurance contract.[148]

10 The Application of "Specific Provisions" Relating to a Given Compulsory Insurance (Art. 7(4) Letter (a) of the Rome I Regulation)—Public Law Aspects

Key importance for the understanding of the normative content the first sentence of Art. 7(4) letter (a) of the Rome I Regulation attaches to the question if the "specific provisions" mentioned in that provision are rules mandatorily applied in the conflict of laws sense or overriding mandatory provisions. At this point, one should be guided by the criterion of the conflict of laws basis for application of the provisions given effect beside the law generally applicable to the contract.

The answer to that question is problematic. The source of doubts is the structure of Art. 7(4) letter (a), first sentence. The hypothesis of first sentence of Art. 7(4) letter (a) is that the law of a Member State of the European Union imposes in reference to a specific type of insurance the obligation to insure. The disposition is the requirement that the parties to the insurance contract follow "specific provisions" on that compulsory insurance type as provided for in the EU Member State whose law prescribes the obligation to insure. In addition, the discussed norm has a sanction in the form of finding an insurance contract which does not comply with the "specific provisions" as non-complying with the insurance obligation. This makes the norm a blanket provision, introducing negative legal consequences of acts which do not comply with very generally named provisions of law. Such rules are "specific provisions relating to that insurance."

It must be resolved if the first sentence of Art. 7(4) letter (a) contains, beside a norm of unified substantive law, a conflict of laws rule requiring to apply "specific provisions relating to that insurance" as provisions mandatorily applied in the conflict of laws sense or if the expression "specific provisions relating to that insurance" should be referred to overriding mandatory rules.

[148] Dominelli (2016).

The source of problems in the establishment of the conflict of laws nature of the "specific provisions" referred to in the first sentence of Art. 7(4) letter (a) is also the relation of the discussed norm with the provisions of the Directive 88/357 (Present: Directive 2009/138). Namely, Art. 8(2) of the Directive 88/357 (Present: Art. 179 (2) of the Directive 88/357) is supplemented by Art. 8(5) letter (a), first indent, of the Directive 88/357 (Present: Art. 179(5) letter a of the Directive 2009/138). Under that provision, "Member State shall communicate to the Commission the specific legal provisions relating to that insurance." It follows that in the provisions of the Directive 2009/138 the concept of "specific provisions relating to a given compulsory insurance" is explained by the contents of notifications made by the Member States introducing the insurance obligation.

Article 179(2) letter (a) of the Directive 2009/138 does not contain any conflict of laws norm. In the same way, it does not belong to "provisions of Community law which, in relation to particular matters, lay down conflict-of-law rules relating to contractual obligations" in the understanding of Art. 23 Rome I. This does not mean, however, that the provision of the Directive is considered as a part of interpretation of the first sentence of Art. 7(4) letter (a). The concept of "specific provisions" in the understanding of the first sentence of Art. 7(4) letter (a) should be assigned autonomous meaning. First, this is supported by the absence in Art. 7 of a norm referring to Art. 179(2) letter (a) of the Directive 2009/138 for the sake of clarifying of the term "specific provisions." Second, the acceptance as authoritative for the clarification of the term "specific provisions" of the contents of notifications made by Member States under Art. 179(2) letter (a) of the Directive 2009/138 would contradict the idea of harmonization of private international law. The content of the notification is arbitrarily decided by each Member State. This may lead to an excessively wide definition of the range of "specific provisions," e.g., by inclusion among them of general provisions on contractual obligations. Moreover, the contents of notification may be decided by such factors as legislative technique or tradition adhered to in the national legal system of a specific Member State. The sources of law on a given type of compulsory insurance may comprise either comprehensive regimes, including in the area of substantive law on the insurance contract, or rules referring to general legal provisions on the insurance contract or to the law of contractual obligations.

The analysis of Art. 7(4) letter (a), first sentence, leads to the conclusion that "specific provisions" belong to the category of rules mandatorily applied in the conflict of laws sense, and not to the category of overriding mandatory provisions.

The requirement of compliance by the parties to insurance contracts with "specific provisions" of a given Member State relating to specific types of compulsory insurance points to the conclusion that the first sentence of Art. 7(4) letter (a) contains the requirement of applying "specific provisions" beside the law generally applicable to the contract. This statement leads to the conclusion that the discussed provision contains the following conflict of laws norm: to insurance contracts in respect of which insurance obligation is introduced by the law of an EU Member State specific provisions of the Member State governing that compulsory insurance shall apply. Further specification of the content of that conflict of laws rule necessitates interpretation of the term "specific provisions." The provision of Art. 7(4) letter (a), first sentence, allows, in my opinion, to make the two following conclusions in his regard. First, "specific provisions" may only be mandatory provisions (*ius cogens*). This follows from the fact that non-compliance with the "special provisions" under the first sentence of Art. 7(4) letter (a) gives rise to the consequence of non-compliance with the insurance obligation. Second, the formulation "the insurance contract shall not satisfy the obligation to take out insurance" suggests that "specific provisions relating to that insurance" are not all mandatory provisions governing a specific type of compulsory insurance but only such norms that form the contents of the statutory insurance obligation. Such provisions will be, e.g., norms on the minimum guarantee cover. Their application does not depend on whether they relate to two or more compulsory insurance types introduced in a given Member State. It is essential that "specific provisions" are rules forming the content of the statutory insurance obligation, which allows to narrow down the designation scope of the analyzed conflict of laws rule, characteristic of a conflict of laws rules designating mandatorily applied provisions in the conflict-of-law sense. At the same time, not every norm forming the content of the statutory insurance obligation will be recognized, under Art. 9, as overriding mandatory rule.

It must be concluded that from the first sentence of Art. 7(4) letter (a) the following conflict of laws rule can be derived: to the insurance contract in respect of which the insurance obligation has been introduced in the law of a Member State of the EU, mandatory rules of that Member State shall apply specifying the content of the insurance obligation relating to that compulsory insurance (specific provisions). This norm is a complete norm. It applies mandatorily. It curtails the consequences of designation of the law generally applicable to the contract either by a conflict of laws rule on the choice of law or conflict of laws rule in the absence of choice of law. Its application does not depend on the comparison of the provisions of the law generally applicable to the contract with the specific legal provisions of the Member State introducing the insurance obligation.

There are also other arguments against recognising the first sentence of Art. 7 (4) letter (a) as overriding mandatory provision. First, if the legislator, when drafting Art. 7(4) letter (a), first sentence, had that category of norms in mind, the legislator would use the expression "overriding mandatory provisions" instead of the term "specific provisions." Second, Art. 7(4) letter (a) refers both to "specific provisions" of the conflict-of-law *lex fori* and to "specific provisions" of a Member State other than the conflict-of-law *lex fori*. However, under Art. 9(3), overriding mandatory provisions of a Member State different from the conflict of laws *lex fori* are given effect only if in that Member State "the obligations arising out of the contract have to be or have been performed." The place where the obligations arising out of the contract have to be or have been performed is not identifiable as regards the fulfilment of a public law obligation to conclude a compulsory insurance contract.[149]

[149] Kropka (2010), p. 231.

The first sentence of Art. 7(4) letter (a) is supplemented by the second sentence of that provision. The disposition of that sentence contains the requirement to apply the "specific provisions" referred to in Art. 7(4) letter (a), first sentence, prior to the law of the Member State in which the risk is situated, designated as the relevant law under the applicable conflict of laws rules under Art. 7(3), first indent, letter lit. (a) (choice of law) or Art. 7(3), third indent (where the applicable law has not been chosen). Such conclusion assumes that Art. 7(4) letter (a), second sentence, shall not apply to situations when the legal provisions of the Member State introducing the obligation to insure and/or legal provisions of the Member State where the risk is situated are given effect as overriding mandatory provisions.[150]

In the same way, Art. 7(4) letter (a), second sentence, contains a conflict of laws rule demarcating the application spheres of "specific provisions" of law of the Member State introducing the insurance obligation and the law of the Member State where the risk is situated, designated as the relevant law. This norm is not a conflict of laws rule of second degree, demarcating the areas of application of other conflict of laws rules under the Rome I Regulation. It does not provide that the conflict of laws rule designating as relevant the law of the Member State where the risk is situated shall not apply when another conflict of laws rule applies under which effect is given, beside the law relevant to the contract, to "specific provisions" on a given compulsory insurance of the country imposing the insurance obligation. The conflict of laws rule encapsulated in Art. 7(4) letter (a), second sentence, resolves only about the course of action when the provisions of law of the Member State where the risk is situated, as the generally applicable law, contradict the "specific provisions" relating to a given type of compulsory insurance of the Member State introducing the insurance obligation, by deciding that the latter norms shall prevail.

A contradiction between the law of the Member State where the risk is situated and norms of the Member State introducing the insurance obligation comes into play only when the application of law of the Member State where the risk is situated and of the "special provisions" of the Member State imposing the obligation leads to different consequences.[151]

It follows from the above considerations that the public law insurance obligation affects the problems of establishing the applicable law.

[150]Kropka (2010), p. 228.

[151]Kropka (2010), p. 234.

11 GDPR in Insurance and Private International Law

Important changes in the insurance business were introduced by IDD[152] and GDPR.[153] It seems that, in practice, application of IDD and GDPR may give rise to certain problems since both legislative acts seem to be based on different assumptions. In case of IDD, one of the most crucial elements is the obligation to identify the customer's demands and needs. On the other hand, the Regulation requires that the least possible amount of personal data be collected to protect rights and freedoms of natural persons.[154]

Disputes concerning personal data breaches on international scale are complex. Despite the application of new, harmonized UE provisions on the protection of personal data (GDPR), the European Union has not filled the gap in the Rome II Regulation[155] relating to the protection of privacy (Art. 1(2) letter (g)). GDPR contains only rules in the area of international civil procedure (Art. 79 and following). On the other hand, there is no complementary conflict of laws regime of liability for violating the terms of personal data protection.

It is not an easy task to designate the law applicable to specific questions relating to personal data protection. Difficulties follow form the following reasons: (1) exterritorial applicability of GDPR (Art. 3 GDPR), wherein doubts relate both to the specification of the exterritoriality scope and its impact on the process of designating the applicable law; (2) mixed, public and private nature of GDPR provisions; (3) use in GDPR of new criteria (establishment, targeting of activities, monitoring of the behaviour of data subjects) in establishing the scope of GDPR's application, which gives rise to a question about concurrence of such criteria with connectors (e.g., breaching party's domicile, place of violation) found in conflict of laws rules on non-contractual liability; (4) introduction in GDPR of rules in the area of international civil procedure, especially on national jurisdiction, favourable to persons asserting claims against data controllers, which, in conjunction with a missing clear conflict of laws regime, increases the risk of forum shopping (manipulations of the applicable law) by data subjects (injured parties); (5) the abovementioned lack of harmonized conflict of laws rules for privacy commitments, whereby in case of Member States of the European Union, privacy commitments were expressly exempted from the scope of application of the Rome II Regulation,[156] this means

[152] Directive (EU) 2016/97 of the European Parliament and of the Council of 20 January 2016 on insurance distribution (OJ L 26, p. 19, as amended).

[153] Regulation (EU) 2016/679 of the European Parliament and of the Council of 27 April 2016 on the protection of natural persons with regard to the processing of personal data and on the free movement of such data, and repealing Directive 95/46/EC (General Data Protection Regulation) (OJ L 199, p. 1).

[154] Pokrzywniak (2018), p. 150.

[155] Pazdan (2009), p. 23.

[156] Regulation (EC) No 864/2007 of the European Parliament and of the Council of 11 July 2007 on the law applicable to non-contractual obligations (Rome II) (OJ L 199, 31.7.2007, pp. 40–49).

that depending on the body examining the case, different national law may apply (regarding matters not expressly regulated in GDPR, e.g., amount of compensation for violation of privacy);[157] (6) the need to assess which of GDPR's provisions are mandatory overriding rules.

There is no doubt that private international law aspects were seriously neglected in the works on GDPR.[158] Emphasis was put on specifying GDPR's exterritorial applicability (Art. 3).

The basic conflict of laws rule under the Rome II Regulation is the principle of applying the law of the country in which the damage was sustained regardless of the country where the harmful event took place or the country or countries in which the event's incidental consequences occurred (Art. 4(1)). Application of that rule in relation to GDPR violations should not raise any major doubts. Moreover, the Rome II Regulation contains additional supplementary rules. In the first place, the court should check if the parties made a valid choice of applicable law, according to the preconditions under Art. 14 of the Rome II Regulation. Also, that solution has advantages in case of claims for violating the rules on personal data protection. It accounts for party autonomy. In the lack of a valid choice of law, it must be checked if there are preconditions to applying rules on separately addressed torts/delicts (Art. 5-9 of the Rome II Regulation). When the answer is negative, and it is so in case of violating the principles of personal data protection, it becomes legitimate to recourse to the general norms under Art. 4 of the Rome II Regulation, starting from the rule under (2) (applicability of the parties' common personal law which, by the way, will be a solution consistent with the rules of jurisdiction under Art. 79 and following GDPR). Only in the absence of a common personal law, one should apply the basic norm under Art. 4(1) providing for applicability of the law of the country where the direct damage occurred. In both above situations, it is expedient that the court establishes if it is possible to correct the designation of law under Art. 4(3) of the Rome II regulation.[159]

12 Conclusions

The purpose of the above considerations was to indicate the mutual interpenetration between EU provisions of public and corporate law, as well as the impact of national provisions of the same type on private international law. The meeting point between public and private insurance law is characterized by the fact that the traditional distinction between private law norms (as law protecting predominantly the private interests of individuals—parties to civil law relationships) and public law norms (as law of the state protecting common interests), originating from nineteenth

[157] Nagy (2012), pp. 251–296.
[158] Czepelak (2010), p. 705 et seq.
[159] Świerczyński (2020), p. 53.

century liberalism, becomes increasingly problematic. Public law regimes increasingly often penetrate the areas of legal insurance relationships previously considered an exclusive domain of private law.[160] In doing so, they are intended both to protect general interests (social and economic or political)[161] and to protect "private" interests. Among others, this refers to: antitrust, administrative sanctions, insurance supervision, information duties,[162] supervision of insurance activities through public law, protection of insured in group insurance,[163] artificial intelligence in insurance, rules specifying the criteria of admission to specific professions (brokers, agents, insurance distributors).[164] At the same time, there is a growing awareness that those areas (as, for example: contractual relationships, delicts (torts)) have a "public" significance. Private law, more and more clearly, also realizes "public" interests[165] because norms protecting "private" interests are also relevant to the social or economic organization of the state.[166] At this point, one should point especially to the rules protecting "weaker" parties to civil law relationships, both in contractual and other relations (delictual tortious).[167] This is the case since private law also fulfils "public" functions—by provisions forcing the parties of civil law transactions to also consider cross-community or general economic interests. As a result, it becomes increasingly difficult to clearly set a demarcation line between public and private interests and, in the same way, between public and private law rules,[168] especially that legislators relatively rarely invoke that distinction expressly and do not introduce its clear criteria.[169]

It must be noted that the division between public and private law provisions, fading in certain legal systems, retains its importance in the context of international relationships. Whereas in purely "national" relationships, the generally formal qualification of a legal norm is irrelevant to the establishment of its preconditions, in international relations the problem of a norm's nature becomes of utmost importance. Derogation of mandatory private law rules of a legal system connected with a given relationship is, one way or another, effected through conflict of laws choice of law or objective designation of the applicable law according to the criterion applied by the judge of the forum.[170] However, such result does not have to be the case in regard to public law norms. This follows from a different "level" of public interest reflected in private law norms and public law norms. Therefore, a public law norm

[160] Merryman (1969), p. 3 et seq.

[161] Zachariasiewicz (2014), p. 447.

[162] Fras (2019b), pp. 113–143.

[163] Fras (2019c), pp. 1–23.

[164] See, e.g., Zachariasiewicz (2014), p. 446 et seq.

[165] See, e.g., Baade (2015), p. 435.

[166] Blessing (1999), p. 46 et seq.

[167] Martiny (2006), p. 87 et seq.

[168] Salomon (2008), p. 1738.

[169] See, e.g., Nowacki (1992), p. 30; Szczepaniak (2015), p. 4.

[170] Philip (1982), p. 92.

may "force" its application, regardless of the law governing the legal relationship. It was assumed that norms protecting public policy have a territorial effect.[171] A similar consequence attaches to the observation that a given public law rule has an "overriding" nature if its application involves a criminal or administrative sanction, which is always strictly "territorial."[172]

Moreover, insurance contact law is harmonized to a certain degree by directives on consumer contract law covering consumer insurances. Mention is to be made of Directive 2002/65/EC (Distance Marketing of Financial Services)[173] and Council Directive 93/13/EEC (Unfair Contract Terms).[174] Council Directive 93/13/EEC (see article 4 para. 2), Directive (EU) 2016/97 of the European Parliament and of the Council of 20 January 2016 on insurance distribution provide EU minimum standards of client protection and allow Member States to adopt more protective measures. Other directives outside the scope of client protection, such as the Directive 2000/31/EC (Electronic Commerce),[175] Directive 2011/7/EU (Late Payment)[176] and Directive 2004/113/EC (Gender Equality)[177] also have an impact on insurance contract law. The provisions of these directives often have mixture nature—public and private.

As opposed to Art. 7 Rome I, in EU legislation the insurance customer is considered a protected party under sectoral directives and regulations. 2016/97 IDD is inconsistent in the specification of the group of parties covered by the protective regime. In Recital (3), the party indicated as protected is the customer, whereas Recital (10) uses interchangeably the terms 'consumer' and 'customer:' "Current and recent financial turbulence has underlined the importance of ensuring effective consumer protection across all financial sectors. It is appropriate, therefore, to strengthen the confidence of customers and to make regulatory treatment of the distribution of insurance products more uniform in order to ensure an adequate level of customer protection across the Union." However, the Directive does not contain any legal definitions of those terms.

[171] von Hoffmann and Thorn (2007), p. 61.

[172] Ellger (2012), p. 1231.

[173] Directive 2002/65/EC of the European Parliament and of the Council of 23 September 2002 concerning the distance marketing of consumer financial services and amending Council Directives 90/619/EEC, 97/7/EC and 98/27/EC, OJ 2002 L 271/16.

[174] Council Directive 93/13/EEC of 5 April 1993 on unfair terms in consumer contracts, OJ 1993 L 95/29.

[175] Directive 2000/31/EC of the European Parliament and of the Council of 8 June 2000 on certain legal aspects of information society services, in particular electronic commerce, in the Internal Market ('Directive on electronic commerce'), OJ 2000 L 178/1.

[176] Directive 2011/7/EU of 16 February of the European Parliament and of the Council on combating late payment in commercial transactions (recast), OJ 2011 L 48/1.

[177] Council Directive 2004/113/EC of 13 December 2004 implementing the principle of equal treatment between men and women in the access to and supply of goods and services, OJ 2004 L 373/37.

Since insurance contracts may have an investment element, one should also address the concept of investor. The legal definition of retail investor was included in Regulation 1286/2014[178] (hereinafter PRIIP), whereby that legislative act refers to legal definitions of clients as provided in other directives, depending on whose clients they are and what kind of services (goods) they buy, i.e., whether that is a packaged retail or insurance-based investment product. Under Art. 4 item 6, "retail investor" means:

- a retail client as defined in point (11) of Article 4 (1) of Directive 2014/65/EU
- a customer within the meaning of Directive 2002/92/EC, where that customer would not qualify as a professional client as defined in point (10) of Article 4 (1) of Directive 2014/65/EU

At the time being, consistency is missing, both of the EU and national legislators, in the specification of the subject of public law protection. In the provisions on the insurance market, the EU legislator does not introduce the customer's legal definition although that term is used, which is a serious shortcoming and gives rise to interpretative doubts about the scope of protective measures. In Regulation 1094/2010,[179] the terms customer and consumer can be found; also, IDD contains both terms and only once uses the concept of professional or retail customer (Art. 30 (6) item (c)).

An exception in this regard is the PRIIP Regulation devoted to a narrow aspect of insurance activities—insurance contracts with an investment element. For that reason, the Regulation contains a legal definition of retail investor, meaning a "customer within the meaning of Directive 2002/92/EC (currently Directive 2016/97), where that customer would not qualify as a professional client as defined in point (10) of Article 4(1) of Directive 2014/65/EU."[180]

Bearing in mind the indicated terminological differences, the existing legislative framework needs straightening. It seems legitimate to introduce, for the EU legislation concerning the entire financial market, a uniform customer definition, introducing a dichotomous division between professional and non-professional customers. This is especially substantiated by the existence of so-called hybrid products, covering services of different financial market sectors and the related systemic threat.

[178] Commission Delegated Regulation (EU) 2017/653 of 8 March 2017 supplementing Regulation (EU) No 1286/2014 of the European Parliament and of the Council on key information documents for packaged retail and insurance-based investment products (PRIIPs) by laying down regulatory technical standards with regard to the presentation, content, review and revision of key information documents and the conditions for fulfilling the requirement to provide such documents (OJ L 2017.100.1).

[179] Regulation (EU) No 1094/2010 of the European Parliament and of the Council of 24 November 2010 establishing a European Supervisory Authority (European Insurance and Occupational Pensions Authority) (OJ L 331, 15.12.2010, pp. 48–83).

[180] Art. 4(1) item 10 of the Directive 2014/65/EU: 'professional client' means a client meeting the criteria laid down in Annex II.

On legal relationships which are especially "susceptible" to public law regimes, the delimitation of the spheres of influence between private and public law is—in the opinion of certain authors—becoming groundless.[181] At the same time, it is argued that nowadays the distinction between private and public law is still of great importance[182]—especially for the law applied in practice—because of the need to demarcate between the spheres of application (among others, with a view to the competences of appropriate authorities) of rules belonging to the former or the latter branch of the legal system.[183] When considering this issue, it should be noted, in the first place, that the distinction between private and public law norms is not consequently followed in all legal systems, and the sense of introducing such division is often put into question.[184] It must be noted that the differentiation between public and private law provisions, although blurred in certain legal systems, retains its validity in reference to international relationships. While in purely "national" legal relationships the formal qualification of a legal norm is generally irrelevant to the establishment of preconditions to its application, in international relations the question of the norm's nature assumes greater significance. Derogation from mandatory private law provisions forming a part of the legal system connected with a given relationship is, one way or another, effected by conflict of laws designation of law or by objective designation of the applicable law according to the criterion applied by the judge of the forum.[185] However, such consequence does not have to be the case with regard to public law norms. This follows from a different "level" of public interest reflected in private and public law norms. As a result, a public law norm may "force" its application regardless of the law governing the legal relationship. Therefore, it was assumed that norms protecting the public policy have a territorial effect.[186]

Nowadays, the most popular criterion is that of interest (public/private) realized through the norm, however, even this criterion is criticized,[187] for example, because the demarcation between such interests—as mentioned above—is sometimes difficult.[188] Besides, more importantly, even if it were possible to distinguish public law provisions on that basis, all of them are a manifestation of certain "common" interests and are intended to protect such interests. The criterion of "interests," in reference to "overriding" mandatory rules of private or public law, implies drawing attention to the purposes realized by the state through specific legal regimes. Consequently, this refers to provisions which are so important to ensure consistence

---

[181] See, e.g., Harlow (1980), p. 241 et seq.

[182] Its importance even grew in places where it had not been recognized before, see Jurgens and van Ommeren (2012), p. 172 et seq.

[183] See Szczepaniak (2015), p. 13.

[184] Szczepaniak (2015), p. 6.

[185] See, e.g., Philip (1982), p. 92; von Biberstein (1981), p. 96.

[186] See, e.g., von Hoffmann and Thorn (2007), p. 55.

[187] Maier (1982), p. 289; Lowenfeld (1979), p. 335.

[188] See, e.g., Kominos (2002), p. 477 et seq.

of the state organization that they must apply, regardless of the law governing the given legal relationship under "ordinary" conflict of laws rules. Therefore, not every purpose of a "mandatory" provision (including public law rules) necessitates its "overriding" application. This refers to special purposes, of great political, social, economic, or moral significance, that is, purposes which are also protected by public order clauses. In this connection, it is pointed out that it is useful to consider, in the process of establishing "importance" of a given provision, such purposes (values) that may be considered an expression of the principles of international public policy. Therefore, attribution to any specific rule of the "overriding" mandatory nature is a consequence of concluding that the values realized by the provision reflect the principles of transnational *ordre public* or of the European public policy.[189] Such solution was adopted in Art. 9(1) of the Rome I Regulation I.[190]

References

Auclair N (2003) The French Report on the implementation of the EC choice of law rules for insurance (in:)

Baade HW (2015) The operation of foreign public law. Texas Int Law J 1995, no. 30

Baker T, Logue KD (2015) Mandatory rules and default rules in insurance contracts, Faculty Scholarship at Penn Law. 582

Basedow J (1991) Drasch W., Das neue Internationale Versicherungsvertragsrecht. Neue Juristische Wochenschrift

Basedow J, Fock T (2002) Rechtsvergleich. In: Basedow J, Fock T (eds) Europäisches Versicherungsvertragsrecht. Bd. I. Hrsg. Hamburg

Bělohlávek A (2010) Rozporządzenie Rzym I. Konwencja rzymska. Komentarz. Tom 1, Warszawa

Bigot J (1989) La liberté de prestations de services en assurance de dommage au point de vue juridique. R.G.A.T.

Bittner C (2000) Europäisches und internationales Betriebsrentenrecht. Grenzüberschreitende betriebliche Altersversorgung im Spannungsfeld von europäischem und internationalem Betriebsrentenrecht. Tübingen

Blessing M (1999) Impact of the extraterritorial application of mandatory rules of law on international contracts. Helbling & Lichtenhahn

Blomeyer W, Otto K (2004) Gesetz zur Verbesserung der betrieblichen Altersversorgung. Kommentar. München

Blomeyer W, Otto K (2006) Betriebsrentengesetz. Gesetz zur Verbesserung der betrieblichen Altersversorgun. Kommentar. München

Bohne A (2004) Kollisions- und Sachnormen der betrieblichen Altersversorgung bei internationalen Personaleinsätzen. Münster

Brownlie I (1998) Principles of public international law, 5th edn. Oxford

Bruck E (1924) Zwischenstaatliches Versicherungsrecht. Leipzig

Bull H (2019) Choice of law for insurance contracts: history of Article 7 of Rome I, particularly regarding the relationship with Directives 88/357 and 90/619 in Light of Directive 2009/138. Oslo Law Rev 6(I)

[189] See Zachariasiewicz (2014), p. 442.

[190] C.f. judgment of the Court of Justice of 23.11.1999, C-369/96, in the case Arblade. ECR 1999, p. I-8453.

Court of Justice of the European Union, judgment of 23.11.1999 in cases C-369/96 and C-376/96 (Arblade). ECR 1999, I-8453
Court of Justice of the European Union, Case C-381/98 Ingmar versus Eaton. ECR 2000, I-9305
Czepelak M (2010) Would we like to have a European Code of private international law? "European Review of Private Law" 2010
d'Avout L (2005) Glosa do orzeczenia francuskiego Sądu kasacyjnego (Cour de cassation) z 24 lutego 2004 r. w sprawie Republique federative du Bresil c. Mme L. de Azevedo Werneck. RCDIP 2005
de Meireles PM (2020) Applicable law to insurance contracts in the light of Rome I Regulation – challenges to cross-border insurance contracts in the EU. ULP Law Rev 13(1)
Dicey AV, Morris JHC, Collins L (2006) The conflict of laws, vol 2, 14th edn. London
Dicey AV, Morris JHC, Collins L (2015) The conflict of laws, vol 1, 15th edn. London
Dickstein PS (1995) Die Merkmale der Lebensversicherung im europäischen Binnenmarkt. Hamburg
Dominelli S (2016) Party autonomy and insurance contracts in private international law. Aracne
Dörner H (1997) Internationales Versicherungsvertragsrecht: Kommentar zu den Artikeln 7 bis 15 EGVVG mit Materialien. Heidelberg
Dubuisson B (2004) La loi applicable au contrat d'assurance dans l'Espace européen. "Revue de droit commercial belge"
Eichenhofer E (1987) Internationales Sozialrecht und Internationales Privatrecht. Baden-Baden
Eichenhofer E (1994) Internationales Sozialrecht. München
Eichler H (1966) Versicherungsrecht. Karlsruhe
Ellger R (2012) Overriding mandatory provisions. In: Basedow J, Hopt KJ, Zimmermann R (eds) The Max Planck encyclopedia of European private law. Oxford University Press, Oxford
European Commission, Amendment of 21.08.2013 to Art. 22 of the draft Regulation on matrimonial property regimes, KOM (2011) 126 of 16.03.2011
Fras M (2008) Prawo właściwe dla umowy ubezpieczenia na życie. "Prawo Asekuracyjne" 2008, No. 1
Fras M (2019a) Contemporary European normative tendencies regarding the essence and typology of insurance contracts. Liverpool Law Rev 40. https://link.springer.com/article/10.1007/s10991-019-09232-0
Fras M (2019b) The Directive 2016/97 on insurance distribution (IDD) and private international law. Rev Eur Comp Law XXXVIII. http://cejsh.icm.edu.pl/cejsh/element/bwmeta1.element.ojs-doi-10_31743_recl_4848
Fras M (2019c) The group insurance contract in private international law. Neth Int Law Rev 66(1). https://www.researchgate.net/publication/337122518_The_Group_Insurance_Contract_in_Private_International_Law
Fras M (2020) The European context of the group insurance contract, Problemy Prawa Prywatnego Międzynarodowego 2020, T. 27. https://www.researchgate.net/publication/337122518_The_Group_Insurance_Contract_in_Private_International_Law
Fras M, Pacuła K (2014) Umowa ubezpieczenia obowiązkowego w prawie prywatnym międzynarodowym. In: Kowalewski E, Mogilski W (eds) System prawny ubezpieczeń obowiązkowych. Przesłanki i kierunki reform, Toruń
Fuchs D (1999) Regulacja koasekuracji w prawodawstwie Unii Europejskiej. Radca Prawny, nr 2
Fuchs B (2003) Statut kontraktowy a przepisy wymuszające swoje zastosowanie. Katowice
Gasińska M (2003) Ubezpieczenie jako metoda zarządzania przez pracodawcę ryzykiem wypadku przy pracy. In: Ubezpieczenia w polskim obszarze rynku europejskiego. Wyzwania i oczekiwania. Warszawa
Gruber UP (1999) Internationales Versicherungsvertragsrecht. Karlsruhe
Gruber UP (2009) Insurance contracts. In: Ferrari F, Leible S (eds) Rome I Regulation. The law applicable to contractual obligations in Europe. Munich
Harlow C (1980) "Public" and "private" law: definition without distinction. Mod Law Rev 43

Harpen I (1991) The small self-administered pension scheme. The Accountant's Magazine. Abstract: www.faqs.org. Accessed 15 Sep 2020
Haynsworth v. The Corporation, 121 F. 3d 956 (5th Cir. 1997)
Heiss H (2008) Insurance contracts in Rome I: another recent failure of the European legislature. Yearb Priv Int Law 2008, no. 10
Hełczyński B (1927) Umowa ubezpieczenia na cudzy rachunek. Kraków
Herzog P (1967) Civil procedure in France. Hague 1967
Holman v. Johnson, 1 Cowp. 341, 98 Eng. Rep. 1120
Jędrasik-Jankowska I (2004) Treść ryzyka emerytalnego. In: Bińczycka-Majewska T (ed) Konstrukcje prawa emerytalnego. Zakamycze, Kraków
Jurgens G, van Ommeren F (2012) The public-private divide in English and Dutch Law: a multifunctional and context – dependent divide. Camb Law J 1
Keller M (1962) Das Internationale Versicherungsvertragsrecht der Schweiz. Bern
Kemper K (2003) In: Kemper K, Kisters-Kölkes M, Berenz C, Bode C, Pühler KP (eds) Kommentar zum Gesetz zur Verbesserung der betrieblichen Altersversorgung. Hrsg. Köln
Kominos AP (2002) New prospects for private enforcement of EC community law: Courage v. Crehan and the community right to damages. Common Mark Law Rev 4
Kowalewski E (1997) Wprowadzenie do teorii interesu ubezpieczeniowego. In: Wąsowicz A (ed) Ubezpieczenia w gospodarce rynkowej, 3. Bydgoszcz
Kramer U (1995) Internationales Versicherungsvertragsrecht. Karlsruhe
Kramer X (2008) The new European conflict of law rules on insurance contracts in Rome I: a complex compromise. ICFAI Univ J Insur Law 6(4)
Kropka M (2007) Prawo właściwe dla umowy ubezpieczenia następstw nieszczęśliwych wypadków. Glosa do wyroku Sądu Najwyższego z dnia 3 lutego 2006 r., II PK 152/05, PPPM 2007, vol 2
Kropka M (2010) Kolizyjnoprawna regulacja umowy ubezpieczenia w rozporządzeniu Rzym I, Katowice
Kropka M (2015) (p:) Pazdan M (ed) Prawo Prywatne Międzynarodowe. System Prawa Prywatnego. Tom 20B. Warszawa
Lando O, Nielsen PA (2009) The Rome I Regulation. Common Mark Law Rev 2008, vol 45
Lowenfeld AF (1979) Public law in the international arena: conflict of laws, international law and some suggestions for their interaction. Recueil des Cours 163
Maier HG (1982) Extraterritorial jurisdiction at a crossroads: an intersection between public and private international law. Am J Int Law 76
Maixner O, Steinbeck R (2008) Das neue Versicherungsvertragsrecht. München
Malinowska K (2003) Kodeks cywilny. In: Brodecki Z (ed) Prawo o kontraktach w ubezpieczeniach. Zakamycze, Kraków
Mann FA (1984) The doctrine of international jurisdiction revisited after twenty years. RCADI 3, vol 186, Hague-Boston-London
Mannington Mills, Inc. v. Congoleum Corp., 595 F. 2d 1287 (3d Cir. 1979)
Martiny D (2004) In: Reithmann Ch, Martiny D (eds) Internationales Vertragsrecht. Hrsg. Köln
Martiny D (2006) Neue Impulse im Europäischen Internationalen Vertragsrecht. Zeitschrift für Europäisches Privatrecht:60–95
Mataczyński M (2005) Przepisy wymuszające swoje zastosowanie w prawie prywatnym międzynarodowym, Kraków
Mataczyński M (2011) Cywilnoprawne skutki naruszenia obowiązków nabywców znacznych pakietów akcji spółek publicznych. Warszawa
Merryman JH (1969) The public law-private law distinction in European and American law. J Public Law 17
Muszalski W (2007) Podstawowe zmiany ubezpieczenia społecznego w świecie. Praca i Zabezpieczenie Społeczne 2007, nr 6
Nagy C (2012) The world is a dangerous weapon: jurisdiction, applicable law and personality rights in EU law – missed and new opportunities. J Priv Int Law 2

Nowacki J (1992) Prawo publiczne – prawo prywatne. Katowice
Pacud R (2006) Oczekiwanie prawne na emeryturę dożywotnią (ekspektatywa). Bydgoszcz
Pacuła K (2014) Przepisy wymuszające swoje zastosowanie jako instrument ochrony „strony słabszej" umowy ubezpieczenia, Problemy Prawa Prywatnego Międzynarodowego 15, https://rebus.us.edu.pl/bitstream/20.500.12128/4789/1/Pacula_przepisy_wymuszajaca_swoje_zastosowanie.pdf
Pazdan M (2008) Prawo prywatne międzynarodowe. Warszawa
Pazdan J (2009) Rozporządzenie Rzym II – nowe wspólnotowe unormowanie właściwości prawa dla zobowiązań pozaumownych. "Problemy Prawa Prywatnego Międzynarodowego". T. 4. Ed. M. Pazdan. Katowice
Philip A (1982) Mandatory rules, public law (political rules) and choice of law in the E.E.C. Convention on the law applicable to contractual obligations. In: North PM (ed) Contract conflicts. North-Holland
Pilich M (2012) Statut umów ubezpieczenia według rozporządzenia Rzym I. In: Grzegorczyk P, Weitz K (eds) Europejskie Prawo procesowe cywilne i kolizyjne. LexisNexis, Warszawa
Piroddi P (2008) The French Plumber, subcontracting, and the internal market. YPIL 10
Pokrzywniak J (2018) Nowe zasady dystrybucji ubezpieczeń, Wolters Kluwer Polska, Warszawa
Polish Constitutional Tribunal, judgment of 10.07.2000, SK 12/99. Dz.U. no. 55, item 665
Polish Supreme Court, judgment of 1.06.2011, II CSK 513/10. Lex
Polish Supreme Court, judgment of 11.05.2012, II CSK 545/11. OSP 2014, no. 2, item 17
Polish Supreme Court, judgment of 30.06.2005, IV CK 771/04. BSN 2005, no. 11/12
Präve P (2005) Versicherungsaufsichtsgesetz mit Europäischen Gemeinschaftsrecht und Recht der Bundesländer. Hrsg. J. Kölschbach er al. München
Prölls, Martin (2010) Versicherungsvertragsgesetz, Kommentar zu VVG, EGVVG mit Rom I-Verordnung, VVG-InfoVerordnung, VVG-InfoV und Vermittlerrecht sowie Kommentierung wichtiger Versicherungsbedingungen. München
Reichert-Facilides F (1976) Versicherungsverbraucherschutz und Internationales Privatrecht. In: Reichert-Facilides F, Rittner F, Sasse J (eds) Festschrift für Reimer Schmidt. Hrsg. Karlsruhe
Richter J (1980) Internationales Versicherungsvertragsrecht. Frankfurt am Main
Riley v. Kingsley Underwriting Agencies Ltd., 969 F. 2d 953 (10th Cir. 1992)
Roby v. Corporation of Lloyd's, 996 F. 2d 1353 (2nd Cir. 1993)
Roth WH (1985) Internationales Versicherungsvertragsrecht. Tübingen
Roth WH (1999) In: Honsell H (ed) Berliner Kommentar zum Versicherungsvertragsrecht. Hrsg. Berlin
Roth WH (2004) Internationales Versicherungsvertragsrecht. In: Beckmann RM, Matusche-Beckmann A (eds) Versicherungshandbuch. Hrsg. München
Salomon D (2008) The private international law of contracts in Europe: advances and retreats, Proceedings of the Duke Law Center for International and Comparative Law and Tulane Law Review Symposium. The New European Choice-of-Law Revolution: Lessons for the United States? Contract and Tort Law. Tulane Law Review, May 2008
Schnyder AK (2004) In: Internationales Vertragsrecht. Hrsg. Ch. Reithman, D. Martiny. Köln
Seatzu F (2003) Insurance in private international law: a European perspective. Oxford
Sieg K (1971) Rechtsgutachten zu den Entwürfen einer 2. Koordinierungsrichtlinie auf dem Gebiete der Direktversicherung. In: Steindorff E (ed) Dienstleistungsfreiheit und Versicherungsaufsicht im Gemeinsamen Markt. Hrsg. Stuttgart
Sodolska E (2005) Europejskie prawo ubezpieczeń. In: Brodecki Z, Serwach M (eds) Prawo ubezpieczeń gospodarczych. Zakamycze, Kraków
Spickhoff A (2003) In: Bamberger HG, Roth H (eds) Kommentar zum Bürgerlichen Gesetzbuch. Band 3. §§ 1297-2395, EBGB, CISG. Hrsg. München
Świerczyński M (2019) Sztuczna inteligencja w prawie prywatnym międzynarodowym – wstępne rozważania. Problemy Prawa Prywatnego Międzynarodowego 25

Świerczyński M (2020) Prawo właściwe dla zobowiązań deliktowych wynikających z naruszenia zasad ochrony danych osobowych przyjętych w GDPR, Problemy Prawa Prywatnego Międzynarodowego 2020, vol 27
Swiss Federal Tribunal, judgment of 29.10.1998 r., BGE 125, I, 65
Szczepaniak R (2015) Przyczyny odwoływania się do podziału na prawo publiczne i prywatne przez polskie organy stosujące prawo. Forum Prawnicze, nr 1
Szubert W (1987) Ubezpieczenia społeczne. Zarys systemu. Warszawa
The first American Restatement of Conflict of Laws. 1934, § 610
Timberlane Lumber Co. v. Bank of Am., 549 F. 2d 597 (9th Cir. 1976)
Von Biberstein W (1981) Limitation of party autonomy in private international law by rules of Ius Cogens in laws protecting agents and distributors. In: Smit H et al (eds) International contracts. Columbia University
von Hoffmann B, Thorn K (2007) Internationales Privatrecht. C.H. Beck
Weigel HP (2005) Versicherungsaufsichtsgesetz mit Europäischen Gemeinschaftsrecht und Recht der Bundesländer. Hrsg. J. Kölschbach et al. München
Wesselmann J (2007) Betriebliche Altersversorgung in der Republik Italien und der Bundesrepublik Deutschland. Münster
Wojewoda M (2007a) Zakres prawa właściwego dla zobowiązań umownych, Kraków
Wojewoda M (2007b) Zakres prawa właściwego dla zobowiązań umownych, Warszawa 2007
Wolff M (1933) Internationales Privatrecht. Springer, Berlin
Zachariasiewicz MA (2010) O potrzebie wskazania w nowej ustawie o prawie prywatnym międzynarodowym podstawy stosowania przepisów wymuszających swoje zastosowanie. Problemy Prawa Prywatnego Międzynarodowego 7
Zachariasiewicz MA (2013) In: Popiołek W (ed) System Prawa Handlowego. Międzynarodowe Prawo Handlowe, vol 9, Warszawa
Zachariasiewicz MA (2014) In: Pazdan M (ed) Prawo Prywatne Międzynarodowe. System Prawa Prywatnego. Tom 20A, Warszawa

The manufacturer's authorised representative in the EU is Springer Nature Customer Service Centre GmbH, Europaplatz 3, 69115 Heidelberg, Germany. If you have any concerns regarding our products, please contact ProductSafety@springernature.com

Printed and bound by CPI Group (UK) Ltd, Croydon, CR0 4YY
30/09/2026
02225496-0012